The Business of Bei

The Business of Being Made is the first book to critically analyze assisted reproductive technologies (ARTs) from a transdisciplinary perspective integrating psychoanalytic and cultural theories. It is a ground-breaking collection exploring ARTs through diverse methods, including interview research, clinical case studies, psychoanalytic-based ethnography, and memoir. Gathering clinicians and researchers who specialize in this area, this book engages current research in psychoanalysis, sociology, anthropology, philosophy, and debates in feminist, queer, and cultural theory about affect, temporality, and bodies.

With psychoanalysis as its fulcrum, *The Business of Being Made* explores the social constructions and personal experiences of ARTs. Katie Gentile frames the cultural context, exploring the ways ARTs have become a complex form of playing with time, attempting to manufacture a hopeful future in the midst of growing global uncertainty. The contributors then present a range of varied experiences related to ARTs, including:

- interviews with women and men undergoing ARTs;
- a psychoanalytic memoir of male infertility;
- clinical research and work with transgender, gay, and lesbian patients creating new Oedipal constellations, the experiences of LBGTQ people within the medical system, and the variety of families that emerge;
- research on the experiences of egg donors (now central to the business of ARTs) and a corresponding clinical case study of successful egg donation;
- the experience of ongoing failure, which is often unacknowledged for ART procedures;
- how and when people choose to stop using ARTs;
- a psychoanalytic ethnography of a neonatal intensive care unit populated primarily with the babies created through these technologies and their parents, haggard and in shock after years of failed attempts.

Full of original material, *The Business of Being Made* conveys the ambivalence of these technologies without simplifying their complicated consequences for the bodies of individuals, the family, cultures, and our planet. This book will be relevant to clinicians, medical and psychological personnel working in ARTs and infertility, as well as academics working in the fields of sociology, literature, queer and feminist theories and at the intersections of cultural, critical, and psychoanalytic theories.

Katie Gentile is Professor and Director of the Gender Studies Program at John Jay College of Criminal Justice, New York. She is author of the Routledge title *Creating Bodies: Eating disorders as self-destructive survival,* co-editor of the *Genders & Sexualities in Minds & Cultures* book series, also from Routledge, and co-editor of the journal *Studies in Gender and Sexuality*.

Genders & Sexualities in Minds & Cultures

Genders & Sexualities in Minds & Cultures is a book series whose scholarship is situated in the transdisciplinary spaces of psychoanalysis and cultural theory. Aiming to illuminate both theorized and lived experiences of gender and sexuality, the series privileges the exploration of human experience as conceived intersectionally, favoring work that sutures categories of difference such as "race," social class, religion, and disability. The series aims to attract leading scholars and practitioners from around the globe who are interested in a dialogue between psychoanalysis and the academic study of genders and sexualities. It also seeks to introduce the scholarship of emerging authors who are engaged with psychoanalytic theory and/or practice.

Several academic presses have created book series specifically examining genders and sexualities from different theoretical and disciplinary perspectives. Whilst many take psychoanalytic theory as a foundational form of inquiry, few are edited or written by trained analysts or clinicians. Most such books rely on the work of a standard array of psychoanalytic theorists, i.e., Freud, Lacan, Jung, Guattari, and Laplanche, but may not consider and integrate contemporary psychoanalytic theory as it emerges from the clinic. What is missed are the unique contributions that advances in psychoanalytic theory and clinical work have to offer and, in turn, a way to compel the interest of practicing clinicians and further the knowledge of academics whose interest is captured by traditional psychoanalytic ideas.

Genders & Sexualities in Minds & Cultures brings together contemporary research, theory, and practice from both academy and clinic, using psychoanalysis as the fulcrum that complicates and deepens our conceptualizations of genders and sexualities. As a series edited by four individuals whose work spans both the clinical and academic domains, Genders & Sexualities in Minds & Cultures offers a wider and diverse engagement with newer theories of psychoanalysis. Further, the clinical sensibilities informing this book series will make it accessible and useful to a wider audience.

Books published in this series:

The Business of Being Made
The temporalities of reproductive technologies, in psychoanalysis and culture
Edited by Katie Gentile

"In this unique, and insightful set of essays edited by Katie Gentile, the experience of assisted reproductive technologies, ARTS, is given a multi-disciplinary treatment that brings cultural criticism and psychoanalysis into an encounter that transforms them both. Taking account of the cultural, political, economic and psychological contexts of ARTS, *The Business of Being Made* refuses a simple taking-sides in debates around biomedicalization and reprofuturism. It not only gives an in-depth view of the potentialities as well as the risks, the disappointments, the trauma for those who engage with these technologies; it does so without forgetting the implications of ARTS for sex, gender, race and class differentiations. The essays are a must read for those concerned with the affects of biotechnology on every aspect of life now and in the near future." – **Patricia Ticineto Clough, Queens College and The Graduate Center, CUNY, Editor of *The Affective Turn***

"Technology is no longer some thing we hold in our hand or a machine that sits on a desk. It threads our minds, it bends our spines. And as this remarkable collection of essays demonstrates, technological bio-power unconsciously pulses, reproducing reproduction and the new world to come. Read and get ready." – **Ken Corbett, Author of *Boyhoods: Rethinking Masculinities* and *A Murder Over A Girl***

"Drawing on the resources of both psychoanalytic and cultural theories, Katie Gentile and her co-authors spotlight the dynamic interplay between neoliberal risk management and cultural narratives of reproductive 'failure' and 'success'. *The Business of Being Made* offers a fascinating, urgent, and – dare I say – *timely* exploration of the sometimes contradictory ways assisted reproductive technologies are remaking kinship, subjectivity, and the experience of temporality itself." – **Ann Pellegrini, Director, Center for the Study of Gender and Sexuality, New York University**

The Business of Being Made

The temporalities of reproductive technologies, in psychoanalysis and culture

Edited by Katie Gentile

LONDON AND NEW YORK

First published 2016
by Routledge
2 Park Square, Milton Park, Abingdon, Oxon OX14 4RN

and by Routledge
711 Third Avenue, New York, NY 10017

Routledge is an imprint of the Taylor & Francis Group, an informa business

Cover photo and piece "My baby Frankenstein" by Dolores Zorreguieta. http://www.sheisanartist.com

British Library Cataloguing in Publication Data
A catalogue record for this book is available from the British Library

Library of Congress Cataloging in Publication Data
A catalog record for this book has been requested

ISBN: 978-0-415-74940-4 (hbk)
ISBN: 978-0-415-74941-1 (pbk)
ISBN: 978-1-315-69408-5 (ebk)

Typeset in Times New Roman
by Swales & Willis Ltd, Exeter, Devon, UK

Printed and bound in the United States of America by
Edwards Brothers Malloy on sustainably sourced paper

Contents

Contributors

Diane Ehrensaft, Ph.D., is an associate professor of Pediatrics at the University of California, San Francisco and the Director of Mental Health of the Child and Adolescent Gender Center. A developmental and clinical psychologist in the San Francisco Bay Area, she specializes in research, clinical work, and consultation related to assisted reproductive technology families and gender-nonconforming children. She is the author of *Gender Born, Gender Made* (The Experiment, 2011), *Mommies, Daddies, Donors, Surrogates* (Guilford, 2005), as well as the forthcoming book, *The Gender Creative Child* (The Experiment).

Katie Gentile, Ph.D., is Professor of Interdisciplinary Studies and Director of the Gender Studies Program at John Jay College of Criminal Justice, New York. She is editor of the Routledge book series Genders & Sexualities in Minds & Cultures. She is the author of *Creating Bodies: Eating Disorders as Self-Destructive Survival* (Routledge), co-editor of *Studies in Gender and Sexuality,* and on the editorial board of *Women's Studies Quarterly.* She is on the faculty of New York University's postdoctoral program in psychotherapy and psychoanalysis.

Orna Guralnik, Psy.D., is a clinical psychologist and psychoanalyst practicing in New York City. She co-founded the Center for the Study of Dissociation and Depersonalization at the Mount Sinai Medical School, where she was funded by National Institues of Health and *National Alliance for Research on Schizophrenia and Depression* grants. She teaches and publishes on the topics of dissociation and depersonalization, as well as culture and the individual in psychoanalysis. She is on the editorial board of *Studies in Gender and Sexuality*, on faculty at the National Institute for the Psychotherapies and the St. Luke's Roosevelt Hospital, and graduate of the NYU postdoctoral program in psychoanalysis.

Stephen Hartman, Ph.D., is a co-editor of *Studies in Gender and Sexuality* and an associate editor for *Psychoanalytic Dialogues*. He co-chairs the faculty of the Psychoanalytic Institute of Northern California and provides clinical supervision for trainees at the Access Institute for Psychological Services in San Francisco, California.

Adam Kaplan, Ph.D., is an attending clinical psychologist at New York-Presbyterian Hospital, where he is also the coordinator of the adult track of the Psychology Internship Training Program. A graduate of The Institute for the Psychoanalytic Study of Subjectivity, he has a faculty appointment at Columbia University and maintains a private practice in New York City.

Susan Kraemer, Ph.D., is a clinical psychologist and psychoanalyst in private practice in New York City. She is Clinical Instructor in Pediatrics and Psychiatry, Columbia University College of Physicians and Surgeons, and consultant to staff and families in the neonatal intensive care unit at New York-Presbyterian/Morgan Stanley Children's Hospital. She is also faculty at the Parent–Infant Psychotherapy Training Program, Columbia University Center for Psychoanalytic Training. She has particular interest in opening possibilities for more reflective consideration of maternal experiences of all kinds, including the mother's hate and aggression.

André Lepecki, Ph.D., is Associate Professor in Performance Studies at New York University and Guest Professor, Stockholm University of the Arts. He is an independent curator and writer. Edited books include *Of the Presence of the Body* (Wesleyan University Press, 2004); *The Senses in Performance* (Routledge, 2007, with Sally Banes); *Planes of Composition* (Routledge, 2009, with Jenn Joy) and *Dance* (Whitechapel, 2012). His single-authored book *Exhausting Dance: Performance and the Politics of Movement* (Routledge, 2006) has been translated into ten languages.

Michelle Leve, Ph.D., is a graduate in Clinical Psychology from the New School for Social Research in New York City. Her research interests center around how healthcare contexts interact with, and impact, individual health experiences. Michelle's current research is exploring the experiences of egg providers within a healthcare context shaped by neoliberalism.

Tracy L. Simon, Psy.D., clinical psychologist and psychoanalyst, is a graduate of the New York University postdoctoral program in psychotherapy and psychoanalysis and adjunct clinical supervisor at the Ferkauf Graduate School of Psychology, Yeshiva University. She works with political asylum seekers at the human rights clinic at HealthRight International and has a private practice in New York City.

Zina Steinberg, Ed.D., is Assistant Clinical Professor of Medical Psychology (in Pediatrics and Psychiatry), Columbia University College of Physicians and Surgeons. Thirteen years ago she created a project, still ongoing, that consults to families and staff in the Neonatal Intensive Care Unit at Morgan-Stanley Children's Hospital, New York-Presbyterian Hospital. In addition, she maintains a private practice in New York City, seeing couples, individuals, and families, and is on the faculty of the Stephen Mitchell Center for Relational Studies.

Dolores Zorreguieta (cover photo) was born in Argentina in 1965. In 1987 she graduated from The National School of Fine Arts. A year later she had her first solo exhibition at Frans Van Riel Gallery. In 1992 she moved to New York, where she started experimenting with installation at New York University. She has received grants from The New York Foundation for the Arts and The New York State Council on the Arts. She has exhibited her work in the United States, Latin America, and Europe. In 2008 she relocated in Campbell, California, an hour south of San Francisco. See http://www.sheisanartist.com.

Acknowledgments

I want to thank the contributors for providing their papers to this unique volume. I also want to thank *Studies in Gender and Sexuality* for allowing me to reprint the case study (Part III in this book) with discussions, and parts of my own paper "The Business of Being Made" from the same issue (Volume 14 #4). I also want to thank my participants for sharing their stories for this research project. Many thanks to Avgi Saketopoulou for comments on Part I and Tracy Simon for her thoughts on the Epilogue. I thank Muriel Dimen for being such an important mentor to me, and now an editorial partner.

Abby Stein, my good friend, is sadly thanked posthumously. She was a reluctant feminist who made me rethink some of my assumptions but, most of all, she was a wonderful friend while I was going through assisted reproductive technologies (ARTs) and dealing with multiple losses. My friends and colleagues have helped so much in day-to-day conversations about babies, fetuses, ARTs, and life in general, in particular Helen Hurwitz, Debra Roth, Elaine Freedgood, Jim Stoeri, Jude Ornstein, and Jennifer Capobianco. Steven Knoblauch, Steve Botticelli, Mary Sonntag, Galit Atlas, and Steve Kuchuck have provided solid and always generative intellectual holding in our reading group. Allison Pease, Liza Yukins, Erica Burleigh, and Kyoo Lee, have provided an excellent feminist theory reading group out of which many of my musings have emerged.

I want to acknowledge Kate Hawes and Taylor & Francis for having faith in a book series focused on inter- and transdisciplinary approaches to gender and sexuality. Thinking and writing between disciplines are key to generating new ideas and I am so thankful to have the support of a great press and a wonderful editor behind this endeavor.

My writing partners Febo and Dumpling are ever-helpful and persistent reminders of lunch, snack, play, and dinner breaks, and they keep me in good company. Lastly, thank you Rob, as always.

Part I

Setting up the context by integrating cultural and psychoanalytic theories to explore ARTs

Chapter 1

Introducing *The Business of Being Made*

Katie Gentile

Stories about assisted reproductive technologies (ARTs) are becoming more and more familiar, and the lingo of ARTs – in vitro fertilization (IVF), intrauterine insemination (IUI), egg freezing, and surrogacy – is at this point commonplace.[1] Celebrity magazines regularly feature J-Lo and her twins, Mariah Carey and her twins, Julia Roberts and her twins, to name only a few. The reality show *The Kardashians* discussed ARTs for one of the sisters, including potential surrogacy or egg donation from another sister. Neil Patrick Harris and his partner, as well as Nicole Kidman and Keith Urban, have openly discussed their respective processes of surrogacy, and Melissa Etheridge openly discussed the sperm donor who contributed to her family. Apple is offering to give money towards egg freezing for its women employees. ARTs in these contexts seem magical and easy, the end to women's enslavement to the biological clock. Now women have no excuse for not "having it all." And, because ARTs take the heterosexual intercourse out of reproduction, now everyone can have a biological child. These narratives of success belie the reality that most cycles of IVF will fail and 40–50% of patients entering fertility clinics will not become pregnant (Spar, 2006; Mundy, 2008). It appears ARTs have become yet another neoliberal trope to imagine a life without limits.

Not surprisingly, given the positive spin, ARTs are big business. When talking to women in their 30s and 40s in the United States, everyone knows at least one person who has sought out reproductive technologies. Central to this increase has been a shift in medical discourse where measures of fertility and infertility are now part of every woman's healthcare (Mamo, 2007; Gentile, 2013). As "infertility services" are rebranded as "fertility services," there is a shift to such clinics providing a service of wellness (Mamo, 2007), reinforcing the new location of ARTs as a central component to ordinary medicine for all women. This emphasis on reproductive medicine follows a market. Fertility medicine is one of the fastest-growing and most profitable areas of medicine. The average cost of one cycle ranges from $8,000 to $15,000, depending on the cost of medications (RESOLVE.org), with an average of three cycles before pregnancy or giving up (Spar, 2006; RESOLVE.org). Many do give up because success rates are still quite low, approximately 20% per cycle (Throsby, 2004; Mundy, 2008). Although the field of ARTs is growing exponentially, the rates of success have remained fairly constant.

This book is the first inter- and transdisciplinary exploration of ARTs. In order to comprehend the role and function of ARTs within individual lives, we must also explore their roles and functions for the cultural body, knowing these are inextricable. As such, this book links different disciplines and theories to understand experiences of ARTs. But these are not the only links this book makes. Psychoanalysis takes linking as a central task, yet it routinely destroys those connections to the outside world. Cultural theories, on the other hand, describe well how affect can function to organize the cultural body and surroundings through specific behaviors and responses. However, we need a psychoanalytic-based inquiry to understand why it is that some of these organizing affects become more contagious and compelling to the cultural body than others. For instance, cultural theorists can describe the role of risk management in creating a compliant social body, but psychoanalytic theory can expand upon this by helping to articulate how it is that, in the face of potential catastrophe or precarity, one might be attracted to the hopeful promise of certainty provided by strategies of preemption and risk management. Thus, integrating cultural and psychoanalytic theories can provide a more complex understanding of subjectivity.

The first part of this book does just this by integrating and expanding upon cultural and psychoanalytic ideas of time to create a transdisciplinary theory of subjectivity where relational linking does not stop at the interpersonal, but extends in networks that include culture, communities, animals, objects, and the environment. As will be described in Chapter 2 and expanded upon in the Epilogue, creating links to the world at large requires a new theory of relational subjectivity, where emergence occurs through a process of coming into being within the vast world of human and nonhuman objects upon which we are dependent, and thus, where the human is not at the center. In this new theory of subjectivity detailed here, temporality – the generation of time and space – is conceptualized as *the* linking capacity: that which creates and shapes the differentiations through which subjectivities emerge. Here, as will be described through this first part, playing with time – manipulating it with procedures of preemptive risk management around babies – can become a compelling form of affect regulation for individual and cultural bodies.

Cultural time, babies, and ARTs

This book is the first inter- and transdisciplinary exploration of the complicated experiences of ARTs. An interdisciplinary approach is necessary because ARTs are changing the cultural landscape in many ways. Certainly, ARTs, when successful, enable infertile, transgender, and/or same-sex couples or single people to birth biologically related children, expanding our notions of family and kinship. But the explosion of neonatal intensive care units (NICUs) and high-risk pregnancy wards is in large part due to the proliferation of ARTs. And, as will be described, ARTs advance a promise fueled mostly by hope for a baby in the face of the high statistical odds of failure. Additionally, in the current pro-natal culture, the category of reproductive technologies that, historically, included birth control and abortion in addition to assisted reproduction now appears to focus exclusively on the creation of babies (see Hassinger, 2014). So the variety of reproductive technologies has been subsumed by those that seek to create, not terminate or avoid, a pregnancy. As will be discussed in the first few chapters, by supposedly taking the sex out of reproduction,[2] ARTs make possible a virgin birth. This accomplishment makes it hard not to understand this shift as representing the ancient Madonna/whore split, where virtuous women go to any lengths to achieve pregnancy, while "fallen women" seek to prevent or terminate theirs. Thus, to explore ARTs requires holding many contradictions.

So this book brings together different methodological approaches to examine ARTs. The first part sets up the cultural context of the technologies by integrating cultural and sociological theories on biomedicalization and queer theories of reprofuturity with a specific psychoanalytic conceptualization of temporality-based subjectivity. Using temporality as the frame, these chapters also create a unique subjectivity assembled around a relational intimacy and accountability not only to other people but to our environment as a whole. These first three chapters are steeped in theory, creating a new transdisciplinary approach to understanding ARTs. They provide the necessary framework within which the rest of the chapters examine ARTs and their potential impact on people, medical systems, and the lives that are produced. Chapters 4–13 then use clinical or interview narratives (Chapters 4, 5, 7, 8, 9), personal memoir (Chapter 6), and a psychological ethnography (Chapter 8) to closely examine the experiences of being ART patients, egg donors, and parents in a busy NICU.

Since the first test tube baby in 1979, these reproductive technologies have been situated in the public imagination as magical and horrific (see Oliver, 2012), creating choices and opportunities for people to time pregnancy and avoid genetic disease or disorders, while flirting with the abject – designer babies and the God-like creation of Frankenstein. According to Freeman (2010), "Frankenstein's monster is monstrous because he [the monster] lets history too far in, going so far as to embody it instead of merely feeling it" (p. 104). In the case of the art installation *My Baby Frankenstein* (Zorreguieta's cover photo), the monstrous registers simultaneously with an uncanny disturbing beauty. But here it is not just historical time that is breached. This monstrosity embodies a present overflowing with times – the nostalgic figure of the baby with the emergence of the promise and horror of a future, the glowing light of potentialities, as Muñoz (2009) might say, enfolded within a layer of transparent plastics, a specter of unchecked consumption and pollution, the human-made substance that will not die/decompose. In a time when our relationship with nature is constructed as a war with humans as the innocent victims, this baby embodies our infantile ambivalence, rage, and terror of "mother" nature. Floating alone in a void, this baby is made and gestated outside the maternal body, breaching our notions of biology and the temporal generational chronology and structure of the Oedipal, while reinforcing its inherent mandate for reproduction.

This temporal breaching is a central aspect of ARTs. The use of donors radically expands the spatial and chronological notions of family and kin (Strathern, 1995). The sperm or egg donors or surrogates become invisible, but perhaps ghostly, presences in the family. With egg donation, the gestational body becomes a second biological mother, a third parent. As the gestational body, this mother, who may be a surrogate or the cultural mother, influences which genes from the donated eggs become expressed to create the infant. If the surrogate uses donated eggs from another woman, you suddenly have three mothers and a father (or potentially two fathers if sperm is also donated). To expand families further, governments are considering legalizing procedures that enable doctors to insert the mitochondria of one egg into another, such that there are three to five genetic parents. How the specters of these parental ghosts influence development is an ongoing question that cannot help but disrupt psychoanalytic ideas of the Oedipal configuration (see Chapter 7). For example, when a mother gestated and birthed her daughter's babies, i.e., her own grandchildren (see Miller, 2013), the Oedipal structure temporally imploded. And these culturally disruptive examples are culled primarily from heteronormative situations.

Because ARTs bring reproduction into a lab, they can be seen as supposedly democratic, providing all people (with financial means) the opportunity for some form of biological parenthood, thus creating even more diverse kinship potentials outside of culturally constructed gender/sex binaries with their nuclear family structures. ARTs then simultaneously stretch and challenge the Oedipal structure while enabling this structure to spread and enfold even more diverse configurations of couples, families, singles. After all, the Oedipal functions to structure the hierarchy of generations, as Loewald (1980) observed, such that parents cede authority to the adult children. This generational temporality can be both challenged and spread through ARTs. Additionally, if Oedipus is the "handmaiden" of capitalism (Chanter, 2006, p. 129), then it should come as no surprise that ARTs are marketed as allowing, and nearly mandating, Oedipal fulfillment to all through reproduction. As Mamo (2007) observes, compulsory heterosexuality has shifted to compulsory motherhood, or I would say, compulsory parenthood. So ARTs, with their rupturing, morphing, and reinforcement of family as some form of biological parenthood, are ripe for projections of horror and promise for the cultural body.

ARTs have been the focus of theory and research for decades, especially in the feminist literature, where they have been embraced by some as the royal road to equality (think of Shulamith Firestone's (1970) dream of liberating the female body from pregnancy) and rejected by others as another biomedical invasion of women's bodies. Yet, as ARTs proliferate, psychoanalytic accounts have been scant and uncritical. Additionally, the psychoanalytic representation of them, like that in the popular culture, has not discussed the fact that many, if not most, patients will not succeed in getting pregnant. The repeated losses and sense of uncertainty have not been a significant focus. Also absent has been discussion of the potential for re-traumatization for survivors of sexual violence. This is particularly glaring given that research shows even women without histories of trauma can develop symptoms of posttraumatic stress disorder when dealing with infertility and the ART system (Bradow, 2012). Given that the focus of intervention is on the woman's body, and that almost all of these interventions involve sometimes daily penetration of the vagina with ultrasound wands, catheters, and the injection of painful dyes and fluids into the uterus and the fallopian tubes, often by a parade of different clinic doctors who are disproportionately male, this particular area of silence is deafening. This silence needs to be understood as ignoring not only female survivors but also male survivors who, as partners or donors, may experience themselves as causing or just witnessing such invasions, and who themselves are objectified as "producers of samples," expected to orgasm on command, often under pressure and outside the context of sexual desire or/and arousal.

This book evolved from my own experiences. Like many heterosexual women, I spent my adult life actively avoiding pregnancy. I believed the high-school health teacher who said pregnancy would occur after only one time without protection. So when my identity as a fertile woman was shattered, my options were shaped by economics: my insurance covered ARTs, not adoption. So my partner and I headed to the clinic.

Engaging in ARTs as a partnered heterosexual patient meant the already loaded decision about having a baby had to be re-established each month. The normal ambivalence of the life-changing decision weighed on us with each month's failure/reprieve. After all, 51% of pregnancies in the United States are unplanned (Teitelbaum & Winter, 2013, cited in Burtman, 2014), meaning just over half of parents may not actually make an active conscious choice. When one engages with ARTs, the already complex question of "do I want a baby?" breaks into "do I want a baby?" "do I want to be a parent?" "do I want to be biologically pregnant?" and "how far am I willing to go physically, mentally, psychologically, and financially to become pregnant/have a biological child?"

As it became obvious that there was only uncertainty about our future and the doctors had no definitive idea of what was interfering with my getting pregnant, I sought out research that might answer some of my questions and help organize my experience. I was stunned to find that most of the psychological research focused on the creation of compliance, helping men and women better interface with the ART system. There was little critique or cultural context. I initiated an interview study with women and men going through the ART process. As I read more research, cultural theory, memoirs, and online diaries and discussion boards, I realized my story was typical. It involved endless invasive and, at times, terribly painful tests, many misinterpreted physical symptoms, dashed fantasies, and years of tracking cycles, only to cede control to a clinic doctor who was not even sure what was wrong. Most memoirs and online discussions described medical mishaps, some costly in terms of money or time wasted on useless attempts, others actually life threatening. For me, these mishaps involved some important medical reports that were not read by the doctor until 6 months after the tests – 6 months during which our insurance paid for four IUIs that had no chance of working. Once the doctor read the report and diagnosed the problem, I had one botched surgery, one reparative surgery, and a total delay of 1 full year of treatment. Time, as will be described, has dense contradictory meanings in ART treatments. Women are rushed into the ART system and rushed to conduct tests that have to be done on specific days of a cycle, only to be told to be patient and to not give up hope as months of failure are racked up.

But my experiences were just the tip of the potential iceberg, as I approached treatment conservatively with a clear line of how far I would go. I was spurred to do research in this area partially as an attempt to make sense of how it is that women in particular are so willing to go through these invasive, re-traumatizing, expensive, life-altering treatments, especially when the success rates are still quite low (20–30%). But as I read articles and books in medical anthropology, feminist, cultural and queer studies, ethics, philosophy, and psychoanalysis, it become clear to me that the only way to begin to make sense of ARTs was to integrate multiple disciplinary perspectives. After all, ARTs involve reproduction and babies, areas of cultural, familial, and psychic experience that, as Bourdieu (1977) might say, are located in "the natural," what psychoanalysis would call "the Oedipal," the space that is beyond questioning. As will be described, this space that appears to be beyond critical reflection is one of commodified nostalgia and sentiment around babies, where babies are associated with happiness (Ahmed, 2007/2008). But the lure of ARTs is more complicated than just being about some ideals of sentiment and Oedipal fulfillment.

Although the practices of biomedicalization are central to the generation of self-experience, psychoanalysts have not often contextualized health-related behaviors, like engaging in ARTs, within this neoliberal culture shaped by risk management. Alternatively, although cultural theorists have explored ways that biomedicalization and the attendant technologies of the self (Foucault, 1988) function to organize and produce self-experiences, few have explored the ways in which biomedicalization and risk management may be psychologically attractive and engaging. In particular, psychoanalytic theory can be used to help explore the conditions under which this future-oriented subjectivity may hold an allure, culturally and individually, knowing these distinctions are co-constructed.

There are also complementary approaches to exploring bodies and spaces in cultural and psychoanalytic theories. In cultural theory, bodies are described as being produced through social interactions and practices. These interactions and practices are shaped by, and in turn shape, the affective spaces within which bodies emerge. For instance, a cultural theorist might consider the body of a cutter being produced through the practice and rituals around cutting. Here, the action and affects surrounding the behavior of cutting produce distinct bodies.

Psychoanalysis, on the other hand, would see the body/psyche producing the action, in response to affects, and these affects are usually theorized as emanating from within the body that "holds the score" of past traumatic interactions (van der Kolk, 1994). For psychoanalysis, the social can be seen as shaping the body/psyche, but not producing it. Relational theories of psychoanalysis can approach the self as emergent through social spaces, but these theories usually cap the social at the interpersonal or/and dissociate the cultural from the psyche. Cultural theory conveys more fluidity and motion, conceptualizing subjectivity as not only multiple, but emerging through a continuous process of assembling and reassembling. Psychoanalytic theory can help deepen exploration of the ways in which this process of (re)assembling – of making the multiple singular, of rendering the asynchronous linear – occur. It is this complex process that enables coherent subjectivity to emerge. This focus on space, in terms of multiplicities becoming singular, and nonlinear times patterned to create meaning, situates temporality as a unique link between cultural and psychoanalytic theories of becoming a subject. Here, it becomes clear that the capacities of ARTs to produce different forms of temporality function as a form of social control, affect regulation, and agency. This transdisciplinary project then sets the theoretical and cultural context for the rest of the book.

Although this introduction may appear to situate ARTs as a form of social control, this control, like all forms of power, is not without its creative and generative resistances and interpretations. Indeed, this book is unique because it does examine ARTs from a variety of different perspectives and disciplines, making it the first multidisciplinary collection discussing ARTs from critical, celebratory, and neutral positions, focusing on cultural and feminist theory, sociology, and in-depth clinical case work. In a culture organized around ideals of reprofuturity (Halberstam, 2005) and biomedicalization (Clarke et al., 2003, 2010a, b), where some babies are objects of consumerism and fetish (Gentile, 2013), while others are cast aside as excessive (Oliver, 2012), or as targets for criminal justice interventions (Paltrow, 2013; Roberts, 2009), ARTs take on particularly loaded meanings in the cultural and clinical spaces. This book attempts to engage these representations to enrich and further complicate the literature on ARTs.

Biomedicalization + reprofuturity + psychoanalytic time = a recipe for complex social control and agency

Clarke et al. (2003, 2010a, b) have described biomedicalization as a systemic process shaping our culture. As will be described in more detail, biomedicalization is similar to what Foucault (1988) described as technologies of the self, where engaging in a series of socially promoted practices of self-management produces a felt experience of the self. Biomedicalization is a complex cycle whereby medical experts identify risk factors and then disseminate these risk factors in their medical research. The lay population is urged to become active consumers of this research as part of becoming a healthy, moral citizen. Thus, being a compliant patient becomes synonymous with being a responsible citizen, and both depend upon the consumption of medical research. Health management becomes an industry marketing behaviors, foods, supplements to help avoid identified risk factors, and we follow the recommendations, purchase the merchandize, and engage in the behaviors, so we can create a sense of a "healthy," i.e., morally responsible, self. Risk management within a neoliberal context is key here, because through biomedicalization, healthcare becomes privatized to individual citizens (Reith, 2004). One can see this complex process in action every Tuesday in the Science section of *The New York Times,* which is usually filled with information such as what foods to eat to help your vision, exercises to avoid stress, how to lose the fat around your middle, and, of course, how to increase your fertility and what not to eat when you're pregnant.

But biomedicalization does not operate alone toward popularizing ARTs. "Reprofuturity" is also at work; queer theorists have long described it as the values of the culture that identify the rhythms of an ideal life unfolding from middle-class ideals of reproduction (Dinshaw et al., 2007). In a culture shaped by reprofuturity, children not only mark the value of life, but they embody the hopes for the future. To be childless is to be without a future, to live without a "for" (Ahmed, 2007/2008), without a deep moral purpose. Reprofuturity ensures that babies are associated with happiness and a meaningful future life.

Biomedicalization and reprofuturity come together like fuel to a fire in the case of ARTs, which rely on educated, compliant patients who understand they must spend any amount of money and time and endure any amount of inconvenience and pain to create a biological child. But this is where psychoanalysis can add depth to the picture.

As will be described in Chapter 2, time is the foundation for the emergence of subjectivity. Through time, affect is structured, experienced, and enacted. We act and make meaning of our experiences from our capacities to create time and space (Gentile, 2007, 2013, 2015a).

Biomedicalization and reprofuturity both involve practices of manipulating this foundational time. The lure of biomedicalization is its promise of certainty – as long as you avoid risk factors in the present (thus creating a risk factor-free past), you will be healthy in the future.[3] Babies, as reprofuturity conveys, hold the promise of this future. As will be described, this promise of a future is particularly attractive in times of cultural upheaval or stress, when social spaces of reflection collapse. During such times, commodified forms of affect may be manufactured and circulated in lieu of meaningful reflection (Layton, 2010, 2014). Babies and fetuses can then function as perfect fetish objects for the cultural body, reinforcing not just gendered, but also race and class-based forms of oppression and privilege (Gentile, 2011, 2013, 2014). Thus, ARTs are located at a special cultural vortex, where two of the most significant social practices shaping our cultural body, biomedicalization and reprofuturity, merge. Because both of these discourses involve the complementary manipulation of affect through the production of temporalities – biomedicalization promotes and quells risk for the future while reprofuturity promotes a hopeful future through reproduction – and temporality is the foundation of subjectivity, both of these practices become socially contagious through their capacities to produce ways of going on being. Thus, when biomedicalization and reprofuturity are combined in the practices of ARTs, our very temporal foundation of subjectivity is engaged and potentially soothed or/and regulated while being re-created.

About ARTs and infertility

According to the American Society for Reproductive Medicine (http://www.reproductivefacts.org/topics/detail.aspx?id=36), the diagnostic criterion for infertility is 1 year of unprotected, heterosexual, vaginal intercourse. However, heterosexual couples (including most of the people I interviewed) are often referred to fertility clinics after only 3–6 months. Recalling Foucault's (1970) critiques of expert knowledges, as new drugs are produced, ART protocols proliferate and the availability of treatments increases. In response, more people are diagnosed with infertility sooner.[4] And, while most doctors will justify this leap to ARTs by quickly drawing a frightening graph of how markedly women's fertility declines after the age of 35, in actuality, statistics in this area are quite messy. According to a recent report (Twenge, 2013), most stats used in current studies are based on French population studies from 1670 to 1830. More recent statistics show that the difference in pregnancy rates at age 28 versus 37 is only about 4 percentage points. As Twenge reports, data culled from a Danish study on women who had at least one child demonstrate no decline in fertility from the 20s to the 40s. Other studies indicate that 66% of women will have a decrease in fertility after 35, with the rest remaining stable until 45 (Mundy, 2008). However, as Twenge (2013) points out, this decrease can be erased with carefully timed intercourse/insemination alone. Just over 17% of women aged 15–34 and 21.4% of 35–40-year-olds are infertile (Cain, 2001). This myopic focus on the woman's "biological clock" (and, recently, but to a much lesser extent, men's) supports biotechnological causes and interventions for infertility, ignoring environmental or structural causes. After all, economic class, not age, is the largest predictor of infertility (Mundy, 2008). This rabid focus on age needs to be seen intersectionally as an operation of misogynous class-based oppression. As will be described in Chapters 2 and 3, the metaphor of the ticking clock is a common trope to reinforce the centrality of reproduction for women, which, given that the United States lags behind much of Europe in terms of maternity and paternity leaves and affordable child care, leaves many women having to choose between professional advancement, financial stability, or reproduction.

Given that class, not age, is the best predictor of infertility (Mundy, 2008), the current structure of ARTs guarantees that those most impacted have limited or no access to expensive ART interventions. Because ARTs remain expensive interventions that are not always covered by insurance (or only components of the treatment are covered; for instance, many insurance plans will not pay for medications that can cost thousands of dollars per cycle), they function to reinforce class and race distinctions, such that upper-class "white women are privileged consumers whose fertility is promoted while black women's access to technology and their reproduction in general are discouraged" (Oliver, 2012, p. 166, referring to Dorothy Roberts). The desire for babies is deemed legitimate for white women while coded as excessive or criminal for women of color and poor women (Roberts, 2009; Oliver, 2012). This racial/ethnic and class disparity will be discussed further in Chapter 2 in reference to the ways fetal protection laws have criminalized pregnant women of color.

Western culture is organized around the idea that women embody materiality and are identified as the bodies of the culture, enabling men to appear disembodied or beyond materiality (see Butler, 1990; Dimen, 1991; Goldner, 1991; Bordo, 1993; Probyn, 1993; Grosz, 1994, 1995; Oliver, 2007, to list only a few). As many have observed, this containment of embodiment in the female means females are socialized to communicate through their bodies, to identify their physical appearance as the site of their power, control, success, and mastery. The body produced by this culture is assembled as a series of measurements such as weight, calories consumed, and clothing size, and it is split into parts – thighs, breasts, butt – that are isolated and judged. Fertility treatments are perfectly structured to exploit this form of objectified subjectivity through its physically and emotionally demanding protocols that categorize and locate the female patient based on procedural measurements – hormone levels, follicle size, thickness of uterine lining, numbers of eggs produced, and, of course, age. Since women are the identified patients regardless of the diagnosis, men's bodies cease to be relevant to the treatment, except as disembodied producers of "samples." Even when the fertility problem is a male factor, it is identified as a problem with sperm (not the male body), and the solution is a more technologically complicated form of IVF – intracytoplasmic sperm injection (ICSI) – identifying one sperm that appears to be good enough and injecting it directly into an egg that has had its shell softened to more easily accept it. Treating the male body in order to increase the quality of sperm is not usually an option in the Western model of fertility medicine (see Franklin and Ragoné, 1998), even though it is in other non-Western medicines (A. Vitolo, personal communication, July 7, 2006).

The language of ARTs is also interesting when it comes to the process known as "egg retrieval." To retrieve is to either bring in wounded or killed game as in a hunt, or to "salvage" or "rescue" something that was previously yours (Merriam-Webster dictionary online: http://www.merriam-webster.com/dictionary/retrieve). The implication here is that, by artificially stimulating the ovaries to produce extra eggs, these eggs then need to be salvaged or rescued from their maternal host by the doctor, who regains rightful possession of them as if on a hunting expedition. And this expedition requires a great deal of time and effort on the part of the woman patient who with each round of IVF, must undergo outpatient surgery with anesthesia. So the patient must fast the evening before and take the day off from work. Throughout the cycle, but especially after the egg retrieval and implantation, women must also monitor their activity and exercise levels. Depending on the number and quality of eggs retrieved and successfully fertilized, this process can be repeated multiple times, sometimes monthly.

Here, the symptom of infertility takes a back seat to the technology designed to produce pregnancy. So, regardless of the identified infertility factor, intervention involves monitoring and/or controlling the woman's hormonal cycle in order to increase follicular production of eggs and time ovulation. This process requires potent hormonal drugs, continuous monitoring of follicles (which can be overstimulated, resulting in a life-threatening condition) and blood levels, carefully timed intercourse, insemination, or invasive egg retrievals (for IVF), followed by embryo transfers into the uterus, and, if multiple embryos implant, sometimes reductions. While other countries have created laws restricting the numbers of embryos that can be transferred (based on research demonstrating that success rates increase with fewer embryos and because some believe it is unethical to selectively abort embryos, and because it can be psychologically challenging for the patient), the United States relies on "guidelines." Those embryos not implanted, if healthy enough, may be frozen for use during another cycle or donated. This use of "guidelines" vs. laws means decision-making power is granted to the patient – who is often driven by the idea of multiple births as an instant family with children – and the doctors who are oftentimes influenced by market demands for higher numbers of births (multiples figure better in clinic success statistics). The complications of these decisions will be discussed in Chapter 8 in terms of the ramifications for NICUs.

Studies of ARTs from disciplines as diverse as sociology, economics and business, legal studies, medical anthropology, and psychology identify most of the same characteristics. First, as mentioned, because it takes heterosexual intercourse out of the process, ART makes reproduction sexually democratic after all: it is a medical procedure for every participant. This opens up biological parenting to same-sex and transgender couples/families and single people, although access to ARTs is limited by state. Of course, this democratizing is based on the fact that reproduction is controlled entirely by the doctor. As the leader of an orientation workshop for a large New York City fertility clinic stated, "pregnancy is much easier once the doctor takes control over your [the woman's] body." The clinical gaze disciplines the body in an attempt to control it, as though it were a predictable reproductive machine. The potential causes of infertility become irrelevant. Ginsburg and Rapp (1995) describe how women's bodies are erased from images of ARTs and replaced by technologies, making interventions appear "natural" and "miraculous" simultaneously (pp. 6–7). Human fertility is pegged as "not very efficient" and in need of scientific assistance (Franklin, 1995), and because fertility, as constructed within Western culture, is located exclusively in the woman, it is her body that is labeled inefficient.

Within ARTs, women's bodies are under constant surveillance, and it is women who undertake significant and unknown medical risk in fertility treatments. In ARTs, each month's period signals both a failed attempt at pregnancy and a need to try something new; and something new is always available. Pharmaceutical companies and the biomedical establishment are central to how infertility is diagnosed, conceptualized, and treated. The medical establishment constructs this as a "never enough" treatment, in which the newest, most technologically advanced techniques are continually evolving and being tweaked, so, from month to month, women and men are given hope that the next treatment, the next month, surely the next attempt will be successful (see Franklin & Ragoné, 1998; Inhorn & Van Balen, 2002). Because infertility often has an unknown cause, and women's cycles can vary from month to month, the possibilities for intervention can seem endless, bound only by the woman's age (sometimes) or the patient's financial resources.

Although the US Centers for Disease Control suggests clinics report their statistics, there is no standardization dictating what gets reported as success. For some clinics success is a live birth, which may increase the numbers of embryos implanted and the number of multiples born, since twins would count as two successes. "Live birth" is also a broad category, including babies born without a problem as well as those born preterm, those with medical problems, and those who die shortly after delivery. Other clinics report a positive pregnancy test as success, even if it results in miscarriage. Also there is no enforcement to report, so only 50–60% of clinics report their statistics (Mundy, 2008). Success rates average 20–30%, meaning it is a medical procedure where over 70% of patients will not be "cured" (Spar, 2006; Mundy, 2008). As will be described, ARTs do not follow typical market patterns. As clinics proliferate, the procedures become more expensive, not less, and with each failure people are willing to pay more, not less, staying with the same clinic and blaming themselves for the failures (Spar, 2006).

With only guidelines as oversight, the ART field has repeatedly been called a "wild west science" (Spar, 2006; Mundy, 2008), where there are no limits to how far one should go in the quest to become pregnant. For instance, some drugs used for IVF do not even have Food and Drug Administration approval for infertility applications (Zoll, 2013). Mundy calls this current state of fertility medicine the beneficiary of a perfect storm, including

> pro-life opposition to embryo research; the demand for total reproductive liberty – absolute freedom of choice – on the part of infertility patients' advocacy groups; and, not least, doctors who benefit from transferring practical, psychological, and moral responsibility for decision-making to patients.
>
> (p. 239)

who are not the experts. There is even a growing industry of companies that will interpret clinic and procedural statistics for patients (Seligson, 2014). Given the economics of ARTs for patients and clinics and our pro-natal culture, patients are not supported to make healthy decisions. This perfect storm is fueled by the medicalization of childlessness that encourages a focus on the biological experience of infertility and finding biological solutions (Letherby, 2002, p. 283), engaging biotechnology in an endless search for causation.

Although conceptualized by some as a "patriarchal bargain" (Lorber, 1989), the essence of the bargain in the context of ARTs is that many of the costs involved are hidden from view. In pointing this out, I am not questioning people's respective choices or the value of or the benefits from ARTs. Indeed, most memoirs I read and the people I interviewed did not regret engaging with ARTs, even when they did get pregnant. I am not entering into the "mommy wars" or attempting to comment on issues of "leaning in." I am attempting to explore how options and agency for choice making are constructed (Petchesky, 1995) and experienced, including the contexts and the material conditions shaping ART interventions, the psychological experience of the procedures, and, most importantly, the ramifications for a repetition for sexual trauma, something that seems obvious, yet few have discussed.

The critiques in this book are less about ARTs in theory than about how they are practiced currently: how they reflect our cultural atmosphere of neoliberalism that squashes collective action and the networks, and the meaningful reflection that simultaneously supports and emerges from it. It is easy when discussing ARTs to cling to one side of the debate or the other, so, in an attempt to hold a third or potential space, I am emphasizing how ARTs and their various cultural contexts foster "collective capacities to act and become" and create "poisonous encounters between bodies that decompose a body's relations of parts" (Parisi, 2004, p. 45). ARTs produce multiple subjectivities that are agentic, traumatized, and colonized. They inhibit meaningful reflection while expanding potentialities of being.

The cultural stereotype of women ART patients is of a rabid, myopically driven woman attempting to control everything around her in her quest for a baby. As will be described, ARTs are all-consuming, requiring that the patient structure her days, months, perhaps years, around the protocols. This myopic engagement is, if not demanded, certainly rewarded by the medical personnel who expect patients to wrap their lives around the ever-changing demands of the treatment. When engulfed in a never-enough treatment atmosphere (see Franklin & Ragoné, 1998), where one is tempted to continue even hopeless cycles because something new is always around the corner, stopping before one is pregnant is not an option (Ibid.). As will be described, we live in a culture shaped by the neoliberal ideals of self-sufficiency and the privatization of failure and success. Heterosexual women, in particular, may have had years of engaging with the body as if it is a highly fertile bomb just waiting to be set off by a poorly inserted diaphragm, a broken condom, or a missed pill. Not being able to get pregnant easily after years of working so hard not to can shatter a significant part of one's identity and sense of subjectivity. Given the economics of treatment, most ART patients have class and racial/ethnic privilege. Many (not all) are high-achieving, hard workers used to seeing success from their efforts. These energies can easily be applied to ART protocols. As Sara, an interviewee, reflected, getting pregnant "was the first thing in my life I hadn't been able to do if I just worked hard enough." Many factors combine to make ARTs an all-encompassing pursuit.

Structure of the book

This book has four parts. The first part explores the context of reproduction, situating the representation of babies and ARTs within the cultural imagination. Ideas of temporality, in particular reprofuturity – how a "normal" life is constructed around reproduction – are central (L. Edelman, 2004; Halberstam, 2005). As will be described in Chapter 2, reprofuturity shapes the temporal rhythm and values of the culture, privileging those events, affects, and experiences associated with children. Here, promise is held in the future, and this temporal motion shapes subjectivities. This focus on temporality is relevant not only because the values of reprofuturity shape subjectivities, but because the process of ARTs requires entering into a new temporal world, where one is positioned in a liminal space of "almost pregnant," engaging in procedures that require the religious fervor of a new convert blindly driven by hope in a certain future trajectory (Franklin, 1998) designed to disavow the uncertainty of the liminality. This futurity is coupled with an intensive scanning of the past for any potential transgressions to be blamed for the failures (Gentile, 2013). And, as will be described, this complex temporal layering occurs with little space for reflection, which compromises capacities for meaning and decision making. This foreclosure of meaningful decision making becomes quite important when one is caught in the machine that is ART procedures.

While queer theorists have deconstructed the temporal normativity conveyed through reprofuturity, psychoanalysts, often steeped in the Oedipal and other canonical developmental trajectories, have held firm to reifying linear temporal development and maturity through reproduction as the sign of psychological health. Placing ARTs within this cultural context helps to shed light on the ramifications of the ART "bargain."

This first part introduces a unique integration of cultural and psychoanalytic theories through the link of temporality. As mentioned above, the cultural and psychoanalytic theories of subjectivity highlighted here privilege time and space in the formation of the self. This transdisciplinary theoretical approach provides a new space from which to examine ARTs. These initial chapters also provide a conceptual analysis of the cultural context of biomedicalization and reprofuturity within which ARTs have not just become an option, but are now cast as a necessary part of women's healthcare. This normalization has very important ramifications. Building on this context, Chapter 4 uses interview data and memoir to situate ART patients as struggling with multiple different temporal positions, highlighting the potential for re-traumatization for survivors of sexual violence.

Part II details and describes some of the complex situations that have evolved with the proliferation of ARTs. Egg donation has become a popular way of staving off uncertainty, controlling or "gifting" time. Chapter 5, by Michelle Leve, describes the complex situation of egg donation. In most ART stories, the egg donors remain the anonymous secret, rendering maternity multiple and/or tenuous. Leve's chapter explores ideas of subjectivity, choice, and agency for egg donors as well as the complicated political and economic issues surrounding the selling of eggs. After all, as Leve describes, most Western countries consider eggs equivalent to organs, and thus, they cannot be sold. As Leve observes, the identified value of the eggs is determined by the qualities and experiences of the donor, as if there is a one-to-one correspondence. These qualities are often ranked in egg donation programs, by the potential donor's race, ethnicity, class, and education. Pictures of the donor are always included. In these and other ways, egg donation is handled quite differently from sperm donation, as will be described. In egg donation, language is key. Eggs are not "purchased"; they are "transferred" between bodies. The egg donor is called a "provider," never a "seller," and the woman buying the eggs is a "recipient," not a "consumer." As Leve describes, the egg donor is forced to walk a thin line between altruism and maternity. Just as psychoanalysis struggles to foster and tolerate ambivalence, Leve is advocating constructing egg donors as exploited, agentic, and oppressed.

Chapter 6, by Adam Kaplan, takes the form of a personal narrative addressing male infertility. Although around 40% of infertility is based on the male factor (Mundy, 2008), discussions of male infertility are few. Just do a search on the psychoanalytic database called PEP and "male infertility" will pull up a mere two articles, one by Keylor and Apter (2010) and the other my response to their article (Gentile, 2010). This silence in the psychoanalytic world in particular is explored in Chapters 2–4. Although the interview narratives in Chapter 5 include men, like most research, theory, and clinical case studies on ARTs, the focus is still on women. There is little research or published clinical work on men participating in ARTs or who are infertile. Indeed, male infertility, a significant factor in the proliferation of ARTs, has been described as a cultural taboo (Webb & Daniluk, 1999; Daniels, 2006) and is usually left unexamined, ignored entirely, or glossed over with phallocentric stereotypes (see Gannon et al., 2004; Gentile, 2010).

Many articles and theories circle around the same issue: the conflation of infertility with impotence, and impotence with the loss of all cultural power. The media and the men themselves struggle to disaggregate infertility from gender and sexuality. Messages from the media about low sperm counts and male infertility describe "shrunken penises," fears of "gay" or "feminized" genitals (Gannon et al., 2004; see also Daniels, 2006). This conflation signals just how enmeshed the penis and testes are with the phallus as a symbol of power. Male infertility is so taboo and unthinkable that the culture collapses masculinity into the penis. Physical function is equated with heterosexuality and gender expression. If a man cannot produce enough sperm, his very masculinity is in question.

Thus, Kaplan's personal narrative provides a necessary rich and complex detail to the literature on male infertility. As a clinician and author, Kaplan tries on established psychoanalytic theories of male infertility, rejecting most as antiquated and phallocentric notions of masculinity. He asks instead if male patients and their analysts can stand in the cultural spaces where men can be vulnerable without either projecting their weaknesses on to others (women, children, and other men) or collapsing into a category of male impotence. Can a man just be human? After all, if, as clinicians, we cannot deconstruct our inherited notions of phallocentric, invulnerable masculinity, what do we have to offer an infertile male other than stereotypes (Gentile, 2010)? With these theories as a bedrock, men should flee to greener, more potent pastures, whether they be younger women or men, or just a different therapist. Kaplan's take on infertility opens up some space, complicating experiences and the theorizing of male infertility. As he deconstructs masculine ideals of isolation and independence, the book editor captures a dialogue with him in the footnotes.

Chapter 7, by Diane Ehrensaft, further complicates the ways in which ARTs can destabilize the Oedipal narrative by detailing clinical work with transgender parents and their experiences of ARTs. As she describes clinical work with transgender couples, the traditional Oedipal model of kinship morphs into what Ehrensaft describes as a complicated circle of networks with multiple different forms of parents and siblings. While anthropologists have described ARTs expanding our notions of kinship, Ehrensaft outlines a new psychoanalytic construction of family, thus, of psychic development far beyond the traditional horizontal limits of the Oedipal.

Chapter 8, by Zina Steinberg and Susan Kraemer, takes the potential of ARTs full circle by describing the work of clinical consultants on a NICU. Steinberg and Kraemer describe this chapter as illuminating the "shadow side" of ARTs, in particular IVF. NICUs (and high-risk pregnancy wards) have exploded with the proliferation of ARTs, yet the very real potential for the creation of tenuous and short lives is rarely mentioned when people enter the world of ARTs. This chapter can be heartbreaking, as the authors expose the underbelly of what they describe as the triumphal narratives of infertility treatment. Here, "efficiency, urgency and calm braid together" in an atmosphere where babies may weigh a pound, their skin bruises with the slightest touch, on respirators that obscure their faces, with lungs barely formed. As Steinberg and Kraemer point out, for most of the parents, the NICU is the culmination of years of IVF attempts. Here, the liminality of "not yet pregnant" gives way to the liminality of a tiny, tenuous life, illuminating the depths of the ART "bargain" (Lorber, 1989).

The first two parts, Chapters 1–8, set a complex cultural and psychoanalytic context for Chapters 9–13, Part III, that is centered around a psychoanalytic case study about a woman recipient of egg donation. Research, theory, and clinical work tend to avoid the unthinkable void of infertility, so few have found ways to write about the unspeakable losses, absence, and experiences of lack in infertility. What do you do when space collapses, such that time cannot move and one is suddenly stuck in not a timeless or spaceless present, but a dense present filled with layer upon layer of heavy time, so thick with lack – lack of potential, lack of spark to ignite, lack of motion, lack of life? Tracy L. Simon's case tells just such a clinical story. Nora, a white, upper-class woman has been on an 11-year quest through the world of ARTs that ends only with the introduction of a donated egg. But this egg is not merely a vehicle for pregnancy – it is a foreign object, sent to abduct Nora's body. She acts almost as if she "knows" what Clough (2004) tells us, that DNA forms networks of information, webs that will have her body producing an "other," as they will also alter her body forever. Nora's affectively charged responses to this pregnancy, held and managed by Simon, resemble a powerful tornado flattening spaces of reflection and dissent.

This case study is followed by three distinct discussions of the case focusing on different aspects of loss and mourning and generativity. Stephen Hartman, in Chapter 10, describes infertility as a claustrum, where the alien from the film *Aliens* turns gestation into abduction. Here, the clinical space is painted as a desolate, treacherous void. Hartman's thick description of infertility and the technologies that overtake the body pulls the reader into a visual realm where the horror of how humans play with reproduction can be felt in all its discomfort.

What Nora does not know, however, is what André Lepecki's discussion in Chapter 11 can bring us. If subjectivities are assemblages, then who are we assembling? His refrain, repeated throughout the chapter, "whose body are we gathering as we come into being?" functions as an unsettling chorus, demanding reflection from different spaces each time it returns. Cellular cleavage will occur; the egg will grow, but it will do so only in a choreographed dance, where Nora's biochemistry creates the conditions for certain genes to be expressed, dulling some while igniting others. This egg will have at the very least three biological parents. As an egg fertilized by Nora's husband, it is an invader, but it is not a discrete body, a discrete alien. It is a body gathered from all the bodies of the donors – Nora's and her husband's bodies, not to mention those of Simon.

Lastly, Orna Guralnik, in Chapter 12, takes a completely different position, one that uses loss for the creation of something new. Guralnik creates a playful space to assemble different approaches to ARTs, where the potentials are unpacked in tandem with a critique of psychoanalysis' continuing romance with Oedipus. She interprets Nora's and her own patients' ambivalences around ARTs to be based in the seeming impossibility of living outside the Oedipal. Although this stance threatens to interpret the psychological, physical, and economic distresses of ARTs as merely defensive, and she does not address the ways in which ARTs also enable the Oedipal mandate of reproduction and generational distinctions to enfold everyone regardless of gender or sexuality, her emphasis on the potentials for ARTs is an important addition.

Wrapping up the case discussion, Simon returns in Chapter 13 to respond to each of these discussants, providing further detail and analysis of her case, enriching our theories about the experiences of ARTs.

Part IV is the Epilogue, a chapter that goes beyond merely wrapping up the main points of the book. Certainly the chapters and their approaches to and descriptions of ARTs deepen our understandings and theories about these technologies. But, in each chapter, it is clear that ambivalence around reproduction in general, not only in ARTs, needs to not just be "tolerated," but to be actively cultivated so patients can create the transgressive spaces necessary to question the Oedipal reproductive mandate and the reprofuturity of the dominant culture. We have to bring intrapsychic ambivalence out into the open as overt conflict and conflicts of interest with ourselves, our cultures, and our environments. As ARTs proliferate they do produce male, female, and transgender bodies more and more friendly to their interventions. But it is crucial in the face of these biomedicalized practices to hold space for reflections and contradictions, the ways ARTs generate possibilities, while making expensive promises they know they cannot keep. Space must be made for alternative forms of parenting and the legitimacy of nonreproductive lives, childfree living, and, lives that are not referenced to the production of children whatsoever. In the face of environmental destruction as a result of rampant human reproduction, which is now coupled with a fetishistic view of the fetus, psychoanalysts in particular need to help create the space for reflection with ARTs. We must challenge ourselves and our patients to experience the intrapsychic, interpersonal, local, and global impact of our choices. It is these links that are erased not just in neoliberal structures of our culture, but by psychoanalysis itself. It is this complex level of analysis that is required to unpack the "patriarchal bargain" (Lorber, 1989) of ARTs.

Notes

1 As will be described, IVF is the go-to "cure" for infertility. It involves having the woman take daily hormone shots to stop, then start, her menstrual cycle and hyperstimulate ovulation. Multiple eggs are harvested and fertilization takes place in a lab. If embryos develop, one or more will be inserted into the uterus in hopes of implantation. This process will be described further throughout this book.

IUI may or may not involve ovarian-stimulating hormones. Sperm is inserted into the uterus through a catheter. Surrogacy usually involves paying a woman to gestate a fetus. The egg and sperm may or may not be from a donor.

2 This depends upon one's definition of sex. ARTs most often take the heterosexual, vaginal–penis intercourse sex out of the equation. Male orgasm, however, is still required for most forms of ART, although there are technologies to extract sperm. So ARTs take the heterosexual sex out of reproduction for everyone while reinforcing the idea that female orgasm is superfluous in reproduction.

3 Here is one of the examples of biomedicalization shaping subjectivities. The avoidance of risk factors shapes not just your time – you will have a healthy future – but also your embodiment – a healthy future/time means a healthy body. This will be explored further in Chapters 2–4.

4 Additionally, ARTs are being used on children as young as 7 who have cancer to save reproductive potential (Mundy, 2008).

Chapter 2

Bridging psychoanalytic and cultural times – using psychoanalytic theory to understand better how reprofuturity and biomedicalization produce subjectivities

Katie Gentile

One would have to be living under a rock to not notice the media's obsession with babies, pregnancy, and what Donna Haraway (1997) termed the "public fetus". As mentioned previously, Mamo (2007) goes so far as to claim that, for women, there has been a shift from compulsory heterosexuality to compulsory motherhood. While it may be easy to explain this grip on reproduction as merely the titillation of popular culture, the lure of the fetus is contagious even to the news media. *The New York Times* has seen a marked increase in articles on pregnancy and maternal health in the past decade (Gentile, 2011). But it is not only the amount of coverage that has increased; there has also been a shift in its tenor. While in the 1990s pregnancy coverage focused on the need to decrease what was often described as the scourge of teenage pregnancy, by 2006 most articles were celebrating and protecting pregnancies, even those of teenagers (Gentile, 2011). Now hardly a day goes by without some new medical report arousing feelings of panic and emergency around threats to fetal health. These studies restrict the lives of pregnant women by emphasizing certain risks over others, those emanating from the maternal body through foods eaten, drinks consumed, exercises attempted, over environmental or structural risks. Pregnancy itself has been celebrated to the extent that there have been articles describing competitive birthing between women (see Kargman, 2007). Keeping up with the Jones' in this area is important because babies have become not just accessories; they are symbols of opulence (Haughney, 2007) for white, upper-middle-class families, as will be discussed.

This focus on babies and pregnancy occurs within a specific cultural context of neodomesticity and reprofuturity– renewed pressures for women's domesticity often centered around children and neoliberalism and its medicalized outgrowth, biomedicalization – practices of embodiment that privatize affect and illness, requiring us to experience our bodies through measurements of weight, cholesterol, estrogen, blood sugar levels, etc. As will be described, assisted reproductive technologies (ARTs) emerge at this perfect vortex, pairing the cultural obsessions with biotechnology, medicalization, and the use of babies as fetish objects (Gentile, 2013, 2014) with a renewed focus on the home as a space of self-transformation for women. The ideologies of neoliberalism, neodomesticity, biomedicalization, and reprofuturity can all come together in ARTs to promote a drive for reproduction at all costs. But the argument that permeates this volume is that experiences situated in spaces the culture deems "natural" can be difficult to critique (Bourdieu, 1977). Wielding the term "natural" keeps the ideological under the table and out of view. Human reproduction and the ritualized medicalization that shapes it function to help define what we consider "the natural," thus, they are quite tough to examine or critique.

This chapter functions to set up a certain cultural and psychoanalytic context for examining the practices and protocols of ARTs. It does so by outlining a new transdisciplinary conceptualization of subjectivity based not only in relationships with other humans, but with those of the environment of human and nonhuman objects with which we are in a continual cycle of co-emergence. Temporality is the link creating and disrupting this vast intimacy. I begin by looking at the roles and functions of the fetal fetish for the cultural body. From there, it becomes clear the culture projects desires and hopes on to the fetus, embodying what queer theorists have termed reprofuturity. But this way of "playing with time" as a form of regulation (Gentile, 2007) calls for a psychoanalytic take on temporality in order to better understand the lure of the fetal fetish and other concepts surrounding ARTs that will be described in the next chapter. After all, affect and queer theorists can describe how reprofuturity functions to organize a cultural body, but psychoanalysis can explore how this organizing is based on forms of time that produce and reify certain self-experiences. Here, temporality not only shapes us through the rhythms and spaces of parental care; our subjectivities are only produced through time. This foundational role of temporality for our very self-experience renders us particularly susceptible to cultural practices that manipulate time and futurity. To explore these functions of time, this chapter uses cultural theory to expand upon psychoanalysis and psychoanalysis to expand upon cultural theory.

The commodification of affect and the corresponding fetish of the fetus

US culture since 9/11 can be described as risk-based (Beck, 2007) and organized by crisis or emergency time (Hesford, 2008). Both terms describe a collapse of social space, limiting reflection and meaning making (Oliver, 2007; Layton, 2010; Gentile, 2011). Without this reflective space, we are unable to transform affect into embodied action, to create and use symbolization and representation. This can result in a dependence on prepackaged commodified experiences that provide an easily digestible, linear, unidirectional temporal narrative. This prepackaged affect can be used to create a fantasy of wholeness in the face of overwhelming anxiety and an inability to have faith in a progressive, better future (Brown, 2005; Gentile, 2011). Through the use of such commodified affects, a neoliberal fantasy of invulnerability can be maintained (Oliver, 2007; Layton, 2010; Gentile, 2011, 2013).[1]

Commodified affects such as nostalgia (Huyssen, 2000) and romantic sentiment (Berlant, 2008) are particularly popular remedies, trading manufactured emotion for innovative meaning making, to create a fantasy of simplicity unencumbered by the pain and anxiety of ambivalence and oppression (Ibid.). Oppression can become erased through nostalgia and sentiment because the past is rewritten, manufactured to create the present that is desired (Love, 2007). Because affect emerges in nonrepresentational social spaces and produces nonlinear networks of transmission (Clough, 2004), it can function as both a space of resistance (Massumi, 2002) and of biopolitical control and manipulation (Clough, 2004). The latter can occur through a particular relationship to time that becomes rigidified through a spatially collapsed, linear repetition. Sentiment and nostalgia about babies and childhood are examples of this rigidified temporal repetition. These forms function to promote an uncritical compliance with increased biopolitical surveillance, especially around reproduction, as women are urged to engage in a vigilant and manic panic about future (in)fertility and the health of their future fetus (see Gentile, 2013).

In this cultural context of limited reflection and temporal collapse, the image of a fetus can be a fetish of citizenship, standing in for the "virtuous private citizen around whom history ought to be organized, for whom there is not a good-enough world" (Berlant, 2010, p. 110). In this scenario, as Berlant notes, the public fetus becomes the fetish object that can be protected without compromising our fantasies of independence or self-sufficiency. We can relate to it without becoming weak as the fantasy fetus is used to contain and carry the relational vulnerability.

This public fetus is irresistible because it is a perfect "lure for feeling" (Whitehead, cited by Shaviro (n.d.), p. 8), visible yet inaccessible, functioning as a container for infinite projections that hold the capacity to produce various effects (Bennett, 2010) for us all, including the capacity to mark time and experience its movement. As will be discussed in the next chapter, in a culture shaped temporally by notions of heteronormative reprofuturity (Halberstam, 2005), the public fetus slips in easily as the fetish object in relation to which we can feel whole and disavow death and anxiety by creating an embodied representation of the future. Images of the fetus not only "entertain propositions" (Shaviro, n.d., p. 9); they hold the potential to phantasmatically embody them, because the container will at some point be birthed into the world. Thus, fetuses contain projections of futurity, embodying temporality.[2]

This temporal function is central when facing potential global catastrophe. Unlike other forms of risk, catastrophe disorganizes rationality and traditional models of decision making because it is based on speculation (Cooper, 2006). There is no exact "when" (p. 125); thus, catastrophe "operates outside chronological continuity with the past" (p. 125). According to Cooper, the only way to face up to such a future is to become "immersed in its conditions of emergence, to the point of actualizing it ourselves" (p. 125). The brilliance of using the fetus as a fetish object is that it enables the cultural body to not just actualize the conditions of emergence, but to do so within a "real" material body – the fetus. But the fetus provides even more defense against catastrophe as it enables us to actualize these conditions *within* ourselves, indeed, *within* the abject (Kristeva, 1982) maternal body. Time and space are central then to the use of the fetus in the face of catastrophe.

Situating the use of the fetus as a fetish in the face of catastrophic unknowing sets up an important cultural context for the analysis of ARTs. But if time and space are central to the production of subjectivity, then catastrophe presents a seismic disruption to being, such that there may be great desperation fueling this fetish object. The fetus may function not just as a "lure for feeling," as described above, but as the only available container holding us individually, and collectively, in time. After all, if catastrophic not knowing disrupts any sense of prediction, it threatens our very psychic organization with annihilation. But if we can pause this cultural theory for a moment in order to trace the foundations of time and space psychoanalytically in the development of subjectivity, we can differentiate *prediction*, which conjures a linear collapse of potentials, from *expectation*, which can create the space necessary to generate nonlinear and multiple potentials. After all, even networks of affective communication in the face of catastrophe can form the potential spaces of resistance as well as those of social control (Massumi, 2002; Clough, 2004).

This chapter, then, seeks to integrate cultural theories of time and space with those of psychoanalysis, generating a contextualized subjectivity for psychoanalysis and a multidimensionally agentic one within cultural theory. This transdisciplinary theory of temporality is required in order to begin to understand how it is that ARTs and their promise of certain futures remain singularly enticing even in the face of constant failures.

Blackman (2008) contends that psychoanalysis is part of the cross-disciplinary romance with the concept of self-regulation, a pairing she sees as having gained ground in the 1990s with the rise of neoliberalism, and I would add, of a renewed cross-discipline attention to affect. She identifies theories of self-regulation emerging as an outgrowth of our cultural need to privatize both suffering and the responsibilities for intervention. This privatization functions to produce psychological subjects that are hindered in their abilities to contextualize the social as a significant area of influence. Blackman warns us to be mindful to identify when regulation is used to order chaos and promote creative meaning making and when it is deployed to produce forms of discipline and compliance. Thus, we must engage in a critique of the reification of affect regulation. So while it is important to describe this developmental regulation through time, we need to do so while holding on to the understanding that the pressures of the culture to individualize and mandate regulation and self-control impact our theories, even as we conceptualize affect and regulation as relationally emergent.[3]

So as I write and theorize ideas of affect regulation, I want to emphasize that my use of "self" or "affect" regulation refers to a complicated contextualized capacity. Regulation is not an individual or privatized practice, nor is it an end goal or neoliberal skill to master, to meet a culturally reified notion of psychological health. Regulation is always relational, meaning it is a process emerging not internally but in the social and cultural space that produces bodies, where networks of affect emerge (Clough, 2004). Further, regulation is always emergent, i.e., one cannot and should not maintain regulation.

Time and the production of subjectivities

> [C]ritical interpretation of actions, desires, and values both requires and results in connecting the present to the past and the future.
>
> (Oliver, 2007, p. 86)

Creative meaning making emerges from a notion of the present as being full and attached to multiple, divergent pasts, presents, and futures (Dinshaw, 2012). These temporal divisions are not rigid, but in continuous motion, shaped through a process of differentiation that is itself a form of connectedness, not separation (Gentile, 2006, 2007). But creating these temporal links, transforming affect into conscious, meaningful behavior, is quite a complicated process that is easily undone.

Trauma and violence can jeopardize our capacities to create the time and space necessary for reflection and representation of experience. We may "retreat into a dissociation of fixed representation – a virtual world of fantasies" (Campbell, 2006, p. 143), resulting in a dependence upon premade cultural narratives that can be swallowed whole to make meaning of experience (Oliver, 2004; Gentile, 2007, 2011). Here, the "lack" or space created between affect and representation can become torturous, and the precariousness of subjectivity that presents opportunities for innovative re-creation is instead experienced as persecutory. There can be little capacity to play with meaning, and instead there is a strong desire/need to arrest it as a "belief to be affirmed at all costs" (Reeves, 2011, p. 384). In this state of temporal rigidity, commodified forms of affect like nostalgia and sentiment can provide containment and certainty. Although the common understanding is that trauma stops time or destroys chronological time, it is important to re-conceptualize this assumption. If we conceptualize time as a process, where past, present, and futures are multiple and nonlinear, what is destroyed in trauma is not chronology, which is already a distortion of time according to Bergson (1913/2001), but the flow of time (Campbell, 2006) or the capacity for faith to go on being within an unfolding duration of time (Gentile, 2007, 2011, 2013) – in other words, our capacities to create ourselves anew through time.

Developmental time

Bion (1962a, b), Winnicott (1971), Loewald (1980), and Lombardi (2003, 2008) each describe time developmentally, theorizing it as being held by the caretaker in her/his rhythms and patterns of satisfaction and frustration.[4] These embodied interactions create the initial patterns of temporality. Beebe et al. (2012) build on this idea, describing these interactions as producing a predictability of behavior over time. This predictability results in the creation of "if–then sequences" (p. 262). These sequences are the foundations for internal and procedural representations of self and other; thus, the sequences are a foundation for the development of a sense of differentiation. Differentiation, as written previously (Gentile, 2007), and as Barad (2007, 2010) has observed, is not just a form of connection but the process through which subjectivities, and thus our surroundings, come into being. The predictability of interactions leads to the development of the capacity for expectation, or what Davoine (2012), in the context of trauma, calls expectancy. Bion (1962b) also focuses on expectation. He contends that preconception creates an expectation that, when not met, results in frustration which can then fuel the creation of thinking. Thus, for Bion (1962b), the violation of expectation in time, the violation of an established pattern of interaction, is the foundation for thought. Presence of expectation itself, however, demonstrates a capacity for gathering and holding experiences, and the capacity to create a future – an expectation. The present emerges from the future; according to Bion, "the future casts its shadow backwards on the present" (Ogden, 2012, p. 106, footnote). In other words, time is necessary in order to have a violation of expectation.

Lombardi (2003, 2008) identifies linear, chronological time as thought, writing that it is "equivalent" (p. 1534) to the work of Bion's *K* (knowledge), as well as to the development of the capacities that facilitate the tolerance of frustration and psychological growth. Lombardi builds on Bion's and Matte Blanco's ideas of temporality, describing time as sequential. Developing the capacity to recognize this chronological structure of time becomes, for Lombardi, a central component of "authentic" mental activity (Lombardi, 2008, p. 1194). Here, being able to experience time as linear is a measure of psychological health. For Lombardi, depersonalization and dissociation are seen as failures of time rather than as different forms of time, simultaneous times, or resistant uses of time, for instance, toward affect and relational regulation (see Gentile, 2007, 2013, 2015a). Time, for Lombardi (2008), functions to convey the limits of reality. In each of these psychoanalytic theories, time is a linear structure we use to organize our experiences in order to think. Accordingly, organizing the self around any nonlinear or nonchronological time is assumed to indicate psychosis.

Developing multiple times

Massumi (2002) describes bodies coming into being through affecting and needing to be affected. This affecting, like Beebe et al.'s (2012) infant–caretaker videos, describes a pattern of interaction where any originating intentionality emerges from within the space between. Here, one can theorize that time is not conveyed to the infant by the parent, but is instead produced by the interaction of the caretaker(s)–infant. Time, then, is emergent, created within what Knoblauch (2011) and Trevarthen (2009) would call polyrhythmic relational patterns of interactions. These relational patterns form a bubble or membrane, as Winnicott has termed it, around the caretaker(s)–infant. According to Winnicott, this bubble enables the infant to create a capacity for going on being.

As caretakers succeed and fail in responding to the infant, the infant gradually begins to develop a capacity for "inner reproductive holding" (Winnicott, 1971) through various times that are accumulated. These accumulations simultaneously produce a felt space of interiority that emanates from the "intermediate territory"

(p. 5) of transitional phenomena. It is from this intermediate, neither inner nor outer, territory (that produces a sense of an internal, which itself is neither inner nor outer) that memorial processes emerge. Memorial processes are not produced by, nor do they produce, linear, singular time. The present is continually being reproduced; it is layered and in motion, while pasts and futures are continually re-created with each new interaction.[5] Returning to the example above of "if–then" sequences (Beebe et al., 2012), with these more layered conditions, there would be multiple "ifs" and potential "thens" that would be continually re-creating each other. Thus, perception in the present is not merely "shot through with memory" (Loewald, 1980, p. 157), becoming what G.M. Edelman (2004) terms the "remembered present." It is, instead, shot through with multiple pasts and presents and futures. Perception emerges through a present with a "reservoir" of multiple, nonlinear links to the pasts, "as well as a close anticipation of the imminent future" (Grosz, 2004, p. 173). Thus, perception and memory emerge simultaneously, but there is a fundamental tension linking and differentiating them (Ibid.). This ensures that time does not collapse into a linear, unidimensional, densely packed present (a common response to trauma). Maintaining this mutual tension is a complicated process, easily undone, as will be described momentarily.

Time is not external, something universal with which we connect. *We come into being with its creation and engage in the continual process of its re-production.* Perception, retention, internalization, and anticipation are always elaborations and integrations, and new. Subjectivity emerges from engaging in a process of temporal motion between pasts, presents, and futures, building layers of continuous and simultaneous, nonlinear relational experience. Thus, the accumulation of affective experiences, i.e., the process of inner reproductive holding (Winnicott, 1971), is based in cultural rhythms of time. For instance, consider the different cultural rhythms of time that would emerge within a caregiver–infant dyad influenced by Dr. Spock vs. Winnicott vs. B.F. Skinner. Freeman (2010) describes chrononormativity creating bodies based on how "people are bound to one another, engrouped, made to feel coherently collective, through particular orchestrations of time" (p. 3). Here, cultural rhythms of "causality, sequence, forward-moving agency" (p. 64) become somatic facts, ways of knowing and being. Subjectivities emerge through a circulation of affect (Ahmed, 2007/2008) that, though seemingly existing in singular bodies and minds, is actually a series of "historically specific circulations that align and differentiate bodies in particular ways" (Murphy, 2012, p. 80). Our embodied subjectivities are produced by specific circulations, or timed rhythms, of affect, such that certain identities are coalesced, called up, interpellated (see Dimen, 2011), in different ways within cultural spaces.

Thus, caregivers are transmitting not only rhythms of interaction, but culturally appropriate rhythms of interaction, times, and spaces that convey culturally mediated practices of embodiment. It is within these particular culturally mediated rhythms of time that the process of accumulation creates the sense of interiority, as "[t]he subject . . . does not pre-exist its feelings but creates itself through them" (Stenner, 2008, p. 100). A "self" experience, then, is merely a particular way of "patterning spatial and temporal co-assemblages" (p. 107). Thus, cultural rhythms, times, and spaces create subjectivities.

Bodies/objects of time

This process of accumulating patterns and the patterns themselves are embodied and not necessarily representational or symbolic, although they are the foundation for these meaning-making capacities. Wittmann (2013), a neuroscientist, contends that our sense of time's duration is based in feeling states of the body, in other words, unrepresented affect. Gallese (2007) links affect and time within relational spaces, describing his notion of intercorporeity – the process of collecting embodied simulations of others. Here, the brain and body mirror other brains/bodies in interactions and register, prerepresentationally, other people's intentions toward us (Modell, 2011). Thus, the accumulations that function to create our sense of interiority are not mere representations, but embodied gestures, actions, responses, conscious and unconscious intentions, and potentials. But if we take seriously the deep layering of temporality described so far, then we are not only collecting our simulations, intentions and those of others in the moment, but also the pasts, presents, and futures of these others with whom we interact and their respective accumulations of interactions and simulations of others in their pasts, even as each of these interactions is being recast in the present moment. As Ettinger (2006) wrote,

> Thing inside my other's other is aching inside me, and where a forsaken Event that took place between "my" unknown others struggles for recognition through me and with me. Such a Thing and Event of the other are waiting to be remembered by me – I who never forgot them in the first place. Such are the traumatic.
>
> (Ettinger, 2006, p. 166)

These complex temporal layers of relational simulations and accumulations are the spaces of transgenerational transmission of trauma. These are the ghosts: what has been termed the haunting of time. But it is not time itself that is haunted, but, as Ettinger implies, it is the "struggles for recognition through and with," the relational spaces of differentiation and connection. These haunted struggles can collapse temporal space, rendering the emergence of the past to be not just *in* the present but *as* the present. And, given that these forms of transgenerational traumas emerge within nonrepresentational spaces, they are particularly difficult to recognize and represent. The collapse of the necessary tension holding the past, present, and future together and apart renders the ongoing creation of the present impossible. Instead, as will be described, one may have to install a temporally rigid notion of the present as isolated from the ongoing rhythms of time.

Given the nonrepresentational status of accumulations, it is clear these complex temporal processes are not located in the brain. Indeed, even the mind is not an isolated sovereign manager or ruler. Instead, it has been described as "a diverse, interconnected system (a mutuality of moods-objects-neurotransmitters-hormones-cognitions-affects-attachments-tears-glands-images-words-gut)" (Wilson, 2011, p. 280). Neurotransmitters are found throughout the body, and in particularly high quantities in the gut (Wilson, 2004), making the gut a particularly responsive area, referred to at times as the "second brain" (Ibid.). Research has also demonstrated how a body's physical reflexes exhibit reflection and meaning making (see Wilson, 2004; Koehler, 2011). Even the process of hearing a sound involves unconscious forms of perception that function to simplify and chunk information (Terranova, cited in Diamond, 2013).

But, as minds become bodies, bodies become unbounded, porous, culturally constructed entities. Object-oriented ontologists (Connor, 2011; Shaviro, n.d.), new materialists (Bennett, 2010), posthumanists (Barad, 2007, 2010), and biologists like Rupert Sheldrake (1990), and to some extent ecofeminists (Donovan & Adams, 1996), have implored us to recognize that bodies themselves are loosely assembled entanglements, interrelated components of social networks extending beyond skin – a superficial and inaccurate boundary of organism and environment. Here, all organisms are rhizomatic patterns of becomings and contagions (Deleuze & Guattari, 1987). Bodies are produced through events, "incorporated" (Massumi, 2014, p. 29) into the world. Indeed, the environment is "expressed in the nervous system and manifested by it through actions" (Koehler, 2011, p. 312). Neural patterns, then, are not located in what we identify as bodies or brains, but emerge from within the networks of relational entanglements and engagements. They are based within temporal layers of relational movements and intentions, each comprised of infinite potential pasts, presents, and futures refracting between and within each other. This interconnected assemblage of subjectivities can render the networks of commodified affect, described previously, particularly powerful and contagious. Separations of self/other, self/world, even human/object, are merely components of our culturally manufactured experience of a supposedly segregated and regulated world.

To complicate time further, temporality also emanates from the interobjective space, i.e., spaces between human and nonhuman objects (Morton, 2013). In other words, objects emanate forms of time that shape human time. Linear time can be seen, then, as the result of our dissociation from the network of objects surrounding us (or/and vice versa). Thus, as I have outlined, space and the rhythms of time emerge through a differentiation of objects, human and nonhuman, as these differentiations create times and spaces. Indeed, one of the early lessons we teach children is not to feed the dog/cat at the table. The table is for humans. This implicates the times of the dog/cat, table, and food. Each object has its own ontological and physical time (Morton, 2013), and these times are cast like "spells" (p. 93), shaping what we experience as human time. Objects act upon us to create "zones of aesthetic causality" (p. 141), but this acting is interactive, for instance, that the table is not for dogs/cats. Much to my mother's chagrin, my table is multispecies. It casts a spell on cats to spread out on it as it casts a spell on me to rest my teacup and newspaper upon it. This use of aesthetic and embodied causality is neither linear nor directional. If we can open up our living of temporality to include nonhuman and human objects (i.e., stand in the spaces between the culturally created categories of human and nonhuman, even as I write the words as if they are two distinct categories of being), we produce a new intimacy with our surroundings (Morton, 2013), a new sense of "being-with" that dismantles the "great divide" of human exceptionalism (Haraway, 2008) that separates us from our worlds, and ideally also produces a new form of responsibility and caring-based subjectivity. Thus, as we differentiate and come into being through complex layers of temporalities, as described here, we are also always co-emerging with all the bodies and objects of our surroundings (this will be discussed further in the Epilogue).

Time as representation and regulation

Although time produces nonrepresentational spaces of affective experience, most psychoanalytic theories of time limit it to being a structure that organizes primary process. Loewald (1980) and Lombardi (2003, 2008) both describe sequential time enabling experience to pass into secondary process. Linear time functions as a "temporal parameter" (Lombardi, 2003, p. 1536), enabling an experience of the infinite within the finite (his quote of Matte Blanco, 1988, p. 171), or, as Loewald describes, enabling an integration of primal density within secondary process. Here time and space facilitate representation. Again, in these theories, time is an external meter that appears universal and stable. Psychological health requires allowing one's reality to be shaped by this external linearity that must then be internalized. According to these theorists, time is not a cultural process that is ever changing, evolving, and existing within and producing relational spaces.

Certainly, temporality lays the foundations for the representation of experience, as symbolic meaning making becomes possible through a process of temporally linking affect to symbol. For instance, the experience symbolized and represented through the word "cold" or "hot" only gains meaning when it can be linked to a particular relational affective experience of discomfort, which then is associated to an experience of intervention or relief that is close enough in time and space (Gentile, 2007). Through the unfolding motion of altered but temporally linked states of being, links of recognition are created. Felt spaces of interiority, interactivity, and intersubjectivity emerge as they become differentiated (differentiation being a form of connection, not separation).

But here again is where time becomes more complicated than that conveyed by psychoanalytic theory. If past, present, and future are continuously unfolding back upon, and re-animating, each other, then it is not the imposition of linearity that is the foundation for symbolic meaning making. Instead, it is the capacity to experience the unfolding of temporal rhythms of relational time. This complex process of meaning making simultaneously creates our sense of going on being. It forms the basis of affect regulation, which becomes a temporal practice involving the ability to create, and thus place the present into a nonlinear, multidimensional, and fractal temporal context where a pattern of discomfort and relief has been established and accumulated and can be called upon to relationally "self"-soothe. But this soothing requires temporal travel into a time and space of relief. Winnicott (1971) observed this use of temporality in his description of transitional objects that have the abilities to travel through time and space. Anxiety is contained with a sense of time and space as durational and ongoing in contrast to the discomfort. In other words, by knowing anxiety is situational, we can create a temporal boundary – it will end. Through this practice we enable a notion of going-on-being, by embracing a future that will unfold and be different than the present state of suffering. This capacity for temporal containment provides the space enabling us to reflect upon our circumstances and make meaning of our experiences in the moment, literally through time. It creates a relational space for representation and coming into being. Because time is a process that is continually re-created, it can be tight, linear, and containing or expansive, nonlinear, and asynchronous as needed. For instance, we most likely do not want to hold the asynchronous potentialities of time when flying in a plane or being prepped for surgery. At these times, most would prefer linearity without creating the space for uncertainty or too much reflection on infinite potentialities.

The centrality of faith and duration

As described elsewhere (Gentile, 2007), this capacity for regulation is founded upon and requires a faith in continuity – that the future will resemble the past in the present, and through this, one will continue to go on being in relation. To hypenate an "if" to a "then," as Beebe et al. (2012) do, requires or/and is simultaneous to the creation of faith in continuity. However, again, continuity is not necessarily linearity. Continuity involves the capacity to emerge in temporal motion, to manufacture linear and nonlinear patterns out of asynchronous temporality. Perception and organization of patterns rest upon the capacity to accumulate experiences, which itself requires the capacity for "if–then." After all, to create an "if", one needs the space to reflect upon one's experiences in the moment, the space to move and shift. To create an expectation of "then" is to travel in time to a particular future that only comes into being via its relationships to presents and pasts. This "if–then" is not only based in some element of expectation and anticipation but also in a prerepresentational, perhaps nonrepresentational, faith to hold oneself within the environment through temporal motion – a sense that one will not cease to be as the future unfolds.

Eigen (1984) also writes of faith as being central in development. In his readings of Bion and Winnicott, faith is akin to a belief in Bion's *O* – the ultimate reality. As such, his notion of faith has not just a futurity, but a certainty or object, a belief in something. According to Eigen, faith is what enables one to connect to the nonrepresentational. My casting of faith here is that it is a foundational process within which to experience or conceptualize Bergson's (1913/2001) notion of duration, the rhythms and speed of unfolding and becoming that "ensures that not everything is given at once, that the universe is not over the moment it is born, that it occupies a duration" (Grosz, 2004, p. 246). In other words, duration is the tension, the agent of temporal tensegrity, at once holding and differentiating multiple pasts, presents, and futures. In this proposed version of development/subjectivity, faith generates the capacity to accumulate culturally created patterns from the rhythms of arousal and satisfaction conveyed in caretaking, from which affect regulation emerges. It creates an experience of a felt interior space of accumulation from which meaning, including representation and symbolization, is generated.

Time, spaces, and symbolization

According to Bergson (1913/2001), affects exist in a "perpetual state of becoming" (p. 130), thus containing them through language and symbolization functions to spatialize them in a way that creates a false sense of coherence in the face of the reality that "[e]very sensation is altered by repetition" (p. 131). Tweaking Bergson a bit, one could consider instead that representation binds these layers of nonlinear affective experience in ways that "delay complicate, and free behavior, even as it inhibits it" (Grosz, 2004, p. 230). Returning to the previous example of learning cold and hot, representation allows the experience of "hotness" to be contained within the word hot, but doing so also limits the experience of hotness by binding it with the word. However, this potentially limiting word "hot" also functions to create a new experience of hot. Thus, the word is both generative and constraining. But, in order to have this re-creation of experience through words, one must have a delay of experience, the time and space for it to reverberate, to echo, for the feedback to collect, accumulate, and layer, to have the feeling of a feeling (Massumi, 2002). This dense yet momentary delay or "hesitation" (Deleuze, 1991, p. 105) indicates an emerging capacity to use space and time to contain and regulate affect, enabling one to create one's world (Deleuze, 1991).

Here, disagreeing a bit with Bergson, I would say it is not the process of representation or spatializing affect that is necessarily problematic. Instead, it is the tendency of certain forms of representation to make affect linear and unidirectional that functions to dampen the "quality" of existence, in favor of the "quantity" of it (Bergson, 1913/2001, p. 43). Linearity requires a form of forgetting (Dinshaw, 2012) the multiplicities and potentials in order to render linearity possible. This forgetting can be functional, such as in the example above when we board a plane, where forgetting all the potentialities of flight is helpful to regulate affect and to get on the plane. However forgetting is also a form of social control. Memory is "a ritual of power" (Foucault, cited in Halberstam, 2011), creating a linear and continuous narrative from the asynchronous and contradictory and, in so doing, it creates a rhythm of time and a structure for a cycle of memorialization (Halberstam, 2011). A socially constructed form of forgetting and remembering, then, does not just "preserve psychic order" (p. 83); it creates and defines it.

As a critic of linearity, Bergson (1913/2001) described time shaped by duration that tumbles like "the notes of a tune, melting so to speak, into one another"

(p. 100). One maintains a faith that the tune is ongoing in a rhythm that guarantees all the notes do not happen at once; they unfold or melt into one another. Composer John Cage, a fan of playing with space, claimed that it was the space between notes that produced the melody. Each note of a melody, then, contains a sense of the past (where the melody has traveled) as well as anticipation for the next, although one does not know exactly where one will go. The tune, then, the intervals, the shapes of the spaces between, produces the notes and not vice versa. Thus, the note holds a form of anticipation that is not prediction so much as a state of openness to the unfolding melody. Similarly, anticipation in terms of duration is a process of maintaining an openness to the endless "potentialities," a term I am borrowing from Muñoz (2009), that are our "conduit[s] for knowing and feeling" (p. 113). Duration may be experienced as a form of succession but this succession is multiple: what Parisi calls "transituational" (Parisi, 2004, p. 32). Duration renders the body merely "a temporary, constantly unfolding collection of momentary, fleeting instances of equilibrium suspended in a field of virtual partialities" (Parisi, 2004, p. 42). Here, actualizing potentialities can be seen as an ongoing process of creating tensegrity between differentiations of being, and expansions within what Deleuze (1991) terms unlimited virtual possibilities. Tensegrity, as I am using it, describes the forces that hold up a tent, where the poles are vertical due to the force and tightness of the canvas, which itself is stretched and held up by the poles. It describes a reciprocal relationship of expansion and contraction. An organism, then, is an entity that emerges as forces close in upon themselves to cohere into a form, while simultaneously expanding within a virtual whole (Deleuze, 1991).

Bergson's notion of duration reflects what Knoblauch (2011) might call a polyrhythmic movement of emergence. The unfolding wash of duration means primary and secondary processes co-mingle and co-constitute each other, such that language and symbolizing processes function as "embodied temporal reminders" (Gentile, 2007), recasting the past in the present, based on and further shaping the emerging future. Thus, one could see duration embodied in a faith in continuity, and this faith in the unfolding of time forms the basis for the capacities to experience, represent, and symbolize embodied relational interactions. Our notion of a creative and innovative "self" experience, then, is generated by creating links or differentiating within these simultaneous, nonlinear, asynchronic (Freeman, 2010; Dinshaw, 2012) times.

To recap, memorial processes, memory, and meaning making emerge from expectation. This expectation is not prediction, nor cause and effect. The development of this seemingly internalized capacity to expect an outcome is the basis of memorial processes. But, as has been unpacked here, the foundation of expectation depends upon the capacity to experience faith in duration, going on being through time and space. Duration enables the "future to come", to remain both with us and ungraspable (Braun, 2007, p. 17), thus always unfolding and multiple. It is this faith in duration that undergirds any capacity for expectation or anticipation, which can then produce memorial processes. Faith in duration is not a linear cause-and-effect development but the capacity to open to the unfolding durations of time.

If subjectivity, therefore, is shaped by our creation of time (and vice versa), then the violence of trauma collapses the space required for duration. This, in turn, re-shapes our capacities for reflection, representation, and symbolization. Chronological time may be destroyed and parts of self-experience may feel frozen, but these are symptoms of the loss of the capacity to hold the optimal tensions, the tensegrity between past, present, and future, as nonlinear unfolding experiences, such that the past becomes equivalent to the present, because pasts can then only emerge in and as the present, as over-determined, unidimensional cause and effect. It is a collapse not of time or space but of capacity. After all, maintaining optimal tensions of times and spaces requires coming into being over and over again within a "push and pull of time" that can be, as Dinshaw (2012) quotes of Augustine, "excruciating" (p. 63). Thus, in certain circumstances of trauma and stress, the simplicity of coherence through culturally sanctioned, commodified, affective experiences can be quite alluring in favor of engaging with the unknown toward an emergent experience of becoming.

Thus, as space collapses and reflective meaning becomes constrained, the capacities for going on being and creating a future melt away. Here, ARTs can step in to save the day. With their linear, predetermined rituals and clear expectations for compliance, ARTs can easily function as a salve for regulating the anxieties inherent in the crisis of infertility. But, unlike other forms of commodified experience, ARTs enable one to engage in a process of creating the embodiment of the future – a baby. ARTs provide a unique, manufactured form of duration that is purchased through the clinic.

The temporal production of biomedicalization

Given time's centrality in producing subjectivities, how the culture plays with time is clearly important. Neoliberalism pre-9/11 was based on the idea of the future as euphoric and unlimited, but since 9/11, a future based on catastrophe has dominated (Cooper, 2008). This rigidly constructed, dangerous future is one that requires a present defined by preemptive actions of risk management (Gentile, 2013). Hesford and Diedrich (2008), too, have described post-9/11 culture as being driven by a "tyranny of emergency," where the specter of catastrophe causes a flight into certainty, and the only certainty available within this collapsed space is based on the repetition of an idealized fantasy of the past, which was described in the previous chapter as nostalgia (Huyssen, 2000) and sentiment (Berlant, 2008). For instance, cultural narratives since 9/11 feature romanticized and sentimental images of domesticity, including "the denigration of capable women, the magnification of manly men" (Casper & Moore, 2009, p. 150). This temporal repetition of the nostalgic renders the rhythm of time redundant. It is not that time ceases to pass, as some trauma theorists claim, but it passes in a repetitive, linear fashion, without the multiplicity of space required for multidimensional motion. Thus, trauma collapses spatial capacities, not time. As noted in the previous section, pasts, presents, and futures are multiple and interrelating;

thus, disruptions in any of them cause a systemic reaction. This obsessive elevation and repetition of a singular fantasized past results in the disavowal of present issues (i.e., global warming, economic instability, and healthcare threats) such that "action, myth and amnesia become the drugs of certainty" (Hesford, 2008, p. 181). Accordingly, the present, in this configuration, secures its future only by "reordering the past" (p. 174) into a myth of simplicity and singularity. The rampant celebration of pregnancy and the celebrity fetus would be an example of the creation of a future based on a past mythology of rigid gender arrangements and a nostalgic ideal of childhood.

If pregnancy is constructed as the embodiment of the future, then it also represents a blurring of temporal boundaries, not only based on women's "troubling tendency" (Haraway, 1997) to produce multiple bodies, but because the temporalities of past, present, and future become merged in one body. This merging provides the unique opportunity to protect the future by controlling the abject – the pregnant, leaking body. This opportunity to target the future and the abject simultaneously renders pregnancy a perfect magnet and catalyst for cultural anxiety and control.[6]

This form of rigid temporal linking results in displaced attempts to control and resolve anxiety. But, of course, as anxiety is repetitively misplaced, it can never be quelled. Instead, it generates an increased need for defensive reaction even as that reaction itself creates more anxiety. This cycle of dissociation sets a stage for the practices of biomedicalization, which slip in perfectly, harnessing denial and displacement through compulsive, repetitive rituals.

Biomedicalization as fundamental to the construction of ARTs

A main focus of neoliberalism is a fluidity between the private and public, such that many functions of the public space are re-cast as private issues (Grewal, 2006) (i.e., individualized retirement funds vs. state-funded social security). The state defines which behaviors are to be seen as empowering, and, within neoliberalism, women's sense of empowerment is tied to their bodies. This can take forms such as body modification through dieting, exercising, plastic surgery, and make-up, all of which are cast as forms of personal power, control, success, and mastery. As the identified bodies of the culture (Oliver, 2007), risk is also embodied by the female. This is clear in ARTs, since they focus their practices almost entirely on women's bodies regardless of the cause of the fertility problem. In relation to fetuses, this embodiment of risk is managed through biomedicalization, where surveillance functions as individual empowerment and security. It is not that male bodies are free from embodied forms of surveillance, but that they are subject to different forms. For instance, Riska (2010) contends that practices of biomedicalization around male bodies focus on *sexual* health while those focused on women emphasize *reproductive* health (Gentile, 2013). Thus, practices of biomedicalization function to reinforce gendered practices of embodiment.

Biomedicalization can be seen as a multidirectional system that functions to produce medicalized subjects (Clarke et al., 2003, 2010b). Clarke et al. (2003, 2010b) identify five interactive processes through which biomedicalization is constituted. First, the culture, including the political and economic context, shapes the medicalization that pathologizes or renders problematic a condition that was previously considered unremarkable or not pathological. For instance, infertility becomes a medical problem with a medical solution. This cause-and-effect temporal linking leaves no room for environmental causes or social solutions like adoption. Second, the identified ideal of health becomes reified, requiring engagement in a never-ending cycle of risk management and self-surveillance. If one's cholesterol level falls, it is because one followed the medicalized regime of risk management and must continue to do so. If it does not, it is because one failed to follow the regimes closely enough. This biomedicalized system of self-blame and self-responsibility changes the standards of what is considered and accepted as normal. So, as will be described, the very presence of a biomedical treatment for infertility actually creates a forced choice where one has to engage with fertility medicine, and fertility medicine shapes all women's healthcare. Third, this new ideal of normality becomes a lifestyle that itself is based not on the avoidance of disease, but on the identification and avoidance of risk factors. Avoiding the risk factors, not avoiding disease, is deemed healthy. This means one is stuck engaging with an unrelenting, singular present. Risk factors and their related behaviors are linearly and rigidly linked to a certain future (disease) while the subject has no capacity to generate futurity or possibility. Agency is located in the risk factors to create the future. Next, with computerization and information management, the identification and cataloguing of risk factors is endless.

Finally, these steps of biomedicalization transform the experience and production of selves through these rituals of self-surveillance and healthy lifestyles, "blur[ring] the boundaries of coercion and consent" (Rose, 2001, p. 10). Because this medicalized ideal of normality demands transformation from the "inside out" (Clarke et al., 2003, p. 181), these behaviors are experienced as being empowering. As Beck (2007) described in terms of risk society, the citizen/biomedicalized subject is made to feel grateful for being given the list of risk factors and the identified practices to avoid them. By producing subjectivities, biomedicalization becomes a central mode of social control, and this control operates through networks of commodified affects – a perpetual cycle of risk and its management. Additionally, although Beck observed anticipation, unlike catastrophe, lacks a temporal–spatial focus, with biomedicalization anticipation is given concrete form.

Biomedicalization constructs the spaces within which risk appears, operates, and can be managed. Thus, its proliferation depends on the contagion of anxiety. As we've already seen in the previous chapter, a risk-based society is a future-based society, one that is organized around anticipation and the calculation of risk to control the future ostensibly by controlling behavior (Reith, 2004). One could see this risk-based organization eliminating the future, replacing it with an "endlessly extended present" (p. 392). However, one could also see risk creating an endless array of futures. In the wake of trauma, this endless production of catastrophes could be seen as an attempt to breathe life into what Bergson (1913/2001) might call a duration-less present. In this psychoanalytic conceptualization, "risk management becomes a salve, a form of affect regulation in the face of intolerable affect" (Gentile, 2013, p. 158). Engaging in calculation and the managements of risk can bring a sense of agency because such planning creates the structure within which to go on being, to create a future (Reith, 2004; Gentile, 2007, 2011). So biomedicalization can feel especially empowering in the face of trauma and uncertainty because it plays with time to organize anxiety and dread, producing patients who take individual responsibility for their wellness while simultaneously supporting medical expertise.

Babies produce "normal" time

> I went to the nurse practitioner at my university health center to diagnose a problem I was having. She gave me what turned out to be an incorrect diagnosis of a birth defect that would render me unable to have children. She delivered the news blandly, pointing out that it didn't really matter for me if I was infertile. She said "after all you're 34 in graduate school. It's not like children are a priority for you." It was her supervisor who requested further tests to figure out that in fact I actually had two large growths, requiring surgery and biopsy. It felt like if I wasn't using my uterus for reproduction, my health didn't matter.
>
> (Olive, an interviewee)

While biomedicalization creates forms of temporal risk management behaviors that complement ARTs, the lure of ARTs becomes even more compelling given the cultural values of "reprofuturity" (see Halberstam, 2005; Dinshaw et al., 2007), where the ideal timeline of life is shaped around a "middle-class logic of reproductive temporality" (Halberstam, 2005, p. 4) or "straight time" (Freeman, 2007, p. 170). The very meter of one's lifetime is punctuated by reproductive milestones. The success of life is measured according to reproduction and wealth accumulation (Halberstam, 2011). Just consider the way the category of reproductive technologies has shifted from including abortion and birth control (avoiding pregnancy), to being focused on ARTs (creating pregnancies). This shift enables a dangerous cultural form of splitting, where ARTs are seen positively while abortion is demonized. In the United States, ART clinics are proliferating while those offering abortion services are being squeezed out of existence. Insurance is expanding to include more ART coverage while coverage for abortion and birth control is being contested and chipped away, if not overtly slashed out of existence (Hassinger, 2014).

Reprofuturity privileges the relationship between parent and child as the most important, equating childlessness to annihilation (Downing, 2011, p. 49). But this "straight time" is not a simple equation where no child equals no future. As Ahmed (2010) writes, "no children" signifies the loss of a fantasy of the future as that which will promise compensation for present suffering. The loss of "the after," the baby, is experienced as the loss of "the for" (p. 183): the purpose of life. Here, the future is only valuable if it is normative – where children or the attempt to have children is the center of one's life.

As the emblem of the future's "unquestioned value" (Edelman, in Downing, 2011, p. 48), children also function to embody the projection of "valorized qualities" (Downing, 2011, p. 60), innocence, the reasons we fight wars (Berlant, 2010). The idea or fantasy of their potential presence functions not only to give value to certain temporalities; it provides the rhythm, propelling one's experiences of time's duration. With a childful future, one's durational rhythm moves unidirectionally and linearly "forward" in what is considered to be a progression. Of course, while the culture's temporality and values may be focused on reproduction, it is an idea of reproduction, the fantasy and fetish of a fetus. Valuing actual children is not necessarily related to reprofuturity. Additionally, as described earlier, duration based in linearity cannot produce creative meaning making.

Placing the reproductive family at the center of social structures functions to "bind the past to the present and the present to the future" (Halberstam, 2011) through the idea that adulthood *means* (heterosexual) parenting as a temporal form of chronological substitutions – son for dad; daughter for mother. Lineage, inheritance, and regeneration mark the cycle of the Oedipal temporality. Inheritance is a form of social control. As Halberstam (2011) observes, the "legacy" of the mother to the daughter (and, I would add, the father to the son) is to reproduce her "relationship to patriarchal forms of power" (p. 124). Thus, maternity produces subjectivities that are temporally linked to histories of mothers, while nonmaternal subjects are left unattached in time.[7]

Reprofuturity also genders time. For women, time with children is valued over other forms of time. This can have multiple negative impacts at work, including the continuing assumption that women will take the time off to care for sick children and family members, and thus should have limited access to leadership. There can also be a tacit assumption that others at a job should chip in to help a parent. This system may balance out for parents, but those who remain childless do not get the benefits (Cain, 2001). For instance, Olive, who was quoted above, described listening to a motivational speaker at work:

> She told us she was a workaholic, unempathetic to her employees who she saw as not working as hard as her. She described how when she was running a meeting if someone came in late she'd stop the meeting and publicly shame them. But then she had a child. Everyone around the room nodded in tacit agreement, smiling. Then she realized people had legitimate reasons for not putting in endless hours and not being on time, and these reasons had to do with children. She said not everyone would agree with her, but these people would be the ones who did not have children. She really said "if you don't have children you couldn't possibly understand her reasoning." I kept thinking, so if my dog is sick, am I allowed to be late? Is this leeway really reserved only for parents?

Months later, Olive described expressing frustration at having worked on a report during a weekend. When she complained to a senior colleague, he said: "Well, you need to respect that others in our department have chosen to have families so they can't be expected to do as much on weekends."

It is important to acknowledge that many parents (men and women) do not work with people who are asked or expected to chip in, and many do not work with bosses who respect parenting. However, as these interviewees demonstrate, reprofuturity assumes time with children is more valuable than time without, and it functions to narrow the public discourse around "work–life" issues, ensuring "life" is code for "family," and "family" is always code for children.

Reprofuturity produces gender

When I was in the throes of ARTs and trying to get pregnant, I remember I saw an article in *Glamour* magazine, of all places, critically analyzing the recent push toward motherhood. Because I had been analyzing representations of and research on pregnancy (Gentile, 2011), I took note. The author, who came out as childless, was describing the glorification of celebrity and model mothers who can now have it all – with money, nannies, trainers, etc. I was so relieved to read a critical article in a mainstream magazine. Then I noticed an "editor's note" at the end of it, as you would see a "correction" to the story. The note was light and airy, an antidote to the article that said that, after trying for many years, the writer had finally given birth to a baby. The existence of the note and its placement seemed to undermine everything she wrote, situating the article and its critique as a form of sour grapes that were now sweet.

This is merely one example of how reprofuturity functions to produce gender as it equates the category of female with that of mother. Thus, maternity confers normality and social acceptance for women (Throsby, 2004). Lou, a male interviewee who had gone through 4 years of ART procedures with his female partner, expressed surprise when his partner described the emotional difficulty in dodging what she experienced as a continual barrage of questions from others about why she did not have children. He said, "I think I have only ever been asked once." The gendered production of bodies through reprofuturity means childless men are not called upon to explain their choices while women without children often have to make the people around them comfortable with their infertility or choice not to have a child (Throsby, 2004). Similarly, women (and men) with children do not have to explain their reproductive choices.

Even nowadays, stereotypes of childless women abound. *New York Magazine* collected various quotes from women celebrities about not having children (Ma, 2014). Many quotes featured women pathologizing themselves for not wanting children, being selfish, deficient in some way, or/and "choosing" to have a career over children, feeling they could not have both. Women without children are still often considered to be "abnormal" (Oliver, 2012, p. 85), "bitter and selfish and morally deficient," objects of pity assumed to be full of regret (p. 109).

Cain (2001), in interview research with women who are childless, found they often described themselves as selfish, childlike, neurotic, irresponsible, and immature. As one participant in Cain's study put it, "I was selfish enough [that] I wanted to be with [my husband] . . . we got comfortable being selfish" (Cain, 2001, p. 124). To not want or to not have a child is a selfish act for a woman.

Stereotypes of childless women are just magnified by psychoanalysts who consider infertility a result of unresolved maternal conflicts (see Rosen, 2002, for a critique of psychoanalytic treatment of infertility) or the absent-minded, narcissistic avoidance of the realities of women's biological time (Chodorow, 2003). In her memoir, Zoll (2013) says the first thing out of her infertility doctor's mouth was "you should have come to see me when you were 30" (p. 7). In a culture shaped by reprofuturity, all reproductive responsibility goes to the woman. For instance, Chodorow (2003) implies that single heterosexual women who wait to have children are too picky: waiting for Mr. Right, or too selfish or misguided: focusing on their careers. This privatizing of the struggles and conflicts of potential parenthood (lack of adequate maternity and paternity leave, lack of adequate child care, lack of adequate models of equal parenting so women don't have to automatically take time off) keeps intact structural inequalities that make reproductive "choices" anything but free.

Childless women are also often seen as channeling a "maternal instinct" into caring for animals ("furbabies," Manterfield, 2011, p. 95) or working long hours. Here, childless women's passions and attachments are interpreted through the lens of pronatalism and reprofuturity. This patronizing attitude insults the choices these women make and renders illegitimate the genuine care and ethical treatment of animals, reinforcing and condoning neglect or abandonment of animals when the "real thing" finally comes along. Additionally, such compensatory behaviors are not used to describe childless men's behaviors (Cain, 2001), i.e., there is no gender equivalent of the "crazy cat lady" for men.

Women are now expected to "have it all" (see Oliver, 2012): children and a fulfilling career, and there are few positive role models or cultural narratives for childless women as most construct the uterus as an empty space awaiting a baby (Throsby, 2004, p. 29) or, as one memoir of infertility is titled, "Empty womb, broken heart."

In this cultural context, public exposure of ARTs makes it more stigmatizing to not have children (Franklin, 1997). It means women and/or couples who stop trying have to make excuses for not going further, not trying harder to conceive. This stigma of childlessness is only magnified by older celebrities who claim their lives are finally fulfilled with the addition of their twins. This creates a fantasy that infertility is always surmountable if you just try hard enough.

But pulling out all the medical stops to conceive is also not the answer to avoid social stigma. Some feel those who pay for ARTs are selfishly wasting money on unnecessary medical procedures (Throsby, 2004). Yet, when infertile people do not seek out reproductive assistance, others assume they are not ready to sacrifice to be a parent (Ibid.). There is also an assumed correspondence between the degree of desire for a child and the extent one will go to get one (Ibid.). Therefore, infertile people are placed in a no-win situation.

Reprofuturity, affect, and desire

As has been described, neoliberalism includes a form of social control that is exercised relationally through affect (Deleuze, 1995; Hardt & Negri, 2000; Clough, 2008). Ahmed (2004) describes an affective economy, in other words, a network of interactions shaped by circulated patterns of affect. These patterns of affect produce uneven worlds, social relations, and differently valued bodies (Murphy, 2012, p. 80). Thus, the generation and circulation of these affects are powerful forms of control, as "our identities and desires get sucked up and commodified: they become fetish selves and wishes" (Campbell, 2006, p. 184). For instance, as mentioned previously, cultural narratives post 9/11 offer up an endless slew of romanticized domesticity denigrating powerful and capable women in order to magnify the power and value of men (Casper & Moore 2009). These narratives reify a value in life "itself over the quality of life, mere survival over meaningful life" (Oliver, 2007, p. 133); in the United States, this is manifested as an obsession with protecting fetuses through the deployment of the state to criminalize women's behaviors while privatizing responsibility for postnatal and child care.

Reprofuturity shapes this affective social control by delineating those things that lead to happiness and manufacturing a desire to accumulate and reproduce them. The "happy housewife" is another example of this, as the happiness functions to erase household labor (Ahmed, 2010, p. 573). Habits associated with happiness can "disappear as freedom" (p. 35), seeming to be beyond critique or analysis. This narrative of happiness cloaks inequalities for, as Ahmed writes, it is assumed people cannot be oppressed and happy. So in commercials, women alone are portrayed as happy – sometimes even euphoric – to find the right laundry detergent, to clean floors, cook, and clean the toilet. This happiness not only "functions to justify the gendered forms of labor"; it situates this division of labor as an "expression of a collective wish and desire" (p. 573), as if women are not only happy to be the ones cleaning; they wish for it. Here, the fantasy of the home as the productive space of happiness is merged with that of the reproductive family, creating an unquestionable link between children, family, home life, and happiness.

Associating happiness with feeling good is a modern construction that temporalizes it, positioning good feelings as progressive and forward (Ahmed, 2010). Happiness functions as a promise of the future, and things and habits that are considered good are those that are associated with future happiness (Ahmed, 2010). Here, happiness is a deferral that promises transformation (Ahmed, 2010). As Bergson (1913/2001) observed, the future as an idea, "pregnant with an infinity of possibilities," is better than the future itself when it becomes present (p. 10). Babies can fulfill this displacement and deferral of happiness easily, as their demands in the present are experienced as a promise of their future. For instance, intense morning sickness is understood to correspond to a healthy embryo. Parents might believe that once the baby is past the demands of infancy, or past the "terrible twos," or in school, they will be happy and fulfilled. This deferral of happiness also functions to give form to the formlessness of time, making time experienceable (Halberstam, 2005).

So happiness around babies is complicated and multilayered. Babies embody the future as goods. They are an idealized, hoped-for, prepared-for project, coming into being in the present only through their projection into the future as a finished product. This product is a powerful lure of perpetual anticipation, as fulfillment and personal transformation can be experienced in the present through its constant displacement into the future. And one must defer this contentment, because if the present experience of the goods, the baby, is less than happy and fulfilling, the promise of the future is shaken and the worth of the baby itself is jeopardized.

Consider the uproar that surrounded Erica Jong's essay "Mother madness" in the *Wall Street Journal* (November 6, 2010). Her article stated what has been stated before: that changing trends toward more active and involved parenting impact women disproportionately. Reader responses took only offense, describing exactly what she was saying: that women have to give up their careers or give up sleep and any pretense at self-care to meet shifting ideals. But giving these things up, according to the readers, should be experienced as a privilege (which it is economically). Instead of following Jong's logic, which identified the expectations of parenting as unrealistic, the responses of the readers demonstrated that to question the legitimacy or value of the expectations was to question their life choices and the value of their children. In this cultural context, a crisis in happiness is construed not as a failure of our ideals of happiness (Ahmed, 2007/2008) or of our stratified institutional structures, but as our own failures to follow the ideals of happiness. We blame ourselves or others for our failures to create happiness and, as Halberstam (2011) contends, this failure extends to many academics who continue to measure the health of a society through the fidelity of the reproductive nuclear family, and I would include psychoanalysts, who continue to hold the reproductive family, the Oedipal narrative, as the center and the indication of a healthy and mature self. This also creates a closed cycle of blame, reifying the neoliberal subject as solely responsible for his or her own happiness.

The winning combo of biomedicalization and reprofuturity

> So we were rushing to get to the clinic in time for an IUI [intrauterine insemination]. I had a container of sperm but we were caught in a traffic jam. The clinic called my cell angry I wasn't there yet and said they would not do the IUI later than the assigned time. It's like military boot camp in that the patients must fit into the office routine, and this is part of the process of becoming socialized to being a patient. You learn that all bloodwork is to be done between 7.30–8.30 in the morning. Period. All IUIs as well. I explained I was caught in traffic, but the structure of the clinic time was unalterable. So

> I found myself ditching my partner in the car, in the traffic and sprinting up 8th Ave. with a cup of sperm in my bag worrying I was irreparably scrambling them, thinking, "I really hope I don't get hit by a car with a jar of sperm in my bag."
>
> (Olive, an interviewee)

Lastly, reprofuturity gains power when it is wedded to biomedicalization. One can see that, with increasing biopolitical regulation, biological life itself becomes an object of technological intervention, and nature then becomes a form of capital to be bought, sold, and regulated (Hardt & Negri, 2000). Components of "natural" processes like reproduction, then, become commercial interests in a new way. The affective economy that commodifies sentiment and nostalgia around babies functions to cloak this commercialization of reproduction as well as the biomedicalization of women's bodies in reproductive medicine. After all, why would anyone not do all they could to have a healthy baby? But with biomedicalization, the focus is on avoidance of risk factors in the service of a limitless future, not the creation of a healthy baby.[8]

This melding of biomedicalization and reprofuturity also has profound ramifications for women's general healthcare. For instance, in 2006, the Centers for Disease Control and Prevention (CDC) created a new medical category called "preconception care" (PCC), designed to identify and monitor all premenopausal female bodies as potential mothers, regardless of women's intentions (Gentile, 2013). Although the guidelines were created to address the steady increase of babies born with low birth weights and physical and cognitive disabilities, and at-risk pregnancies, they ignore the growing use of ARTs and the related multiple births that are directly related to these rises (see Spar, 2006; Mundy, 2008). In addition, intimate-partner violence, a significant cause of birth defects (Jeanjot et al., 2008), is not a primary target of the guidelines (Gentile, 2013). Instead, PCC is a set of protocols that create surveillance practices for women organized around the temporal categories of "preconception" (basically a female's lifetime from birth to the point at which she decides to try to become pregnant, or to the time she enters menopause and/or is infertile), "pre-pregnancy" (defined as the time after a woman decides to try to become pregnant but before she actually is pregnant), "pregnant," "postnatal" (after the delivery of a baby), and "between pregnancy" (for women who had a difficult or dangerous delivery or pregnancy). Naming the category "between pregnancy," not "after a dangerous pregnancy," a woman is defined not based on the recent past of medical difficulty which may render her to be in a compromised state in the present. Instead, she is located in time purely based on the idea of a future pregnancy – she is *between* pregnancies, whether or not she plans to have another child. The proximity to crisis is projected into the future, instead of being addressed in the present. The medical interventions at this point are not based on the new baby or the present state of the mother, but instead on getting the woman's body prepared for a fantasized future pregnancy. Medical protocol is based on urging her to focus on regaining her health in order to become pregnant again (Gentile, 2013). These temporal stages then shape women's medicine, so that all premenopausal women are labeled not only based on their potential to reproduce, but on their temporal proximity to the fantasized fetished fetus. Here, all women's healthcare is recast as reproductive healthcare, organized around risk management and surveillance of women's bodies. As Clough (2004) observes, biopower is deployed through networks of information that function to control not individuals but populations. Through the PCC guidelines, "premenopausal women" becomes a category for reproductive medicine, and all such women are encouraged to engage in "empowering" biomedicalized behaviors focused on the health of a future fetus.

Producing racial/ethnic and class disparities

As mentioned previously, not all fetuses are fetishized equally. Current images celebrating pregnant bodies reflect "stratified reproduction" (Ginsburg & Rapp, 1995) whereby middle- and upper-class (in particular, white) women's reproduction is spectacularized, depicted as avenues for self-transformation and empowerment. For poor women and women of color, having multiple children is seen as a threat to the cultural body, a mark not of opulence but of poor self-control (Ginsburg & Rapp, 1995; Roberts, 2009). Low-income women and women of color are criminalized for having children (Roberts, 2009; Paltrow, 2013), depicted as "undisciplined breeders" taking advantage of the system (Ginsburg & Rapp, 1995) or illegal immigrants with "anchor babies."

The fetal fetish succeeds in part based on the capacity to erase the mother's body, depicting the fetus floating alone in a void, as if an independent object, or one neglected by its host and in need of care or legislative intervention. Yet the adoption of personhood amendments stem from a law passed to protect, not criminalize, pregnant women.

The Unborn Victims of Violence Act was passed in 2004 as a response to the killing of Laci Peterson, a white woman who was 7 months pregnant, by her white husband. Since then, 36 states have extended the range of this Act to feticide, with the provision that it not be used to persecute the women who are pregnant. However, the Act opened the doors for personhood amendments that, although having only passed in a couple of states (Oklahoma and Virginia as of this writing), have impacted public consciousness and medical protocols. For instance, the CDC now urges doctors not to prescribe to women of reproductive age drugs that might cause birth defects, even when the woman has no intention of getting pregnant. Here, women's intentions are overridden by their potential for pregnancy, and girls' and women's healthcare is re-conceptualized as not just maternal but fetal healthcare (see Gentile, 2013, 2014).

This melding of biomedicalization and criminal justice has serious ramifications for all women, but in particular poor women and women of color. Despite the provision the law not be used to prosecute pregnant women, 77% of criminal cases involving pregnant women since 2005 do not even mention potential threats by the father, male partner, or any other person. They are focused exclusively on the criminalization of the pregnant women (Paltrow, 2013). The majority of cases were of poor, African American women who were arrested or/and reported to state authorities by hospital and other medical staff, oftentimes when the women attempted to gain access to drug treatment programs upon realizing they were pregnant. Instead of treatment, they were subject to felony charges and oftentimes imprisoned as the fetus was deemed a ward of the state (Dubow, 2011). And, demonstrating that the fetus is merely a fetish object, and that even fetuses are subject to segregation, the concern for fetal health stopped at imprisonment, as the majority of these pregnant women did not receive prenatal care while being held. (Paltrow, 2013). Paltrow (2013) also details a number of cases where pregnant women of color were detained based solely on their supposed *potential* for harming their fetus even when they did not harm it and even after the fetus was born as a healthy baby. Here, the potential catastrophic future overpowers and rewrites the present, producing a maternal subject who, although she birthed a healthy baby, might not have, and it is this latter potential present that is the most salient.

As mentioned in Chapter 1, the fantasy fetus depicted in cultural images floats alone in a void, but this fetus has translucent, usually white, skin. It is this fetus that is typically used to indicate vulnerability and the need for rescuing. The cultural values placed on bodies is clear. As the criminal justice system incarcerates pregnant, economically disadvantaged women, primarily women of color, under the pretense of "protecting her fetus," they are merely succeeding in imprisoning multiple generations simultaneously. While at this point in time it seems all women are cast as being potential or even inherent threats to their respective fetuses (preconception care guidelines make that very clear), white women are steered toward biomedicalized interventions that function to patrol their appetites and curtail their behaviors. Poor women of color are subject to government systems – child protection, home visits, and the criminal justice system. It is a facet of the new racial caste system, except as Alexander (2010) would also note (see below), it is not really new.

In the United States, there is a horrific history of black women's reproduction being controlled and interfered with by white men of economic means. As Alexander (2010) describes, earlier systems of slavery exploited and controlled black labor. The criminal justice system and the new caste system, in contrast, just function to "warehouse" the black population, who are seen as unnecessary to the growing global market (Alexander, 2010). By incarcerating pregnant women of color, the system is "warehousing" two generations simultaneously, damning both, rigidifying the future of both. As Paltrow (2013) terms it, these are the new "Jane Crow" laws, as these laws take away the mother of the family. In communities that have been disemboweled by the incarceration of men, wedding drug laws to fetal protection laws is the nail in the coffin. It completes the picture of mass incarceration.

So this fetal fetish impacts all women. However, there are differential impacts based on race/ethnicity and class as to whether one enters the biomedicalized realms of PCC and ARTs surveillance, where reproduction is supported and cultivated, albeit patrolled, or whether one's reproduction is criminalized and women are imprisoned and separated from their fetuses in laws that render it a ward of the state (see also Roberts, 2009; Paltrow, 2013). This racial-ethnic/class context that stratifies reproduction, segregating fetal and maternal care, also shapes ARTs. For instance, lower economic class is the most significant predictor of infertility, yet ARTs are geared toward and accessible to the wealthy.

The next chapter continues describing the culture, but focuses on dispelling the myths and cultural fantasies surrounding and supporting ARTs, while providing a framework for understanding their protocols. This chapter also illustrates some ways people stop ARTs, finding an end in a durationless present.

Notes

1 I am highlighting 9/11 as having functioned as a catalyst, increasing the intensity of commodification of affect. Certainly, commodification of experience dates back to the rise in industrialization, so it is not a new phenomenon.

2 One could also interpret the obsession with fetuses and babies as a very dangerous displacement of anxiety in the face of global climate change, perhaps based also on the guilt of realizing the devastated planet these fetuses will inherit. In this context, controlling the uterine environment through fetal personhood amendments and pregnancy exclusion laws is easier than doing the work necessary to provide a healthier, less toxic postnatal environment. I am not justifying these misogynous legal maneuvers, just pointing out some of the complexities of the fetal fetish. I thank Steve Botticelli for highlighting the complicated role global climate change and environmental destruction could play here.

3 As described elsewhere (Gentile, 2015), this privatization is exemplified in the now infamous Stanford "marshmallow" study. In this study, 4–5-year-old children were left in a room with a sweet treat. The researchers told them if they could wait to eat it for a certain amount of time they would get two of the treats. If they could not wait and ate it immediately, they would not get an additional treat. Thus, they were rewarded for exercising self-control through what was assumed to be a form of self-regulation. Although the study was conducted in the 1960s, recent articles and a popular radio show have revived it (see Lehrer (2009), and the 2010 WNYC Radiolab episode, "Your future in a marshmallow" (www.radiolab.org), to name only a few). The study is fascinating, but it also demonstrates how the US culture in particular reifies individualization and privatized self-regulation as affect regulation. Here, psychological health and one's future accomplishments are "embodied" by the capacities of a child to practice self-denial, self-control, and the containment of an appetite alone in a room.

4 Psychoanalytic theories tend to reinforce the Oedipal and reprofuturity by focusing myopically on the maternal. Certainly, the initial experiences of caretaking shape and produce subjectivity; however, psychoanalytic theory and its use of terms like the "maternal function" naturalize this caretaking within female-identified bodies, further tethering women to reproduction and child care, while leaving differently-gendered bodies out. It is difficult to deconstruct the Oedipal and reprofuturity while centering psychoanalytic theory within the "maternal"–infant relationship.

5 Although Freud's notion of *Nachträglichkeit* similarly proposes the idea that the present recasts the past, the past that is recast here is continually refracting to re-create the present and in relation to both the multiple pasts and presents, multiple futures.

6 There are ancient associations between women, death, and abjection, positioning reproduction well for use as a cultural fetish. Kristeva (1982) claims the maternal body is the ultimate abject signifier. Pregnant and postpartum bodies exemplify the leaky abject

(Ibid.), embodying the limits of life, death, and sexuality that fuel cultural anxiety in the time of emergency management where the rigidly gendered use of bodies prevails as a central form of anxiety regulation (Gentile, 2011). So we see pregnancy celebrated manically and sentimentally, but this pregnancy can only include expanding bellies and breasts, no swollen legs, ankles, or puffy faces, and postpartum bodies must return immediately to the pre-pregnancy state as if having a baby is such a natural process it leaves no trace when done "correctly" (Ibid.). Focusing biotechnology here is to control the very process at the foundation of this symbol of the abject itself, the symbol of the limits on our being. And to illustrate how practices of biomedicalization are not about health, while the public devours pictures of swollen milk-filled breasts stretching the material of ball gowns on the red carpet, the public act of breast feeding, one of the ultimate body boundary-blurring activities, is still legally regulated in a number of states.

7 This relationship reflects Deleuze and Guattari's (1977/2009) notion of the Oedipal functioning to support the cultural structures of power and control, and not vice versa.

8 The surveillance of women's bodies has also expanded due to our "growing tendency to . . . designate genetics as the source of all human 'defects,' weaknesses, and limitations" (Browner & Press, 1995, p. 307). This attitude toward genetics is apparent in ARTs, where people do not purchase sperm or eggs; they purchase qualities they want their child to have. Hair and eye color, attractiveness, height, weight, intelligence, talents – all these are listed in sperm and egg donor profiles (Spar, 2006), and these traits are taken to represent the future baby. So one is purchasing not an egg or sperm, but the qualities of a potential baby. Here, the booming industry is not only drugs, but diagnostic testing and the production of databases to "informationalize" these donor eggs and sperm, reduce them to multiple lists and measurements.

Chapter 3

Situating ARTs in the cultural imagination

Katie Gentile

In the United States, where the occupational structure is not family-friendly and many women are forced to choose between promotions and pregnancy, being able to time babies is an important component to any kind of gender equality. Toward this end, assisted reproductive technologies (ARTs) have been cast as enhancing women's reproductive choices. For many women in traditional cultures, ART can rescue them from a culturally unacceptable or potentially dangerous situation of childlessness (Benjamin & Ha'elyon, 2002). Given that ARTs take the act of heterosexual intercourse out of the process, they have also functioned to democratize reproduction, enabling transgender, lesbians, and gay men to become biological parents (Franklin, 1997; Mamo, 2010). Others are clearly critical of what they identify as a new and more insidious takeover of women's bodies by science and the medical establishment.[1]

As mentioned in Chapter 1, this research evolved from my own experiences. Like many ART patients, I went to a specialist initially just to find out what was going wrong. But we fell into the large pool of patients for whom infertility had an unknown cause, which in the end meant more procedures and protocols for me. ARTs are like an uncontrolled snowball, attracting and gathering new procedures with every visit. The idea of entering a clinic just to find out what is wrong is naïve, first because much of the time there is nothing identifiably wrong, and second, because whatever the diagnosis, in vitro fertilization (IVF) is the go-to money-making procedure for what ails you. Although not apparent from the photos of twins in celebrity magazines or from the exploding number of multi-infant strollers on city sidewalks, going through ARTs is no picnic. You often have daily appointments with long waits in crowded waiting rooms that do not always have enough seats, while waiting to see a doctor you may have never met who will be conducting some procedure on your reproductive system, under the adoring gaze of the many photos of smiling (usually white) babies hung like awards on the clinic walls. Only after reading many studies and interviewing others did I realize this surreal experience was quite common. I found many excellent writings describing ART protocols and the experience of them from cultural and feminist theory, but little in psychoanalysis. The case studies I did find often blamed women for their situation, either through the age-old line that unconscious conflicts about the maternal functioned to wring the life potential out of the uterus, or blaming women (never men) for irresponsibly putting off reproduction as if in a hysterical fantasy of endless fertility. Yet this limitless fantasy of fertility is exactly what is marketed to men and women by fertility clinics and the media. Another glaring void in the psychoanalytic literature was any exploration of ART attempts, the repetitive failures and the unspeakable loss(es) usually involved, the demoralizing and sometimes dehumanizing aspects of treatment, and the tricky social interactions that can emerge when one is situated as "not yet pregnant."

This chapter and the next tell stories of infertility culled from published memoirs and interviews I conducted. This research project was driven by a desire to complicate and integrate different disciplinary ideas about ARTs in hopes of contributing to a literature that desperately needs to grow and diversify. It began as an interview study with the goal of engaging ethnically/racially and socioeconomically diverse men and women, heterosexual and lesbian, gay, bisexual, and transgender people who sought out ARTs. But, after 3 years of data collection based partially on the snowball method while reaching out to and posting on relevant diverse websites, blogs, and listserves, I found only eight women and three men to participate, and no one who was not heterosexual and white.[2] The men who participated did so with their female spouses and typically said very little. The possible reasons for this small homogenous response rate and deferral to partners will be discussed momentarily, as it is a form of data that says something important about the experience of ARTs. Although lacking diversity, these interviews do bring to light experiences of those many people who do not succeed in getting pregnant. Eight of the interviewees did not succeed, although one of those adopted a baby. One couple (Steve and Mari) became pregnant after ending ARTs. The rest remained without children as of the interview. Seven interviewees used IVF, four intrauterine insemination (IUI). One withdrew from treatment after finding out through the assessment process that she had a chronic condition that would make pregnancy difficult. Although a disappointing response rate, I think the interviews and research here are important because exploration of the impact of these treatments has lagged far behind their growth, and only one study, in sociology, has focused on people who fail to become pregnant (Throsby, 2004).

As mentioned, ARTs are conceptualized by some as a "patriarchal bargain" (Lorber, 1989), meaning that consumers have limited capacity to exercise choice. The focus in this research was on people's experiences of their treatment and, when relevant, the ways in which they decided to stop. The small sample limits generalization, but the narratives culled here bring up important points about the psychological experience of the procedures and, most importantly, as will be described in the following chapters, the ramifications for a repetition for sexual trauma, something that seems obvious, yet no previous research or case study has discussed. Additionally, the process of ARTs requires entering into a new temporal world, where one is positioned in a liminal space of almost pregnant, while engaging in procedures that require the religious fervor of a new convert blindly driven by hope in a particular future trajectory (Franklin, 1998), while scanning the past for any potential transgressions to be blamed for failure (Gentile, 2013). And, as will be described, this complex temporal layering occurs with little space for reflection; thus, there are limited capacities for meaning and decision making.

Blackman (2008) notes how suggestibility has increasingly been seen as reifying the ideal of an individual impervious to social influences. Describing cultural trends necessarily implies some suggestibility and an observation that people are doing what they are told. Subjectivity involves not just ambivalence but the understanding that we are not always aware of our feelings in the moment and, of course, many of our responses remain unconscious. As I attempt to observe and create theoretical links between cultural trends and events and interview data, I am not labeling people as unreflective lemmings, nor questioning the values of choice or the benefits of ARTs. I am trying to explore the experiences of these technologies, as they are situated within a cultural context.

It's all about the woman's body/erasing men's bodies

> It wasn't until our third and last doctor, as we were getting ready to quit, that they did an actual sperm analysis and they found that only 2% were viable. I felt like I was hit by a truck. What the fuck were those other infertility doctors doing? This percentage of bad sperm is when they usually say, "use a donor," not to mention each and every doctor had blamed me and my age for the infertility, when in fact it was probably my partner. We wasted 3 crucial years of attempts.
>
> (Olive)

As mentioned earlier, ARTs paint human fertility as "not very efficient" and in need of scientific assistance (Franklin, 1997). Because, culturally, fertility has been located within the female body to the exclusion of the male, women are the identified patients regardless of the problem; the focus of ART protocols in the West is on female bodies.[3] Women often comply with this focus, and, even when infertility is due to the male factor, they commonly take at least part, if not all, of the responsibility for the problem, demonstrating "courtesy stigma" by calling themselves as well as their partners infertile (Miall, 1986, quoted in Lorber, 1989). The scant research that exists on men and ARTs describes male infertility as a cultural taboo (Webb & Daniluk, 1999), an assault to masculinity that undermines virility and potency (Webb & Daniluk, 1999; Gannon et al., 2004). Indeed, as will be discussed further in Chapter 6, male infertility is often conflated with impotence, perhaps indicating a cultural fantasy of castration that undermines any attempt to acknowledge it. Thus, it is not surprising that men's bodies cease to be relevant in ART treatment, except as disembodied producers of sperm samples. In this study, three couples had male-identified fertility issues and all were directed to IVF as the only option. While this myopic focus on the female body can be disempowering and alienating for men (see Keylor & Apter, 2010), it also protects them (Gentile, 2010). In the discourse of ART, men are not tested – only sperm is tested. And sperm is tested only as to its ability to fertilize an egg, the assumption being that this is the entirety of its participation in conception. Consequently, we know little "about its role in embryo development and implantation" (Daniels, 2006, p. 147). Even intracytoplasmic sperm injection (ICSI), a procedure developed during the 1990s for use in cases of male infertility, focuses the intervention exclusively on the woman's body, medically enhancing its ability to become pregnant with a potentially genetically or physically challenged sperm. The procedure takes a sample (either through a syringe into the testes or from masturbation) and identifies and extracts potentially viable sperm. The egg is then treated chemically to soften the shell or/and a hole is made in the egg membrane. Sperm is injected directly into the egg, thereby making it easier for the challenged sperm to fertilize. ICSI is one of the more popular forms of IVF, even when a male factor is not identified (Mundy, 2008). So women's bodies and the eggs they produce are the sites of intervention to attempt to make up for the problems of the male body. As discussed, the structure of such procedures ensures that embodiment is contained within the female, liberating the male from its limitations (Gentile, 2010).

As the focus of intervention, women's bodies are instrumentalized and managed as so many disembodied measurements and lists to be analyzed, predicted, and controlled. Visit any fertility blog or website, or observe that, when women discuss treatments, they describe their bodies in terms of measurements of different hormone levels on specific days of the cycle, numbers of eggs produced, and size of follicles. Here, information management is internalized and women live their bodies as numbers and measurements. This is not a difficult task for many women, who may already have learned to live through calorie counts, pounds on a scale, and/or commodified clothes sizes. Here, as with disordered eating behaviors, the numbers and measurements can constrain and confine female bodies while providing a temporal holding, a numerical skin within which to go on being through time and space (see Gentile, 2007).

As women's bodies are under constant surveillance, they are subject to invasive and painful assessments and procedures as well as significant and unknown medical risk in fertility treatments. Mundy (2008) calls ARTs an "extreme sport" and cites a number of studies linking ovulation-inducing drugs to cancer in women and diseases in children. All my interviewees (and myself) were asked by doctors to sign a waiver that stated we understood the potential cancer risks involved in taking ovulation-inducing drugs. But when doctors were asked to explain these risks, many of us were told there really were none; studies were inconclusive; they would not give us any drugs that were not safe. None of us asked why, if that was the case, we were signing this consent waiver.

Doctors monitor and/or control the woman's hormonal cycle through daily hormone injections in order to predict the timing of follicular production of eggs and ovulation, even though these times may differ in each ovary. Women must have regular vaginal sonograms to be monitored for overstimulation of the ovaries, a condition that can be fatal, and, oftentimes, daily blood tests to check hormone levels. If a partner's sperm is required, sexual activity must be carefully timed to maintain optimal sperm production, insemination or surgical egg retrievals for IVF, followed by egg fertilizations and, if after a few days embryos have developed in the lab, they are injected into the uterus. If multiple embryos implant, selective reduction may be an option. As mentioned previously, the United States, unlike other countries, relies on "guidelines," not laws, to govern the number of implanted embryos. There can be pressures from patients (based on their finances, life circumstances, and desires), as well as from clinics and organizations, to implant multiple embryos. Each daily or weekly appointment involves a long wait in a crowded clinic room that was described by all but one interviewee as standing room only.

ART procedures often require women to miss work, which many just cannot afford to do. This structural component can also reinforce women's responsibility for the treatment and men's alienation from it, since it can be prohibitively difficult for both partners to miss that much work. Treatment can result in women putting careers or promotions on hold for years of treatment (Throsby, 2004), while the male partner may end up working longer hours to pay for it.

Given that medical protocols like preconception care (described in the previous chapter) cast all premenopausal female bodies as always potentially reproducing, whether or not they plan to, it is an obvious extension that women alone must eliminate all imaginable risks to potential children. Here, a woman's temporal–spatial orientation is stretched such that, with any present decision or behavior, she should be oriented in the future body of her potential baby (and, in some medical reports, she should situate herself in the fetus of her potential fetus, worrying about the damage her choices could have on the reproductive capacities of a future female fetus (Gentile, 2013)). The present is filled with audits of past behaviors and their potential impact on a future fetus. So the future is not embodied in the woman's body, but instead projected into the future body of her potential fetus and baby. In this temporal configuration, the present is a collection of multiple, successive, catastrophic futures embodied in multiple potential fetuses, and each is tethered to the mistakes of the past. Within this dense culture of time, when actions are immediately tied to reproductive potential, it seems natural and normal for ART procedures to be focused exclusively on the female body, for that is where all the cultural attention to and anxiety about reproduction is focused.

In fact, the discourse on fetal protection shifts dramatically when it involves men's behaviors. For instance, the vast majority of genetic defects are passed by the sperm (Daniels, 2006), and "despite the scientific research that has shown potentially damaging effects [on sperm] of men's cigarette smoking and drug and alcohol use, public attention has focused almost exclusively on the toxic effects of pregnant women's behavior" (p. 143). And, as mentioned previously, although the Unborn Victims of Violence Act was created in the wake of an intimate-partner violence case (and intimate-partner violence is a significant cause of birth defects), it is women who have been targeted as threats to fetal health. This particular focus of surveillance casts mothers as "ideologically meshed" with their biological children (Casper & Moore, 2009) and fathers as ideologically distinct, dissociated and spatially separate from theirs, reinforcing the need to maintain surveillance on women's fertility while ignoring men's. Daniels (2006) claims that a focus on male-mediated fetal harm threatens "men's reproductive self-sovereignty – their right to do whatever they please with their own bodies" (p. 153). Additionally, male reproductive vulnerability creates such panic and denial it can only be met with maternal blame as deflection (Daniels, 2006).

As observed elsewhere (Gentile, 2010), this reflex to turn our collective heads to disavow the vulnerable phallus was clearly demonstrated in the rewriting of the plot of *The Children of Men* for film. In P.D. James' book from 1992, humans have lost the capacity to reproduce because adult men are unable to produce sperm. Men's bodies are subject to monthly monitoring by the state in hopes of finding sperm. In the book, men's bodies are the objects of regular medical surveillance. In the movie, this central plot was changed, making women infertile. Few, if any, reviewers discussed this major plot change. This change is eerily similar to Margaret Atwood's novel, *The Handmaid's Tale* (1986), where the words "male sterility" are outlawed, never to be verbalized in public.

By associating the female body with "flesh, contingency and becoming" (Cavarero, as quoted in Oliver, 2007), i.e., the future (Dinshaw et al., 2007; Gentile, 2011), the male body is maintained as an "abstract image of proportionality, perfect balance and timeless stability" (Oliver, 2007, p. 15). The male body produces a steady, predictable flow of sperm while the female body has oftentimes unpredictable cycles that ebb and flow (Martin, 1991). As Martin noted, female reproduction is identified as a system of interdependent hormones and organs while the male system is viewed as "autonomous, operating independently and in isolation" (p. 490), the ideal neoliberal citizen dependent on and influenced by no one.

> So the male body is an abstract image of perfection that never has to be tested for certainty as it is timeless. It remains unchanging and still while the female body is full of time, full of the future, full of unpredictability, just plain full and threatening in its temporal density.
>
> (Gentile, 2013, p. 169)

This fantasy of impenetrability stands in face of the reality that sperm counts have declined across the globe, and many evolving reproductive disorders in men are also being found in animals in surrounding geographic locations, lending support to environment causes (Daniels, 2006, p. 45). Yet biosurveillance strategies skip over men, focusing instead on women (Daniels, 2006). When men do have to participate in biomonitoring practices for ARTs, they consider the experience to be humiliating and shameful (Webb & Daniluk, 1999, p. 13) and do not readily comply with medical orders (Throsby, 2004). Olive's partner Lou, like another male participant, Steve, described being humored by the experience of masturbating in a clinic room to produce "samples." Both joked when describing the variety of pornography available, distancing themselves from the use of the media in their respective everyday lives. But this humor evaporated immediately for Lou once he became a focus of surveillance. As Olive (not Lou, who was also a participant) shared separately:

> We went to two different clinics, each of which focused all their intervention, pity, and judgmental comments on me, my diet, my exercise regime, my age, my noncompliance when I didn't want to take too many hormones. As a last try we went to a private doctor who discovered Lou's sperm had some significant problems that no one had considered. Suddenly he had to have an extensive series of blood tests, which he complained about. I'd had endless blood tests for the past 4 years. Then when he had to go to a specialist he refused to go alone. I had to wait during one exam that involved an ultrasound of his scrotum. When he reappeared he was white as a sheet and would not speak to me. He just kept saying "I don't want to talk about it," and he hasn't to this day. I just kept thinking wow, he never would have made it through one vaginal ultrasound, let alone daily ones for years, not to mention the unbearable pain of having dye shot up your fallopian tubes, and multiple strangers inseminating you like cattle.

Centering intervention on women may support a fantasy of impenetrable and stable masculinity, but it also alienates them from the treatment. Lou initially felt he had nothing to offer this study since the procedures had all focused on his partner, Olive. Similarly, Leanne's husband talked very little during the interview, saying his wife had more important information. For Steve, this gendered focus on Mari left him overwhelmed. He described the pain of watching Mari become more and more sad after each failed procedure. As he noted, they were both going through the losses, which meant he couldn't support and help her as he usually would. Additionally, he described feeling he had to protect her from his sadness since she was going through all the physical demands of the interventions. Similarly, Lou also described being overwhelmed with feelings of intense sadness throughout the process but, for him, he said, "I was afraid Olive would see my sadness as my desire for us to continue, to try harder or to do more invasive procedures. I felt I had to hold it back for fear she'd feel it was pressure to go further." Throsby (2004) found men often felt their roles to be those of traditional masculinity, being the emotional rock for the couple and the one who would keep one foot in reality in order to assess the viability of each proposed protocol. Of course, this need for the rational partner hints at the ways ART procedures are not just an uncontrollable downhill snowball, collecting protocols along the way, as I described earlier. This snowball is barreling down a mountain shaped by those cultural pressures for reproduction that identify babies as the promise of the future, especially for women. Thus, there can be a need for a guide who will keep one foot out of the fray, who will be, or pretend to be, unaffected by the intensely emotional and vulnerable situation.

So the protocols of ARTs function to reproduce traditional gender roles where the woman is the vulnerable, patient body and the man is the objective, rational, decision-making mind. Of course, these gendered roles hurt both partners. Although these men described feeling intense sadness, they said they could not always express or share it with their respective partners, leaving them alienated from the process itself as well as potentially alienated from their partner and from their own emotional responses. Clearly, there is a need for more research and support for male partners, as Keylor and Apter (2010) have also noted.

In ARTs, women, who are raised to police their bodies as objects (Gentile, 2007), rigorously follow the medical advice and participate in much more invasive and painful inconvenient procedures. In their interview research with pregnant women, Browner and Press (1995) found most of them were preoccupied with what they ate and drank, believing it directly impacted their developing child. They also tended to believe they were at fault if there were any problems, including miscarriage. They described feeling little confidence in their body's abilities to handle pregnancy and to develop properly without medical intervention and monitoring. Here, a cycle of dependence has been perfectly fostered. Preconception care and prenatal services function to educate women about all the potential problems, then they claim to provide the services to monitor and reassure women that all is OK. They create anxieties that only they can quell (Browner & Press, 1995). Rejection of technology and testing is seen as a rejection on the part of the expectant mother to do all she can to ensure a healthy baby (Browner & Press, 1995) and can be punishable by criminal prosecution (Paltrow, 2013). Feminists have described the medicalization of childbirth, but here we see the medicalization of preconception, fertility, prenatal care, in addition to birth. Basically, healthy babies can no longer be created outside the medical gaze, which now includes lifelong surveillance of female bodies. To include men in this cultural narrative of reproduction would require embodying them, which would threaten the culture's separation of mind/body, male/female, and the myth of male invulnerability that undergirds patriarchy. But not including men alienates them from the process and threatens their reproductive, physical, and psychological health (see Chapter 6).

ARTs transcend the body

Although focusing on the female body, ARTs also transcend the body. With ARTs, conception is not assisted but "achieved . . . in the laboratory by professionals . . . constituting an unfamiliar primal scene" (Franklin, 1995, p. 328). Reproduction is not the result of messy, out-of-control, merging bodies, but, instead, a carefully calculated and controlled procedure complete with white lab coats and sterile instruments. ARTs, then, erase sex from reproduction. If pregnancy was/is a shameful display of carnality (Oliver, 2012), the telltale sign that a woman has had sex, then ARTs bring into possibility a virgin, sexless birth. Related to this, Franklin (1997) notes the religious symbolism in infertility treatments, where the desperate infertile woman is made pregnant with a miracle baby via the intervention of the God-like medical doctor. "Science and nature are unified in an act of pro-creation" (p. 207) that renders the medical doctor divine. "The omnipotence of the doctor turns reproduction into a monogenetic process" (Helmreich, 1998), where the doctor becomes the sole/soul creator (Gentile, 2010), the masculine (the vast majority of fertility doctors are male) God who "sparks the formless void of the earth to life with a kind of divine seed" (Helmreich, 1998, p. 211). And, as with the most famous virgin birth, paternity in the case of ARTs becomes ambiguous: Is it the partner (male/female/transgender)? The sperm donor? The inseminating doctor? The doctor who retrieved the eggs? The laboratory technician who fertilized the eggs in the case of IVF? Or the doctor who implanted them? All of the above? And what about the participation of the pornography available to men at the clinics to help them produce the "samples"?

As bodies are transcended, or perhaps dispersed, the embryo is further individuated and separated from the maternal, which becomes merely a container that, only through biotechnology, can be coaxed to allow implantation and gestation. The doctors become the paternal heroes, creators of the "little fetus that could" (Franklin, 1991, p. 195), soon to be the miracle baby, as long as the maternal body submits to the biotechnological interventions.

This erasure of bodies through ART plays well in a culture where media representations of fit, skinny, postnatal bodies function to erase the process of gestation, rendering the baby a product of patriarchy, unencumbered by the abject maternal body (Gentile, 2010, 2011). Such a process of erasure creates a public suspicion – did she really have a baby? Was she really pregnant? Did that body reproduce? And with ARTs it can include: Did she have sex (heterosexual intercourse)? How could it have happened? It creates a magical spin on the primal scene by taking bodies out of the process of reproduction itself. As the female body becomes a collapsed space of absence (literally collapsed, concave stomachs), we could actually believe the baby dropped from the stork. It brings us culturally to a pre-Oedipal state of mind where babies just appear; the primal scene has not reared its exclusionary head, forcing us to deal with our ambivalence and limits. The Madonna has reappeared; women can have babies not only without sexual contact or pleasure, but through procedures of suffering and inconvenience. ART babies, then, are not conceived through "original sin."

This unique status of ART babies not being tainted by desires of the flesh may also play into the spread of these technologies. As global climate change and other catastrophic futures rain down on reality, there may be an unconscious desire to create the perfect messianic baby who will once again cleanse "man" of "his" sins. (This possibility will be taken up further in the Epilogue.) Because the ART baby is created outside of the flesh, it can function to enact an aggressive act not just against the abject maternal, but against *the* abject maternal – mother nature, who can be not just dominated, but bested (now we can eradicate genetic diseases; take that, evolution!) and rendered irrelevant through ARTs. Further, by promoting the absolute importance of babies, creating them in labs and then disavowing their gestation, the culture creates a form of temporal linking that symbolically erases women as productive beings.

The bodies ARTs transcend are also temporal, as they can alter or collapse the chronology of genealogical embodied time, transgressing (Oedipal) lineages. Consider cases of (grand)mothers who have gestated their respective daughters' babies. Also, in ARTs, units of reproductive time are rearranged (ejaculation can occur moments or years before fertilization; eggs can be harvested and prepared for fertilization as sperm is produced and washed; fertilization occurs in a lab; and embryo development can begin weeks, months, or years before implantation). Time is slowed or sped up (monthly cycles are slowed, accelerated, or magnified, i.e., "superovulations," with shots), and even suspended (freezing embryos and stopping cycles).

Additionally, we must situate ARTs within a culture that stratifies pregnancy not only by race and class, but also by age. The glorification of teenage pregnancy can function as titillation, for it creates an irresistible combination of innocence and sexuality (Oliver, 2012). In this light, the sexlessness of ARTs can function to reinforce the assumed barrenness of older female bodies, bodies within which sex no longer works (even if ARTs might) and within reprofuturity, where sex no longer matters because it is now all about the production of the baby. While ARTs in younger women can conjure fantasy images of the immaculate conception, with older women, this sexlessness can function to reinforce the culture's misogynous ideas about older women's asexuality and abjection. And because women's bodies are the site of intervention, it is women's bodies that may be cast as useless and sexless. Again, even in ARTs, male orgasm is still required (usually).

One might observe that this is a setup for an experience of alienation and commodification. However, women are not being disconnected from the product of their labor: their babies, so much as being disconnected from their bodies as the producers of these babies. They are being separated from their labor itself. As babies take center stage in the culture, the media celebrates women who erase the proof that they produced these valued commodities, rendering women's bodies (again) merely objects in a patriarchal world.

ARTs as a process of exercising choice

Choice is tricky, and I have no illusions about simplifying it here. ARTs have been described by many as a wild west science and a never-enough treatment focused on women's bodies (see Franklin & Ragoné, 1998), where each month's period signals both a failed attempt at pregnancy and renewed hope for a new protocol, and something new is always available (see Franklin & Ragoné, 1998; Inhorn & van Balen, 2002). The possibilities for intervention can seem endless, bound only by the woman's age or the couple's financial resources. Observing from this perspective, one might be hard-pressed to see ARTs as anything but a new form of medicalized colonization, and certainly, considering the critique of biomedicalization, such a view is inevitable. Yet feminist critiques of ARTs have been tricky because reproductive choice is a central tenet of feminism. Firestone's (1970/1979) early vision of equality was based on reproductive technologies.

Haraway (1997) identifies technology as a resource, freeing women from the cultural constraints of embodiment, including reproduction. ARTs are positioned as enabling women to control their reproductive system, as noted previously, extending the biological clock.

Ideals of agency, however, often assume ownership of one's body, which, given the centuries-long history of white, patriarchal "appropriation of others" (Petchesky, 1995, p. 395), means choice and agency are complicated for women and people of color. Historically, women have been manipulated in ways that foreclose the potential for collective action (Spivak, 2010, p. 38), used to support, not shift or deconstruct, neoliberal patriarchal social structures. For instance, neoliberalism locates agency within individual behaviors such that eating disorders, stripping, prostitution, self-mutilation, and cosmetic surgeries have each been read as forms of agency and complicity with little attention to systemic change or relational forms of being. A contrast to this individualized notion of ownership of the body is that proposed by Collins (1990), where women have a "bodily integrity" that is "communal and extended rather than individualized and privatized" (Petchesky, 1995, p. 398). Subjectivity is historically contingent, but not essentialist or fixed (see Chapter 2). It is in a constant process of becoming through time. However, even collective and process-based subjectivities engage with discourses and affective networks that function to provide differing levels of agency and choice making (Petchesky, 1995). As Bollas (1987) wrote, agency is not located in the "caller" or the one who is called, but rather in what is "called up" (p. 240), what the affective economy or affective patterns of the culture demand. In other words, agency needs to be spread not only to the women and men who may be "called" into the ART system, but to what is "called up." The power of the affective content of babies cannot be underestimated in a culture shaped by reprofuturity.

Integrating Spivak's approach to agency as collective engagement with what Parisi (2004) describes as "collective capacities to act and become" (p. 45), it is clear we need to disaggregate choice making from agency. Although, in capitalist terms, more choices means more agency, as Franklin's (1995, 1997, 1998) extensive research has indicated, choice making in the context of ARTs is not in and of itself a form of empowerment. Indeed, as will be described in the next chapter, choice making in the context of ARTs could be described as the creation of "poisonous encounters between bodies that decompose a body's relations of parts" (Parisi, 2004, p. 45) – in other words, fostering levels of dissociation.

Choice making is further complicated by selective cultural representations of ARTs that reinforce its miracle status through a process of erasing failure, risk, and the physical and time demands. ARTs become a normalized part of women's reproductive medicine (Mamo, 2010). They become part of what Freeman (2010) terms chrononormativity, the ways in which the body is ordered and timed in the service of productivity. By hailing healthy people into a medical process, ARTs become an assumption, like taking insulin for diabetes (Throsby, 2004). In this context, questions about safety seem paranoid, and deciding not to participate or deciding to what extent to engage with ARTs are both interpreted as limiting one's options, thus jeopardizing one's empowerment and agency. ARTs produce a "forced choice" (Kalbian, 2005, p. 108), where refusing any form of ART is positioned as refusing medical treatment, and thus, refusing to have a child (Ibid.). Public exposure of ARTs not only makes it more stigmatizing to not have children (Franklin, 1997); it creates an assumed correspondence between the degree of desire for a child and the extent one will go to get one (Throsby, 2004).

A central component of biomedicalization is the creation of a felt sense of identity that gains agency and empowerment through choosing to follow and purchase medicalized lifestyles. As mentioned, just as many women can find agency through the instrumentalization of the body through caloric and weight management; the practices of ART, too, involve objectifying the body as a series of measurements to be controlled. And ART clinics and the media position ART patients as empowered agents taking control over their fertility. However, as my interviewees and many memoirs describe, agency in relation to ARTs can be limited to making the choice to surrender one's body to the expert discourse of the doctor, resulting in a form of dissociation of the body. This has significant consequences, especially when we consider the potential for re-traumatization of survivors of sexual violence.

Lastly, choice in the context of ARTs is also difficult to assess because the growing surveillance around reproduction and the proliferation of ARTs supposedly function to create healthy babies, which, as described in terms of reprofuturity, confer unquestioned happiness.

ARTs as an effortless panacea

> IVF as it is culturally constructed is a great process – success goes to clinic, failure to the woman.
>
> (Throsby, 2004, p. 59)

Approximately 36% of infertile women or/and heterosexual couples seek treatment (Spar, 2006), and, of those, only 50–60% of the couples will successfully birth a baby (Webb & Daniluk, 1999). Eighty per cent of all IVF cycles will fail (Throsby, 2004). Statistics are complicated here because cause and effect is not linear or clear, and information can only describe probabilities and uncertainties. For instance, the estimate that one in five cycles results in conception does not mean you can embark on five cycles and guarantee success (Throsby, 2004). Percentages are amassed through generalizations based on a "universal" cycle, the assumption being that not only is each woman's monthly cycle the same, but that cycles are the same in different women. It is a medical procedure where close to 70% of the patients will not be cured, yet with each failure more hope for the next cycle is manufactured (Spar, 2006). This investment in the hope of the future as an object is described by Cooper (2008), who situates neoliberal forms of biotechnology as primarily concerned with capturing the promise of accumulation and life, an investment in the future of futures (e.g., pre-conception care guidelines, a focus on the reproductive capacities of a potential female fetus).

Given that patients are paying for hope, ARTs involve a different kind of market speculation where the fundamental rules of supply and demand are "conspicuously absent" (Spar, 2006, p. xvi); people are willing to pay almost anything, and they are apt to decide to pay more, not less, with each failed cycle. They do not give up on the process and they tend to stay with one doctor or clinic, blaming themselves for the failures (Ibid.).

While there are more options than ever for IVF, more potential drug choices, more eggs and sperm available for sale, the prices have actually risen, not fallen (Spar, 2006). This perfect storm has resulted in a global market (see Ginsburg and Rapp, 1995; Spar, 2006) for ART and its components, driving prices up, not down.[4]

With increasing technological advances come increases in overheads for doctors (Spar, 2006), who evoke "reproductive liberty" to justify any procedure at any cost for a baby (Mundy, 2008, p. xviii). As mentioned in Chapter 1, IVF is about $8,000–15,000 per round, with an average of three rounds before conception or giving up (Spar, 2006; RESOLVE.org). It is the most profitable procedure for clinics and also the one most likely to be tracked in clinic statistics and researched diligently by prospective patients. So it is no surprise that doctors often leap immediately to this intervention. Although all my interviewees described the desire to just know why they weren't getting pregnant, most doctors did not seem to share their curiosity, focusing instead on IVF as the panacea. Olive described being prepped for insemination – in stirrups, naked from the waist down – when a doctor she had never seen before walked in, glanced at her chart, and said loud enough to be clearly heard, "IUI? Well, this is a waste of my time." He proceeded to grill her about why she wouldn't do IVF.

All interviewees who went to clinics described the mandatory orientations, typically about 4–6 hours long. These workshops list the tests needed for treatment; they go over the basics of IUI, but spend the bulk of the time on IVF, including, at some clinics, teaching women or/and their partners how to give daily hormone shots. This approach brings ARTs into the home, further normalizing the process. Even if patients are there only for IUI, they are required to stay for the entire workshop and learn about IVF and practice giving shots. The message is clear: everyone will eventually wise up and go for IVF. Put in the language of biomedicalization, such workshops function to produce bodies that are friendly to IVF. Olive said the nurse leading the workshop repeated as a mantra: "once your body is under the control of the doctor with hormone shots, conception is much easier." As Olive reflected,

> I had spent the past years tracking my cycle, taking morning temperatures, identifying ovulation through a kit, the feel of my vaginal mucus, and the orientation made it clear that I was barking up the wrong tree. I had to cede control to the doctor. Unfettered access and control was the key to fertility.

The booklet she had from the workshop also stated this verbatim, as did those materials Sara, Jordan, and Hannah had from theirs.

Lastly, as Spar (2006), Mundy (2008), and Roberts (2009) each point out, ARTs also take a toll on other areas of the healthcare and the education systems. Largely unregulated clinics often implant multiple embryos, leaving women to choose either to deliver multiples or to reduce. Having patients successfully birth multiples positively impacts clinic statistics that count the number of births, not how many women get pregnant (Cain, 2001; Spar, 2006). But women carrying multiples are more likely to require high-risk maternity wards, and babies born from IVF are more likely to be multiples, premature, have lower birth weight, need care in the neonatal intensive care unit (NICU), and to have more developmental problems requiring more cognitive-based educational interventions (Spar, 2006; Mundy, 2008). ARTs are directly related to the explosion of high risk maternity wards and NICUs in hospitals, the most expensive unit.[5]

By focusing intervention on the symptom, not the cause, ARTs create a cyclical market of repeat consumers where people have to return if they want more children. Additionally, because ICSI has been linked with congenital malformation and infertility in boys (Mundy, 2008), IVF is creating the next generation of infertility patients.

ARTs reinforce while seeming to transcend the Oedipal

The power of ideology is its ability to remain invisible while shaping affective networks, and thus, experiences and subjectivities. Similarly, Oedipal ideology is both visible and obscured in ARTs, leading some to cast the technologies as a revolutionary way of transcending the Oedipal. But, as has been detailed in these first three chapters, and as the rest of the book will demonstrate, this relationship is much more complex. On the one hand, ARTs do complicate traditional notions of kinship and parenting. Even linear generations can be rearranged with these interventions. But, in opening up biological reproduction to so many different configurations of family and nonfamily, ARTs are also a servant of the Oedipal, enabling the Oedipal to spread into new domains, new relations. As mentioned previously, if ARTs bring the (spurious) promise that now everyone can have a biological child, they are also spreading the reproductive mandate from which the Oedipal emerges: now no one has any excuse not to have, or actively try to have, a biological child. Certainly, there are many different aspects of the Oedipal that are challenged by ARTs, but the foundational ideology of reprofuturity from which the Oedipal is created is only reinforced and strengthened by ARTs. Indeed, as described in the next chapter, ARTs create and spread a psychological desire for reproduction (Franklin, 1997). If the creation of desire for reproduction does not serve the very foundations of the Oedipal, then what does? Given the number of potential parental figures (egg and sperm donors, surrogates, doctors who perform the inseminations or implantations, lab technicians fertilizing eggs, nurses/partners giving hormonal shots), how does one generation even know who it is they should displace in the "waning" (Loewald, 1980) of these new Oedipal hierarchies?

So it is within this cultural maelstrom of reprofuturity and biomedicalization that ARTs produce bodies willing to choose to undergo invasive procedures driven by hope for pregnancy. But, of course, lived experiences are always more complicated. Additionally, as will be described in Simon's chapter, even success in ARTs does not resolve the potential complicated feelings of loss that infertility can engender.

Notes

1 The more organized critiques of ARTs originate in the UK and Australia, home to the organization FINRRAGE – Feminist International Network of Resistance to Reproductive and Genetic Engineering. FINRRAGE calls for doctors to explore environmental causes of infertility and seek nonbiological interventions to infertility. They see ARTs as producing "mother machines" (Corea, 1985), "test tube women," and "living laboratories" (Klein, 1989). They see ARTs functioning to enforce pro-natalist agendas and exploiting a desire for children by marketing hope more than successful reproduction. Of the feminist critiques, they alone discuss overpopulation as a central concern fueling resistance to ARTs and the need for more accessible processes for adoption.

2 Each person participated in an interview lasting approximately 1–2 hours. The interview protocol focused on general questions about reproductive history, decision making around ARTs, experiences with ARTs, and, when relevant, questions about how they decided to stop treatments. The protocol was approved by the John Jay College of Criminal Justice/City University of New York Institutional Review Board. Participant names were changed for confidentiality.

3 This approach, avoiding intervention with men, is not the norm throughout the world. In Chinese medicine, for example, there are detailed diagnoses and multiple different interventions for male infertility (Ann Vitolo, personal communication, July 7, 2006).

4 For instance, while other countries have equated selling eggs to selling organs, making the practice illegal, the United States has not. So international brokers can pay unlimited fees for designer US eggs. As more donor eggs become available the price increases, not decreases, because the market has begun to differentiate eggs with "ideal" qualities. Here, people do not purchase sperm or eggs; they purchase the qualities of the donor that match those they want their child to have (Spar, 2006). The fact that genes need to be activated by an environment is not considered. Genes are not seen as webs, but reduced to units, entities in isolation – again, the fetish of individualization and independence and the disavowal and disgust with interdependence ring through. Human traits are instrumentalized, reduced to DNA and information. Cells become "objects of knowledge and practice" (Haraway, 1997, p. 142), with DNA that can be categorized like any other information to be archived, edited, and subject to computational procedures (Clough, 2008). As we instrumentalize biological entities and functions, we erase the processes that enable them to come into being as we attempt to control and reproduce them through our own technologies (Clough, 2008). This booming industry of "bioinformatics" (Ibid.) is not only based on donated eggs and sperm, but also the information catalogued in order to enable ART practices.

The hormone market, too, is another booming success, with 75% of sales being total profit, around $390 million annually (Spar, 2006). Medical profits alone are estimated to be about $3 billion per year and this does not include profits made by consultants, therapists, lawyers, equipment suppliers, or laboratory workers separate from the office. According to Spar (2006), the only aspect of the ART market that has remained stable is that of surrogacy, but only because there is a large supply of poor women in the United States and in developing countries who are willing to serve as inexpensive surrogates.

Gestation, the cheapest form of labor, is that conducted outside the lab and purview of the doctor. Additionally, reproductive labor is developing similarly to other transnational systems of women's labor, such as domestic, sexual, and maternal, and these spheres are fluid in that women in one often migrate from one to another (Cooper, 2008).

5 Medical costs for twins are three times those of single babies for the first 5 years (Mundy, 2008). In 2004, 12.5%, or one in eight, of all live births were premature, a 33% increase in the past 30 years. The average premature baby costs $42,000, a significant increase of healthcare costs; 20% have severe learning disabilities, and 45% need special education. In 2003 there were more triplet births than ever before, rising from an average of 37 to 200 per 100,000 births at a cost of more than $500,000 per baby (Mundy, 2008, p. 217).

Chapter 4

Producing temporalities through assisted reproductive technologies

Katie Gentile

> The surgical procedures were surreal. I remember getting there at 7.30 prompt, and waiting, waiting, waiting in the reception area that was standing room only, as usual. Then they call your name, you strip, don a gown and get on a hospital bed that is wheeled into a public hall in the clinic. There I waited for what seemed like an hour, in a line of women on beds that snaked down the hall. I was one of like eight women and there were more waiting to get into this line. Each of us in a bed, lined up down the hall outside the surgery room. It was so surreal it reminded me of a scene out of *The Handmaid's Tale*[1] or something. When it was finally my turn I remember wanting to make a joke to the doctors in the room who must just keep doing different procedures all day like a factory, you know, all these women being wheeled in one after the other . . . Something like, "you do remember what I'm here for, right?" but they put the mask on so fast I couldn't think. The funny thing is, they actually did botch that surgery and I had to do it all over again a couple months later at a different clinic. Thanks to them we lost more than a year.
>
> (Olive)

If it isn't obvious at this point, ARTs are a challenge. However, research on them, including this study, is complicated by the fact that the difficulties of the treatment procedures themselves cannot be disaggregated from the trauma of infertility. Research on infertility and ARTs focuses almost exclusively on white, heterosexual couples (see Chapter 1). The studies that do exist have found that, for these heterosexual couples, the diagnosis contributes to difficulties in sexual functioning and satisfaction, disrupting marital communication, creating interpersonal relationship difficulties and emotional and psychological distress for both partners (Webb & Daniluk, 1999).

Just as the protocols of ARTs erase men's bodies, research in the area tends to focus almost exclusively on heterosexual women. According to these studies, heterosexually coupled women going through ART treatments often begin to associate sex with disappointment, guilt, pain, shame, and failure. ART processes can result in feelings of anger, betrayal, powerlessness, isolation, depression, suicidality, hostility, low self-esteem and unfairness, and lack of justice (Webb & Daniluk, 1999). One's meaning of life is questioned, and issues of mortality can loom large. As will be described here, these feelings can trigger previous experiences of trauma, particularly responses to sexual abuse.

Paraphrasing Oliver (2004), women are often expected to carry and contain the affective burden of shame for the culture. Given the cultural burden and responsibility placed on women for reproduction and the gendered structure of assistived reproductive technology (ART) protocols, it is not surprising that women can develop significant psychological distress, somatic problems, and hypersensitivity and hypervigilance regardless of the source of the infertility. Greil (1997) found infertility to severely impact women, who often felt an inability to control their body or life. They felt defective and alienated from the world that felt fertile – bursting with displays of pregnant women who seemed the recipients of special attention, attention these infertile women felt they would never deserve or receive. Women described avoiding friends or/and situations with children. They felt stigmatized and unable to make meaning of their treatment that took over their lives. Women tended to blame themselves for their infertility, willingly deferring to medical advice and control in hopes of an answer (Browner & Press, 1995). Although men experienced stress when infertility was due to a male factor, they were less apt to lose trust in themselves (McLeod, 2002), whereas women were stressed and lost trust in themselves regardless of the identified cause (Greil, 1997; McLeod, 2002).

On the other hand, engaging in ARTs is to be enveloped within a culturally sanctioned health regime that can become a source of self-concept, identity, and achievement. This containment can be especially attractive after a diagnosis of infertility that can usher in a time of uncertainty and feelings of being out of control. ARTs enable one to identify as a patient and, in doing so, become linked to layers of communal experiencing that provide meaning making to one's experience of infertility. They also shift one's temporal position from being infertile to being a patient receiving fertility treatments. ARTs can provide a trajectory of hope and a feeling of motion, progressing toward a culturally sanctioned sense of futurity. But this externalized temporal containment comes at a price.

ARTs and the temporality of uncertainty

> Olive went for the blood test to find out it [an intrauterine insemination (IUI) procedure] had failed. That afternoon, when they called to tell us it had failed, they pushed us to do IVF [in vitro fertilization]. They pushed us by giving us no time to make decisions. They said if we wanted to do IVF we had to let them know that day on the phone. We were floored and distraught. We couldn't think about next month.
>
> (Lou)

Time in the world of ARTs is complex and contradictory. On the one hand, the doctors will remind patients how the time of fertility tick tocks away rapidly, marked by each month's period that signifies opportunities missed and eggs lost. But clinic time is framed by a "hurry up and wait" temporal structure, where one rushes for early appointments to sit for sometimes hours before being seen. ART tests must be timed to specific days of the menstrual cycle, marking time cyclically. But these are interspersed between recovery times, which slip linearly away. If one uses donors, time can anxiously stretch out even longer. Zoll (2013) described having to wait a year between choosing an egg donor and beginning a cycle.

These diverse temporal structures are framed by an overarching present marked by the liminal state of "not yet pregnant" (Sandelowski & de Lacy, 2002), living in an ambiguous space of being expected to plan for an indefinite future. Some women described living events in the present as they imagined they would be "next year" with a baby (Greil, 1997). Here, the experience of holidays and occasions became framed through a form of "proleptic haunting" (T. Catapano, personal communication, 1 August, 2014). For instance, Olive developed a playlist of songs she imagined singing to and with her baby. Each time she heard these songs, including after she and Lou decided to stop their attempts, she experienced a tsunami of temporally based affects, bombarding her with multiple pasts, presents, and futures. Because infertility is so often unexplained and "lasts for an indeterminate length of time" (Whiteford & Gonzalez, 1995, p. 28), "it can become *chronic crisis,* with no identifiable onset or solution, creating . . . a prolonged crisis state" (p. 28) that can result in high levels of posttraumatic stress disorder (Bradow, 2012). This crisis state is managed privately, rarely shared with social support networks. So time becomes marked and shaped by a daily, weekly, or/and monthly cycle of procedures, that pile uncertainty upon uncertainty in a culture where the capacity to generate meaning is dwindling and the abilities to tolerate frustration without disavowal increasingly absent. It is a setup for lack of reflection and capacity to make meaning or agentic decisions.

"It's like buying a lottery ticket" (Steve) – ARTs producing affect

This ongoing crisis state can be made more confusing because it co-occurs with a present where there is a mandate for experiencing hope for the future. Obviously, attempting to shape the future is a key motivation for participating in fertility treatments, but not in the way one would most likely imagine. Four of my interviewees echoed what Franklin (1995) found in her initial research, that they chose ARTs not necessarily because they believed the procedures would be successful, but so they could tell themselves they had done all they could to become pregnant. This, again, illustrates the complexities of choice. ARTs become a practice with which to engage in order to avoid regrets in the future. But, as Franklin also found, fertility treatments function like a craps game, in that, with each unsuccessful round, women were situated by the doctors as being somehow closer to pregnancy. A common theme echoed by the interviewees was "I kept thinking just one more time," or "we're so close," implying a spatial movement toward the goal, even though none of the doctors could articulate what went wrong. Like predicting a coin flip, doing more rounds of IVF does not increase the probability of conception, yet the participants' assumptions were that with each try they were *closer*. So, like gambling at a craps game, the hope for and anticipation of success did not dissipate with failure, but instead compounded, leaving the women wanting pregnancy more than before they began the process. As Steve said,

> The IUIs were like lottery tickets – you buy it, it gets you excited, you begin to fantasize about how it will feel to have a baby. You visualize the baby, your life with that child. Then when it doesn't happen it's much worse than it was before we did the ARTs. You are even more crushed, more disappointed and more depressed. It was like the worsening of hangovers with addiction. Each failed cycle felt more devastating. I never felt that level of anticipation and disappointment when we were just trying on our own.

So procedures that were initially attempted to forestall regret actually created the conditions for it. The dynamics of the procedure itself altered women's desire for offspring, making it harder, not easier, for them to live with the impossibility of becoming pregnant. As Zoll (2013) described in her memoir, the process of ARTs fostered regret. Additionally, they can create a form of anticipation and futurity that is narrowly constructed around pregnancy, often with no alternative. As Steve described, pregnancy was the only end imaginable, making failure that much more painful, shocking, and jarring. So ARTs produce affective experiences.

In fertility medicine, the mantra, either internal or expressed by the medical staff, is that you waited too long. This can focus the regret not just on waiting, but, as Zoll (2013), Hannah, and Olive noted, on everything you did in the past instead of having a baby. Events from your past are then weighed against the value of a baby. For some, this means a past that is recast as being filled with mistakes and poor (i.e., non-fertility) choices. This re-creation of the past can also function to erase professional successes or fill them with shame. Zoll (2013), in her memoir, describes re-experiencing her past writing awards as almost shameful since they symbolize that she was not focused on having a baby. So the affects produced can turn even professional successes, accolades, and one's chosen career track into shameful symbols of infertility or/and events now marked only by regret. This has significant ramifications for subjectivities that may become reassembled in ways that evacuate success and competence.

Given the complex ways that pasts, presents, and futures create the conditions for subjectivity (Chapter 2), ARTs can also function to undermine faith in going on being and shake one's confidence in decision making. As mentioned, ARTs negatively impact self-esteem and confidence, and increase anxiety, depression, and sense of lack of control (see Rosen, 2002). One can become fixated on thoughts of death and looming mortality. These negative experiences can be compounded by the isolation that also occurs, as people tend to privatize their coping with ARTs and avoid social situations, especially those that might involve pregnant women or children (Throsby, 2004). Add to this the biomedicalized practices that promote dissociation of the body and you have a picture of someone at risk of losing the capacity to generate meaning. As patients cede control over their bodies, their minds cling to the only future trajectory that can possibly make meaning of their current situation and the one constantly held out, like a carrot, by the clinic: "I kept my eyes shut and kept my mind on my baby, imagining how it would feel to hold a child of my own against my breast, and knowing that any pain now would be worth that feeling" (Manterfield, 2011, p. 104). The present, filled with pain, discomfort, inconvenience, and growing expenses, becomes singularly experienced through the future body of being a mother. When this biomedicalized hope takes over within a culture of reprofuturity, one's durational trajectory, spaces for meaning making, and reflection can collapse into the notion that a baby is worth any amount of pain. Here, any divergent past, presents, or futures disappear, leaving the only remaining possible future that of parenthood. So the only way a patient can experience time's duration and a future is through the reproductive body. Within the culture of ARTs, no pregnancy is equivalent to no future.

"I should have had gold-plated tampons" (Mari)

The collapse of meaning-making capacities is also impacted by the complicated experiences of embodiment during treatments. Physical sensations of pregnancy are also those of premenstrual syndrome and some ART hormone treatments. So physical signs are not only untrustworthy; they can be experienced as misleading. Like the sword of Damocles, a period hangs over fertility treatments, threatening the end of any potential pregnancy. As Mari described, "I felt like I should have had gold-plated tampons for my $800 periods after each failed IUI." The arrival of a period announces simultaneously the failure of the procedure and the loss of a potential pregnancy, as well as new hope for the next month's procedure that is now attached to the future pregnancy. The period becomes a monthly reminder of the body's failure and potential to reproduce. This contradiction and ambivalence can be intolerable, resulting in a turn on the body as a tantalizing object of persecution that holds out the promise of the impossible. This experience can be shattering to one's identity and entire sense of self. As Jordan noted, "I tried not to get excited when I'd feel bloated or swollen, hoping I was pregnant. Then when I saw my period I just felt contempt. Thanks for nothing." Most interviewees and memoirists said it was a reminder each month of failure, a sign that they had to start the painful, difficult, time-consuming process all over again, as well as an indication that pregnancy was still possible . . . next time. Additionally, each menstrual cycle without a pregnancy or without intervention can be experienced as valuable eggs being lost from an already questionable reserve (Zoll, 2013). These contradictory experiences of the body can contribute to even more ambivalence and distress.

This turning against the body completes a cycle of dissociated dependency on the doctor and the ART procedures, a point to which I will return shortly. The discourse of ARTs, as we've already seen, is such that it is not the procedure but your body that failed. The body is clearly working against your efforts and desires. Trust goes to the doctor and the clinic. This turning against the body can be dangerous, especially in the context of IVF. Two interviewees experienced life-threatening side effects from IVF, and both described having their pain minimized as being merely a response to the treatment. For Jordan, as her abdomen distended, she retained pounds of water overnight, and she experienced intense pain. Yet it took a number of calls to the doctor to get him to do an ultrasound, during which it was clear her ovaries were close to rupturing due to hyperstimulation, a potentially fatal condition. One woman had an ectopic pregnancy after an insemination procedure. She had not been verbally warned about this potential, and had to seek emergency treatment. While in the hospital, she found out that both IVF and IUI increase the chances for this condition. Additionally, ectopic pregnancy often results in blocked fallopian tubes, meaning one is more likely to need IVF after an ectopic pregnancy in order to become pregnant. Thus, ART procedures themselves function to generate their own customers.

All of my women interviewees and every research study I read indicated that women felt that if they did not do all they could, follow all medical and scientific advice, they alone were responsible for whatever problems developed. So the procedures of ART contribute not only to a further distrust of the body and self, but also self-blame, again showing the complicated dynamics of responsibility: one needs a medical intervention to get pregnant but it is the body alone that holds the blame when the procedure fails. Of course, this complicates the situation further and fuels the lack of confidence with decision making, cycling back again to further buttress the authority of the doctor and ARTs.

Self-surveillance is a key to biomedicalization and, as noted, surveillance of past behaviors in an attempt to manufacture certainty in the face of the unknown is a common response to feelings of helplessness in the present (Gentile, 2013). Throughout the interviews, as we discussed their experiences, the female interviewees would change course, suddenly associating to the past, scouring their behaviors for any potential transgressions in behavior that might have compromised their fertility. The men, even the two with male-factor infertility, did not do this during the interview. It is important to note that this scouring of the past usually co-occurred with another mantra of pained disbelief: "I've been so good. I've done everything right, how could I not get pregnant?" (Jordan). So the interviewees alternated between attempts to create certainty through the past, to fanning the flames of distress as they failed to find satisfactory reasons for their infertility. It is also important to point out that, although all the female interviewees engaged in this attempt at temporally based meaning making, in only one case was the female body the cause. In most of their cases infertility was unknown, and in two it was an identified male factor. Even in the cases where there was a certain male factor identified, the participants (Olive and Jordan) still engaged in this temporal sweeping, as if their bodies should be able to make up for their partner's diagnosed deficit.

The present, too, was a focus of surveillance, especially in terms of "stress." All of the interviewees alluded to the idea that maybe they didn't conceive because they were too "stressed." Each also had numerous stories of other people, usually well-meaning, saying something akin to "relax, have a glass of wine and enjoy it and you'll get pregnant," implying not only that the participant was too stressed, but that she didn't enjoy sex enough to get pregnant. And this advice, like the ARTs themselves, focused exclusively on women as the source of difficulty. Everyone described hearing the urban legend: "You know, a friend of mine tried for years and then when she adopted a child she got pregnant." The moral being either adoption is a proven form of fertility treatment, or your stress is the only thing standing between you and a pregnancy. While one cannot underestimate the power of stress on the system, stress became another way the body and mind were to blame. Olive, Sara, and Jordan each reflected on the conundrum of having to schedule the endless series of tests and doctor appointments sandwiched in with work and other responsibilities, all the while monitoring prenatal vitamins, food, drink, and exercise, while trying not to get stressed about the money being spent and time ticking by. Time, in the context of fertility medicine, only ever ticks toward aging out – "ovarian failure", as normal aging is called in this field. Stress is inevitable. Olive also made a point of noting that her friends never seemed to be concerned about the impact of stress on sperm quality or production, even though research indicates it is a significant factor (Daniels, 2006).

ARTs as a training in dissociation

> I could only dwell on the relentless planning, the chilling sensation of the vaginal probe, and the vulnerability of the stirrups. There was no longer a whole me engaged in this process. There was just the shell of me going through the motions.
>
> (Zoll, 2013, p. 105)

> It was strange. There were different doctors up your vagina each day and none were my own doctor who I knew. Measuring follicles, timing ovulation, dosing meds, to invade, take over, control and dominate your body. They tell you to let the doctor control your cycle. So different from the books I read before when I was supposed to check the cervix, fluid, tune in to learn all the potential signs of ovulation. I felt like they were training me not to trust my body since it hadn't managed to produce anything on its own.
>
> (Olive)

All but one interviewee, every memoir, and most studies describe clinics as cattle factories where nameless patients become statistics awaiting their times to be inseminated.[2] McLeod's (2002) participants described being "only another procedure to be done" (p. 3). Benjamin and Ha'elyon (2002) described treatments as "the violation of privacy, the violation of time, and most of all the violation of body" (p. 667) that can easily cause "feelings of distrust of self, not knowing what you deserve, how you should be treated and what you need" (McLeod, 2002, p. 120). Mari and Steve tried to have a child for 3 years before going to a clinic, where they went through six failed rounds of IUIs. Although skeptical of IVF, Mari did take two different follicle stimulators for three of the IUI procedures. She became pregnant with her son on their last official attempt that was made on their own, without any assistance, after her doctor finally suggested and conducted surgery to remove endometriosis. Although a preliminary test showed significant endometriosis, the surgery to clear it only occurred *after* six rounds of IUIs. After giving birth, Mari refused to go to the doctor for her own healthcare for 3 years, saying "I didn't want anyone touching me, poking holes in my body. I did not want to be confined in those stirrups and vulnerable again." Whether it was a way of reclaiming her bodily integrity or a form of traumatic response, or both, Mari was clear and emphatic about her choice. She took her son to his appointments but she did not want to be the patient.

ART procedures foster a form of depersonalization in that they actually create a model for how women should relate to their own bodies through dissociation, objectification, lack of trust, and ceding control to the doctor. Of course, given the objectification of women's bodies in the general culture, ARTs can easily slip in to create an additional level of patrol and self-surveillance. Patients have no privacy; heterosexual coupled patients are expected to engage in sexual intercourse on command outside of arousal (or to masturbate on command for men); women are subject to constant vaginal ultrasounds, inseminations, extractions and implantations, daily blood tests, and an endless series of invasive tests. The body begins to be experienced "as a collection of defective measurements" (Olive). As a patient, one can feel like a "vessel to which anyone could have access" (McLeod, 2002, p. 3). Anyone, indeed. Because fertility medicine is a 24-hour, 7-day-a-week business, many clinics retain multiple doctors such that patients may never see their chosen doctor, only an unpredictable parade of different experts. Olive, who specifically chose one of the only women doctors in the area, ended up seeing her only twice in 2 years of procedures. Not having been told she would most likely see different doctors, she recalled being half-naked, in stirrups anxiously awaiting her first IUI when a male doctor she had never met entered, asked her name, the name of the sperm donor/father to be inseminated, and the procedure (standard checks), without even looking at her. "I felt like I was floating above my body watching it all unfold. I wanted to stop it and say wait, who are you? Why are you here? Where is my doctor? But I fell mute." She described experiencing flashbacks shortly after this from an experience of sexual abuse as a child. She said:

> I felt like I was right back to being 10, after it [the sexual abuse] happened when everything that went wrong felt like validation that I deserved to be abused. It was like my infertility, all the pain of the procedures, it all just felt like justification, my abuser was right, there is something innately wrong

> with my body. It deserves to be punished. I started watching my food, my exercise, doing everything I did as an adolescent to gain control. I felt so weak, like I couldn't deal with a simple insemination without remembering being in that room, feeling held down and unable to respond. I hadn't thought of it for years and there it was. I got sick to my stomach because I knew there was a really good chance I'd have to do it all again next month, probably with yet a different doctor.

During the second year going to the clinic, she recalled running into her doctor in the clinic hall, smiling and saying "Hi," only to realize her doctor had no idea who she was. Although she spoke to her doctor on the phone, the doctor knew her physical body only as a series of measurements, test results, and procedures, a "body" of information. Here, ARTs can be a particularly malignant sleight of hand, where the advances of biotechnology claim a transcendence over the body, but this transcendence is only possible with a sacrificed female body. This sacrifice is enacted by all parties, including the female patient.

Confusion of tongues

Here, we have another perfect storm, this time one of traumatic repetition. I feel hard-pressed to imagine a more perfect potential repetition of sexual trauma in the medical field. ARTs involve ritualized cycles of physical invasions, most involving, for women, feet restrained in stirrups, with procedures occurring in one's vagina and uterus, while one is most likely experiencing some feelings of vulnerability and/or helplessness in the face of the uncontrollable. Since, within a culture shaped by reprofuturity, no baby means no future, no forward trajectory of purpose (Ahmed, 2010), feelings of annihilation can get re-ignited. Treatments take over and invade all daily activities. Physical privacy is invaded again, and part of this invasion is focused specifically on sexuality. If one is heterosexual, one may have to ritualize sexual activity, timing intercourse or ejaculation outside of any notion of arousal. And within this cycle, the blame can fall overtly or covertly squarely on the woman, who often blames herself for the infertility and feels powerless in what Zoll (2013) called the face of existential nothingness.

Despite the clear and obvious similarities of ART procedures to the dynamics of sexual abuse, I found only a small handful of studies that even mentioned sexual abuse (McLeod, 2002; Katz, 2008), and only one explored it (Bartlam & Woolfe, 1998). Letherby (2002) compares the procedures of infertility treatments to rape in that both involve a lack of social support, delayed feelings of crisis, and stereotyping and blaming the victim. Certainly, each of these factors was described by my interviewees, but there is also a "confusion of tongues" (Ferenczi, 1933/1980) apparent here, where the painful and degrading procedures are re-cast as the positive means to the end of having a baby. This act of colonizing one's experiences and meaning making can be devastating, especially when the success rates of the procedures are still so low, at 20% (Mundy, 2008).

In ART, failure from month to month is met by the doctor with hope for the next treatment, and this hope does fly in the face of reality, which most patients know. There is no space or recognition of the loss (Tsigdinos, 2010; Manterfield, 2011), especially when faced with the mantra, "it will all be worth it once you have your baby" (Manterfield, 2011, p. 192). Manterfield (2011) describes not just doctors but women themselves participating in this collapse, as her internet communities were filled with a discourse of forced hope which went contrary to her own feelings that her body had let her down and her need for space and time.

This immediate forced feeding of hope after defeat leaves no time for mourning, disappointment, or even reflection. The last day of a cycle only becomes the last day of a cycle with the first sight of blood that indicates failure and loss. But this sight of blood also indicates the first day of the next cycle, and the following days are, of course, numbered chronologically, enabling only the forward trajectory of hope for the next cycle, evacuated of the past. Failure, loss, and disappointment butt up directly to hope and a clinic and cultural mandate for positive thinking. There is no space for reflection or regulation. Decision making is immediate. Jordan recalled that, as she was lying in the stirrups after a vaginal ultrasound confirming a miscarriage, the nurse said, "we need to know now if you plan on trying again next month because we have to order the meds today." She said, "I wanted to stop for a second to think about what had happened but then the nurse was so emphatic that we not waste time so we had her order the meds." This story was echoed earlier in a quote from Hannah, who had a very similar experience with a somewhat "forced" choice. Here, taking space to reflect on and mourn is cast as "wasting reproductive time," and, given the overbooked clinic schedules, it might mean missing a month. So, instead, one is pulled into a rigidly defined future with no way of kicking free to take a breath without being seen as a difficult or noncompliant patient. As Olive said,

> if I didn't follow the doctor's orders he would make comments suggesting I wasn't ready to make the sacrifices necessary to get pregnant. So if I missed a blood test because I couldn't get out of a work meeting, I wasn't flexible enough, didn't want to be pregnant bad enough or something.

As a number of interviewees and memoirists noted, it was impossible to complain about being treated like cattle, enduring painful tests and interventions, and dealing with loss each month, because fertility treatment is optional; it is a "choice" and an economic and class privilege. The interviewees felt they had only themselves to blame for any discomfort. Lastly, as most interviewees found out, complaining about treatments can come back at you not just in terms of questioning one's commitment to having a baby, but questioning one's capacity as a potential parent – "if you can't handle some medical appointments, how will you deal with having a baby?" Similarly, the most common question I heard during the interviews was: "I know the treatments are demanding, but how could I not be willing to give up my lifestyle, autonomy, friends, job promotions, etc. if it will get me a baby?" There is no limit to what one should do to have a baby. Here, complaining was interpreted as self-indulgent, and placing limits on treatment interventions was interpreted not only as noncompliance, indicating a lack of commitment, but as not wanting a baby badly enough and not having what it takes to be a good parent. Here, the confusion of tongues is quite colonizing, as expressions and experiences of pain, frustration, loss, and retraumatization are all reframed based on the schedule of a clinic, the structure of ARTs, and a culture shaped by reprofuturity and biomedicalization.

The lack of space for reflection and push to move "forward" also limits the amount of questioning women can do about the hormones they take. This means the potential dangers of hormones or the impact of them in the moment are wiped away as the paranoia of a difficult patient (McLeod, 2002). Jordan said when she had researched a procedure her doctors acted like it was quaint, but to question the validity of it or the impact of the hormones, even after being asked to sign a waiver by the clinic that she understood the risks involved in taking them, was to incur hostility and sighs of frustration from the doctors. Olive said:

> whenever I asked too many questions my doctor would respond curtly that if I had that many questions I should speak to his nurse. I get it, he's busy, he has a waiting room filled with patients after me. But it made me feel like there are legitimate and illegitimate questions, those for him and those for his nurse.

And all this pressure seemed to be privatized and individually held.

My interviewees, the research, and the memoirists all described a situation of not being able to discuss what was really going on with most of the people in their lives. And, while most of my interviewees and the memoirists described getting a great deal of support from online communities, they all noted that this support was not in person at the clinics. Two interviewees participated in clinic-sponsored support groups, but otherwise they all made note of the deafening silence and tension in waiting rooms. Jordan noted: "it was surreal. We were all there for the same reason, perhaps even the same procedure, and yet we rarely even made eye contact, let alone talked." So the clinic itself can feel akin to a family that collectively holds a secret, and, as in such families, the secret's function is in part to destroy any sense of our relational and collective capacities to emerge through action. Zoll (2013) described her clinic staff actively advising patients to keep their treatments a secret because so few people understand. Additionally, as she and my interviewees noted, it can be difficult to talk about the pain and unbearable experiences of repetitive loss that treatments entail.

This idea of a secret is important. I have already alluded to how difficult it was to find participants for this study. Although, in social gatherings, whenever I discuss my research I always hear at least one, if not multiple, first-hand stories about ARTs, this prolific network of anecdotes did not translate to the research setting. The silence in this context is striking and reminiscent of the deafening, electric silence of crowded clinic waiting rooms. So I began asking the interviewees if they had any ideas about why this might be so. Each one initially responded saying they could not understand why because it was so important to talk about and publicize this experience. But each of them also followed this up with emphatic statements that people should not feel shame about engaging in ARTs and that they did not feel ashamed. When asked what this shame might be about for others, the interviewees all described the potential shame of having to reach out for help to do something others can do so easily. The shame in this context may also express the heterosexual privilege of the interviewees (and myself) and the corresponding assumptions of entitlement to a cost-free, easy, and pleasurable reproductive experience. The participants implied that people might feel ashamed that a personal defect was discovered, that the women might not feel whole or normal. One of the two women who had had significant progressive illnesses diagnosed through the process of testing suggested that perhaps the process of ARTs had resulted in other problems that rendered infertility and babies less important in shaping their lives.

Martha, the only participant who did conceive through IVF, reflected on how much harder ARTs were than she had anticipated, and suggested that people who become pregnant do not want to remember the process for fear of re-experiencing the stress and pain or tainting their baby as not being natural, not a "real" Oedipal object, somehow. Women who have babies through ARTs may be positioned in a different liminal space, somewhere between "normal" and "deficient." These maternal subjectivities are shaped by the capacities to gestate and produce a baby but not to conceive one outside of the biotech system. This may render the maternal too tenuous for revisiting experiences of ARTs, especially if one is wondering about how they will have future children. (See Chapter 9, by Simon, for a case discussion of egg donation and the resulting feelings of vulnerable maternity.) Again, however, these aspects may signify the cracks of heterosexual, partnered privilege. For single, transgender, and same-sex couples, ARTs may be seen and experienced more positively as enabling reproduction and not necessarily as a sign of biological failure. However, Mamo's research on "queering reproduction" (2007) describes some similar responses by lesbian patients engaging with ARTs.

The eight interviewees who had not gotten pregnant through ARTs considered how difficult it was to talk to me about it, how it brought the experiences back, and conjectured that those who did not get pregnant do not want to talk about and re-experience the loss and pain. Perhaps they did not want to go back to reliving the experience of core-shaking disappointment and mourning of the monthly reminders of failure that do not end when one quits trying to conceive (M. Hadley, personal communication, July 10, 2013). Indeed, for Olive, the idea that her periods continued even though she stopped trying to become pregnant felt like a monthly form of torture, continuously pulling the scab off the wound. Of the male interviewees only one contributed to this aspect of the discussion, saying that since all the treatments focused on his partner, he didn't feel he had much to offer a researcher. Lastly, all but one participant kept their treatment a secret from all but close friends and family, which meant that to participate in the study was to talk to a stranger about an experience they had not shared with many people in their lives. ARTs may take over one's life, but they do so in a privatized way. So participating in a study would break that boundary, bringing a biomedicalized "failure" into the social space. So as ARTs proliferate throughout the culture, the shame patients feel for their infertility, for having to seek assistance for something others do so easily (and go to such lengths to avoid doing), for feeling defective in some way, is silencing.

Finding an end in a durationless present

> We had spent $50,000 with nothing but heartache to show for it. But perhaps the greatest consideration was the realization that losing more IVF offspring was just too much to bear – especially in a "support-deprived vacuum" where "the rest of the world (minus our immediate family and a handful of close friends) didn't know about or recognize our losses.
>
> (Tsigdinos, 2010, p. 82)

It is exceedingly difficult to make decisions to stop ARTs because new technological options "produce a forced choice" (Kalbian, 2005, p. 108). Thus, refusing any form of ART is construed as refusing medical treatment, and refusing to have a child (Ibid.). ART brings healthy people into medical process and erases the failure rates, leaving the majority who do not have babies holding the bag, attempting to make sense of what went wrong. ART fuels the attitude that you must try everything before you can allow yourself to remain childless, especially, as noted, for women who are "vulnerable to the suggestion that [they are] unwilling and perhaps too selfish, to make the necessary sacrifices to be a mother" (Throsby, 2004, p. 40). Stopping comes with judgment. When I told the doctor I was done trying, he replied, "I can see you just aren't ready yet." Women's choices "including stopping before the goal of the treatment has been achieved . . . have to be carefully managed, negotiated and accounted for to others in order to avoid exclusion" (Throsby, 2004, p. 40).

How do you stop treatments when the decision requires acknowledgment of a possibly childfree future, a form of futurity that is denigrated in the culture (especially for women) and seriously under-theorized and still over-pathologized within psychoanalysis? Throsby (2004) quotes a study participant, "and I think to myself, right, this is it. You know, this is it forever, until we get taken into a home and we die. That's what life is. It'll just be work and more work" (p. 184). In addition to this existential struggle, Daniluk and Tench (2007) found people had difficulty adjusting after so many years of invasive medical procedures that left them feeling depleted. It involves a significant life transition from the state of "not being pregnant yet" and living in the potential future, to not trying any more and acknowledging there will be no pregnancy. One is forced into a very dense present where duration and the movement into the future can be and feel stalled. Here, the past looms large as one is left in an endless state of not knowing *why*, and thus, never knowing *if* maybe the next cycle would have been the one.

Tsigdinos (2010), Manterfield (2011), Olive and Sara described initially feeling useless as women. Manterfield reflected on her body as a failure, seeing her breasts as "useless appendages" (p. 159). Olive described the monthly appearance of her period as "a cosmic joke" reminding her that her body was a "parody of a woman's."

As described, the conditions of ART treatments often function to collapse the reflective space necessary to make healthy decisions about what is enough. This can limit one's ability to act toward self-preservation, contributing to engaging in more self-destructive behaviors, and it might result in women participating in treatments they might not otherwise agree to or want. As noted, 40–50% of people who seek treatment do not end up having a baby. Yet few studies have looked at the impact of infertility stresses for the majority of patients, let alone how they decide to stop treatments. One of the few studies found that people were able to accept the decision to stop only after they had demonstrated to themselves and others that they had done all they could (Throsby, 2004). Benjamin and Ha'elyon (2002) found as long as women could make sense of their pain, loss, and the procedures as being for a baby, they could continue the process. Mari said she knew they had to stop when "it became more painful to continue." When patients could no longer make meaning of their experiences through this lens, i.e., when they could no longer manufacture faith in a particular future, they could no longer tolerate the procedures. Women often stopped when the potential baby of the future could no longer be conjured up in the present to act as a third, making meaning of pain, loss, fear, anxiety.

Additionally, for interviewees whose IVF procedures had resulted in multiple fertilized eggs, continuing treatments became a way of dealing with the presence of their embryos. Fertilized eggs became a concretized representation of their future, luring them into more cycles. This decision was made even more complicated for the interviewees who were treated at clinics that took pictures of the embryos before they were frozen, so the couples could "hold" them while they were frozen. These pictures created a connection to the embryos, making it more difficult to process loss when they did not implant. One couple named the embryos, which made it even more difficult not to continue IVF attempts, if only because, as Hannah said, "what were we going to do with these 'babies'"? The embryos were babies to her, which made it impossible to imagine disposing of them in order to create a time that was "post"-treatment. The only solution seemed to be to keep trying, even when she didn't really want to.[3]

Franklin (1997) asks "[h]ow can you reach the end of the story when neither the causality nor seriality of events can be ordered as a progressive sequence" (p. 13), when both causality and seriality are necessary in order to create meaning in our culture? Indeed, the procedures of ARTs tax our capacity for faith in going on being in a number of ways. First, it is destabilizing that failure must be met with an immediate hope-filled plan for the next cycle. Second, there is an assumption that, with each failed cycle, doctors know/learn more about what is causing the difficulty and are able to identify problems and remedy them. It is assumed they are refining each cycle with more finely tuned complexity. But many people will never know why they could not get pregnant. This sense of progression toward a knowable better future when the problems will be fixed keeps the patient on the hook. It is unthinkable to consider that doctors might just be throwing darts blindly at a board; progression might not be occurring, and, after all this struggle and expense, you might still be in that large but invisible, childless post-treatment population with an unknowable problem.

Most importantly, ARTs proceed by collapsing space, making room for only one potential future. This one future is produced through its own series of linear connections structured through the discourse of biomedicalization, where an objectified female body takes center stage. Sustaining the potential for only one particular future may make the treatments and one's present sense of sadness bearable, but it also makes it hard to find resolution and decide to stop treatments. While each month's period shatters one's attachment to this singular future, each month's treatment immediately reinforces it, meaning one is stuck in a perpetual, cyclical present shaped around preparing for the only future that is given space to exist. And within a culture shaped by reprofuturity, for some this is the only future available for consideration. Additionally, as psychoanalysts know, the tenuous tantalizing quality of this one future, its ritualized re-creation and destruction, can itself become an irresistible cycle of abuse. One is unable to move or embrace the potential for multiple potential futures, because the only future allowable is that which cannot materialize. Because, as Franklin (1997) noted, treatments create the desire for a baby; they then function to erase attachments to different pasts and presents. ARTs, then, do not just collapse the space of potential futures; they erase our attachments to multiple, diverse pasts and presents: the same temporalities that help us sustain connections to multiple potential futures, futures where we continue to go on being without treatment, without children, without linear narratives. Here is the cycle of trauma where any sense of meaning making is collapsed to a linear cause and effect: one past (you've always wanted a baby), one present (you are filled with the desire to have a baby and will do anything), one future (I have a baby).

> "I look at toddlers and say, wow, that will never be us. This is it, there is no developmental event to plan for" (Lou).

Ending ARTs involves a significant life transition from the state of "not being pregnant yet," living in the liminal potential future, to being suddenly dropped into a very thick, motionless present. The teasing liminal future of pregnancy created by the constant hovering "what if" needs to be joined to or/and displaced by other potential futures (and their multiple nonlinear pasts and presents) for creative, meaningful decision making.

Adoption . . . now?

> There had been no ceremony to mark the passing of my motherhood . . . no cards of sympathy . . . Concerned friends and neighbors hadn't rallied around, bringing casseroles and offering assistance, because my loss was not visible. There were no framed photos on the mantelpiece to show what had been taken away from me, and no ritual outlet for my grief.
>
> (Manterfield, 2011, p. 210)

Although adoption is usually not discussed in ART clinics (in the United States), it is a common suggestion socially for those who are failing to conceive through ARTs. Indeed, as a number of interviewees and memoirists described, well-meaning people usually bring it up when ART patients are in the depths of despair and unclear, ambiguous mourning – "Why don't you just adopt?" As Cain (2001) so aptly notes, after spending years on an "emotional rollercoaster", it is tough to embark on yet another emotional risk. As one of her participants expressed: "I was tired of people making decisions that affected my life. During infertility treatments, we had to deal with insurance companies and doctors. I wanted to be able to decide what happened to me without having to beg others for help" (Cain, 2001, p. 77). Tsigdinos (2010) writes:

> even if babies were freely and readily available (which they were *not*) I wasn't going to risk entering into the equivalent of a rebound relationship. I was going nowhere until I was willing and able to come face to face with my failure, loss and emptiness.
>
> (p. 89)

Manterfield (2011) wrote that her lack of emotional stamina post-ART treatments kept her from setting out on another "treacherous" (p. 195) and uncertain journey. Additionally adoption is not a panacea for infertility itself and the mourning and loss that may need to occur in relation to the realization that one is unable to reproduce.

Adoption is anything but certain, and it is yet another system where women/couples are subject not only to forms of surveillance, but scrutiny. Instead of one's body being pried open for medical procedures, adoption typically takes a microscope to every aspect of one's life. Olive, who, with Lou, went to some adoption agencies, reflected on the different quality of invasion necessary for adoption, including examinations of your physical and mental health records, the state and quality of your home, your perceived parenting skills, friends, family, job/career, body mass index, sexual orientation, marriage (or lack thereof), age and how they are all weighed, evaluated by someone else after you pay an extraordinary amount of money. She said:

> infertility treatments can feel less invasive and more in my control in comparison. At least in the end I knew my body had made the decision not to have a baby, not someone else who had judged me as unfit to parent.

Zoll (2013) described ARTs having a certain agency within their protocols. As mentioned earlier in reference to biomedicalization, the practices of ART can produce a sense of agency as one feels one is *doing* something. In adoption, Zoll notes that she felt she had to cede control and wait. And while consumers of ARTs are the consumers, which under capitalism translates as some amount of control, shifting to adoption means shifting to becoming the one being consumed, the object being judged by a pregnant woman or agency.

It is important to note that one interviewee, Sara, vehemently disagreed with people who complained about the rigors of the adoption process. She and her husband began the adoption process as they began their IVF cycles. They successfully adopted a newborn baby within a year. It is important that, for this couple, adoption was an option pursued with as much rigor as ART; however, their story is not the norm in adoption circles.

Being healthy, not just pregnant

"Living childfree and wanting children are not mutually exclusive" (Throsby, 2004, p. 180) and they do not necessarily or automatically signify unhappiness or desperation. Instead, the presence of these conflicting desires highlights the complex work people who stop treatments have to engage in when making meaning outside the dominant pronatal cultural narratives. Success in terms of fertility treatments needs to be expanded and redefined from unquestioningly having a baby to creating the capacities to make meaning in one's life within, beside, with different forms of, or just without parenthood.

Hardt and Negri (2000) contend that resistance to the biopolitical emerges in the forms of struggles to create new public spaces and new forms of community and relating. Lemke (2011) suggests that, in order to identify and engage with resistances, we need to explore how "subjects adopt and modify scientific interpretations of life for their own conduct . . . and how can this process be viewed as an active appropriation and *not* as passive acceptance?" (p. 120). Women who decide to end fertility treatments provide an interesting vision of such resistance, as they have engaged with very strict forms of biomedicalized regulations through ARTs and then extricated themselves, and come into being through different cultural discourses. "Feminism involves political consciousness of what women are asked to give up for happiness" (Ahmed, 2010, p. 585). ARTs ask women to give up their bodies, time, lives. And, as with any insidious patriarchal request for submission, the "promise" is said to be worth almost any amount of discomfort or even suffering.

Throsby (2004) uses Probyn's (1996) term of "outside belonging" to describe couples who decided to stop fertility treatments before conceiving. This outside belonging is described as "a site of 'ongoing in-betweenness' which offers 'immense political possibilities' in its capacity to both capture and propel the movement not only between categories, but also of the categories themselves" (Probyn, quoted in Throsby, 2004, p. 79). Although the "other" is "always buried in the dominant" (Halberstam, 2011, p. 73), a refusal to reproduce or to pull out all the stops to get a child may be seen as a "perversion of desire" (Halberstam, 2011, p. 111), where the value and commodity of the female body as the reproductive body of the culture are denied. As a "symbolic site of failure, loss, rupture, disorder" (Ibid.), perhaps the infertile female body can become available for queer signification where it can destabilize, if only a little, the patriarchal, heteronormative reproductive mandate. Thus, infertility can present opportunity; as Halberstam writes, "the maps of desires that render the subject incoherent, disorganized and passive provide a better escape route than those that lead inexorably to fulfillment, recognition, and achievement" (p. 130).

However, as noted earlier, "critical interpretation of actions, desires, and values both requires and results in connecting the present to the past and the future, and putting those actions and desires into a context that can make sense of them" (Oliver, 2004, p. 86). In other words, without the space and time within which to make meaning, those outside the traditional maps of reprofuturity can be more vulnerable to incorporating external forms of meaning making (Gentile, 2007), even if their very presence helps to down the patriarchy "one brick at a time" (Halberstam, 2011, p. 133). "[I]t is crucial for women to be able to create new meanings for their lives outside of patriarchal conventions that continue to link women, sex, and death. Otherwise, women's freedom is reduced to the freedom to kill themselves" (Oliver, 2007, p. 40), either literally or symbolically. De-centering fertility is key, then, to this endeavor.

Not being able to conceive on command, whether through heterosexual intercourse or some form of ART, makes the decision to have a child more conscious and ongoing. You have to go through endless medical hoops that require a great deal of motivation and patience. Many people can engage in the process rabidly and myopically without question while, for others, the expectable ambivalences can be paralyzing or at least a constant additional struggle. There is a great deal of positive growth that can come from not being able to reproduce according to plan. You are forced to look at how you make meaning of your life in a way others may not. You cannot escape the existential fright of mortality and, thus, the limits weighing on us all.

While two of the interviewees described intermittent states of frustration and disgust with their bodies and lives, Manterfield (2011), in her memoir, and three interviewees described gaining appreciation for the knowledge their body held by not getting pregnant. As Olive put it:

> My body knew better. I'd rather have miscarried repeatedly early on than to have faced what could have been genetic problems and a horrible decision down the road. My body knew; it just took me a while to listen. I think seeking out acupuncture and other alternative therapies helped my physical self make the choices it needed to become healthy, not just pregnant.

Here, the body appears separate but not dissociated. The body is a subject with desires and knowledge and, when "listened to" and supported, can lead to educated, reflective decision making based on multiple, heterogeneous potential temporalities. But this isn't easy. Dinshaw (2012) describes asynchronous temporal experience as "individually traumatic and socially disruptive," an "excruciating temporal exercise" of a ceaseless "push and pull" of times (p. 63). That in turn involves engaging in a process of continual re-creation of self-experience. If, as Freeman (2010) contends, part of heteronormativity, and I would add reprofuturity, is the process of not just identifying with a same-sexed parent, but becoming him or her, then failing to become a parent is a failure in this temporal system. Freeman posits that this temporal system functions to erase time, rendering the past now the present, as the son or daughter now becomes the father or mother. I would say it functions not to erase time but to collapse space. So not becoming a parent means this temporal system is, instead, robust, filled with potential times – pasts, presents, and futures – within which one may or may not have the capacities to make meaning. After all, experiencing one's body as a temporary, constantly unfolding collection of momentary, fleeting instances of equilibrium "suspended in a field of virtual partialities" (Parisi, 2004, p. 42) can be freeing, exhilarating, and intolerably stressful.

Throsby (2004), Manterfield (2011), and three of my interviewees described experiencing a new motivation to make life changes, leaving a boring, overly demanding or unfulfilling job, switching careers, and spending more time in activities that were enlivening. Leanne rekindled her love of body surfing and hiking, spending more time enjoying the outdoors with her husband. Zoll (2013) describes the healing power of yoga and walking in the woods. Perhaps it is not a surprise that physical activities were commonly described. As Leanne put it, "In body surfing and hiking I can feel my body do something I want for a change, but I also get to experience the joy of moving. It was a perfect compromise where I could feel in my body for the first time in a long time." Olive described physical activity giving her the "feeling of my body as alive even if it couldn't create life." But each memoir and interviewee emphasized that resolution was an ongoing process. Jordan said: "Whenever a friend or colleague gets pregnant, it's like I start all over again, the questioning, the wonder about what if, what could I have done differently, did I make a mistake?" All described occasionally or often making up excuses to avoid baby showers and other related celebrations. Olive said: "I seem OK but whenever I hear about someone getting pregnant I obsessively calculate their age. Am I too old? How come they had a baby at age, whatever, and I was even younger and couldn't?"

"To become conscious of possibility can involve mourning for its loss . . . you have to be willing to venture into secret places of pain" (Ahmed, 2010, pp. 585–590), and create different temporalities where happiness and "the narrowness of its horizons" (Ahmed, 2010, p. 585) is not automatically linked to what is considered to be good. In relation to ARTs, this includes creating futures, presents and pasts that shift and de-center the "proleptic hauntings" (T. Catapano, personal communication, August 1, 2014) fueled by the ideologies of reprofuturity. The possibilities of failure in the case of ART can hold the potential for great pain and loss and retraumatization, but this failure also holds the potentials for transformative and transgressive meaning making, where we can "disrupt and alter the conditions of [our] own emergence", opening to "something other than what we might have hoped for" (Puar, 2009, p. 169). One can be positioned to create the space to deconstruct biomedicalization, reprofuturity and its strangling linear temporality, shifting ideas of health and happiness, mourning, and loss. Here, we need to create space to "embrace the unfolding future" (Bergson, 1913/2001), a futurity that is not over-determined, neither forward nor backward, but unfolds like the notes of a tune, with each note embodying infinite attachments to other tones and spaces between and their potentials (Muñoz, 2009).

As Cvetkovich (2012) asked in relation to depression, can there be a story, a narrative of ARTs and infertility that can provide hope without also doling out the usual perfunctory happy ending and resolution? I'm still sad. I can still feel ripped open by the sight of a baby's wispy hair, the sound of the tortured cry of a scared or hungry or dissatisfied infant, or when witnessing the impenetrable gaze between a caregiver and a baby. Yet I am also fulfilled in my life and relatively content. I enjoy playing music, doing open-water swims, and having the freedom to travel, things I know I could not do if I had had a child. Thus, ending treatments requires multiple continuous resolutions but few clear happy endings.

In the words of Lou:

> Through time I've found a balance so now when I see parents and their children I still might think, "wow, I'll never hold my own baby" and it can still strike me down. But now those are more balanced with times I'm out late and I think, I wouldn't be doing this if I had a child, and now I even have times that aren't referenced to children at all.

Although this research represents the experiences of a self-selected and limited group of people, it demonstrates the importance of holding the cultural context when working with patients undergoing ARTs, including monitoring not just our own stereotypes based on reprofuturity and biomedicalization, but recognizing the ways in which we emerge within and through them. Reflecting on the ways we are all produced through these discourses is also imperative to being able to recognize the significant potential for retraumatization around sexual and physical abuse and the confusion of tongues that can emerge around the quest to have a baby through ARTs as they are currently structured.

As ARTs grow and proliferate within a culture shaped by reprofuturity and biomedicalization, they produce bodies more and more friendly to their interventions, interventions that do not include the space and time required for reflection, generating meaning, and making decisions. Halberstam (2011) claims we need a form of optimism that does not rely on positive thinking or is an "explanatory engine for social order," where one is urged to always see the bright side. Instead, we need "a little ray of sunshine that produces shade and light in equal measure and knows that the meaning of one always depends upon the meaning of the other" (p. 5). We need, in other words, not just the capacity to tolerate ambivalence, frustration, and unhappiness, but the appreciation of them as integral components of meaningful experience. Meaning itself emerges from forms of ambivalence, conflict, and collisions. Through these capacities to cultivate and revel in the shade, we can work to maintain a constant-evolving critique about the "assistance" of reproductive technologies, their linear temporality that erases pasts, presents, and futures, failure or alternatives, their costs and benefits, in order to begin to illuminate the essence of the "bargain."

Notes

1 Atwood, M. (1986). *The Handmaid's Tale.* New York: Random House.
2 An apt metaphor, since ARTs emerged out of experiments and protocols used with farm animals, in particular breeding cattle – meat – using superovulation, IUI, and forms of IVF (Corea, 1985).
3 Frozen embryos have also become issues in divorce where partners vie for custody and the possibility to have them implanted in the future. Recently, as part of a divorce case, a New Jersey woman asked her ex-husband to pay to have her eggs frozen, since she felt they put off family for his career (see Richards, 2013). ARTs create new complicated networks of affective entanglements to sort through.

Part II

Filling in the gaps of ARTs

Chapter 5

The bodies and bits of (re)production

Dilemmas of egg "donation" under neoliberalism

Michelle Leve

Throughout the past three decades the use of assisted reproductive technologies (ARTs) has been increasing in the global North and South. One technology that has proliferated in use since the mid-1990s is egg donation. Egg "donation" involves the retrieval of eggs from one woman (the provider); these eggs are fertilized and implanted into another woman (the recipient) (Shanley, 2002). The United States in particular has seen growing use of third-party eggs for pregnancy. From 1995 to 2009 the number of donor egg cycles in the United States increased from 4,783 to 17,697 (Klein & Sauer, 2010; CDC, 2011). Moreover, only a small fraction of these eggs in the United States were actually "donated" or provided without payment by family or friends (Shanley, 1998; Spar, 2007). The majority of "donor" eggs were sold by women between the ages of 21–34, for an average of $5,000 per harvest (Spar, 2007) and sometimes upwards of $50,000 (Spar, 2007). It has been suggested that the use of third-party gametes (eggs and sperm) is tempered with the euphemism "donor" to mask psychological discomfort associated with the role of compensation (Shanley, 2002) in these particular transactions. Thus, some scholars (Shanley, 1998; Beeson & Lippman, 2006) have argued for a shift in language from egg "donation" to egg "transfer," and for the use of "provider" instead of "donor." Although this language in many ways still obscures the financial exchange, following those scholars noted above, I will employ the language of "egg provider" and "transfer," aiming to (at least partially) move away from this dominant language.

Throughout the past three decades, feminist scholars have debated the gendered, sociocultural, political, and economic consequences of ARTs. Prior to the birth of the world's first test tube baby in 1978, Shulamith Firestone (1970) suggested that ARTs could liberate women from biologically rooted gender inequalities and motherhood. Other feminist scholars contend that ARTs contribute to the increasing medicalization of women's bodies (Thompson, 2005; Mamo, 2010), exacerbate the "motherhood mandate" (Russo, 1976; Thompson, 2005), commodify the maternal body (Mahjouri, 2004), and further twine women to the biogenetic aspects of motherhood under patriarchy (Mamo, 2010). Of particular concern to feminist scholars is third-party reproduction, which in the United States primarily involves the buying and selling of eggs and/or sperm. Although ARTs, like egg donation, represent a promising option for women (and men) wishing to have a biological child, these technologies also raise a variety of new dilemmas concerning motherhood and consumer citizenship within a healthcare context shaped by neoliberalism.

Neoliberalism and bodies

The United States represents an ever-expanding market for ARTs, with revenues of $4 billion a year (Ryan, 2009). With no national regulation, it has been called the "wild, wild west of reproductive care" (Spar, 2007). Unlike Canada, Australia, China, Denmark, and some Shi'a branches of Islam, which equate gametes (eggs and sperm) with organs and thus prohibit their sale, the United States does not currently regulate this aspect of third-party reproduction (Mamo, 2010). This market-based approach to medicine, in combination with a lack of regulation, resonates with the neoliberal ethos. Neoliberal policies (or lack thereof) function to shift responsibility from the state to the individual. For instance, as will be described in this chapter, the industrial North has seen delayed and declining childbearing among (mostly) white middle-class women in response to increased healthcare costs, deregulated wages, and the need for two-income families (Waldby & Cooper, 2008). In a culture shaped by neoliberalism, the intervention for this decline focuses on assisting women to become pregnant, not shifting policies to make it easier to sustain a family. ARTs, like egg transfer, are then marketed as an individualized solution to a social problem. However, this "solution" is primarily trafficked through the bodies of other women, and has led to what some call the "commodified maternal body" (Mahjouri, 2004, p. 14), encouraging new forms of exploitation of women's reproductive bodies and parts (Gupta & Richters, 2008). Tyler (2011) refers to our current cultural climate as a "disciplinary neoliberalism" whereby "our most intimate bodily experiences have become thoroughly capitalized" (p. 22). Conversely, others (Weinbaum, 1994; Waldby & Cooper, 2008) argue that we need to understand third-party reproduction as a form of *labor* within biocapitalism, so as not to reproduce notions of women's self-sacrifice or deny women rights over their bodily material. Moreover, Nahman (2008) suggests that egg sellers are "savvy participants" of the neoliberal economy where citizenship is equated with buying power. Thus, it could be argued that egg providers are capitalizing on their potential maternal bodies to participate in the market-place, a key value of neoliberalism. In addition to concerns about commodification of the maternal body, a dilemma emerges concerning whether ARTs disrupt or reinforce biogenetic notions of motherhood. Strathern (1992) questions how ARTs might blur the binary of nature/culture, by drawing a distinction between social and biological parenting, through the assistance of third parties. Gupta and Richters (2008) argue that women's maternal bodies are broken down into their component parts and utilized for profit making within patriarchal capitalism, fostering a view of women as childbearing machines. Further, concerns have been raised that, within the context of patriarchal neoliberalism, it is women, and their bodies, who are called upon to bear the burden of reproductive technologies and the ensuing surveillance: what Roberts (2009) refers to as "reproductive responsibility." In this chapter I will map out these dilemmas, as I argue that what is missing from the aforementioned literature is the materiality of egg providers' experiences within a healthcare context shaped by neoliberalism.

Background on egg transfer

Any discussion of egg donation requires an introduction to the process of egg production, harvesting, and transfer. Some recipient women use the eggs of a "known donor," typically a sister, relative, or friend (Borrero, 2001); however, it is also possible at some clinics for a recipient to meet a paid provider. Alternatively, eggs are provided by an anonymous woman who, in the United States, typically provides her eggs for payment (Shanley, 1998). Anonymous transfer occurs in infertility clinics or egg donor programs that recruit women through advertisements in college newspapers, the internet, or word of mouth (Borrero, 2001; Shanley, 2002). It is also possible for anonymous donation to occur in the context of egg "sharing," in which women undergoing infertility treatments agree to provide half of their ova to another woman in exchange for reduced fees on their treatment. Additionally, some programs offer identity release, which gives the option of releasing the provider's contact information when donor-conceived children turn 18 (if they are told).

Regardless of whether egg transfer involves an anonymous, identity release, or known provider, there is a lengthy screening process. Initially, a potential provider fills out an application, upwards of 30 pages long (Haylett, 2012). The application includes questions concerning the potential donor's physical appearance (i.e., nose shape, skin color, body type/weight), educational background (sometimes including GPA and SAT scores), self-description of temperament, reproductive history (i.e., date of first period, past pregnancies, and/or abortions), talents or hobbies, medical illnesses, alcohol/drug consumption, family health/illness history including mental health, number of sexual partners, and sexual orientation. Although women who identify as lesbian or bisexual are allowed to donate, there is some research (Pollock, 2003) that suggests that queer women have both worried about, and experienced, exclusion from egg transfer when they share their sexual orientation.

Following this initial application, the provider must submit to extensive medical and psychological screening. This includes a comprehensive physical examination, psychological testing, blood tests, sexually transmitted infection tests, and genetic screening. This screening includes testing for the cystic fibrosis gene and may include other chromosomal analyses, as well as testing for fragile X syndrome (ASRM, 2012). In commercial egg transfer, the medical and psychological histories are typically given to the potential recipients in addition to the information from the initial application. Clinics often try to "match" providers with recipients, based on each party's respective profile and the recipients' desire. This matching typically centers around physical characteristics, as it has been noted that, under the dominant genetic imperative, "looking like a family" is important to both egg and sperm recipients (Jones, 2005; Martin, 2010). Further, some clinics create provider profiles for all eligible providers at a given clinic and then allow the recipients to view all the profiles in order to select a provider themselves, while others (typically research hospitals) give the recipients a single profile and they then can decide to select that provider or wait for another.

Once a recipient selects a provider, the "cycle" can begin. For the provider (the recipient has a much more complicated process of intervention, as described in Chapter 7), this process takes around 3 weeks. It begins with daily self-injections of hormones to suppress the menstrual cycle. These are followed by injections to hyperstimulate the production of the ovaries (Borrero, 2001) in order to harvest a high number of eggs. The side effects of these injections range from mild to severe and can include hot flashes, breast tenderness, mood swings, cramping, nausea, dizziness, nasal congestion, fatigue, bloating, and headaches (Curtis, 2010). There is also a small risk of ovarian hyperstimulation syndrome, which can result in severe pain, permanent injury that can negatively impact the provider's fertility, and, in rare cases, death (Borrero, 2001). It is important to note that the long-term risks of egg transfer for both provider and recipient have not been sufficiently researched (Curtis, 2010).

Egg retrieval occurs 7–12 days after beginning the initial injections. The provider is sedated with a general anesthetic. The doctor retrieves the eggs by a transvaginal oocyte recovery (Borrero, 2001), inserting a needle through the vaginal wall and amassing eggs by sucking them into a needle. Because the provider has received a general anesthetic, she must fast the evening before, cancel her usual activities for the day of the procedure and have a friend or family member escort her home. The provider cannot exercise for 2 weeks prior to and following the retrieval, to avoid the potential for ovarian torsion, which is the twisting of the stimulated ovary that can then cut off blood supply to this ovary. If this occurs, surgery is required to untwist the ovary. Following the retrieval, providers have one medical exam and then typically do not hear from the clinic again, unless they are asked to provide eggs another time.

Reproductive technologies and neoliberalism

Neoliberalism has a direct bearing on the ways in which reproductive technologies are situated within the US cultural climate. Neoliberalism is a political-economic ideology and practice that promotes individualism, consumerism, deregulation, and transferring state power and responsibility to the individual (McGregor, 2001; Galvin, 2002; Newman et al., 2007). Neoliberal citizens are expected to "be empowered to take control of their lives" (Galvin, 2002, p. 117) and their bodies, with such empowerment usually expressed through consumptive practices. Proponents of neoliberalism conflate citizenship with buying power in the market-place (McGregor, 2001). The dominance of this privatizing ideology has had well-documented effects on healthcare experiences (McGregor, 2001, Galvin, 2002; Newman et al., 2007), in addition to increasing commercial investment in the body (Waldby & Cooper, 2008; Pitts-Taylor, 2010), especially women's bodies.

In relation to reproduction, Mamo (2010) argues that fertility biomedicine is constitutive of the neoliberal ethos as it "becomes another do-it-yourself project enabling us to transform our selves, identities, and social lives through consumption" (p. 176). Further, within biocapitalism, reproduction has been broken down into its component parts (eggs and sperm, fertilization, implantation, etc.), privatized, and deregulated (Waldby & Cooper, 2008). It has been argued that, within the global economy of neoliberalism, the female reproductive body is fragmented and commodified, leading to the exploitation of women as "mother machines" (Corea, 1985, cited in Gupta & Richters, 2008). However, Waldby and Cooper (2008) argue that feminists should locate egg donation, or "vending" as they call it, as a form of *labor*. They suggest that this understanding increases women's rights over their tissue and bodily integrity by highlighting how reproductive and "intellectual" pursuits within biocapitalism are both forms of labor (Waldby & Cooper, 2008). However, Waldby and Cooper (2008) argue that there is a hierarchical positioning to these forms of labor, in which academic/scholarly labor is more acknowledged and protected within biocapitalism. Alternatively, situating these practices under the rubric of gifting and generosity institutionalizes the bodily sacrifice of women, whereby:

> gifting under contemporary conditions of highly capitalised life sciences is often simply a way to expropriate donors and deny them rights over bodily material. On the other hand, when we consider tissue vending as a form of labour, even of the extremely coercive kind, we avoid these romanticising and victimising tendencies and open up the possibility that present labour relations may be subject to contestation.
>
> (Waldby & Cooper, 2008, p. 67)

As such, Nahman (2008) argues that we should turn our attention to the global forces of neoliberalism, which places women (and men) in conditions where they feel the need to commodify their reproductive bodies. Moreover, it has been suggested that one of the unintended consequences of the "neoliberalisation of life" (Waldby & Cooper, 2008) in the industrial North is delayed and declining childbearing among (mostly) middle-class women (Waldby & Cooper, 2008). This delay is complicated. There has been a growing need and desire for two-income families, in part in relation to increased access to the public sphere by women, but also related to deregulated wages, and increasing costs of healthcare and child care, and lack of adequate parental leave. In this context, there have been increasing economic, affective, and temporal costs to childbearing (Waldby & Cooper, 2008). ARTs, including egg transfer, are then represented in this context as an individualized "solution," rather than a consequence of neoliberal policies (or lack thereof). So, in relation to egg donation, we can see how neoliberal ideologies and practices play out in, and interact with, material bodies, as the bodies of the women are the focus of intervention, not the social, political, and economic factors.

Bodily commodification and egg transfer

A growing body of feminist literature has begun to explore concerns about the commodification of reproductive bodies, and body parts, within a gendered market-place (Gupta & Richters, 2008; Nahman, 2008; Mamo, 2010; Almeling, 2011). The medical context that is of special interest has been referred to by Ratcliff (2002) as the "stork market," while Mamo has dubbed the field "Fertility Inc.". Of particular concern is third-party reproduction, including egg transfer.

Rene Almeling's (2011) ethnographic research at commercial egg agencies and sperm banks reveals the gendered construction of third-party reproduction, where sperm donation is considered to be a job, while egg donation is considered a gift. Both egg and sperm donors are primarily motivated by financial compensation; however, the ways in which paid donors talk about their experiences – either as gift or job – is shaped by gendered conceptualizations of reproductive bodies (Almeling, 2011). Further, Almeling argues that, through organizational framing (gendered practices and discourse) and interactions with clinic staff, egg providers are encouraged to draw on gift rhetoric when discussing their decision to "donate." However, locating their motivations as altruistic has consequences. Donors expressed emotional investment in caring about the outcomes of the recipients and often felt guilty if the recipients did not become pregnant (Almeling, 2011). Almeling's research illustrates how constructions of gender land in the narratives, and bodies, of providers.

Feminist scholars have also debated whether payment for reproductive body parts is exploitative. Farquhar (1998) argues that those who promote ARTs are oppressive, while consumers and providers are oppressed. For Corea (1985), reproductive technologies represent instances of patriarchal appropriation of women's bodies. Further, Papadimos and Papadimos (2004) argue that female students in the United States who sell their eggs to cope with rising tuition costs are not making autonomous decisions. Since college students are constrained by their financial limitations, they in turn cannot give informed consent, which is possible only through autonomy (Papadimos & Papadimos, 2004). In comparison, Weinbaum (1994), in her discussion of surrogacy, understands these women as "enterprising poor women . . . [in] a newly found cottage industry" (p. 101). Nahman (2008), in her ethnography of Romanian egg sellers, echoes this sentiment and warns against seeing the women she interviewed as "brutalized victims" of the global egg trade. Rather, Nahman suggests that these women are "savvy participants" of the ova trade, where certain individuals want to reproduce with providers' eggs, and sellers want to supplement their income. Yet herein lies a paradox of egg selling: egg providers attempt to improve their economic status and gain a sense of dignity within global capitalism by selling their eggs, yet these desires are indicative of contexts that promote agency through participation in markets, whether as buyers or sellers. As Tyler (2011) argues, "within neoliberal society the ability (and desire) to work and to spend are key measures of value and ideal neoliberal subjects cooperate with their subjectification within these markets" (p. 22). Thus, commercial egg transfer is a practice befitting the neoliberal ethos, where success is measured through continuous work and consumption (McGregor, 2001) at the site of the body.

Egg donation, discourses of motherhood, and neoliberalism

As mentioned previously, some feminist scholars have raised concerns about the commodification of maternity and potential and actual maternal bodies under neoliberalism (Gupta & Richters, 2008; Tyler, 2011). For Tyler (2011), maternity has been capitalized within neoliberalism, whereby "international 'maternal markets' trade not only in clothes, beauty products, pregnancy belly casts, photo shoots and foetal film, but in fertility treatments, eggs, fetuses and children" (p. 31). Concerning ARTs, Gupta and Richters (2008) hold that, under neoliberal economic globalization, these technologies have transformed women's (potentially) reproductive bodies into *productive* bodies, with sellable parts. Through developments in reproductive biotechnology, including the replacing of "flawed" body parts like eggs, there has been an increased readiness to see women as reproductive bits and "childbearing machines" (Gupta & Richters, 2008). Despite these concerns, little is known about how egg providers negotiate discourses of commodification at the site of the maternal body.

In addition to concerns about the commodification of the maternal body, a dilemma has emerged within feminist scholarship concerning whether ARTs disrupt or reinforce biogenetic notions of motherhood. Some view these technologies as intentionally or unintentionally perpetuating motherhood mandates (Thompson, 2005), further twining women to the biological aspects of motherhood (Mamo, 2010; Martin, 2010) and reinforcing notions that women's bodies "should" be employed in the service of motherhood, even if it is not their own. Martin (2010) argues that the extensive "matching" process in egg transfer, as well as the technology of egg freezing, functions to prioritize a *genetic connection* within fertility biomedicine. While Mamo (2010) notes that despite the "vast array of choices (IVF [in vitro fertilization], egg donor, sperm, home insemination, IUI [intrauterine insemination], etc.) [for lesbian reproductive practices], the choice is the same: biological reproduction" (p. 189). Conversely, Carsten (2007) and Strathern (2005) locate motherhood in the context of ARTs as a *process* – flexible and under construction – rather than an essentialist given. Here, motherhood as a form of kinship is understood as something you *do*, whereby individuals must work to establish boundaries of relatedness, moving away from fixed notions of kinship rooted in reproductive bodies (Thompson, 2005; Carsten, 2007). Further, Thompson (2005) argues that, within the context of ARTs, biological motherhood can indeed be partial. Inhorn and Birenbaum-Carmieli (2008) discuss new kinship studies that call attention to the potential for ARTs to redefine notions of relatedness, including motherhood. For example, Strathern (1992) questions how ARTs might blur the binary of nature/culture, by drawing a distinction between social and biological parenting, through the assistance of third parties. For instance, the egg providers in Almeling's (2011) research refer to their contribution as "just an egg," demarcating a boundary between social and biogenetic parenthood, to position themselves as "not-mothers." While Becker et al. (2005) note how, in the United States, the normative folk model of kinship prioritizes "genetic" or "blood" relationships, and certainly in the context of donor gametes this model is difficult to disrupt.

In the context of neoliberalism, Thompson's (2005) ethnography of ARTs outlines the complexities of disambiguating kinship relations, particularly as they relate to commodification. She notes that, within commercial ART clinics, payment is critical in constituting procreational intent, in turn locating the folks who seek out these technologies as biological kin (Thompson, 2005). Moreover, women using egg providers position gestation as the activity that renders kinship and they work to minimize the biogenetic contribution of the egg (Thompson, 2005). This indicates the additional labor undertaken by recipients to establish themselves as the maternal body.

Further, complex questions arise as to which women are encouraged, or even expected, to utilize these technologies and which women are denied access. Ginsburg and Rapp (1995) have used the concept of "stratified reproduction" to denote how society values certain women (i.e., white, middle-class, educated, married) as mothers, while disparaging and despising "others" as mothers. With regard to egg transfer, Pollock (2003) argues that egg providers in the United States are similar to recipients in terms of education, occupation (or future occupation), and class standing. Although at the time of transfer they are less wealthy than providers, they are "junior members in prosperity" (Pollock, 2003, p. 247). While there are no national statistics in the United States on the demographics of egg providers, research conducted on this group suggests that the "typical" provider is white and educated (Kalfoglou & Gittelsohn, 2000; Curtis, 2010; Almeling, 2011; Haylett, 2012); however, details on the socioeconomic status of providers is lacking. In turn, the notion of stratified reproduction is useful when attempting to understand who is considered to have "suitable" eggs and how these constructions can lead to the reproduction of privilege. Further, Rapp's (2011) concept of "reproductive entanglements" reminds us that, despite this potential of ARTs, like egg transfer, these processes are intertwined with sociocultural, historical, and political contexts. Rapp (2011) states:

> any transformation of child-making proceeds not only through the medicalization of women's bodies; it always and also involves simultaneous entanglement with gender and generational relations, kinship, religious, and governmental regulation at both the local and the international level.
>
> (p. 4)

In turn, it is within the intersecting contexts of neoliberalism/patriarchy/reproductive biomedicine that (some) women's bodies are mobilized for other women's motherhood.

Despite a growing body of feminist literature on the possibilities for ARTs to disrupt or reinforce biogenetic notions of motherhood, there has been little research on how providers negotiate these representations. Two exceptions are Haylett's (2012) and Almeling's (2011) research. Haylett conducted interviews with egg providers and clinic staff, as well as participant observation at fertility clinics in California. The egg providers Haylett spoke with prioritize pregnancy as signifying motherhood, minimizing the connection between genetics and motherhood. They present their motivations for "donating" as wanting to help other women become mothers. It should be noted that egg providers will be rejected from the process if they locate themselves as the mother or imply any filial connection with potential offspring (Haylett, 2012). Haylett begins to highlight the complex dance that egg providers negotiate whilst attempting to be selected for transfer. She explains there is:

> often a very fine line because . . . the women need to care and be invested and altruistic, yet they cannot be too invested, because at the end of the day they do not get to meet the recipients, and they need to be able to let go of their eggs without any emotional or filial attachment.
>
> (p. 230)

Thus, egg providers must navigate a complicated discursive terrain. They must not identify themselves as the, or a, "mother" within the context of egg transfer in order to become an egg provider, while simultaneously expressing gendered norms of selfless motherhood, an ideal of (hetero)normative femininity.

Almeling's (2011) research sheds light on how egg and sperm providers conceptualize notions of parenthood, as well as how they create links to potential offspring, within an American context of gamete transfer. Sperm providers think of themselves as "fathers" while egg providers position themselves as "not-mothers," drawing a distinction between social and biological parenting (Almeling, 2011). Further, the dominance of gift rhetoric in egg agencies functions to emphasize what the provider is giving to the recipient – *her* motherhood. Almeling (2011) suggests that, given the tremendous social pressures on women to be "good mothers," it is in the interest of both agencies and providers to position these women as not-mothers. She explains: "if egg donors were categorized as mothers, then, culturally speaking, they would be the worst kind of mothers. Not only are they not nurturing their children, they are selling them for $5,000 and never looking back" (Almeling, 2011, p. 163). Almeling's research begins to address the question of how providers conceptualize and talk about notions of motherhood within the context of egg transfer. However, more empirical and clinical work is needed to bolster the mostly theoretical work that has been addressing these issues, particularly as they relate to consumer citizenship within the gendered market-place.

A (suggested) feminist psychological framework for studying egg transfer

Much research in feminist and critical psychology has been informed by constructionist epistemologies that see discourses, not individuals, as the primary unit of analysis (see Pilgrim & Rogers, 1997). These approaches arose as a reaction to dominant positivist and post-positivist paradigms in psychology. Positivist frameworks, influenced by biomedical models, aim for supposedly controlled and objective observation of "reality" (Yardley, 1997a). Positivist approaches narrowly define the gaze of science (Ussher, 1997) in their attempts to observe "facts" and "truth," typically through quantitative methodologies. As Ussher notes, this is evident in areas of reproduction, "where the material body stands at the centre of the scene" (1997, p. 2). These frameworks position the body as existing outside of discourse and culture. Positivist and post-positivist approaches have been criticized for attempting to isolate experience from the contexts in which they are embedded (Yardley, 1997a). Moreover, this "individualising framework" (Ussher, 1997) negates sociocultural and historical discourses, which shape our representations of categories like "woman" or "mother" (see Ussher, 1997 for a discussion). In contrast, social constructionists argue that individual experiences and attitudes can only be understood within discursive customs and constraints (see Yardley, 1997b), which open up or close down possibilities for action (Willig, 2008). However, this exclusive focus on discourse has been criticized for ignoring the materiality of experience (Sims-Schouten et al., 2007), leading to what Pilgrim and Rogers (1997) have referred to as "epistemological nihilism" (p. 37). Thus, some have raised concerns about the inadvertent disavowal of the material body within feminist and/or critical circles (Sampson, 1998; Fausto-Sterling, 2005; Pitts-Taylor, 2010). I would like to suggest that a critical feminist analysis turns its gaze towards the materiality of egg providers' experiences, in particular their bodies. As noted above, the (potentially) maternal body within neoliberalism represents a site to examine complex tensions concerning commodification and motherhood as they relate to egg transfer. It follows that, when studying egg transfer, the women who provide eggs, and the contexts in which transfers occur, an approach that can simultaneously investigate the physical aspects of women's lives, as well as the social contexts in which these experiences are embedded, is needed.

As noted, within feminist scholarship there has been concern that (some) social constructionist analyses have (unwittingly) negated the corporeal body (Ussher, 1997; Fausto-Sterling, 2005; Pitts-Taylor, 2010), through a focus on discourse. Pitts-Taylor (2010) notes that much feminist scholarship has positioned the female body as a "docile body" and a passive object, upon which meaning is inscribed by patriarchy and medicine. Within contemporary embodiment theory, there have been calls to acknowledge materiality when studying the body (Colebrook, 2000; Budgeon, 2003; Pitts-Taylor, 2010). However, caution must be taken not to reify bodies as independent entities outside of the sociocultural and historical contexts of women's lives. Ussher (1997) encourages us to acknowledge that "they [material factors] are always positioned within discourse, within culture" (p. 17).

As such, Blackman (2007) argues for an approach that conceptualizes "the body as discursive, material, and embodied without reinstating the notion that discursive and material are two separate pre-existing entities that somehow 'interact'" (p. 1). Further, Sampson (1998) suggests, the body "carries within its very tissues and muscles the story of ideology" (p. 49). In turn, our embodied experiences cannot be separated from the discourses we use to talk about the body.

As a result of developments in reproductive biotechnology, bodily boundaries and experiences have shifted, which in turn has implications for embodiment (Gupta & Richters, 2008). As mentioned previously, within the capitalist framework of reproductive biomedicine, body bits are typically located as (re)movable things, whereby social and individual identities are stripped of meaning from bodily tissues (Waldby, 2002). Moreover, these discursive frameworks can affect how providers experience their bodies within the context of egg transfer. For instance, an egg provider who shared her narrative in the book *Eggsploitation*, which followed the documentary of the same name, stated: "I felt used and just like an egg producer. I felt like that all they cared about were my eggs, and not me and my health and well-being" (Rosa & Lahl, 2012, p. 725). This provider's narrative highlights a mechanistic-like way in which the body is employed within the context of transfer, which in turn leads this provider to feel like a "producer," whose main value is her bodily material. As Katz-Rothman (2004) argues, at the intersection of the dehumanizing discourses of technology and capitalism, women are encouraged to adopt a mechanical self-image that positions the body and its parts as commodities.

Moreover, for those who have bodily matter removed, or receive tissue from others, these bodily bits are not impersonal or without signification (Waldby, 2002). As Waldby (2002) argues, despite the dominance of the commodity model in tissue transfer,

> human tissues are not impersonal or affectively neutral; rather, they retain some of the values of personhood for many if not most of the donors and recipients. Hence, circuits of tissue exchange are not only technical and therapeutic, but also relational and social.
>
> (p. 240)

Gupta and Richters (2008) explain that, as material is moved from one body to another, we develop new meanings of embodiment, in particular one that is "intercorporeal." Waldby (2002) refers to this as "biomedical intercorporeality," whereby the material mixing of bodies produces novel, risked, and fractured forms of embodiment. This new and somewhat (dis)embodied experience, under neoliberalism, is highlighted in the narrative of a journalist and egg provider who published her experiences online:

> I was learning that once I signed my name on a contract, I was no longer in charge of my own body. My time and medical care belonged to someone else, someone who only knew me from the photos they'd seen in an

> online profile and as a series of letters and numbers that replaced my name in legal contracts.
>
> (http://costoflife.heraldtribune.com/chapters.aspx?page=2)

Here, we see the complex interplay between the neoliberal ethos, which expects individuals to engage in continuous work and consumption (McGregor, 2001), and the ways in which egg providers come to experience their bodies. This provider appears to adopt the neoliberal ideology of "productive" citizenship (Weibe, 2009) through her contract labor. Yet it is through engaging in this (re)productive labor that she experiences a loss of control over her bodily agency, whereby her embodiment is located as fragments of photos, letters, and numbers. In turn, this narrative provides some initial insights into the interwoven relationship between neoliberal ideologies and the corporeal body, within the context of egg transfer.

The aforementioned narratives from egg providers highlight the (somewhat troubling) ways in which sociohistorical forces "converge upon the body" (Malson, 1998, as cited in Gurevich et al., 2004). Nonetheless, I do not want to fall prey to the discursive production of women's bodies as "suffering bodies" (Abu-Lughod, 2002, cited in Liebert et al., 2011), as some Western feminism has. In turn, I argue that Budgeon's (2003) notion of bodies as "becoming," whereby bodies are made, unmade, and remade, can carve space for an understanding of egg providers' bodily experiences beyond the "docile body." Here, the body is understood as a process, an *event* instead of an *object* (Budgeon, 2003). Following Budgeon (2003), I would like to suggest an ontological strategy that "can accommodate the possibility of thinking beyond a division of materiality and representation . . . not about what the body means, but how it becomes through a multiplicity of continuous connections with other bodies" (p. 51). This is a call to feminist psychologists and clinicians to conduct research (in its broadest sense) that accounts for both the corporeal bodies of egg providers, and the discourse they use to talk about their bodies under neoliberalism. However, I would also like to acknowledge other actions beyond the academy/clinical sphere, which have begun to address issues of commodification and the (reproductive) body within the context of egg transfer. For instance, the artist-activist and past egg "donor" Raquel Cool employed performance, video, and self-portrait paintings in her exhibition *Live Nude Eggs* to call attention to the ways in which egg providers, and their bodies, are frequently written out of the transfer stories by clinics and recipients. Cool served "ovary martinis" as part of her performance, highlighting the material bodies of egg providers, which are often rendered invisible following transfer. This work is a critical example of "giving voice" to egg providers, their experiences, and bodies. However, as noted, more work is needed to broaden our understandings of egg transfer and the women who provide eggs to others. As such, an approach that not only acknowledges the material body, but pays attention to the meaning in reproductive body fragments, as well as new and fluid forms of embodiment within egg transfer, is necessary.

Conclusion

The tensions outlined above resonate with a long-standing dilemma in feminist scholarship which questions whether individual agency or social structures shape women's lives – a dilemma often referred to as the "structure" vs. "agency" debate (see Leve et al., 2011). In this paper, I have sketched out these tensions and illustrated the complexities of these debates without falling prey to these potentially immobilizing binaries. Before concluding, I would like to suggest that attention to the material body/embodiment in an analysis of egg transfer and the women who provide eggs furnishes a space for agency and resistance (as well as exploitation) within the reproductive market-place of neoliberalism. In attempting to move beyond these tensions, it is important to acknowledge that agency operates within the neoliberal epistemology, rather than outside it (Nahman, 2008); and situating an analysis of egg transfer and the bodies of the egg providers within this reality is essential. Within the context of egg transfer, recipient women's (potential) motherhood is indeed trafficked through the bodies of egg providers. As Thompson (2005) argues in her discussion of surrogacy, women's bodies *are* the infertility treatments. Yet, if we acknowledge that techniques (and technologies) of domination may also become sites of resistance, we open up a space for reconfiguration (Foucault, 1978). Mahjouri (2004) suggests that we locate agency as operating *within* the market-place whereby:

> networks of power interact to produce bodies that actively desire to take part in the disciplinary practices of biopower . . . [and it is then] possible to rewrite the commodified maternal body as a body that possesses an agency that allows it to subvert and reproblematize Marxist binaries of production/reproduction.
>
> (Mahjouri, 2004, p. 14)

Indeed, there is potential for alternative possibilities to swirl within the milieu of reproductive technologies. Both Rubin and Phillips (2012) and Sawicki (1991) warn us against the polarizing representations of ARTs, like egg transfer as *either* inherently repressive *or* libratory. As Sawicki (cited in Rubin & Phillips, 2012) explains, "although new reproductive technologies certainly threaten to reproduce existing power relations, they also introduce new possibilities for disruption and resistance" (pp. 175–176). Following Sawicki (1991) and Rubin and Phillips (2012), it is important to look for such possibilities within the context of egg transfer, examining this space for challenges to biogenetic and patriarchal representations of motherhood.

In turn, I am arguing that it is at the site of the maternal body within neoliberalism that we can begin to move beyond the aforementioned tensions when conceptualizing egg transfer. Although the technology facilitating egg transfer is just over a quarter-century old, for those providing and receiving eggs, there are implications for embodiment. The material mixing of body parts within the context of reproductive biomedicine can lead to "biomedical intercorporeality," which "creates new circuits of relationships[s] in ways that are often neither anticipated nor recognized by medical researchers or liberal bioethicists' (Waldby, 2002, p. 251). It is these potentially novel relationships and forms of embodiment that can be explored at the site of the material body. The experiences of egg providers, noted above, are but an initial step in shifting our understandings of egg providers away from these binaries. Further, following Pitts-Taylor (2010) in her discussion of fat, I suggest that we locate the tissues in egg transfer as bodily matter that *matters*. As Waldby (2002) argues, despite the commodity model of tissue transfer, bodily fragments are imbued with meaning and personhood, for both providers and recipients. Yet, as I have suggested, it is only by focusing on the (maternal) body of egg providers that we can begin to understand the meaning in these body bits, beyond merely the (potential) creation of a child.

In sum, I am suggesting that, rather than characterizing egg transfer as either oppressive or libratory, perpetuating motherhood mandates or subverting biogenetic notions of motherhood, commodifying women's bodies or offering women new ways to join the labor market using their reproductive bodies, we instead take an approach that recognizes the complexities in women's decision making to sell their eggs. I see the maternal body within the context of third-party reproduction as a site of analysis that carves out a space for discussions that move away from "either/or" binaries to what McKenzie-Mohr and Lafrance (2011) refer to as "both/and" discussions. The "both/and" position promotes a space to acknowledge egg providers' agency, while at the same time not downplaying the influence of (oppressive) social structures and discourses. Indeed, gendered sociocultural and sociopolitical contexts shape and constrain the choices women make, and the kinds of stories women can tell about these choices. It follows that a feminist psychological analysis of egg transfer requires a gaze that zooms back and forth (and in between) bodies and culture. Moreover, complex questions arise as to who benefits when we focus our discussions of egg transfer within the aforementioned binaries? What is ignored through these arguments? And whose interests do they serve? Before concluding, I would like to attempt to provide a brief answer to these questions by suggesting that, like other ARTs, egg donation is not a "neutral" technology (Martin, 2010). It is a "socio-technical product" (Inhorn & Birenbaum-Carmieli, 2008, p. 178) that is shaped by its technical features, in addition to the economic, political, cultural, psychological, and moral contexts in which it is utilized. And it is in the US context of neoliberalism, where inadequate (or nonexistent) family leave policies make pregnancy and parenthood disruptive, difficult, and at times impossible, that technologies like egg transfer become a market-oriented "solution," which masks social inequalities.

Chapter 6

Male infertility

The erection of a myth, the myth of an erection

Adam Kaplan

I suppose I should start with two disclaimers: first, this essay is rooted not in research or clinical theory, but in personal experience. This is largely because I found very little in the literature that spoke to my experience of infertility. And with that in mind, second, that I don't really know if I officially qualify as "infertile" (at least in the medical sense, but more on the social and cultural implications of this term to follow).[1] But I do know, after a number of visits with reproductive specialists, that I am sufficiently challenged in terms of my procreative potential that it is fairly certain I am the reason that my wife and I were not able to have a biological child.

While my experience is, of course, singular, the cultural and scientific rabbit hole into which I have fallen reveals common cultural, social, and gender themes that beg for exploration. And it is from within this rabbit hole that I begin my discussion. I want to help other men (and the therapists with whom they might work) navigate the emotional experience of challenges to their reproductive potential and, in doing so, provide a window into this experience to any interested person anywhere along the gender continuum. But here is where things become confusing and sticky; down here in the rabbit hole, how exactly do I feel? There is a simultaneous experience of being firmly grounded in information yet feeling distant from any mirror that truly reflects the emotional complexity. Contemporary scientific understanding of infertility seems fairly advanced in comparison to current psychological formulations, which are worse than nonexistent. If there was nothing but a psychological and psychoanalytic void regarding male infertility, then any perspective could begin the process of creating meaning out of raw experience. But, rather than a void, we have many, many assumptions that are not acknowledged as outdated or severely limited as constructs. The very existence of these constructs can serve to impede the potential for men to find personal meaning in the experience of infertility, as the space for exploration and being can collapse under the weight of these antiquated, dominant ideas. It is a confusing hole in which to sit. It seems, while the medical technology has, for better or worse, advanced to the point of modern machines, psychoanalysis has barely evolved beyond the wheel and axle socially/psychologically/psychoanalytically/politically. In this confusing and destabilizing context, what do I feel? How do I separate, or can I separate, what I feel from what I think I should feel?

What are my issues versus the issues that I assume I must have? In one sense, I don't think these can be differentiated because, as Muriel Dimen (2011) said so well: "Culture saturates subjective experience" (p. 4). Our sense of self, our experience of who we are, cannot help but be shaped by cultural influences. But I also think that a heightened awareness of the sometimes insidious and invisible hand of culture can lead to shifts in experience and, as a result, help rework the intersection of the cultural and personal.

In this chapter I discuss male infertility from a personal perspective. Some of my thoughts are not original. But, given the paucity in the literature about male infertility, it seems important to underscore and apply them again, to provide a foundation and context to help give form and shape to my own and perhaps others' experiences with infertility.

My view from inside the rabbit hole

I have been asked many times how I feel about my problems with fertility. The question usually strikes me as one asked with hesitancy and apology. Brows give the impression of furrowing, words seem chosen very carefully, and a form of social tight rope walking appears to be taking place. (I have not perceived a similar degree of caution regarding inquiries into a variety of other medical issues.) For me, this has always suggested that what is at play is that care must be taken not to insult me. Of course, my perceptions might be influenced by projection or my contribution to the overall dialogue. But I can only emphasize and report my experience – at the root of the dilemma is that I am being asked, "how does it feel to be less manly?", to be somehow, in a way that is essential to my gender, "lacking?"

I can have this conversation. But I don't find the idea engaging or thought provoking, primarily because it feels emotionally distant. I understand the questions being asked, both explicitly and implicitly. But the assumed assault to my manhood that is infertility, the themes of castration, inadequacy, and humiliation that immediately come to mind, feel like museum pieces. These emotional display items certainly make sense to me and reference a familiar idiom. As I said, I undoubtedly could have this conversation in a way that might seem convincing and honest. But, even as I write these words, I lose energy and get bored. I find I don't have anything to say. This is because these ideas, while potentially relevant, don't speak to my life or struggle. I don't doubt that there are many men who would find their pain or sense of loss reflected or/and embedded in these constructs. The problem, therefore, is not that these ideas are a part of the overall discourse, but that they too frequently define and encompass the discourse. I believe that the social connection between manhood (whatever that means) and the capacity to procreate (as iconic image as well as practical reality) is so engrained in our culture that we don't even question the relationship between the testicular symbol and the amorphous experience of manhood grasping for symbolization.

In my mind I'm also having an argument with this volume's editor. She is telling me that I need to outline, define, reference, defend, cite, and "prove" the phallocentric qualities of our culture. After all, if I'm claiming that culture and sense of self intertwine in a dizzying systemic manner, and that men often can't separate who they are from who the dominant cultural paradigms tell them to be, don't I have to document this aspect of modern experience? I see her point. This is academia. But can't I just point to *Seinfeld* (US TV show), that great social barometer, and quote a triumphant George Costanzo when he believed he had impregnated his girlfriend: "My boys can swim! I did it!" George didn't actually want to be a father. He was rejoicing in the fact that his masculinity was proven to be intact. (In general, we should not equate the sense of masculinity rooted in the power to impregnate with an actual desire to be a father.) Can't I just leave it at that? Will the citations make the point any stronger?

I don't think it matters how many sources I cite to support the idea that manhood equals strength, strength equals potency, and potency equals everything from the knees up and the waist down. The fact that I can still say this now, after decades of critique from feminists, gender and queer theorists, is saying something. For many people, infertility has actually become conflated with impotency – despite the fact that these are two different issues (and the connotations attached to the word "impotent" are so varied as to be beyond the scope of this chapter, but in their own way they all contribute to "the myth of the erection"). If your problem involves your penis in any way, your status as a man is demoted. We live in this world with these images and know their dominance. From an experiential perspective, I think it is obvious. I would like to believe that part of what makes us laugh at the scene from *Seinfeld* is that we now perceive it from a vantage point that highlights how George's views about masculinity are increasingly outdated. For some people this may be the case. But my belief is that far too many people still resonate with what George is saying on a gut, intuitive level. I choose not to emphasize citations, as this would: (1) suggest that "proof" remains necessary; and (2) emphasize looking back at where we have been theoretically rather than casting our gaze forward. I am attempting to stay experience-near in my effort to contribute to both cultural deconstruction and theory building.

Instead, I want to argue a negative and speak to what, disturbingly, still isn't experientially available. I want to wind back the clock, point to the limited constructs of self available to men that lie ahead, and say that we need to be smarter, more fluid, more creative, more open to experience, and expand pathways and roads of possibility not yet imagined. When I was in high school in Northern Westchester in the 70s there were no gay kids in my school. Which means they were all in the closet. But I couldn't perceive the importance of the negative – that the absence of gay peers meant that they couldn't express who they were and I was too dense, unaware, and uneducated to see what wasn't there but was obviously all around me. In these same areas of New York, high schools now have LBGT groups, gay marriage is law, and the possibilities for expression of gender and sexuality have reached places my high-school imagination didn't even know to wonder about. And that's the point – in some spheres of experience we are reaching for a place far beyond what my limited teenage vision could imagine.

So why, seriously, is the discourse around male infertility stuck in a circular, self-perpetuating quagmire of castration, lacking "balls," and being less of a man? To quote Peggy Lee: "Is that all there is?"

The search for enlightened context: comparing social science research and psychoanalytic theory

OK, fine – a little proof. But only because it is so important to document, that you believe me, that my old high school is now more creative regarding gender and sexuality than our clinical literature is regarding male infertility. First, there is actually little in the psychoanalytic field on masculinity in general. Sure, there are Ken Corbett (2009) and Bruce Reis and Robert Grossmark's (2009) respective books, a handful of papers, but for the most part masculinity has remained an unquestioned, unexamined category of experience. In terms of male infertility, practically no psychoanalytic writing on the subject exists. At the time of this writing, there were a total of two articles that came up in a PEP search on male infertility: one article (Keylor & Apter, 2010) and a critical reply (Gentile, 2010). There has also been a surprising lack of dialogue and intellectual advancement in public forums and the culture at large. I wonder if anyone reading this can remember ever hearing these issues discussed on public radio, written about in more thoughtful magazines like *The New Yorker*, or raised anywhere on the ever-expanding range of television. It would be a mistake, therefore, to think that the equation of manhood and testicular fortitude is due to the influence of longstanding informed and reasoned thought on the social and clinical perception of male infertility. In many respects, a psychological exploration of men's experience of infertility brings us into largely uncharted and unexplored waters.

That being said, in my reading of the little bit that is out there, I found greater openness and flexibility of thought in the social science-based research than in the theoretical psychoanalytic writing. As an example, Culley et al. (2013) wrote in their article "Where are all the men? The marginalization of men in social scientific research on infertility": "Thus, it guides researchers to look for notions of masculinity that are pervasive as well as diverse notions of masculinity which are open to challenge in the stories men tell themselves" (pp. 228–229). These authors also state how "pervasive masculine norms (such as control, stoicism, strength) can impact on the emotional wellbeing of men who do not live up to these cultural ideals" (p. 228). These few sentences include mention of narrative construction, culture, and the room for differing conceptualizations of masculinity. This degree of creativity and openness is not, however, mirrored in the psychoanalytic writing on the subject. Rather than cast stones at specific psychoanalytic and psychological theorists and, in doing so, reduce their thinking to mere archaic sound bites, I will return to personal experience and state that, in my reading of the theoretical literature, I was confronted with a steady stream of references to castration, inadequacy, potency, intrapsychic conflict and, only occasionally, relational context. Why did the scant available literature reflect such a divide, whereby the research seemed to embrace what I might actually feel? Instead, the psychoanalytic literature seemed to reinforce what I was reflexively afraid might turn out to be true if one were to delve deeply into the experience-distant realms of my unconscious: that the complexities of my felt experiences of masculinity were actually just some reaction formation against the realities that it's all castration anxiety and the universal male quest for phallic dominance. And, of course, in even asking this question, my way of thinking about unconscious process is suddenly uncharacteristically rooted in a one-person psychology devoid of culture. What is this gravitational pull into formulations of the past that is experientially part of reading the available theoretical writing on male infertility? Why must we all regress?

The intersection of personal narrative and the effort to unpack male infertility

I am actually not entirely sure how I feel about my fertility problems, at least in part because I lack a context with which to think, feel, and live with them. Again, what is available must work for some people out there (although, and I can't stress this enough, the chicken-and-egg quality between culture and self-experience makes me wonder how much men's reported struggles with fertility reflect growing up within, and therefore thoughtlessly and wordlessly integrating, an antiquated narrative). Perhaps offering some of my own trajectory might help explain how the dominant paradigms of male infertility feel so unsatisfactory.

I did not grow up wanting to be a father and it wasn't a dominant part of my feelings about marriage. I often struggle with abstract ideas that are disconnected from their specific life context – for example, I don't necessarily think that monogamy is "right," but in my experience of my own marriage, it is right for me/us. I felt similarly in regard to having children, in that I could never separate the thought of whether I wanted to be a father from whether I would want to be a father with a specific person. I enjoy children. I get them and am good with them, and have no doubt that I would love my child with a full heart, but I have always remained ambivalent. I never felt the desire to have a child in the same largely wordless, ultimately inexplicable way that I feel the desire to be with my wife. This left the idea of children seeming more of an intrusion than an addition. That, however, didn't stop us from trying to conceive for roughly 2 years. I bristle when my complex uncertainty is reduced to a version of the cultural stereotype: "men don't feel the need to reproduce as strongly as women." Some men, some women, perhaps, but only if we insist on being willfully simplistic about such a complex topic. I wonder, however, if it would be more precise to say that the overly simplistic cultural stereotype regarding men is actually: "men don't feel the need to be a parent as strongly as women." Men require the capacity for reproduction (which is distinct from actually reproducing or parenting) to maintain their masculinity. I think this is why the subject of male infertility is largely unmentionable and stuck in place. But for me, down here in the rabbit hole, sitting amidst swirling personal emotions and iconic cultural images of gender, I can't shake the disconcerting sense that I am somehow less of a man because I am less of an evolved person – and the distinction noted above is at the heart of the issue. I wonder if I am less of an evolved person because my sense of being in my world, with my wife, in this place and time, doesn't lead me to prioritize fatherhood. Thus, my physical infertility is not nearly as much of an issue as my fears of what I call psychological infertility: the inability to fully desire children. But – do I actually believe that I am developmentally inadequate in an intellectual, academic, logical sense? Not at all. Can I find a place of emotional resolution that feels equal in comfort to my thoughts and convictions? Not fully. Am I confused as I write this? Hell, yes. But I do know that, in my felt experience, this "psychological infertility" feels more like a cultural assault than an aspect of self that I can't bring myself to embrace. So, in regard to the available literature, my opinion is that the maps available to help me navigate this terrain have put a few of the land masses in the right spots but also present the earth as flat.

If I want to discuss my own struggles in a context that can help breathe life and depth and emotional fluidity into my experience, then a conceptualization of men and fertility that places "phallic potency at the center of masculinity" is insufficient (Gentile, 2010). It's not that we don't know anything. The problem, even more insidiously, is that outdated cultural constructs continue to dominate our ways of making meaning around infertility (in other contexts, we have begun to realize that gender is fluid and the world is round). This needs to be acknowledged, and every clinician's ethical responsibility to return to the theoretical drawing board needs to be addressed.

The problematic relationship between psychoanalytic theory and the paradigm of male power

Theory, in any form, is a construction. It is meant to help organize, but should not be equated with truth. I am hardly the first to point out that theory can be an agent of social control. The benefits to men in conceptualizing gender relations in phallocentric terms are obvious – if the very passive act of simply having a penis and testicles carries with it automatic metaphoric and actual interactions of power, then the perpetuation of the theory offers men nonnegotiable access to dominance. I could discuss Freud and Lacan as examples of where this position finds its way into psychoanalytic theory, but so many others have already done so (Dimen, Layton, to name only a few). I also think that would be missing the immediate point I want to make. Yes, there are many examples where psychoanalysis as a field has evolved too slowly. But the primary issue at this point in my discussion is that these ideas are engrained aspects of culture that are so pervasive that they are barely questioned. Men's institutionalized power and images of "the size of his dick" routinely go, if you will, hand in hand. We receive this message in countless ways on a daily basis. Consider as just one example how, when reporting on violence, even media outlets as progressive as National Public Radio will discuss the number of "women and children" harmed, but often leave the number of men injured as a nongendered category.

Men are powerful and there is no need to mention when they are injured or vulnerable, or perhaps we consider this part of the cost men pay for the power inherent in their gender. Women, on the other hand, are equated or/and associated with children. This construction attempts to tug at our heartstrings as this category ("women and children") suggests that women, like children, are weak and vulnerable, undeserving of attack, and defenseless. The words float by over the airwaves, bolstered by the prestige of their source, and the power differential between men and women is embedded into our cultural unconscious a bit more deeply.

Of course, to actively deconstruct this relationship between having a penis and power is simply not in men's interest. It is giving up a mode of contextualization that provides access to power and dominance. Again, it is hardly a source of power that is, by definition, "factually true," but it is certainly deeply felt and experienced in Western culture. Where does this leave me and other men who are challenged in terms of fertility or categorically unable to have a biological child? Castrated, impotent, and inadequate? In the minds of many, and in much of the current literature on male infertility, yes – this is where the inquiry begins. But to anyone reading this, and especially men who have problems with their procreative potential – and the therapists who work with them – this is the moment to stop, wait, think, and, most importantly, look inside and feel. What are some of the prevailing meanings of these terms? Do you actually experience your penis and testes as removed – useless to the point of being gone? Do you suddenly feel as if you are fully without force or effectiveness? Are you, indeed, no longer adequate as a man, as if all of the other self-defined masculine (and human) qualities that you value are no longer of relevance? As stated, history and culture encourage us in the direction of these feelings.

In my own experience, it became clear that problems with my sperms' morphology were primarily responsible for our inability to have a biological child. I quickly became a candidate for all of these "demotions in power and influence" that allegedly come with a fertility problem. And, without question, the diagnosis raised issues for me that initially and somewhat mechanically took on the quality of being "less a man." But as I looked inside and explored my experience, as I implore men in a similar position to do, I was surprised by what I found. The strongest feeling was that I had let down my wife. Not as a man, but as a loving partner who wants to help provide the experiences that she/we value and desire. Yes, we were both, to differing degrees, ambivalent about having a child. But my morphology problems took the choice off the table of proceeding without medical intervention, which had been important to us. (While this was painful for me in my role as a husband, it did not foreclose the option of having a child as much as change the nature of our conversation.) My experience was one of guilt in the context of the relationship far more than the culturally and historically defined starting points of phallocentric power. The former strikes me as more relationally based, while the latter would have much more to do with a "one-person" relationship to my penis and testicles, experienced through the lens of outdated and moldy iconic images. In a sense, for me, seeing the problem more in terms of my marriage took the issues of demotion in manhood out of the forefront of the discussion – which makes sense, as I argue that they shouldn't by necessity be there in the first place. One could counter that, in doing so, I maintain my access to male power because I artfully shift the emphasis in a different direction. Possible? Sure. But not a maneuver that feels experientially consistent with my sense of who I am as a man.

Too many of the ideas from psychoanalytic theory suggest that infertile men are, as a result, less powerful, less able, lacking in something essential to being a "man," and "lesser" in every way that matters to how we feel about being men. I want to stress again that this may, indeed, reflect many men's deeply felt experience of infertility and, unequivocally, that experience is to be respected. But why, by definition, would we continue to equate infertility with these constructs of powerlessness? How does this make sense? And what does it do to our patients if these stereotypes about masculinity are where we consistently meet them, and perhaps even keep them there? Certainly there have been many advancements in psychoanalytic theory as a whole, but, as I will discuss, in my opinion this evolution in thought continues to influence too little of the overall psychoanalytic discourse and has made far too few inroads into our culture at large. As I stated earlier, there were gay kids in my high school. But I didn't expand my thinking sufficiently to question what seemed to simply be my "truth". In actual fact, there were most likely a number of gender-questioning kids of all varieties. Many of us accept this now. In some respects, our equation of infertility with male inadequacy reflects a lack of imagination and an acceptance of limited status quo thought that is similar to my high-school experience of binary gender and heteronormativity.

Sometimes a phallus is just a penis: challenging male authority

I want to return to the issue of power. Infertile men who reflexively embrace the culturally dominant phallocentric theory of manhood have little choice but to admit their failure. To choose to seek therapeutic treatment will likely confront them with, and therefore reinforce, their significant limitations of manhood (see Keylor & Apter (2010), and Gentile's (2010) response to this matter). This is where psychoanalysis and other domains of mental health treatment must accept at least some responsibility for the pathologizing and humiliating predicament in which infertile men find themselves. Our ways of conceptualizing the relationship of power and being a man must be rebuilt from the ground up. To theorize manhood in different terms means all men must, as a starting point, sit with the discomfort of their felt failure and powerlessness – in essence, to embrace their demotion. (Of course, this demotion impacts men differently based on race, class, and other markers of male power.) To theorize differently is to embrace lesser power. While my focus is on male theorists and their self-reinforcing access to power, members of all genders must be willing to question the extent to which they embrace phallocentric conceptualizations of manhood and ask the challenging question: "do I have an investment of any kind in this way of thinking?" or, more explicitly and honestly, "what is my investment in this way of thinking?"

Many years ago I was walking down the street with my wife and we saw a group of men leaving a bar. They were obnoxious and, to my sensibility, luxuriating in the excess amount of audible and physical space that they were occupying. I remember remarking to my wife that I felt that, as a man, you have two choices and they are both exhausting: engage in that kind of behavior, or spend your life coming to terms with the social and self-perception of being "less manly" that comes with refusing to do so. I am 5 foot and 7 inches (1.70 meters) in height – far from a physically intimidating figure. And I believe this lack of stature costs me. For example, I perceive that when in the company of taller men, I have to work harder to take up intellectual and physical space. But even in a male world, where "size matters" (and I say this not to make a cheap joke, but to demonstrate again the ease with which phallic imagery remains readily accessible when discussing male power), I understand that, regardless of my physical stature, I still benefit from male access to power. On many occasions, being perceived as "in charge," in settings as varied as restaurants and/or professional meetings, has been a "right" that is mine to give away if I choose. The assumption of male authority existed implicitly. But I have just as many anxieties and fears as the next person, and I am aware that by deconstructing male access to power I create distance from this unspoken cultural perception of authority that can provide comfort when I am faced with bouts of self-doubt.

I have written elsewhere (Kaplan, 2014) on these next two thoughts, but they should be repeated in this discussion. As a practice, psychoanalysts are trained in a modality that steeps them in history. These old constructs of phallocentric power are spread throughout seminal psychoanalytic and psychological readings. And, as I have suggested, they are compelling. To ask candidates and students to "accept what is helpful and leave the rest" is insufficient. We reinforce, through what is emphasized in our teaching methodology, outdated concepts of manhood and, in doing so, contribute to the way in which psychoanalysis is often a lagging indicator of social change. We need to lead – to not simply deconstruct and question, but to stop simultaneously acting as agents of phallocentric power and therapeutic witness to the pain it produces in all genders. My focus in this chapter may be on the experience of male infertility, but the damage created by reinforcing the phallocentric assumptions that underlie it is far more widespread.

Along these lines, consider the role of "individuation" in our culture and theory. Certainly, psychoanalytic theory, especially those circles influenced by feminist theory, has discussed individuation in recent years within a context of relatedness. But my opinion is that the felt sense of the term in the literature (as well as the culture in which we live) reflects an emphasis on imagery of male power – the capacity to create, cope, and achieve without the influence or support of others. Think about how most of us, at least in large part, experience what it is to be emotionally "strong." It is not how effectively we access social support; rather, it is how well we manage without the need to "rely" on others. This value placed on individual "strength" may well influence men and women differently in a number of ways. But, in my clinical and personal experience, nobody seems to be free of this value system. Again, in their formative educational years, psychoanalysts continue to learn older, less relationally oriented conceptualizations of "individuation" that reinforce this individualistic distortion. These concepts, which integrate historical conceptualizations of manhood, while certainly at odds with subsequently developed theoretical perspectives, can't help but be read with a reinforcing familiar air of cultural "truth." They are consonant with the ideal of male power that has been with us for generations.

As I consider these explicit and implicit beliefs regarding male power that help define the accepted understanding of male infertility as primarily an experience of impotence, castration, and powerlessness, it occurs to me that to challenge these beliefs that reinforce access to male power is beyond difficult – it is seemingly taboo. Questioning this taboo could have a potentially destabilizing influence that extends beyond men simply losing a firm grip on their access to power. If we adopt the challenge to question the idea that a man must be powerful, question how power is defined and symbolized, and in doing so redefine a seminal gender ideal, then I suspect that constructs and organizing principles that contain the already illusory experience of a coherent self could begin to disintegrate for many people. But as I consider this thought, I realize that I may be grouping far too many people under the umbrella term of "men" as I have been using it thus far. In this chapter, exactly whose experience am I attempting to capture?

We all have to start somewhere: first steps at deconstructing my experience of masculinity

I am writing from my own perspective – that of a straight, white man who not only does not resonate with the dominant paradigms provided for infertile men, but who feels caught in a cultural straitjacket every time I am categorized as, well, straight. The issue is not how I define myself sexually, but my lack of identification with the many assumptions and limits that create the outline of how the term "straight" is automatically experienced in our culture. It wasn't until I was halfway through this chapter that I realized I might be writing primarily to heterosexual men with fertility issues – the men who I believe are, in a unique way, automatically and forcefully defined by limiting and damaging cultural rules regarding masculinity. Admittedly, I'm not sure about this, as many gay men also accept the phallocentric notion of masculinity, and many try to reproduce. But when discussing the specific issue of male infertility, I wonder if heterosexual men experience the straitjacket of cultural definition in a more constricting manner. Yes, as an identified white, heterosexual male, I have automatic access to power. But there is a flip side to this coin – one that does not make me deserving of sympathy, but a reality that must be acknowledged by heterosexual men attempting to navigate infertility (or any number of life experiences). The boundaries of what is considered normative behavior for straight men, in general, are very narrowly defined. The gender and sexual fluidity that some women and some other men might enjoy seems to be unavailable to the heterosexual man. It is as if male heterosexuality demarcates the end point of the gender continuum – a place of very limited options, not to mention isolation. As just one personal example of what I am discussing, I often comment that I would check the "straight" box on the questionnaire, as I'm married to my wife and exclusively have had sex with women. But I also enjoy the affectionate relationships that I have with many of my male friends. I experience a bond, a warmth, a sharing of something past words with these friends in a way that has led others to wonder if I'm gay, or at the very least present me with the now thankfully outdated term "metrosexual." All I know is that these friendships feel right to me. And I know I'm not alone. But it feels like it takes a force of will to carve out this space for myself on the end of the continuum that I occupy labeled "straight."

I suspect that all men who struggle with infertility find themselves trapped within the culturally defined definitions of self that are demeaning, but sometimes I wonder if heterosexual men face specific challenges in this area. These men, and I still count myself amongst their ranks, are influenced to varying degrees by a particularly rigid sense of gender self-definition. Because of this, there is a long road to travel before any man who finds himself facing fertility issues can arrive at a point of locating his own mourning, loss, relief, doubts, ambivalence – this list could go on for quite a while – and extract them from a cultural definition that rigidly contains/constrains his experience.

While I never found an approach to exploring my fertility problems in the psychoanalytic literature, I did come across a passage in a collection of essays that connected me to a space where unknown possibilities exist. In *The Book of Men: Eighty Writers on How to Be a Man* (2013), Michael Cunningham writes in his essay:

> maleness, true maleness, isn't really about genitalia at all. It's a conviction. It's a costume that weds itself to our skin and, ultimately, penetrates your very being.
>
> Men. I mean, what are we, anyway?
>
> (p. 73)

Maleness as conviction instead of category, or even a continuum. A continuum is problematic because, even if a spot on the continuum is allowed to shift, it is an overall conceptualization that contributes to the idea that we are identified one way at any given moment. I think the construct of a continuum allows for movement, but not multiple simultaneously existing qualities of self (that cohere, contradict, etc.). But conviction is where feeling and experience meet to create a personal narrative. It integrates and holds the cultural and the personal. It does not imply a category or place, but leaves a space to explore what is deeply personal. It is where I believe we must arrive at when we dial back the clock to reconstruct our conceptualizations of masculinity. And it is where we need to begin when we, or our patients, are faced with male infertility.

I'm not sure I resonate with Cunningham's idea that maleness is a costume that weds itself to our skin and ultimately penetrates the being. But because I'm not going to assume I understand his full meaning, I'll leave open the very real possibility that these words could speak to me. But the idea of "conviction," the possibility that we don't even know what men are ("anyway") are the words that jumped off the page when I read them. These words express freedom. Or at least they do to me. Admittedly, "conviction," strictly defined, has a rather masculine edge ("a strong belief or opinion, a feeling of being sure that what you believe or say is true"). But, in the context in which Cunningham presents his thoughts, I do not experience "conviction" as macho stubbornness. Rather, it feels to me that any felt relationship to being a man, however unnamed or marginalized in our culture, is valid and real. In this light, categories not only expand but also become, in the end, unnecessary. As just one compelling example of this freedom, in a recent conversation a colleague of mine pointed out how:

> once you move on from all the phallic nonsense, there are so many notions traditionally allied with maleness that are ripe for exploration in the culture: doing the right thing; taking responsibility; giving of yourself without complaint; sacrificing; providing, nurturing, encouraging, supporting.
>
> (J.P. Cheuvront, personal communication, September, 2014)

In every circumstance of daily living, including that of "being a man," concessions are made to adapt to cultural, internal, systemic, and historical expectations. I'm not sure that some of these concessions don't serve a necessary purpose, and they would never (or very slowly) fully disappear even if they didn't. But I think that one of the tasks of psychoanalysis can be seen as helping each person identify and find vitality by moving closer to, and embracing, their own conviction of who they want or need to be in their world (and I don't intend to suggest that this is a process devoid of mourning or loss). This idea would, of course, take a different form for each dyad embarking on the therapeutic process. But, in terms of masculinity and the extent to which male infertility presents a challenge to that identity, incorporating the idea that each person's masculinity takes the configuration of an individual conviction boldly validates each experience. It gives permission to start examining, and perhaps removing, some of the historical, cultural, and personal scaffolding that keeps constructs such as castration and impotency so unmovable in the male psyche. "Maleness as a conviction" is an experiential starting point that I find helpful in my own efforts to understand how I feel about my problems with fertility. Even beyond that, this starting point of "conviction" is freeing in my desire to locate a space for myself as a (culturally embedded) man that feels enlivening and authentic.

Note

1 Male infertility can be caused by a number of factors, including low sperm production, misshapen or immobile sperm, and blockages that can interfere with sperm movement and ejaculation.

Chapter 7

Baby making

It takes an egg and sperm and a rainbow of genders

Diane Ehrensaft

Recently, I was sitting in a restaurant having a conversation with two young friends – transgender men, a couple – who were sharing with me their angst about building a family. They want to use assisted reproductive technology (ART). They have plenty of eggs and two uteruses at their disposal. They were in need of donated sperm. They had decided on which one of them will carry their first baby, but they have a problem. The father-to-be who plans to carry the child wants to appear neither on the front pages of *Time* magazine nor at his workplace as the pregnant man. He fantasized about a ranch somewhere that he could retreat to after his pregnancy began to show. Being of an older generation than these two men; I immediately associated to the homes for unwed mothers that pregnant girls were shipped off to in my youth, in shame and ignominy. Then I came up with the bright idea of a transcendent new model of proud rather than shameful retreats for pregnant fathers who would want privacy and freedom from scrutiny during their "lying-in" months. I fully realized the contradiction in the fathers' retreat as a "proud" solution – in a future time when our cultural reproductive discourses recognize the normativity of pregnant fathers or sperm-producing mothers, such privacy would no longer be needed and parents-to-be of all genders could feel free to enjoy their conceptions and gestations with community celebration. However, we are not there yet. So, for the present, the story of my transgender friends puts us on notice that the new convergence of ART (which, through gamete donation and surrogacy, expands the horizons of baby making far beyond mother, father, baby) and gender-affirming medical technology (which affords increasing numbers of people the opportunity to affirm a multitude of genders through hormone treatments and surgery) creates a major challenge.

In the words of Judith Butler:

> we see that technology is a site of power in which the human is produced and reproduced – not just the humanness of the child but also the humanness of those who bear and those who raise children.
>
> (Butler, 2004, p. 11)

Considering the intersection of reproductive and gender medical technologies, we can ask, "What is the nature of that power?" For those of us who think or practice psychoanalytically, to answer that question we by necessity have to unpack, deconstruct, and rework both our theories of reproduction and our theories of gender to make room for the growing phenomenon of same-sex parents and transgender parents who build their families with the aid of ART. From there, we have to put these new theories into practice to facilitate the well-being of these new families of the twenty-first century, and I offer this chapter as a step in that direction.

The reproduction of mothering: a generation later

In 1978 Nancy Chodorow published *The Reproduction of Mothering,* in which she concluded that, as long as women continue to be the gender responsible for the primary rearing of children, we will continue to regenerate a bifurcated, binary, male-dominated gender organization in our culture, based on daughters identifying with their nurturing mothers and sons disidentifying from those same mothers, culminating in the intergenerational transmission of mothering capacities and predilections from mother to daughter to granddaughter and so forth, but not to sons, grandsons, and so forth. The solution: to create a more egalitarian society and demand that men share the primary tasks of child rearing with women in order to break the cycle of gender bifurcation both in parenting and in personality formation. Assumed in Chodorow's discourse is the idea that mothers would be cisgender[1] women and fathers would be cisgender men. Assumed, also, was the idea that the sex listed on the baby's birth certificate, based on visual presentation of genitalia, would be the gender that the baby would claim, so the Fs would become daughters and the Ms would become sons. Twenty-first-century gender transgressions have alerted us that, while these assumptions might apply in a majority of cases, they are not universal. Same-sex couples raise families; the gender of the parents may not match the sex label put on their birth certificates, or the affirmed gender of the parent may not match the label they give themselves as either mother or father. As a society, as parents, and as professionals, we have been learning to listen to our smallest transgender children who let us know they are not the gender reflected on their birth certificates, but rather the other or some other gender combination altogether (Ehrensaft, 2011a), further challenging binary and linear thinking about mothers and daughters and mothers and sons.

At the time Chodorow published her book, caught up in that same binary and linear thinking myself, after reading *The Reproduction of Mothering*, and through personal conversation with Nancy Chodorow, I came to the realization that, in select communities across the United States, subcultures of families already existed who were engaged in this egalitarian endeavor: heterosexual men and women in intact families committed to fully sharing the primary responsibilities of parenting their children. I took it upon myself to research these families, who could provide a social laboratory to investigate whether such an arrangement was possible, particularly within a culture that still demarcated clearly differentiated roles for mothers and fathers and operated within patriarchal hegemony and in which most of the men and women I studied would presumably have themselves grown up in households where women took on the primary responsibilities of parenting. I organized my research project around a singular question, "Can men mother?" Although I took some criticism for gendering the parenting in that way, I held my ground, arguing that I used "mother" in this project as an action verb, not a noun, and meant by that verb all the tasks, responsibilities, and attributes involved in the work of being the primary rearer of a child, characteristics that, in the context of Western culture, were best known as "mothering". Upon completing my research, the answer to my question, "Can men mother?" was yes, most definitely, but, at that moment in history, not exactly like the women. In line with Winnicott's developmental and existential concepts of being and doing (Winnicott, 1971), I concluded that men *do* parenting while women *are* parents (Ehrensaft, 1980, 1987).

This many years later, I chuckle as I realize that, in the context of my present intersectional work on both ART (Ehrensaft, 2005, 2007) and gender nonconformity (Ehrensaft, 2011a, b, 2012), my 1970s question, "Can a man mother?" now seems so antiquated, with future implications that I could not even begin to imagine as I sat down with heterosexual men and women in couples to pursue who changed the diapers and who held the baby in mind. Today, as I engage in my clinical work, either in my private practice or at the gender clinic where I work at the University of California, San Francisco, my mind is bombarded with questions like: Can a man become a mother? Can a father carry a child? Can a mother donate sperm? and so forth. Bob Dylan's lyrics "Makes love just like a woman" run through my head as I come to terms with the fact that a transgender man can mother a child just like a woman, not just emotionally, but physically, carrying the child to term and breast feeding the baby, even after many years of taking cross-sex hormones to bring his body in line with his affirmed gender.

As these myriad possibilities of gender and parenting dance in my head, I am left with only one conclusion: there's a whole lot of shaking going on, leaving the field of psychoanalysis with a whole lot of revamping to do to make psychological and social sense of gender, conception, and parenting when a baby is not a product of a sexual union between a cisman and a ciswoman, the only way that psychoanalysis has heretofore conceived the experience (no pun intended). Even if related to only a small number of parents, the fact of men who become mothers and women who become fathers and the fact of two women or two men who come together to make a baby without sexual intercourse, forces us to make room for these new realities in our psychoanalytic paradigm. So, instead of my now seemingly simple single question, "Can men mother?", I now have four twenty-first-century questions about the intersectionality of gender and parenting. In my own training I learned that the question is often as important as the answer, so in that spirit I do not pretend to offer definitive answers to each of these questions, but rather to invite us to explore them together, as we rework our gender, parenting, and child development theories and practices in light of the more recent parents on the block: gay, lesbian, and transgender parents who make their baby with a combination of their own and outsiders' reproductive material. For the purpose of this discussion I am limiting myself to two-parent families in all of these combinations of gender and sexual identities, so that we can hold steady the variable of two parents but compare these new families in a fertile new world to the "mother-father-have sex-make baby" paradigm emblematic of both traditional and contemporary psychoanalytic discourses.

Here are the four questions:

1 Can a man mother and can a woman father?
2 Is there something missing when a child has two mothers but no father, or two fathers but no mother?
3 What are the psychological implications when a father has a vagina or a mother has a penis?
4 What are the psychological and social effects on all of these children and their parents when a baby is not the product of parents' sexual intercourse but is conceived by science – with the aid of sperm donor, egg donor, surrogate, or gestational carrier?

To even begin to address the four questions, we have to first investigate the manner in which each of these new parents on the block go about having a baby.

Medical, social, and induced fertility

Historically, we have known infertility to signify the failure of a woman's or a man's body to have a working uterus or functioning gametes to make the conception and gestation of a baby possible. In other words, some part of their reproductive apparatus is broken. For the purpose of this discussion, this form of failed reproductive functioning will be referred to as medical infertility. With the advent of reproductive technologies that stimulate fertility or allow parents-to-be to obtain gametes or the use of a uterus from an outside person to create a baby, some individuals have been able to transcend their medical infertility. With the introduction of those same technologies, particularly gamete donation and gestational surrogacy, an entirely new form of infertility came to light. Represented here are the single women, single men, lesbian and gay couples who have reproductive bodies that are working just fine, but are missing a body with which to reproduce. Through the participation of an outside party – donor, surrogate, or gestational carrier – all these people now have the opportunity to create their own babies. For the purpose of this discussion, the lack of a reproductive partner to have a baby will be referred to as social infertility (Ehrensaft, 2005).

Now we add on our third form of infertility: induced infertility. Transgender individuals who choose to take cross-sex hormones to bring their bodies in alignment with their identified gender will put a cap on their fertility as long as they continue to take the hormones. This is a reversible infertility, medically induced. If they have had no reproductive surgeries, by discontinuing their hormones, their fertility can be reinstated. They can also choose to freeze eggs or sperm before hormone treatment or surgical interventions, depositing their gametes in the bank for use in the future with the aid of ART. The exception to the banking option will be younger transgender people who have had the opportunity in their youth to take puberty blockers before the full onset of puberty of their assigned sex, and then go directly to cross-sex hormones to align their bodies to their affirmed gender. These individuals will be rendered permanently infertile, although medical advances are on the horizon that may afford the opportunity for these youth, prior to the administration of blockers, to extract prepubertal gamete material that will be able to be frozen and used for conception later, if that youth should so choose. So keep in mind these three forms of infertility – medical, social, and induced – as we explore both the expanded birth story and the answer to the four questions.

All of these three forms of infertility may be transcended with the participation of an outside party in baby making – sperm donor, egg donor, surrogate, gestational carrier. In traditional surrogacy, a woman is inseminated by a man's sperm and then carries the baby to term in her uterus. In more recent times, traditional surrogacy has been replaced in many places by gestational surrogacy, where one woman carries the child to term, while another woman donates her eggs for the purpose of conception. The underlying reasoning is that this division of labor, so to speak, is a safeguard against the surrogate getting too attached to the baby she is carrying, and the arrangement also offers the opportunity for prospective assisted reproductive parents to choose an egg that fits their family-building goals and then find separate warm and experienced housing for the baby-to-be through a woman who has already birthed children successfully, which often translates to a significant class difference between egg donor and gestational carrier. A gestational carrier may also offer her services to help a couple who can create an embryo between them but lacks a working uterus to gestate the baby. I am aware as I write these descriptions that I am gendering the egg donors, sperm donors, and surrogates, which contradicts what I am about to lay out in the twenty-first-century birth story, a story that highlights the shake-up in gender and conception. So bear with me in the moment as I stay within the confines of the gendered language used in existing guidelines on ART, as outlined within the context of binary cisgender categories.

One last item about the ARTs and the three forms of infertility: to avoid the cumbersome verbiage in referring to the outside parties in all of their iterations each time I make reference to them, I am going to call on a term I coined previously for donors, surrogates, and gestational carriers combined: birth other. I lit on this term by accident, writing notes on birth mothers, making a typo by leaving out the "m" in mother, and then declaring: "I've got it. A perfect term for the person who helps make the baby, not a parent but an other, yet someone involved in the birth process" (Ehrensaft, 2007).

To understand the liminal status of parenting and gender in all its present permutations, we can now add on to the ARTs the effects of a completely separate set of medical technologies. Simultaneous to the era in which reproductive medicine forged ahead to establish ART services so that heretofore infertile parents-to-be could create children of their own, the medical fields of endocrinology and surgery have developed protocols for the administration of puberty blockers, cross-sex hormones, and gender-affirming surgeries, both genital and nongenital, that have allowed increasing numbers of individuals the opportunity to align their gender identity with their bodies (WPATH, 2011). These individuals would be the transgender and gender queer people who choose medical interventions to align their bodies with their affirmed gender selves; other gender-nonconforming people will socially transition to their affirmed gender, but without the use of either hormones and/or surgeries. Many of the individuals in both categories are of child-bearing age and desire to start a family. They may face induced infertility as the result of the hormone or surgical gender interventions; they may face social infertility as the result of missing a body to reproduce with; and they are not exempt from medical infertility as well. Whether it is medical, social, or induced infertility, these transgender individuals setting out to build a family provide the final shake-up in our traditional theories of reproduction – man, woman, sex, baby. Now a man with a uterus can have a baby; a woman with a penis and testes can make a baby with her female partner or with an egg donor and a gestational carrier; a lesbian couple in which one of the women is transgender but retains her penis can have sex and make a baby the old-fashioned way in a two-mother family; a single transgender man who is on testosterone but has had no surgical interventions can go off testosterone, find a sperm donor, and carry his own baby to term. To highlight the complexity of the new combinations and permutations of gender and baby making in the twenty-first century, I would like to present the updated story of the birds and the bees that we would theoretically have to convey to our children if we were to reveal the true and whole story.

The twenty-first-century birth story

If men can bear children, and women can deposit sperm in a bottle so their baby can be born, our traditional, scientifically accurate, child-friendly birth stories have to be radically amended to include all the myriad new possibilities of baby making. Addressing the convergence of medical advances for the transgender community and ART, we now have to acknowledge that not only is there no baby without a mother (Winnicott, 1960, 1971); with new forms of conception using an outside party, including sperm donors, egg donors, surrogates, and gestational carriers, there is now no baby without all the persons involved in making that baby – genetic parents, social parents, gestational parents, gestational carriers, surrogates, egg donors, sperm donors. As this is so, we also have to amend the traditional developmental model based on mother, father, and baby, and, along with it, the standard birth story for young children. Absent ART and gender-affirming medical interventions, the traditional birth story one might tell a child stands as follows:

> Mommy and Daddy decided we wanted to have a baby. It takes a sperm and an egg to make a baby and then a place for the baby to grow before it is born – that would be inside mommy's womb/uterus. Daddies have sperm. Mommies have eggs. The egg and the sperm have to come together to make a baby. So Mommy and Daddy put the sperm and egg together to make the baby and then the baby grows inside Mommy's womb/uterus. And then out comes the baby 9 months later.

The expanded story that dispenses with binary gender categories, heterosexual pairings, and sex as the means of reproduction goes something like this:

> It takes an egg and a sperm to make a baby and a place for the baby to grow, called a womb or uterus. People born with XY chromosomes have sperm and people born with XX chromosomes have eggs, unless their bodies aren't able to make sperm or eggs. People born with XX chromosomes also have a uterus, and that's why babies grow inside those people, and not the people who have XY chromosomes, because they don't have a uterus. Most of the people you know who have XX chromosomes are women, but some are men, and some are somewhere in between. Most of the people you know who have XY chromosomes are men, but some are women or somewhere in between. In some families, there is a mommy with XX chromosomes and an egg and a daddy with XY chromosomes and sperm. If that mommy and daddy want to have a baby, the mommy's egg comes together with the daddy's sperm to make a baby, who then grows inside the mommy's tummy (or uterus or womb) until it's ready to come out.
>
> In some families with a mommy and a daddy who has XY chromosomes, the daddy has sperm but the mommy doesn't have an egg, either because she only has one X chromosome or because her two XX chromosomes didn't work to make eggs. In those families, someone with XX chromosomes and eggs that work can give eggs to the mommy and the daddy so they can have a baby, using the daddy's sperm and that other person's eggs. In some families, the mommy has eggs but the daddy doesn't have any sperm, either because he doesn't have a Y chromosome or because his XY chromosomes didn't work to make sperm. So that mommy and daddy can find someone who has XY chromosomes and sperm that work and ask that person to give them some sperm so they can have a baby together. Sometimes, in mommy–daddy families, it's both things – the mommy doesn't have an egg and the daddy doesn't have sperm, so another person with an XX chromosome can give them an egg and another person with an XY chromosome can give them some sperm so the mommy and daddy can make a baby. In some families, there is only one parent. If it's a parent with XX chromosomes and that person has eggs and a womb, that person will need some sperm to have a baby. So that person finds someone with XY chromosomes who can help by giving some sperm so that person can make a baby and then grow it in her uterus.

> In some families, there is only a mommy and she doesn't have any eggs, either because she does not have XX chromosomes or she has XX chromosomes but her body doesn't have eggs that are working. That person will need both some eggs and some sperm, so two different people, a person with XX chromosomes and eggs, and a person with XY chromosomes and some sperm, can help her by giving her eggs and sperm so she can have a baby. In some families, there are two parents with XX chromosomes and they both have eggs, but they need some sperm. So a person with XY chromosomes helps them by giving them some sperm that come together with one of the parent's eggs so the two parents can have their baby.
>
> Remember that babies also need a place to grow before they come out, the place called a uterus. In some families, the mommy's uterus can't grow the baby or her uterus had to be taken out, or she's a person with XY chromosomes who doesn't have a uterus, because you need XX chromosomes to have a uterus, so a person with a uterus helps by letting the baby grow inside her uterus. In some families where there are two mommies with XX chromosomes, both mommies want to help make the baby, and they can do that, because they can use one mommy's eggs and the other mommy's uterus to make a baby, after they get the sperm from a person with XY chromosomes who is going to help them.
>
> In some families, there is only a dad with XY chromosomes. He has sperm but he needs to find both an egg and a uterus to have a baby. Sometimes that will be the same person, sometimes it will be two different people with XX chromosomes – one who gives the daddy eggs and another who has the baby grow inside her uterus once the egg and sperm come together. Sometimes there will be two dads with XY chromosomes. They both have sperm, but they, too, will need an egg and a uterus for the baby to grow. Like the single dad, sometimes the same person with XX chromosomes will give the dads some eggs for the sperm and also grow the baby in her uterus. Sometimes one person will give the daddies their eggs and another person will have the baby grow inside her uterus after the egg and sperm get put together. Sometimes the two dads with XY chromosomes decide that, since they both have sperm, they'll mix their sperm together to make their baby, and since it takes only one sperm, they know it won't be both of their sperm but only one of their sperm that makes the baby, but they wanted to do it that way so both daddies got a chance to make the baby.

We have definitely left the land of cabbage patches and storks in this story of parents-to-be, the birth other, and conception/gestation in all its iterations. The only remaining gendered category in the story is the social role of mother and father; sex as a means of reproduction is left out of the story, not to protect young children from what they may not be ready to hear but because it is not a universal factor. If we project into the future, the story may become even more complicated as we develop new technologies, just on the horizon, that allow body cells to be transformed into reproductive material, making it possible for two people with XX chromosomes or two people with XY chromosomes to genetically conceive a child together, which may well become reality within the twenty-first century (Regalado, 2004). Even now, the universal birth story is already more complicated than the one I just laid out. As for the purposes of our investigation of the intersectionality of gender and ART, I have left out intersex people, who may have an even more complex picture of chromosomes and reproductive capacities, limiting myself to transgender and gender queer parents-to-be. I am certainly not advocating telling this whole unwieldy tale to a small child, yet the ever-expanding tale stands as the full and scientifically correct story that turns traditional conception, gender, and parenthood on its head in one fell swoop, forcing us to re-examine our heretofore simpler and outmoded conceptualizations of family formation and child development. I would like to embark on that re-examination by addressing each of the four questions posed at the beginning of this discussion.

Question #1: Can a man become a mother? Can a woman become a father?

I am now leaving the realm of my twentieth-century investigation of shared parenting, where my question of men mothering was organized around the concept of gender role expansion, in which men who were fathers could take on, or not, the primary tasks of parenting that had traditionally been assigned to women. I should mention that, in addition to concluding that shared-parenting men of that era *did* mothering while women *were* mothers, one factor came out consistently in the parent interviews: the fathers, committed to equality in parenting and deeply attached to their children, felt deeply jealous of their female partner's ability to both carry a child to term and breast feed the baby. They typically suffered from a hyperboled sense of breast and womb envy, but accepted the biological reality that, until further technological advances, these (cis)men were not able to have the biologically based parenting benefits of pregnancy and breast feeding that would allow them to fully share the parenting experience with their (cis)female partners (Ehrensaft, 1987). The first of my questions about gender, medical technology, and parenting is no longer a question of gender role expansion, but of bodily capacities of men and women today, as they leave the sex assigned to them on their birth certificates to affirm an alternative gender identity. If there is anything that will fully substantiate Freud's understanding that "pure masculinity and femininity are constructions of 'uncertain content'" (Freud, 1925, p. 257), it will be the answer to the question: "Can a man become a mother or a woman become a father?" In the combinations and permutations of gender, conception, and parenting that provide the answer to this question, Adrienne Harris's concept of gender as a personally idiomatic "soft assembly" (Harris, 2005) will stand out in high relief.

Let me illustrate with a clinical account. A request came to me from a family for a psychological consultation in preparation of the birth of their second child.

Involved in the consultation would be the following individuals: (1) a lesbian mom who is the genetic mother of her first-born child, a little girl; (2) the little girl's transgender nongenetic legal father who had been a lesbian mother when the little girl was conceived but has now transitioned from female to male; (3) the sperm donor for their little girl, a gay family friend who is donating sperm again so the lesbian, now heterosexual, couple could conceive their second child; and (4) another family friend, a transgender man, who has birthed three genetic children of his own and is donating eggs so the mother and her transgender male partner can conceive their second child (the egg donation is necessary because the mother, some years older than when her first child was conceived, is now confronted with medical infertility, as her eggs are no longer viable, and the XX father had induced infertility from testosterone use and did not want to discontinue his hormones). At the time of the request for the consultation, the sperm from the gay family friend and the eggs from the transgender family friend had been joined in an in vitro fertilization procedure, resulting in viable embryos that were soon to be transferred to the mother, who will carry the fetus (or fetuses, as the case might be in multiple embryo transfers) to term. So what we have here is a mother–mother parenting couple that turned into a mother–father parenting couple, with no switch in partners; a man who sleeps with men donating his sperm so that first two mothers, and then two mothers morphed into a mother and a father, could have their second child; a woman transitioning to a man who had given birth to three children never as a mother but as a father and then becoming a birth other to his friends who were originally two mothers but now a mother and father so that they could have their second child; a little girl whose mother is now her father, but still has a mother, just gained a father, with no substitution of parents, and with one birth other, a sperm donor, involved in her conception; a baby-to-be who will have a mother and a father, but no parent with a penis, and two male birth others, a sperm donor and an egg donor, involved in the baby's conception, which took place in a Petri dish. Because I had a professional relationship with one of the parties involved, I declined the consultation due to conflict of interest, so I cannot report the outcome for the gender-diverse ART family complex that encompassed these two parents, their birth others, and their offspring. I cite the situation here to emphasize that, although a rare phenomenon, it is within present reality that: (1) mothers can become fathers, but XX fathers with no sperm; (2) with no need for breast or womb envy, just a transition from female to male, fathers can mother in the biological sense, if we hold to the definition of pregnancy and breast feeding as a mothering rather than a fathering activity, but revamp our gender categories so that fathers can be the ones to produce eggs or gestate children; (3) parenting couples of all genders and sexual identities can create their own babies with no sexual encounters, but, instead, with a little help from their friends and the medical community: a situation of sex in the lab, if you will; (4) the gender of a child's parents will not necessarily equate with their mothers having vaginas and their fathers having penises. In my own thinking, for all these four reasons, it would be impossible to impose the traditional concept of the primal scene and the Oedipal configurations that subsequently unfold, a concept based on baby witnessing or fantasizing the sexual union between a penis and vagina attached to its father and mother respectively, and then all the desires, disappointments, and disillusions that unfold as the child puts both gender and family triangles together in the experience of self and others and their sex-assigned reproductive apparatus. Instead, we have a much more expansive terrain of gender possibilities in both baby making and family formation, based not on anatomy but gender affirmations.

To imagine this more expansive terrain, I want to highlight the de-sexing of reproduction and parenting and the deconstruction of binary gender/parenting configurations that occur as people affirm their authentic genders that are separate from their chromosomal or genital make-up, but call on their chromosomal and reproductive constitutions in the endeavor of baby making and baby growing in all kinds of gender and sexual identity combinations and permutations. Let us now return to the paradigm that has been the bedrock of much of our psychoanalytic thinking on sex, reproduction, and child development: a man and woman come together in sexual union; a baby is born; the baby must negotiate dyadic and triadic relationships with same- and opposite-gender parents, mother and father, in the establishment of individuality, relationship, and gender and sexual identities. So what happens when we change the key elements, which is what has occurred in twenty-first-century baby making – no sex, no opposite-sex partners, fluid rather than indelible genders of the partners?

Question #2: Two mothers, two fathers – is something missing?

A few years ago I sat in on a study group of psychoanalytic professionals who are interested in understanding the psychodynamics of ART. None of them works in the field of reproductive medicine. They were interested in understanding the function of paternity – in the infant, in the child, in all of us. They defined the father as the protector of the family, the author of separation and individuation for the child, the representative of culture, and the person who modifies the endless back-and-forth between the mother and the infant (cf. Cath et al., 1982). In their discourse, they identified the father as the parent who gives meaning to the chaotic parts of the personality. They then tried to make sense of a family where there is no father. As an illustration, they chose clips from the movie, *The Kids Are Alright,* the story of a two-mother lesbian family, their adolescent son and daughter, and the sperm donor who helped conceive both their children. So we have two mothers, one genetic, one social (no genetic or biological ties to the children[2]), two children, one heterosexual cisgender sperm donor who inserts himself in their lives. The presenters in the study group zoom in on Laser, the teenage son in the film. They ask what it means that he is growing up in a family with two women who have repudiated men. What will it mean for Laser's masculinity? They show the scene of Laser sitting in the car with his sperm donor, whom he has just met for the first time. Laser queries the donor about the things the donor liked to do in high school. The interpretation by the two presenters, fully accepted by the other attendees: Laser is searching for his lost father, the one his mothers denied him by repudiating men and entering a same-sex union into which their children were born. I was taken aback by the fervor, exactitude, and assuredness of this understanding of Laser's interchange with his donor. Having spent many clinical hours with children in birth-other families, and having written about the phenomenon of identity formation in adolescents who were conceived with the aid of an egg or sperm donor (Ehrensaft, 2005, 2007), their interpretation of father searching by a sperm donor son with two mothers did not match my observations and understandings of the same film clip that they were watching of Laser querying his sperm donor in the care. On the other hand, their commentary did match my perception of hard-core beliefs based on developmental theory of gender development that is clung to as bedrock, in this case that every boy longs for a father and will be suffering from a deficit and a challenge to his masculine development if missing one, beliefs that can have the effect of blinding people to alternative possibilities and to the empirical reality before them. Referring to the film clip, I invited people to imagine a different scenario: Laser looking for a mirror of himself, reflected in the person who holds half his genes, who shares the same gender identity, and was once a teen just like Laser. Laser already has two parents. Where is the evidence he is looking for another?

To quote from one of my earlier writings on the topic of birth other offspring and their search for identity:

> Adolescents, while fervently separating from their parents, are simultaneously using them as a mirror as they investigate all the components that have gone into the mix to make them the individuals they are. It is an exercise not just of the mind but also of the body. Typically, infancy is the locus of the concept of the parent serving as mirror in order to reflect back to the baby a sense of well-being and aliveness. We often forget that the mirror surfaces again in adolescence as youth investigate their changing bodies and develop more sophisticated understandings of the genetic contributions to personality. When a parent of an adolescent cannot provide a "genetic" mirror because that parent has no biological link to the child, the son or daughter will have to look elsewhere for the reflections. The quest to establish one's adult-bodied self, in conjunction with changing cognitive capacities that foster greater interest in psychological meaning and motivation, may lead the adolescent to either search out his or her actual donor or surrogate or grow curious about the path the birth other took to decide to become that child's donor or surrogate.
>
> (Ehrensaft, 2007, p. 135)

As I watched Laser querying his sperm donor, that is precisely what I saw, corroborated by many observations of the same phenomenon in my clinical work with birth other offspring and their families. Further, if we take this concept of birth other as genetic mirror for the youth, the gender of the birth other may be relevant, but not essential. If Laser was an egg donor baby, he might easily ask the same questions of an egg donor about the genetic commonalities between the two, and that egg donor may or may not live in the world as a woman, as we saw in the story of the two lesbian parents, now a mother and father, conceiving their baby with the help of another man's eggs. If we stay encrusted in the traditional model of mother, father, child, and see anything other than that as a deficit for the child, we will do a disservice to all the parents who are expanding the boundaries of parenthood to include parent–parent combinations of all genders and all sexualities, using ART where needed to make those possibilities reality. We will both pathologize and fail to recognize the creativity and expansiveness in the children's exploration of both their own identities and all the members of their family complex, regardless of gender.

Simultaneously, by holding to the original psychoanalytic paradigm as the cornerstone of family normality, we instill in parents of birth other children a fear that the children's search for either the whereabouts or personalities of the people who helped conceive them is a repudiation of their own status as parents and as people who can provide the children what they need in life. This will be particularly true in families where there is "too much" gender – too many mothers, too many fathers – or in families where this is a missing gender – no father, no mother. To fully develop a post-modern model of gender and sexual multiplicities, that model requires expanding to include parenthood, with the following understanding: with the advent of ART, the multiple possibilities of both gender and sexual identities repatterns parenthood to create ever-expanding possibilities of family formation, including the possibility of men bearing children, women impregnating their partners, children being conceived within loving same-sex partnerships but not as a product of sexual intercourse, chromosomes and gametes commingling in multiple configurations to create new family complexes consisting of all the people who intended to have the baby and all the people who participated in either conceiving or gestating the baby, regardless of status as parent or as birth other.

In these family complexes, there is not a question of missing pieces (the child without a father, the child without a mother), but of multiple pieces of varying genders, and to highlight the limitations of the traditional paradigm of mother–father–baby as the baby-now-has-enough model, let me demonstrate with a story, another account of two mothers, a baby, and a gender transition in a parent. Pat and Mindy were a lesbian couple. They had a baby together, using an anonymous sperm donor and Mindy's egg and womb. Sophia was born and, 3 years later, Mindy was pregnant again, using the same sperm donor. Sophia was attending a preschool where every other child had both a mother and father. At the same time that Mindy became pregnant with their second child, Pat, having come to the realization that she was transgender, began cross-sex hormone treatment. As Pat began to get facial hair and a deeper voice, both parents decided it was time to explain to Sophia that Pat would soon be her daddy rather than her mommy. Mindy was somewhat apprehensive about both the turn of events (as a lesbian, she had chosen a woman as her romantic partner, and she was not sure about being in such a relationship with a man) and the effects on their daughter of Pat's transformation from mother to father. In contrast, Pat, exuberant to finally be evolving into the gender that felt authentic, experienced it otherwise, articulating that Sophia would be happy to finally have a "normal" family, with a mommy and a daddy, like all the other children in her preschool. With Pat taking the lead, Mindy and Pat explained to Sophia that soon she would have a daddy like all her classmates, because Pat was taking some medicine to help her become the man Pat had discovered Pat was. Sophia listened intently and then burst into tears, crying, "But I don't want a daddy, I want my two mommies!" Pat, either governed by her own internalization of mother–father–child being the "right" way to have a family, or caught in her own anxieties about how accepting her daughter would be of her gender transformation, became captured in the illusional belief that Pat, in the gender transformation and role or at least labeling shift from Mommy to Daddy, would be providing their daughter with the father Sophie longed for. Yet Sophia felt quite differently, and perhaps Mindy had astutely anticipated Sophie's negative reactions in her own apprehensions. In contrast to the myth of the perfect mother–father–child configuration, Sophia, like so many children in the families they are growing in, wanted what she had, not what was supposed to be right or what she was missing, and the only missing piece for her would be the loss of one of her two mothers, who was to become her father.

The children become our strongest teachers as they teach us that it is not gender constellations that shape their attachments and identifications in the family, but rather their established intimacy with the people they grow to love and depend on. We are bound by two-gender hegemonic thinking about parenting and family when we reflexively perceive deficit for children if one or the other gender is missing in their parent constellation, and fail to see what is right in field of vision: that children may very well want what they have, or not want to lose what they know, rather than want what we or others assume they are missing when there is no father, but two mothers, and so forth. Returning to the members of the psychoanalytic study group, by reflexively perceiving deficit – as when Laser has no father, just a sperm donor, or gender repudiation (or even hatred) – attributed to two women because they prefer to sleep with women, we bear witness to the projection of one's own anxieties about these new ways of making babies, angst stemming from both homophobia and what I have come to label "reproductive technophobia." If we just stay with lesbian families for a moment, we can turn to Susan Golombok and her colleagues' research on the developmental outcomes for children from birth other families to substantiate that, indeed, the kids are alright. Their research has demonstrated that the children in these families, all of them having used a sperm donor to conceive their child, show healthy development in attachment, relational capacities, social behaviors, identity, and cognitive abilities (Golombok et al., 1999, 2001; Golombok & MacCallum, 2003). So, at a macro-level, the lack of a father figure appears to be doing them no harm. In answer, then, to the second question,

"Is there a missing piece?" the answer is: not for the children, not for the parents; only for those who have yet to stretch their horizons to the expansiveness of twenty-first-century parenting beyond the gender binary dyad.

Question #3: What if a father has a vagina, or a mother has a penis?

We have not only sexed the body in our psychoanalytic discourses; we have also gendered the parenting by tying it to the sexing of the body: mothers have a vagina, breasts, and a uterus, and were born with an F on their birth certificate. Fathers have a penis, testicles, and hair on their faces and chests, and were born with an M on their birth certificate. These so-called facts are the prerequisite for the offspring's journey down the road in which children identify with their same-sex parent, disidentify with their opposite-sex parent, and internalize over time that penis = boy and vagina = girl, expanded to penis = boy = father, vagina = girl = mother, with all the implications for personality formation, gender and sexual identity, eros and desire, object choice, and future parenting roles. The transposition of gender among transgender parents and the removal of opposite-sex sexual pairings from the act of conception highlights the limitations and cultural biases in these equations while simultaneously signifying the quintessence of the liminal here – the removal of binary opposites and the phenomenon of in between, neither one nor the other – in the creation of family and the outlining of gender. It is not just that fathers can have a vagina and mothers can have a penis, and two women or two men through their own desire can partner to make a baby, albeit with sex in the lab rather than in their bedroom; it is that the entire enterprise of making and raising babies becomes a terrain in which expanded opportunities for sex, love, gender, and kin move beyond futuristic fantasy to the realities of the ART/transgender/gay/lesbian parents and their children who enter our offices for understanding and support, or who simply live their lives in the communities in which they locate themselves.

In *Assuming a Body* (2010), Gayle Salamon offers a compelling exposition of the body as more akin to a verb than a noun, exemplified by the gendering of the body among transgender people. One area that was not addressed in her discourse, however, was when reproduction and parenting are part of those actions. What happens when the person with XY chromosomes authenticates himself as a woman with a penis who desires to be a mother, and with the aid of ART becomes one, using her stored sperm to conceive her child? Who is she to her child? What, in turn, is transmitted to her child in their parent–child relationship that affects that child's understanding of sex, gender, love, parenthood, and the self? Ken Corbett cautions us about the foreclosures if we remain wedded to our outmoded equations:

> The heterosexual singularity that is instantiated in most discussions of parental union and family formation serves to foreclose our understanding of a child's capacity to form and flourish within multiple circulating narratives.
>
> (Corbett, 2009a, p. 75)

If we also accept gender and, more generally, human development as a lifelong unfolding, never fixed at any moment in time, I would extend Corbett's foreclosure not just to the child's capacities but also to the adult's: both child and parent will co-construct not only multiple circulating narratives but also fluid and multiple sensibilities of gender and of parenting positions when we transcend heterosexual gender-binary hegemony in family building.

Recently, I served as an expert witness in a custody battle between two divorced parents over the gender position of their child. The mother listened to her child, who told her he was a girl and that everyone was getting it wrong; she supported the child in an affirmed identity as a girl. The father perceived this support as the mother's perverse agenda to get herself a daughter and accused the mother of child coercion and abuse, suggesting that the mother might be suffering from Munchausen's by proxy. The custody evaluator, living in a conservative state, having no training as a gender specialist, and biased by his own genderist sensibilities, queried the child, rather aggressively, while observing at the child's father's home: "How can you be a girl? You have a penis." The child ran out of the room and escaped to the swings in the yard. In another family that I have worked with, a young transgender child responded to a playmate who asked, "If you're a boy, where's your penis?": "Oh, for heaven's sake, haven't you ever heard of a boy with a vagina?" In yet a third account, a colleague of mine transitioned from male to female when her two children were adolescents. She and her wife separated, but remained close friends. Because she had always been the children's father, she remained their father, even after legally changing both her gender markers and her name and going through several surgical procedures to align her body with her female gender identity. As a post-divorce family, she, her ex-partner, and their two children all attended a wedding together in another city and all sat at the same table. Someone at the table asked the children, now young adults, where their father was. They pointed across the table to my colleague, a strikingly beautiful woman dressed to the nines. The guests at the table looked totally confused, and persevered – "No, not your father's partner. Where's your *father*?" The daughter pointed again, and finally in frustration, she stood up and, like the little boy with a vagina, in irritation, responded, still pointing: "Right there. *She's* my father."

Going back to the story of the little girl with two mothers who was now going to have a mother and a father, children not only want and accept what they have; they can assimilate in their consciousness not the improbability but the fact that their father is now a woman, no longer with a penis but with a constructed vagina, but still their father. The small child who is in the throes of his own gender discovery does the same – for him what defines his gender identity as male is not what he has, but who he is, with gender formed not by what is between his legs but what is between his ears, by the interweaving of nature, nurture, and culture that allows him to shape his own "gender web"[3] and to communicate to others the standing reality of boys with a vagina, girls with a penis. That child will have no problem accepting that a daddy can have a vagina or a mommy can have a penis, because that is the very projection that child might make of his own future life as a person having a family of his own. There may, of course, be some developmental and cognitive confusions along the way, as when a 7-year-old transgender girl asked her parents with excitement and glee when her uterus would grow so she could have a baby of her own. Yet, absent distress or anxiety, those very confusions reflect the plasticity and creativity of the young child's gender dreams, rather than the child's gender disturbance or dysphoria. In fact, it is often we who become gender-dysphoric when asked to push ourselves beyond the bedrock of binary male–female based on chromosomes and genitalia, while the children skip along with their greater gender freedom. So the father with the vagina, or the mother with the penis, or the woman who is a father transmit to the next generation and to those around them that sex, gender, reproduction, and parenting come in a multitude of narratives, and the transgender child does the same in the declaration: "I craft my body to fit my psyche to become the gender I know myself to be, which might be a girl with a penis or a boy with a vagina, and I then locate myself in my dreams of a future parenthood as that self I know myself to be."

Transgender parenting is not a lab experiment in gender diversity and its transcendent possibilities for gender, motherhood, and fatherhood. It is simply people living their lives, wanting to become parents just like anyone else, or becoming parents first and then later discovering in their ongoing development that the gender they thought themselves to be turns out not to be a good fit. With an evolving social discourse on gender diversity, or even infinity that comes with the sea change in gender sensibilities in Western culture over the past decade, these people have the opportunity not just to do "scrambled-egg" parenting, but to experience for themselves and demonstrate to us a transcendent and generative panoply of multiple circulating narratives of procreation and family formation.

Question #4: What are the effects when a baby is made from science, with the aid of birth others?

The parents under consideration here are gay, lesbian, and transgender individuals who partner with someone to have a baby together, using ART, which means the participation of a birth other or birth others, to bring that baby into the world. So we are running the numbers here – numbers of individuals participating in a child's conception or gestation, number of genders of the parents.

Sigmund Freud developed the construct of the Oedipus complex: the fantasy of incest with the opposite-sex parent combined with envy and rage toward the same-sex parent. Melanie Klein wrote of the precursor to the Oedipal stage, the combined parental figure, which is the baby's fantasy that the parents, or more precisely, their sexual organs, are locked together in permanent intercourse. Anna Freud warned that the lack of a father could lead to dangerous Oedipal victory for a young boy: "Where the father is absent owing to divorce, desertion, death, there is the lack of a restraining oedipal rival, a circumstance which intensifies anxiety and guilt in the phallic phase and promotes unmanliness" (A. Freud, 1965, p. 210). In our twenty-first-century families, there may not be parents of opposite genders. There may be parents of opposite genders, but they may be lacking the sexual apparatus to make a baby through a sexual union with each other. The mother may be a man and the father may be a woman. The father may be growing a big tummy in which baby is growing. There will be no sexual intercourse as the "cause" of the baby. There will be more than two people involved in the baby's conception, so no more Oedipal triangles based on mother–father in sexual union and the baby having to figure out how to fit itself along the triangle. Instead, the Oedipal triangle becomes stretched to a circle, along which are arranged the baby with all the people who went into the creation of the baby and all the people who raise the baby, which could conceivably consist of all women, all men, or a multiple combination thereof.

Given recent controversy about Oedipal as a Western social construct vs. Oedipal as a universal phenomenon, for the purposes of our discussion I would like to temporarily place Oedipus at the side of the road and simply speak of the *family* circle, morphed from the traditional triangle of mother–father–child. Within this family circle, members will definitely discover triangles, and, along with triangles, squares, pentagons, even hexagons in all the combinations of relational matrices between baby, parents, and birth others within that relational circle, and the sum of the embedded relational shapes will depend on the number of participants along the circle and the child's knowledge of their existence (some children are not told of the existence of one or another birth other in their life). For those who have held to the premise that the human species is phylogenetically wired to think of procreation and family life in terms of mother, father, and child, my own clinical observations inform me that we now have a whole cohort of children conceived with the help of birth others who have had that phylogenetic wiring tweaked as a result of the nature of their own conceptions and family complexes. The challenge for each of those children, along with their parents, is to find a psychic space within themselves for each of the participants in the process.

We have already documented that the theories built on the assumption of mother, father, sexual intercourse, and child have been rendered obsolete, or at least incomplete, by the advent of both reproductive and gender-affirming medical technologies. This realization is not simply an academic exercise. Bringing in the concept of the family circle to replace the Oedipal triangle holds clinical urgency, for without adjusting the theories to fit the new circles and to support same-sex couples and transgender parents building their families with the aid of a birth other, the tendency to jump to conclusions about the losses to the boy without a father or the confusion for a child with two mothers or the insistence that every mother has a vagina and every father has a penis pays no heed to the evidence before us. Such assessments also mirror back to the children a distorted image of the ways they are not alright because they fail to conform to the norms of the cisgender male–female–baby triangle – they are circle kids. So, for example, like the members of the study group responding to Laser in *The Kids Are Alright,* if we insist that all children need a father and search for one either in reality or fantasy if missing one, especially if they are flooded with too many mothers, we deny the realities of the very children in front of us who are being raised in lesbian families and render their parents, who have creatively expanded the boundaries of gender and family building, as less than good enough in providing for their children and building a robust life for themselves as parents. If we privilege a male sperm donor over two involved mothers as the critical piece in a teen boy's masculine development, we not only disparage the family the boy has; we dictate to that boy the form his gender development must take – boys turn to men, girls turn to women to both assimilate and accommodate to the binary mores for male and female socially constructed in our culture.

So now I would like to bring Oedipus back from the roadside, specifically to get a picture of the changes that occur when a baby can have parents of a myriad of genders and also more than two people involved in creating that baby. The traditional theory of Oedipal triangles has undergone many renditions. In its original account, the child comes upon the shock that there is not just a mother–child dyad, but a father who has an independent relationship with the mother. Disillusioned, the child discovers the Oedipal triangle, in which he or she must negotiate the exclusion from the marital couple's sexual union and the love–hate affair with each of the parents. Developmentally, the discovery of this triangle is crucial for mental development, eventually leading the child to a sexual and gender identity and acceptance of reality.

In contemporary theories, numbers have replaced sex as the crux of Oedipal development (Britton et al., 2007). In these theories, the child's discovery of the Oedipal triangle is a prototype for *all* human relationships: two can be together; a third looks on. The two are seen by the third person. The child is now ready to take the position of the third person. This is crucial for the child's discovery of the world: to be able to observe, to see without panic that things exist outside the child, new things about which the child did not know. The child learns to observe, to see reality, and not split between objective reality and subjective experience, but rather integrate both domains. As numbers have replaced sex, the centrality or even validity of the Oedipal drama to human development has been challenged. Whether central or not, I am proposing that birth other children experience something more complex than triangles as they incorporate all the members of their family circle while negotiating the tasks of individuation, reality testing, personality, and gender formation, and this becomes even more complicated when we factor in parents or birth others along the circle who do not conform to either the gender binary or the heterosexual coupling that continues to remain hegemonic in Western culture.

From my own observations, I have found that both numbers and sex go topsy-turvy for the children who live within family circles. Let us focus first on the numbers issue: the participation of the birth other in the process of making a baby. This could include up to three people – an egg donor, a sperm donor, and a gestational carrier. This alone – the triangle stretched to a circle – presents the child with a far more complicated developmental task than in the mother-father-have sex-make-baby family triangle: the child is definitely full-on negotiating the multiple circulating narratives to which Corbett refers, incorporating not just a third, but a fourth, a fifth, and maybe even a sixth into relational life. I am recalling the case of a young girl with two mothers conceived with one of her mother's eggs and the sperm of a gay friend of theirs, who became an active part of her life. In no way did she see him as her father, and yet in her relational life she perceived him as more than just a donor, given how active he was in her care. So he became her "duncle," which is how she referred to him well into her young adulthood. Other children in these new family circles do not know who their birth others are, or only meet them later in life, so new shapes embedded in the children's family circles will continue to emerge as the children learn more about the participants in their origins and arrive at more sophisticated understandings of their place in the family complex and the role of each of the players in the family drama – birth others, parents, and child.

Now let us weave in the second factor: multiple gender possibilities for their parents, who will be the romantic partners with whom the child is living. Again, I am going to reference something I wrote a while ago, in response to a paper by Marsha Levy-Warren (2008) on Oedipal configurations in adolescence:

> In reference to the Oedipal stage, which we must remind ourselves is a Western social construct and only questionably a universal human phenomenon, abiding by a fixed and linear formulation is a particularly damaging formulation in the twenty-first century as the gay, queer, transgender, and intersex communities provide vital testimonials to the fluidity of gender and the lifelong journey of integrating sexual orientation, sexual identity, sexual preference, and gender identity into a healthy adult experience.
>
> (Ehrensaft, 2008, p. 361)

Let us bring that adult experience to baby making and the new family circle. Not only does the availability of ART extend the triangle into a circle; when coupled with either two cisgender people in a lesbian or gay parenting couple or at least one person along the family circle calling on gender-affirmative medical interventions to claim his or her authentic gender identity, the convergence of the two simultaneously throws in disarray the binary boxes of gender that are supposed to position themselves at two of the points on the traditional three-point triangle – the mother and father who are in sexual union with each other. So, in the new family circle, not only are triangles morphed into circles; the binary boxes of gender are challenged and sexuality comes in all shapes and forms, and never as the concrete nexus of the child's creation through an act of sexual intercourse. If every child is supposed to have two parents of opposite genders in sexual union with each other to grow up whole, we have a new cohort of children who are growing up unwhole, yet with no evidence of any breakage.[4]

I would like to finish this discussion with a clinical example of a two-father family and a complicated family circle:

> Jason and Ken have two daughters, Felicia, age 4½, and Grace, age 4 months. The two girls were conceived with Jason's sperm and eggs from a donor known to the fathers, found through an agency. Each girl was carried

> by a different surrogate. When Felicia was born, Sarah, the donor, took an active interest in the baby. Both men were more than happy to accommodate her. When Jason and Ken decided to have a second child, they turned to Sarah a second time. By this time, Sarah was engaged to be married and her interest in hearing news about Felicia had notably dwindled. Her fiancé did not want Sarah to be an egg donor again, but Sarah went forward anyway, as the dads explained that she needed the money, and the dads were only too happy to go forward so they could assure a full genetic connection between their daughters (Jason was to be the genetic father again) and because they felt confident in Sarah as a donor. Both fathers were very firm in their desire to allow the girls access to Sarah over the course of their lives. But when Grace was born, they heard nothing from Sarah. Soon after, however, they received a letter from Sarah's fiancé, demanding that Ken and Jason's daughters make no contact with Sarah and that the fathers stay out of his and Sarah's family life. By his report, he and Sarah wanted no connection between the children they hoped to have and the two girls conceived with Sarah's eggs and Jason's sperm. The fathers expressed distress, not for themselves, but for their daughters. They sought out professional advice to sort out how to explain to their daughters the vagaries of their family circle with a donor who shunned interest, under the influence of her fiancé, and two surrogates who, according to the fathers, carried their daughters only for the money and then absented themselves. They felt a particular urgency because Felicia, right on the mark developmentally, had just come to them and asked, "Daddy, Papa, whose tummy did I come from?" It is this question from little Felicia that I want to zero in on.

At age 4, Felicia was not looking for a mother, just as Laser in his two-mother family had not been looking for a father when he met up with his donor. According to Dr. Anne Bernstein, in the preschool years, "Children assume that babies, like themselves and all those who people their world, have always existed. The problem is only to discover where the baby was before it came to live wherever it is now" (Bernstein, 1994, p. 51). It is a question of geography, not mother searching. In Felicia's case, the uterus she came from was attached to a woman, but it could also have been attached to a man. In her developmentally appropriate search for the place from which she came, which she learned could not be either of her fathers because they were two XY dads with no uterus, that place could conceivably have been within another man, a transmasculine surrogate who agreed to help the fathers out by carrying their child. In her case, it was located within a woman who had always identified as female, and what little Felicia wanted to know most about her surrogate was the whereabouts of her own earlier housing, not the whereabouts of her missing mother.

To take the sex out of reproduction is to paradoxically open up the expanded possibilities of gender for all of the members of the family circle – two women can have a baby, two men can have a baby. To keep one's sex while changing one's gender and then become a parent has the same outcome – a man can mother a child, not just emotionally, but physically; a woman can father a child in the literal sense, by offering her sperm so that a baby can be born. The children so created are exposed to ever-expanding possibilities that transcend binary mother–father parenting categories and allow children to explore gender in all its possibilities as they are the progeny of the gender shake-up in making babies. And so are those around them, as they look on.

Conclusion

To quote Virginia Goldner, "To experience gender as permanently unsettled, to deploy gender categories as consciously provisional, to know as fact that gender is socially constructed, and to live it as personally assembled: this is something new under the sun" (Goldner, 2011, p. 157). Children conceived with the aid of ART in families that can come in any combinations of XX and XY chromosomes or gender or sexual identities are definitely living under that new sun, along with their parents and with the birth others who helped them come into being. To make sure that we give them a chance to bask under that sun, rather than eclipsing that sun with outmoded theories of man-woman-sexual intercourse-baby, it behooves us to de-link sex from gender and sexual intercourse from reproduction in order to rework our theories of family and child development and acknowledge the rich multitude of possibilities of baby making and family building in a gender-fluid, ART world where triangles have morphed into circles, men can be mothers, women can be fathers, and birth others can enter the circle to help make babies from science, not sex.

Notes

1 Cisgender refers to those whose sex marker on their birth certificate matches the gender they identify with, or know themselves to be.

2 As referenced above, in the twenty-first-century birth story, in some lesbian families, the two mothers will share biological mothering by using one mother's eggs and the other mother's womb to create their child, referred to by Susan Vaughan as "scrambled eggs" (Vaughan, 2007).

3 I came upon the notion of the "gender web" (Ehrensaft, 2011a) as a three-dimensional replacement for the concept of a gender spectrum, giving us a three-dimensional image of a web containing three major categories of thread: nature, nurture, and culture, which are spun together in various formations to create a gender that is unique to each individual, like fingerprints, but which, unlike fingerprints, is not immutable and can change over the course of an individual's lifetime.

4 I am aware that this statement can apply equally to single-parent families, but since they are not the object of our investigation of the intersection between gender and reproductive medical technology in parenting couples, I have not referred to them in the text.

Chapter 8

The shadow side of ART

Babies and parents in the neonatal intensive care unit (NICU)

Zina Steinberg and Susan Kraemer

Introduction

Mothers and babies in the NICU. Fathers too.[1] So many catapulted there quite unexpectedly. Precipitously. Too early, too soon, not ready. A tenuous life, which for some has followed a tentative pregnancy. Parents who have lived on edge, learning early on about the congenital anomaly or genetic defect that would require their baby to be rushed out of reach to the NICU for immediate life-saving surgery, or for deliberation, further testing, or for complicated, perhaps tortured, decision making. Many have had "fingers crossed" all along, made wary by years of infertility or prior perinatal losses, hopes checked, the story of one's self already grievously disrupted. Some had already been counseled to terminate the pregnancy – "too risky," they are told, "you can always try to get pregnant again." Those pregnant with multiples were cautioned about the possibility, or likelihood, of early delivery. They may be among those who, after multiple cycles of in vitro fertilization (IVF), became pregnant with quadruplets and were faced with a decision about selective fetal reduction in order to improve the outcome. They may have spent weeks or even months on some form of bed rest, straining to protect their vulnerable pregnancy. First oneself, one's body, and now one's baby, all subject to surveillance, monitoring, and intense scrutiny. Each test, each scan deemed necessary, yet this invasive technology threatens to flatten one's sense of personhood, creating enormous unease, perhaps adding even to uncertainty and fear.

As psychologists consulting in a NICU at a major urban teaching hospital (Kraemer, 2006; Kraemer & Steinberg, 2006; Steinberg, 2006; Steinberg & Kraemer, 2010), we have had the privilege of working with and learning from these families. It is a highly acute environment gathering newborns from hours away that need the specialized expertise and technology this unit can offer. About 1,000 babies a year, with a range of diagnoses and gestational ages, are cared for here. There are babies who might weigh less than a pound, born at the limits of viability, and some, "feeders and growers," just needing a dose of medical care before they can go home to their families. There are babies with severe life-threatening congenital defects, some of which will be operable, others not. Some

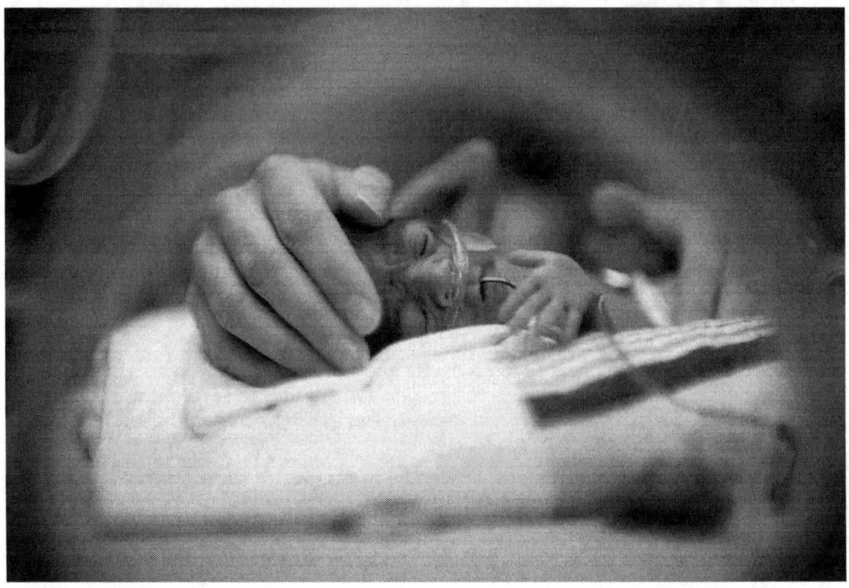

babies have congenital anomalies, some rare and others less so. Many have uncertain futures; families are stunned, often in traumatized shock. About 60 babies die per year, a fact that haunts the unit.

This chapter is written in multiple shifting voices, reflecting in part our co-authorship. We have worked together for 12 years, read the same literature, and continuously processed our many clinical encounters in the NICU. We have learned to speak a similar language, yet at times still retain our individual idiom. We want the reader to be immersed in that co-authorship. In addition, the shifting voices reflect, at times, a desire to create a mood, an affective context, if you will, while at other times a more academic review of the literature calls for a significantly different voice. Interspersed are vignettes that come from our clinical notes. Working psychodynamically in a critical care medical context can produce a constant shift of registers, often jarring for all. (See Mishler (1984) for a description of this.)

From ART to NICU: from life creating to life saving

A certain significant proportion of parents in this other world, what one might call the "underworld" of newborn care – neonatal intensive care – have conceived through assistive reproductive technology (ART). As sojourners in this world, we have learned a great deal about the complex, often ambiguous, and sometimes heartbreaking underbelly to the triumphal narratives (Frank, 1995; Conway,

2007) of infertility treatment. When a couple is going through ART, their primary question is necessarily: "Will we be able to conceive? Will we have the baby we so desperately desire?" In the NICU, the questions are shifted and we become aware of the steady drum roll from infertility to ART through to these births. Most centrally, we hear, "Will my baby live? Will my baby be normal?" And, heartbreakingly, "What did I do wrong? Is it my fault?" The answers to these questions are often frustratingly and wrenchingly ambiguous and uncertain. Most parents are not bludgeoned by a catastrophic or lethal diagnosis (forcing them into a "narrative of closed borders and tragic endings": Zoloth & Charon, 2002, p. 29), but many do face grave uncertainty about medical, neurodevelopmental, and cognitive outcomes. Typically, the answers to these will be revealed only over time, sometimes months, more often years. How does one live in a world of such murky ambiguity? We are surprised to learn that many of these same NICU parents who frantically and compulsively search the internet for answers about risks and outcomes likely for their newborn seem not to have pursued these same kinds of questions about the risks and outcomes with respect to ART. Was this knowledge available but sidelined? Camouflaged by economic considerations or buried by desperation and despair?

In the NICU, one crosses a threshold from life creating to life saving. The promise of the triumphal narrative moves from infertility to conception, to birth into life, albeit a life that may remain tenuous for some time. One is suspended still in the liminal space ascribed to infertility, straddling knowing and not knowing, certainty and ambiguity, afraid to call oneself a parent to this baby or claim this baby as truly one's own. Carson, writing about illness narratives, describes the profoundly unsettled states of mind created: "Liminal space is a place of ambiguity and anxiety, of no longer and not yet. To enter such a space is to slip one's moorings, and be carried by currents towards one knows not where, to be in limbo" (Carson, 2002, p. 180, in Charon & Montello, 2002). A limbo of no longer, not yet, and perhaps, *of never*. The omnipotent hopes offered by ART – the redemptive resolution to the "loss of control, ruptures to the self, disruption in the life story" (Conway, 2007, p. 9) suffered by these parents – are abruptly shattered. The unbearable uncertainties and daily fears are devastatingly real. With so much that is out of anyone's reach or control, even the reach of the most cutting-edge technology, many find themselves in a mindless fog. Our experience has shown us that such mindlessness is a function of complex psychic, interpersonal, cultural and institutional, systemic phenomena.[2] This dynamic web conspires to create conditions in which imagination is shuttered and reflection and thinking are strained, even foreclosed, by feelings of vulnerability, helplessness, shame, guilt, and anxiety.[3]

Disrupted reproduction

> I guess I'm just your typical macho oblivious guy. She got pregnant with our other kids, now 6 and 8, and at least for me, I never thought much about it, no worries. Her mom came to help and we were a family. And those

> kids are great. This time with the IVF and all . . . not so easy. Now I've passed through a secret wall – you know those walls that you touch and they magically open and another world appears. This is a "not real" but "so real" world and suddenly we are in it. I'm trying to be strong, but man, this is hard.

Disrupted reproduction, expectant hopes, and miscarried expectations. Couples who conceive following fertility treatment and land in the NICU may feel they are moving from one place of abjection (Kristeva, 1982; Tyler, 2009) to another: to a world apart, away from the smiling congratulations, flowers, and balloons that greet parents of full-term, healthy newborns. Mothers often meet their babies for the very first time in the NICU, pushed in wheelchairs with IVs dangling, draped in faded, unsightly hospital gowns, unready for the public space. Moving slowly along the corridor of the postpartum floor, up the elevators and through the heavy secured doors of the NICU; they may finally glimpse their baby through the plexiglas of the isolette (incubator), but often are not yet able to hold or even touch their infant. In the uncanny parallel worlds of ART and NICU, privacy is yielded, boundaries are confused, plans and dreams upended. Couples who have kept their infertility struggles and treatments a secret from friends and family may now seek to keep their baby's birth a secret as well. But, like so much that one might have hoped to hold close and secure, the center has not held. So much has ruptured, opened, tumbled out – babies, membranes, amniotic fluid, blood, a cervix, and yes, even a dangling tiny foot. The integrity of one's body has been compromised and then surrendered, as has one's sense of confidence and certainty as a procreative couple and as a fertile woman or man. The mother whose body has been poked and prodded, and the father whose sperm is counted and evaluated, now witness their baby subject to the same scrutiny. Parents are cheated of the sensual pleasures of getting to know their baby in a private space and in accordance with their own rhythms. The technology that supported the creation of life now sustains it; mother's milk may be pumped by machine and fed through a tube; the heated isolette maintains the premature newborn's body temperature. Breasts, arms, and laps waiting. The risk of alienation, of feeling like an imposter mother/father with an unrecognizable imposter baby hovers. The arms that ache to hold the baby, to feel skin against skin, may hang helplessly: sometimes restrained by the baby's fragility, sometimes halted by shame, ambivalence, and fear. The experience of oneself as mother or father – to this baby – can feel perilous, at risk of easy rupture.

It is remarkable really that the majority of parents are able to grow a relationship with their baby under the conditions of this "not real" world. Tenuous reproduction, followed by tenuous birth, may lead to fractured parenting, and intervention and support are critical. As will be discussed further in this chapter, mothers in the NICU (and fathers too) are at high risk for postpartum depression, and a high percentage meet the criteria for acute stress disorder and then for posttraumatic stress (Shaw et al., 2009, 2013). Leckman et al. (2007) found that mothers of full-term, healthy infants spend 14 hours a day preoccupied with their babies, immersed in their care and highly vigilant to their needs. This special mental state, which Winnicott (1956) called primary maternal preoccupation, while referred to as "almost an illness," reflects the intensity of the mother's vigilance, the extent to which thoughts and feelings about her baby and his needs fill her mind and shape her reveries. And fathers too are preoccupied, though, as the research suggests, not as insistently (Leckman et al., 2007). At 2 weeks postpartum they spent 7 hours per day in thought about their infant. But in the NICU, staying open to thought and feeling involves risk; the balance between what is bearable and what is not shifts constantly and unexpectedly. The father in the vignette quoted above had the well-being to even feel "oblivious" as his two older children were born. But this ability to take life as it is, to feel confident about one's luck or one's god is impossible in the world of the NICU. And existing through this ordeal and thinking through this experience can feel sharply at odds from one another in this "not real" and "so real" setting.

In the shadow of the rainbow: meeting Ms. Y

What follows is an account taken from notes made about an initial meeting with Ms. Y, whose baby Z was born at 26 weeks, weighing less than 2 lb (0.9 kg). On the day I meet Ms. Y, baby Z is 17 days old.

> In our weekly psychosocial rounds today, I learned this was an IVF pregnancy, that Ms. Y had several prior losses, that her baby was tiny and had an infection. I made a mental note to seek Ms. Y out.
>
> As I approached her baby's bedside, I felt a familiar hesitation about going over to her, moving into her space, sensitive to the possibility of intrusion. Many parents are initially reticent, cautious. Some uninterested, others suspicious. Am I yet another person coming to deliver bad news, or even, non news? Oh, you're the psychologist. Yes.
>
> She gets up heavily from her chair, holding her belly; she is a large woman, and still carrying a great deal of pregnancy weight. I learn she has a wound vac [vacuum]; the incision from her c-section has reopened; this will help, but there is pain still. Sit, I say. No, I need to check on Z anyway. It is so nice to meet you, and your baby. She's beautiful. Ms. Y smiles broadly, her dark eyes luminous, but her beautiful face is creased with anxiety. We look at her daughter together, exclaiming over her perfectly formed but exquisitely tiny body, speculating what she may look like if we could really see her face, if her features weren't so scrunched by all the paraphernalia supporting her in her too-early arrival. "She's my rainbow baby," she tells me. "The storm has passed. But I don't really believe it, I'm so frightened."

As I ask her about this, inviting her to tell me the story of her pregnancy and her baby's early birth, the words tumble out. The story is a bit jumbled, and I realize I am hearing two stories: the story of this pregnancy and this early birth, and the story of a twin pregnancy that ended in stillbirths at 25 weeks, 10 months ago. Last year at 21 weeks, a cervical cerclage [a stitch to try to keep the cervix closed], 4 weeks of bed rest and then, the babies were suddenly still.

> Can you see why I desperately wished that this pregnancy could be monitored 24/7 from the beginning? My cervix started to shorten at 19 weeks this time. When my membranes ruptured prematurely I came here and they put me on the most high-risk floor where they monitor you all the time. After things calmed down a bit, they wanted to move me to the floor where they don't keep you on the monitor the whole time. I pleaded with them not to. It was like they were going to just drop me, I was a nervous wreck. I guess I am still. You just never know what might happen.

Of course, I say to her, so much has already happened; you can't help but brace for the worst. You're holding your breath; it is so hard to escape your worries about what has happened before.

> I wish you would explain that to my mother! She doesn't understand; she doesn't get that I don't want to tell anyone yet that Z has been born. I can't help it, but I keep thinking about J and K [the stillborn babies] all the time. My mother says it is making me worry too much, to try to put it out of my mind. That maybe it won't be good for me, or maybe even for Z. Maybe that's why I am having so much trouble getting much breast milk. You should see what the other mothers are getting; with my large boobs, I certainly never expected that on top of everything else!

Smiling with her, appreciating her humor, and her envy, I nodded: you didn't count on any of this even though in some ways you have been so worried for a long time. And I thought to myself: perhaps if she could feel her mother worrying with her, or for her – "monitoring" her states of mind – perhaps she could feel a little more steady, a little less alone.

I had noticed the name and date and tiny footprints tattooed on her forearm and asked her if she would tell me about this. She tells me her husband has the same tattoo: his memorializing baby K, and hers for baby J. "They induced me; it was the hardest thing ever, but I guess I did give birth to them." Yes, I said to her, they were born, some like to say "born still" (Crawford, 2008). Her eyes welled up then, and she smiled tremulously.

"Yes, yes; thank you for saying it that way." (She pulled out some skin lotion then, telling me of her ritual creaming of her skin in order to make it "soft and slippery." I noticed the tenderness with which she lotioned the tattooed area, how her fingers lingered there as she spoke.) "You know, Z's due date was 8 days before the twins died, but then she [Z] came 14 weeks early. It can get all jumbled up." I asked her then if she had been able yet to hold Z. Has the baby been stable enough? Did Ms. Y know about skin-to-skin care, where she could hold her baby unclothed against her naked chest? Her eyes grew wide; she shakes her head, suddenly silenced. It has been 17 days. I turned to the nurse sitting near by and ask her when she thinks this might be possible, even to just hold the baby in her arms (which requires less time out of the isolette, less intense monitoring by the nurse). Surprisingly casually, the nurse replied, "we can do it today!" In the minutes in which the nurse finished up taking care of the baby in the next isolette, Z's respiratory status became a bit unstable and it wasn't clear if today was going to be the day after all.

I needed to move on then, but, as I did, I thought about the ongoing challenge of making room for the soft touch of skin-to-skin holding within the hard technology of intensive care. I pictured Ms. Y's lotioning her skin, softening and readying her body in anticipation. I imagined the arm with J's tiny footprints encircling Z tenderly. I wondered why it seemed to take my asking about skin-to-skin care to open the mind of this young, warm, and competent nurse to this possibility. I wondered if she had noticed Ms. Y's tattoos, or her lotion, and if she had thought about her sitting and waiting, and waiting, to hold her living baby for the very first time.

And a further note:

After consultation with my colleagues, and after continuing to hear more from nurses about Ms. Y's ongoing anxiety (even as the baby stabilized and moved towards going home), I became more curious about her comments about her "slippery skin." Was she also cueing me to think about her anxiety about being able to hold her baby safely, to keep her from sliding off, about her fears about helping her baby latch on, to enable her baby not only to survive but to thrive? How best to help her feel that despite the infertility, despite the earlier stillbirths, she could hold this baby in life?

Shadow knowledge

Mrs. R, dazed and confused, sits in the NICU weekly parent group.

> It was the best and worst day of my life. After five rounds of infertility drugs and treatments, miscarriages – early and late – dashed hopes and dark moods, I had my babies, twins. But they were born at 26 weeks and now my son has a cerebral bleed and his head is growing dangerously

> large. They tell me that they need to put it in a shunt. I no longer know what to feel, except terrified. Nurses call me "mommy," but am I? I was a woman who longed to be a mommy, but I never expected this.

The parents in the group nod in solidarity. Like her, many of them have been on the express train of treatments propelled by the powerful hope of having a biological child.

NICUs have been described as "the triumph of modern medicine's investment in technology" (Parikh, 2012). More than 500,000 premature babies are born in the United States each year (Ibid.). The most vulnerable, the micro-preemies, are born between 23 and 26 weeks, with the tiniest of these weighing approximately 1 lb (0.45 kg). Their skin is paper-thin, almost translucent, with their filament-thin veins threaded with IV lines. Their breathing is supported mechanically, their faces masked by breathing tubes and tape, and their tiny chests heave with each ventilated or pressure-supported breath. In a fragile balance, the same oxygen needed to aid their lungs may cause blindness. For many it will be a long time before their immature guts can tolerate even a few drops of preciously pumped breast milk, and they are fed instead with a nutritional formula called TPN (total parenteral nutrition). Even once they can tolerate breast milk (or formula), it will be weeks before they can coordinate sucking, swallowing, and breathing, so the milk will snake through a tube that goes through their nose or mouth down into their stomach. These babies can't yet regulate their body temperature, and their neurological systems too are drastically immature, making many sensory experiences over-stimulating; parents need to be cautioned how to provide "good touch" for their babies. Brain bleeds, never good, and sometimes severe, can cause lasting damage, though most often the effects are not known till the families are home. All neurodevelopment hangs in the air. Skeletal, alien-looking, injured flayed bird, are just some of the images evoked by first glimpses of these tiny babies.

As we navigate the NICU, meeting mothers, fathers, siblings, and grandparents, we hit dark spots: places where the air grows heavy and voices dim. Bewilderment, confusion, a sense of unreality; it is what we have come to call the "blinkered" (Silverman, 2004) shadow side of ART. When a mother tearfully tells us that she understood that she was at increased risk of multiple births and that multiples would likely result in prematurity, she says,

> But I thought a preterm baby would just be smaller. I didn't think a preterm baby would be kept alive by all these tubes and wires, be so scrawny, not even look like a baby. I never connected prematurity and all these scary problems.

Only after consulting for a number of years in the NICU did we start to recognize the ways in which we were also subject to startling disconnects. After hearing an NPR (National Public Radio in the United States) interview with Liza Mundy about her book, *Everything Conceivable* (2007), we began to feverishly research the possible shadow side of ART. We sought out a maternal–fetal medicine specialist and, as we inquired about this, she looked anxiously over at her clinic administrator. "Well, perhaps," she said vaguely. "We don't exactly know. But some procedures, I suspect, might turn out to be especially questionable." We heard veteran nurses gathered over lunch wondering about the increase in rare congenital anomalies that these infants have. "What's goin' on here? We used to see maybe one or two of these kinds of syndromes in a year, now we get one a month!" In weekly psychosocial rounds we begin to pay closer attention to the number of pregnancies vs. the number of live births each woman experienced. These numbers are read quickly along with other medical information. Gravida 5, para*2-5 pregnancies, 2 live births; this shorthand notation of a woman's obstetric history leaves one scrambling to fill in the gaps, to line up the misaligned numbers.[4] Were there miscarriages, stillbirths, multiples, reductions, terminations? There are other numbers recited in code: for example, 4 vtops (four voluntary terminations of pregnancy). Under what circumstances? Why, or how to think about all of this? No attention is paid, no stopping to consider what this might mean for the mother, father, and their newborn now. This is but one of many gaps that flagged our attention. We began to focus on the casual way ART dropped into their quick summary; "this was IVF, this is a surviving twin, yes, mom is 46, after four failed IVF trials, these were donor eggs," etc. Our questions gained heft and urgency. We read further and found evidence for what Debora Spar calls the "fertility-industry complex" and learned that, among developed nations, the United States has one of the least-regulated fertility practices, what Spar calls the "wild west" (2006). While in the United States there are ever-increasingly stringent "guidelines" for clinical and ethical practice cautioning the transfer of fewer embryos, even strongly recommending single-embryo transfers for younger couples with a good prognosis, there are no legal ramifications if a clinician chooses to act differently. In 2011 the California medical board revoked the license of Octomom doctor, Michael Kamrava, noting that he had acted with "gross negligence" but he had not broken any laws: there are no laws to break.[5] In fact, there is incentive to cloud the issues.

Every clinic wants to headline high "success" rate and that usually means pregnancy – not live birth or healthy baby.

Medical researchers however have not ignored the pursuit of answers to questions about the associated risks of ART (see, e.g., Merritt et al., 2014.) Even a cursory examination of journal article titles demonstrates the range of concerns. "In search of safer IVF" (Kovacs, 2012); "Hormonal effects in infants conceived by assisted reproductive technology" (Rojas-Marcos et al., 2005); "Risk of borderline and invasive ovarian tumours after ovarian stimulation for in vitro fertilization . . . " (Van Leeuwen et al., 2011); "Adverse perinatal events associated with ART" (Skora & Frankfurter, 2012); "Are there subtle genome wide epigenetic alternations in normal offspring conceived by assisted reproductive technologies?"

(Batcheller et al., 2011); "Assisted reproductive technologies linked to birth defects" (Hedwick, 2012); "Epidemic of multiple gestations and neonatal intensive care unit use: the cost of irresponsibility" (Janvier et al., 2011); "Reproductive technology and the rise of birth defects" (Davies et al., 2012); "Sperm injection procedures may increase birth defects"(Waknine, 2012); "Earliest of early term births at higher risk for mortality" (Henderson, 2013); "Adverse neonatal outcomes associated with early term birth" (Sengupta et al., 2013); "Injecting sperm more popular but does not improve outcomes: (Henderson, 2015).[6]

Generally, the studies conclude that more research is needed, with larger samples and longer-term follow-up. Compounding the difficulty in getting clarity is that protocols are constantly changing; modifications are being made, with each taking into account the recent scientific evidence and advances. Researchers are then in a position of playing catchup, often reporting data from several years prior. New techniques are being introduced just as health outcomes based on older studies are being reported. And in the United States there are no mandated central registries that compile longitudinal data on children and mothers.[7]

We need to know, and yet we make knowing partial. This "not knowing" (or "kinda knowing") is sometimes voluntary, but often it is the result of unconscious and/or dissociative processes. Information about ART and its attendant cautions have never been so public or so hypervisible, but still the responses remain deeply incoherent. Parents seem to avert their eyes or hold back their questions, focusing sharply on "just get me pregnant. Go for broke." The omnipotent promise of ART, so media-hyped and coupled with parents' deep desires to have their "own" biological child, overwhelms and overshadows, sometimes with deep consequences.

> I was given a large stack of papers to sign. You always get them at a doctor's office these days. You know, you don't really read them. I knew that some of these were important, like the form that said that there could be birth defects. But when I had surgery years ago, there was also something I signed about knowing risks. Did I really know? Could I even fully understand them? When I asked the doctor, he said, "we need to tell you these things, like the paper in the Tylenol bottle tells you the side effects, the risks. They are small." And we wanted a family. Now, I wonder. Is my baby's prematurity and heart defect somehow related to IVF? Will I ever know? And does it matter any more?

The impact of social media, including parent blogs, contributes and confuses as well. There are postings about miracle conceptions and miracle babies and postings of grief and heartbreak that make one look back, question, and wonder.

Multiples – risks to mothers and babies

The most conclusive evidence on the potential morbidities of ART is in the realm of multiple births. Many European countries recognize the serious risks to both mother and baby and legally restrict the number of embryos transferred per reproductive cycle. While there has been some movement to restrict the number of embryos transferred in the United States, there continues to be sharp reluctance to mandate regulation, and consequently the United States has a multiple birth rate that is almost twice that of Europe (European Society of Human Reproduction and Embryology, 2014). In the United States, 43.6% of ART infants are multiples, whereas only 3.4% are born multiples in the general population (Centers for Disease Control and Prevention, 2015; Lowry, 2015), And, while the infertile couple may be delighted to find themselves pregnant with twins or triplets – finally to have the family they hoped for – there are distinct risks in multiple births, risks we see actualized regularly in the NICU. Women are more likely to have pregnancy complications including high blood pressure, preeclampsia, postpartum hemorrhaging, and increased risk of miscarriage. Multiple births are at high risk for prematurity and prematurity is a strong risk factor for neonatal mortalities and morbidities such as intrauterine growth retardation, low birth weight, chronic lung disease, cerebral hemorrhages, retinopathy, infections, and even eating aversions. Lifelong chronic conditions such as hypertension are associated with preterm birth and low birth weight, leading, among other things, to enormous healthcare costs. The annual economic burden of preterm births has been estimated at $26 billion (Behrman & Butler, 2007). Preterm and low-birth-weight infants have the highest mortality rates, greatly contributing to the overall US infant mortality (Lau et al, 2013; Matthews & MacDorman, 2013). Also noteworthy is the fact that racial disparities compound the impact of prematurity. The preterm rate and infant mortality rate for black women in the United States significantly exceed that of white and Hispanic women (MacDorman, 2011).

Single embryo and the problem of cost

Countries such as Belgium and Sweden, with regulations requiring that only one embryo is transferred in initial ART cycles, have seen a marked decrease in multiple births. In 2003 Sweden adopted legislation making single-embryo transfer obligatory (Bergh, 2005). In just one year, single-embryo transfer increased from 25% to 71% of all IVF procedures in Sweden. While the frequency of successful pregnancy was unchanged, the rate of twin pregnancy decreased, from 23% to only 6% (Barrington & Janvier, 2013).

Economic considerations are among the reasons that seem to be at play to account for what has been a different approach in the United States. The difference in cost for each additional child conceived with ART is vastly more in the United States vs. in Sweden or, indeed, anywhere in the world. Furthermore, in the United States, insurance coverage for ART is mostly spotty and/or inadequate, complicating for hopeful parents and doctors the weighing of risks and benefits of implanting multiple embryos (Kovacs, 2015).[8] (Ironically, some insurance companies require three to six cycles of intrauterine insemination (IUI) before paying for ART. IUI is often accompanied by Clomid in order to stimulate egg production.

As this increases the possibility of multiple eggs being fertilized, there is a greater likelihood of multiple pregnancies. In contrast, with ART, the number of embryos implanted can potentially be controlled.)

With costs so high and the age at which many couples or people first start trying to have a baby ever rising, and the desire to have pregnancy made more convenient with fewer life interruptions, the pressure is great to transfer more than one embryo. As one NICU mom, mother of twins born extremely premature and suffering severe neurological damage, said, "I was older and my husband traveled a lot. So we decided to 'go for the kill' and hopefully get our two children."

ART singletons – still some risk

Adding further complexity, studies now show that the outcome of singleton births achieved through IVF is poorer than that of singletons conceived naturally (Tepper et al, 2012; Declercq et al., 2015). These ART singletons are still at increased risk of adverse obstetric and perinatal outcomes, including elevated risks of birth defects, genetic, and epigenetic abnormalities (Bukulmez, 2009; Reefhuis et al., 2009; Marino et al., 2014). Evidence is pointing to the fact that infertility, not the technology, might be at cause. Current research has demonstrated an increased risk of birth defects among women with a history of infertility who conceive spontaneously, i.e., without the support of ART (Davies et al., 2012). Researchers are arguing that greater consideration must be paid to the fact that infertility is a disease that confers independent risk, and that adverse outcomes associated with IVF may be confounded by this inherent fact. Maybe we can use technology to make babies, but perhaps we can't get the infertility out of the equation; both male and female infertility continue to produce adverse complications (Davies et al., 2012).

"Instant family"?[9]

A mother of newborn triplets recounted her long, 5-year journey to this pregnancy:

> We tried to get pregnant for 5 years and our lives were tethered to protocols, shots, hormones, legs in stirrups. Some pregnancies ended in miscarriage, early and late. So then I become pregnant with twins and we couldn't have been happier. At an OB [obstetrics] appointment, the doctor says she hears three heart beats, that one embryo had split! My husband's heart stopped! In the following few weeks we have appointments with several doctors who implore us to do a reduction. They tell us about risks to me in trying to carry three; one doctor angrily tells me that the babies might be disabled like pictures on a March of Dimes poster. Can you believe that? And another doctor looks my husband

> and me in the eye and piercingly reminds us that we had entered his office pleading for just one healthy baby and that he could likely give us that. But if we kept the three embryos, he was far less certain. But how could we take this in our own hands after all that trying and losses?

We linger on these hopes and despair-infused infertility stories, feeling pricked by the insouciance of "going for the kill" and moved by the laser focus of wanting a biological child. With emotions raw and hormones disrupted, they continue to search – one more trial, this time a change of drugs; this will be better. Having fought so hard, their definition of success changes.

Some couples, filled with the memory of loss, make a clear choice to birth multiples while others seem not to consider the risks, consumed as they are by the powerful psychological press for an "instant family" (Baor & Blickstein, 2005). Still others perhaps choose not to hear. "Humpty Dumpty's buddy" is what Zoll (2013) calls herself in her memoir, *Cracked Open*. Fragmented states of self, cycling between hope and crashing despair, lead inevitably to dissociation, the adaptive process by which we disconnect from unbearable feelings and thoughts in an effort to cope with overwhelming stress. While emotionally protective in the short run, dissociation dismantles critical thinking processes. Said one parent, when you're feeling desperate, envious, you're not thinking, "well, I don't want to risk a multiple pregnancy," or think about the risk of reductions. You're just thinking: "I should be so lucky as to have the 'problem of multiples.'"

Parenting multiples: depression, stress, and interactional difficulties

The risks of parenting multiples extend beyond birth and probable prematurity with potential developmental delays and behavioral problems. A small but growing body of research finds that mothers of multiples, as compared with moms of singletons, have a 43% increased odds of having moderate to severe depressive symptoms 9 months postpartum (Klock, 2004; Choi et al., 2009). Multiples also bring an increase in child abuse (Bryan, 2003). In addition, when twins are first-born children and are conceived through ART as compared to those born spontaneously, mothers were found to experience higher levels of parenting stress and lower levels of psychological well-being (Baor et al., 2004). These mothers are more likely to talk about "tiredness," "stress and depression," and to even find themselves "questioning parenthood," whereas mothers of singletons in this study were more likely to express delight in parenthood. (Sheard et al., 2007). Researchers caution that couples pregnant with twins can be "unrealistically optimistic" and consequently unprepared for the emotional as well as practical realities of parenting multiples (Bryan, 2005). Again, compared with mothers who conceived spontaneously, IVF mothers of twins had more positive prenatal maternal expectations during pregnancy, but 6 months postpartum they had higher maternal stress and fewer coping skills (Baor and Soskolne, 2010). There are studies, as well, of preterm NICU families, a group that includes multiples, that find that a significant percentage of mothers and fathers meet the criteria for posttraumatic stress disorder and postpartum depression while in the NICU and then again, though fewer, postdischarge (Shaw et al., 2009, 2013; Lefkowitz et al., 2010). Anxiety, depression, and posttraumatic stress disorder can negatively impact parental behavior, leading to difficult parent–infant interactions affecting, as well, the baby's sleeping and eating patterns and longer-term cognitive and emotional development (Murray et al., 1996; Pierrehumbert et al., 2003).

Studies comparing mother–infant interaction with preterm singletons and twins find that mothers of twins touched, lifted, patted, and held their babies less often and talked to them less frequently than mothers of singletons. At 18 months the twins had less advanced cognitive development (Ostfeld et al., 2001). Parents of medically ill babies, now no longer in need of medical care, continue to anxiously perceive their children to be physically vulnerable, leading to overprotectiveness and a high utilization of healthcare. These "perceived to be vulnerable' children tend to have more behavior problems at 1 year and then again at school age (Allen et al., 2004; deOcampo et al., 2003).

Parental perceptions and attributions have also been studied in a body of work called "prematurity stereotypes." Stern et al. (2006) recruited two groups of infants when they were 6 months corrected age – infants born preterm and infants born full-term. She *randomly* labeled some infants preterm and some full-term, so that some actual preterm babies were called full-term and vice versa. Mothers, not knowing the "true" birth status, were told to interact with and describe one of the babies.

Even mothers of preterm babies viewed the preterm-labeled baby less positively than the full-term labeled baby, and the baby labeled preterm interacted with the mother less positively, illustrating the compounding influence these stereotypes can have on dyadic behavior. Psychoanalytic "infant watchers" such as Dan Stern and Beatrice Beebe have clearly shown bidirectional effects in the interactions of mothers and infants as young as 3 months (see, e.g., Beebe & Stern, 1977; Stern, 1977).

Multiples – risks to children's mental health

Multiples are also more likely to be small for their gestational age and this poses even greater risks to their mental health. In a study of triplets, the babies who were >15% smaller at birth had lower cognitive and executive function performance, decreased social engagement, and more internalizing symptoms than their siblings and peers at age 5 (Feldman & Eidelman, 2009).

Other studies highlight substantial and worrisome controversy linking prematurity, low birth weight, and multiples to attention deficit disorder and anxiety disorders, and they even posit an association risk between autism risk and IVF (Johnson et al., 2010; Vanderbilt & Gleeson, 2010; Pinto-Martin et al., 2011; Zachor & Bern Itzchak, 2011; Mahoney et al., 2013; Treyvaud et al., 2013; Sucksdorff et al., 2015).

In 2012 researchers looked at a data set of more than a million Swedes and found that there was an association between being born prematurely and an increased risk of a range of significant psychiatric disorders and that the younger the gestational age, the greater the vulnerability (Nosarti et al., 2012).

More research is needed, especially prospective large sample studies. Currently, Columbia University, funded by the National Institutes of Health, is creating a population-level database to ascertain the potential links between ART and autism and to identify the mechanisms of the association (Lowry, 2015).

Multiples and late preterm health risks

Though the effects of preterm birth and low birth weight are potentially most serious at the earliest and lowest ranges, research is now alerting us to the more subtle but significant problems that arise when babies are even "late preterm," defined as >34 and <37 weeks' gestation. Seventy-one per cent of all preterm births fall into this category and multiples are highly likely to be in this category. These babies, though they look and seem as normal as full-term babies, have been found to have a "constellation of problems that require as much skill and planning as any complex NICU patient" (Phillips, 2013). These babies have increased risks for potentially serious health problems, as the lungs and brain are the last systems to fully mature. Respiratory distress, sepsis, feeding difficulties, learning, developmental and behavioral challenges are just some of the known sequelae. Indeed, the morbidity rate approximately doubles for every week that a baby is below 38 weeks' gestational age and the infant mortality rate is three times higher than the rate among term infants (Loftin et al., 2010). These infants, if they are in the NICU at all, command relatively less attention from the staff as their acuity, compared to the other babies, is low. Called "feeders and growers," these babies do not require the same constant intervention or conversation with staff. If things are going well while the babies are in the NICU, staff will be generally reassuring on behalf of these babies' outcomes, particularly with respect to the immediate future. But many of these parents, especially those with prior losses and an infertility history, have difficulty with this reassurance and optimism. Their vigilance has been heightened by the trauma of the premature birth, exacerbated following infertility, and their anxiety is not so easily assuaged. They are addictively "googling" and their anxiety is often seen as "micro-managing" or "endlessly questioning" by the medical staff and perhaps also by their pediatricians when they are discharged. They may feel even "crazier" for being told that their feelings are out of proportion and sometimes even that their anxiety can "hurt" their baby. But so much has gone wrong, how can they not be on guard?

Knowing and not knowing

Accrued knowledge about the risks of birthing and parenting multiples has compelled many of the world's developed countries to impose regulations and has propelled the American Society for Reproductive Medicine to promulgate new and tougher guidelines that have begun to impact the rate of multiple births (Kulkami et al., 2013). Yet, in the United States, where parental desire mixed with economic concerns can influence treatment, 20% of women, even when informed about basic medical risks of a twin pregnancy to both baby and mother, rank a twin birth as the ART treatment outcome they most long for (Ryan et al., 2004).

Before the evidence that single-embryo transfers would successfully produce a viable pregnancy (especially for women under 35), multiple births were called an "iatrogenic multiple pregnancy," as treatment for one medical problem – infertility – yields another – multiples. Though the ever-increasing corpus of studies on ART outcomes often ends with an exhortation to better counsel couples on the risks, especially the more certain risks of multiple birth, what is known seems fragmentary and shadowy, seemingly illusory and hard to grasp and certainly, we learn, difficult to design counseling protocols around. Counseling often consists of pro forma meetings with social workers, lists of statistics too dense for most to penetrate, and sheaves of consent forms to sign that often do not include explanations of how little is understood about the long-term health consequences of particular ART drugs or procedures (Zoll, 2013, p. XVII; see also Janvier et al., 2012) or, as we are increasingly discovering, the brutal stony fact of infertility itself. In 2005, at a federal conference on fertility treatment outcomes, a perinatologist, Ronald Wapner, cautioned attendees that parents have no idea about most of the potential real-life complications that go with premature birth (Wapner in Mundy, 2007, p. 244). In large measure, counseling, as currently offered, can't begin to move the desperately hoping mind that focuses on anything that agrees with the outcome it most forcefully prays for.

Neonatal bioethicists remark that "even when well counseled and when there is clear understanding of the statistical chances of poor outcomes, there is often a form of magical thinking, that after such difficulty getting pregnant, the 'bad outcomes couldn't happen to us'" (Barrington & Janvier, 2013, p. 346).

Tali Sharot sheds light on these powerful phenomena. As director of the Affective Brain Lab at University College London, she researches how the experience of emotions affects human cognition and behavior, determining our expectation of the future, our everyday decisions, and our ability to learn. Healthy individuals are prone to believe that they will have more control over events than they do, her research highlights, and this can motivate them, certainly make them feel good, but it can also lead to suboptimal decisions. When most of us are presented with evidence that contradicts what we see as the likelihood of desired positive outcomes, we do not correct for this evidence. But when we are presented with confirming evidence, we readily accept that (Sharot et al., 2011). This "optimism bias," as she calls it, makes our lives more pleasant and increases exploratory behavior. Without it, mild to severe depression (mild depressions also correlating with a more realistic perception of the world) flourishes. To complicate things further, the "evidence" itself carries enormous ambiguity. As Janvier et al. (2012) explain, "Disability is a continuous, uncertain outcome" (p. 801). Parents want to know about the outcome for their baby ("either 0% or 100%"), but such questions, we also learn in the NICU, are often unanswerable as the risks are population-based and thus, for any individual baby, they are uncertain.

The limits of the physician's ability to make prognostic estimates in terms of long-term chronic health problems or neurological deficits (Lantos & Meadows, 2006) leaves some parents confused, frightened, frozen, and vulnerable. There is both the tension around what information can be taken in, what kind of knowledge is tolerable, and the tensions around the borders of what is known and what is not-yet-knowable. Throughout the course of the NICU stay, parents are challenged to make sense of the daily fluctuations in their baby's status – the moment-to-moment monitoring of organ systems and the attention to small but critical variations in numbers that are reported to them, let alone the times of crisis (e.g., blood or bowel infection) that require acute intervention, sometimes even surgery, or the unknowable future. Communication around all of these can be extraordinarily difficult, the information complex to process under heightened states of anxiety. This information is shared by a medical team that rotates constantly and by a parade of medical subspecialists who seem to drift in and out. At the extreme, parents cope with heightened hypervigilance or with avoidance. Those who back away need the most active support in connecting to and being with their baby, even strenuous encouragement to come to the NICU and to learn how to best care for their infant.

"Not knowing" and "shadow knowledge" are themselves built on shaky ground. Consider a recent study of college undergraduates in the United States that found that two-thirds of women and 81% of men believed female fertility did not decline until after age 40 and 64% of men and 53% of women overestimated the chances of couples conceiving following only one IVF cycle (Peterson et al., 2012). The discrepancy between what the students know and what is known about the science of reproduction is vast. It is not only young people in the United States; research in Sweden, Canada, and Israel replicates these findings (Lampic et al., 2006; Bretherick et al., 2010; Hashiloni-Dolev et al., 2011). These same students might find their way to the fertility clinic with shame and desperation that they had waited too long and with determination to make right what they had neglected. Without regulatory controls that more objectively consider the medical and emotional short- and long-term risks and therefore limit the number of embryos transferred, potentially traumatized couples are left in a dissociated state, unable to think critically, prey to their guilt, shame, and longings, finding themselves first on the "treatment train" of ART and then, if they have a preterm low-birth-weight baby, on an analogous very frightening treatment train in the NICU.

Really scared and waiting – once again: meeting Ms. F

Ms. F is breathing at the top of her chest. That, combined with a waif-like presence, creates an air of immense fragility. It takes a few days of short, quiet introductions before she tentatively tells her story, and I slowly see that she is terrified to breathe deeply; she needs to be on hyper-alert. "I don't know who I am, what time it is, certainly not the day of the week." A, her daughter, was born at 30 weeks but with two significant difficulties that complicate the more "straightforward" problem of being born 10 weeks too early. She suffered intrauterine growth restriction so her birth weight was much lower than a 30-week baby. "And no one knows why," she says. And, she continues, her 20-week ultrasound showed that A had a life-threatening defect that would demand surgery.

> The surgery is serious for any baby. It's 8 hours! They say that it is really risky for a preemie. They can't do it now; she has to weigh at least 3 lb and now she is less than 2 lb. We have to wait for her to gain weight. So we are waiting once again.

I ask about the other waiting.

> For the past 3 years I have been waiting and hoping. We started at one infertility clinic and I tried Clomid and IUI and had one tubal pregnancy. Then IVF and I got pregnant with triplets. We then had to make a decision to reduce one of the embryos – they said that that would be safer. That was hard to do, but we also wanted to do the best thing. Our families knew we were going to the infertility clinic, but they don't know about the reduction. We couldn't bear their possible disapproval. We were hopeful, but at 21 weeks they were born dead. We named one for my husband's dead father and one for my dead mother and we had a wake and a cremation. They were so real to me so the wake really helped me.
>
> I then went to a different infertility doctor with a different protocol and got pregnant again, with one embryo this time, as I didn't want to go through any multiple pregnancy again. My doctor said that my body couldn't hold multiples. Then the ultrasound showed the heart defect! The doctors tried to convince us to terminate the pregnancy, to start over and put this behind us. But how do we do that? I already lost 21-week twins. I didn't know that A would be premature at that point.
>
> I am now really, really scared. I can't get the image of A on a bypass machine out of my mind. I have read all about the surgery – all the steps. I want to know all the exact statistics on doing this surgery on a preemie, but I am also too afraid to ask.

> My husband won't talk about it at all. He says we have to just trust the doctors and pray. But the other day I came into the room and he was deep into googling about all the diagnoses and surgical procedures. Why won't he talk to me about it? I think that until he knows that A will come home and is healthy, he can't attach to her. I understand this, but it hurts me as well. And I'll have to go back to work soon because I have the better health insurance. Who will visit A? Who will watch over her? And he is freaked out about money. I guess I am too. We were going to use a good daycare center, but now we've been advised that that wouldn't be safe for her because of all the germs. You know how little kids are always sniffling. And I don't have my mother to help. I'm so alone. So we will need to get a full-time baby-sitter and, though I have decent health insurance, my job doesn't pay well. And neither does my husband's. But I can't think about all of this. I guess that's what he's thinking about.

Together we look at A in the isolette. She has lovely pink and brown polka-dotted bedding and an incredibly soft blanket covers the isolette. We notice that A is sleeping calmly, but mom says that the other day she turned blue in her arms and "now I'm scared to hold her. But what if she doesn't survive the surgery and I haven't held her tight?"

The *claustrum*

> About suffering they were never wrong
>
> The old masters; how well, they understood
>
> Its human position; how it takes place
>
> While someone else is eating or opening a window or just walking dully along.
>
> W.H. Auden, *Musée des Beaux Arts*

There are days the unit teems with focused, piercing energy. Medical teams in white coats rounding by each baby's isolette, reciting lab results, blood gases, oxygen requirements, plan for the day with detail and specificity. Organ systems monitored; maybe a mom sitting quietly in the chair will ask a question, more often not. Medical rounds, though open to families, are not really conducive to the questions of parents, the big-picture questions: "Will my baby be OK?" "When will he be discharged?" Unanswerable questions at this point. Parents are left on their own, ruminating, afraid to be hopeful, trapped in minds that are airless, echoing, and even claustrophobic. Sometimes, of course, the questions are too uncomfortable to be engaged. Down the corridor is a group of doctors in scrubs and masks, bright lights shining into the isolette. A procedure is being performed. Next to this is a baby getting an eye exam to monitor for potential blindness.

Eye exams are hard to watch and babies are very fussy and unstable for a time afterwards. Parents generally leave the bedside. Turn to the right and see the unit doors swing open and a medical transport team brings a new 25-week-old transferred from another hospital, trailed by the stunned and weary dad; mom is still an inpatient at the hospital where she gave birth. He will hurry from one hospital to another, unsure whom he should worry about more – his new tiny son, yet unnamed, whom he has not held or even touched, or his wife who was rushed into delivery when her blood pressure became dangerously high. The nurse moves into high gear, readying the spot for her new charge.

Efficiency, urgency, and calm braid together. Physical and occupational therapists move decisively through the unit, as do respiratory, feeding therapists, lactation consultants, and nutritionists. It is busy, but never chaotic. In corners are parents reaching into the isolette, holding their baby's fingers or texting friends or maybe napping. Sometimes a mom and dad are together, taking a picture of the first time their daughter is held or the first time real clothes are worn, even if they dwarf the tiny torso. How exciting it is to buy those preemie onesies! Will they really ever be too small?

Two isolettes over a young mom who has just given birth is wheeled into the NICU to see her baby for the first time. No smiles: thick tension and fear. She looks, averts her eyes, and tries to look again. Her husband had prepared her, so he thought. But really, how can you prepare a woman who just had an emergency c-section to meet her 2-lb baby? The nurse chirpily explains the monitors and all the lines hooked up to the baby. Tears puddle on mom's cheeks. She tells her husband to take her back to her room; she's tired. He wheels her past two nurses huddled around the computer looking at vacation condos to rent, soon joined by a social worker who shares birthday photos of her son. A mom and her two school-age children arrive and they take out their homework while mom cleans her hands and open the portholes of her baby's isolette, "Hi honey, mommy's here." Teenagers visit their friend, 16, now a mom to a preemie and next to that isolette is another preemie with a heart defect, his orthodox Jewish family praying fervently. And still another dad, muscular and well dressed, leans into his infant's porthole and reads the 91st Psalm off his smartphone. A bigger baby, soon to be getting a tracheostomy tube,[10] now 4 months old, is sitting in an infant seat with a cartoon DVD playing just inches from his face. No parent is around, but thankfully soon a volunteer "cuddler" arrives and starts to play with him.

Seventy babies are cared for by a large medical team. Two hundred nurses working in shifts, dozens of doctors at all levels of training and authority, and endless ancillary professionals keep time in the well-choreographed movement of the NICU. It is their professional home. These are their colleagues, their friends. Some nurses have worked there for more than 35 years, and move with great certitude; others are freshly out of school, eager but hesitant. The parents from all social classes – homeless to hedge funds – multiple ethnicities, religions, and ages – from teenage to 45-year-olds – all stunned and overwhelmed, enter this opaque environment not knowing the implicit rules, often not knowing what exactly has happened to them. They have met scores of medical caregivers and have heard complicated explanations of their baby's problems, but it will be a while before they get their bearings. For now, they are lost.

Sometimes the unit is surprisingly silent. Nurses may be at their computers or sitting and staring off. On these days, very few parents seem to be around. Some we understand live far away, have other children, need to be back at work. But too many stay away. Some are pacing themselves; some, victims of their traumatized states, struggle to avoid being retriggered. Those who have been through the trials of ART are especially vulnerable to such retraumatizations. Preoccupied by the loss of prior pregnancies or babies, perhaps even of the twin or triplet of this precarious newborn, are off at the cemetery, or just elsewhere in a perhaps deadened space in their minds (Tracey, 1991; Tracey et al., 1995), unable to bring their attention to the baby in the NICU. Tragically, some are so burdened by shame and guilt that they fear the toxicity of their touch, or even their presence. The babies are alone in their isolettes, tucked in nests formed by rolled receiving blankets, their life support system intermittently beeping. The older babies in cribs may be crying, a somewhat unexpected and painful sound in the quiet. (The tiniest babies' lungs can't yet produce a cry.)

The bright daylight that floods in through floor-to-ceiling windows contrasts with the heaviness that suffuses the unit, the heaviness of time, the eeriness of the quiet. For parents present on such a day, or even on a day when the unit swarms with activity, the density of such feelings burdens their experience. Feelings which parents describe as almost impossible to convey, so isolated do they feel within them. A mother reports:

> Today, groups of doctors came over, stand over me, "mommy," they say, and tell me how my baby is doing. There were so many of them, speaking quickly, and in their medical language, and I felt, I'm literally under water, these are just strange whooshing sounds, so very far away.

Other parents adapt by becoming proficient in the medical language, obscuring the complexity of their feelings, fearing that their emotional states will not be fully acknowledged. It is a long journey from ART and now into the NICU. In so many ways parents feel cut off from their babies, from others, and even from themselves. For so many, the stigma, the shame, the sense of feeling alien and alienated leave them silenced and, even when in the NICU, in hiding. One woman confided, "The only people now I talk to are my RESOLVE group. So many also had premature babies".[11]

Airless, breathless, ruminative. Shamed, guilty, and waiting. Always waiting. Braced for the worst, hoping for the best. Cut off from their friends and partners, parents, and siblings. "No one understands what you are going through except other NICU families," says a parent. Couples cycling through the many treatments of ART say similar things. For so many, the NICU can feel like a bell jar; a *claustrum* (see also Chapter 10, which describes ARTs as a *claustrum*). This evocative term, deriving from the Latin to describe a fence or the space it encloses, was also used by Chaucer as a synonym for womb and, linguistically, is related to cloister, the sequestered living space of a monastery (Willoughby, 2001). Psychoanalyst Donald Meltzer developed the idea of the *claustrum* to represent an inner psychic world that is dominated by claustrophobic fear: a stagnant closed system stripped of vital interchange (Meltzer, 1992). Willoughby, following Meltzer, conjures this space as the dark inverse (the "Gothic avatar"), the "shadow" of the reflecting, meaning-making mind of the mother-as-container (Bion, 1962a). How strange these multiple meanings that invoke a place of refuge and potential growth (cloister, womb), as well as a trapped space of dread and no-exit. How closely they capture aspects of both the physical surround and the internal experience of many NICU parents. One mom described herself as having the "neurological equivalent of a cardiac arrest. A brain arrest. I stopped thinking. The air in my lungs hung suspended" (LaScala, 2009, p. 193).

Threatened vitality – time, shame, and desiccation

The shadow side of ART is poignantly reflected in three themes that echo in this *claustrum*, this world apart, this NICU: the foreclosure of time, memory, and imagination, shame and abjection, and the medicalization and desiccation of parenting. Vitality is threatened.

There is a confused and mystifying relationship to time, memory, and imagination in the NICU, perhaps especially so for those who have endured long sieges of IVF treatments. Pregnancy after fertility is a complex experience; women describe feeling simultaneously "infertile" *and* "pregnant." In the NICU, mothers speak similarly: "I don't feel like a real mother; who are they calling Mom?" For others who conceive following ART, the experience does shift and the discourse of desperation recedes. Becoming pregnant finally heralds passage into a world where time is marked by incremental developmental events happening within one's body that one can anticipate without dread. Websites show pictures of fetal development at each step: Are you 13 weeks pregnant? This is what your baby looks like now! And once past the first trimester, anxiety dims, hope expands, and reveries grow.

This baby-to-be, now affectionately called "nugget," "bundle," or "peanut," not only grows in the mother's uterus; she grows in the parent's mind as well. Reveries and fantasies become more embroidered and elaborated from between 4 and 7 months of gestation. Mother, spurred by feeling the baby move, elaborates her reveries and fantasies, and these representations of the baby-to-be proliferate with increased texture and specificity (Ammaniti, 1991; Benoit et al., 1997).

What of the mother who gives birth prematurely? Infant researchers have found that between 7 and 9 months, the last trimester, there is an undoing of this specificity – the fantasies and representations become less clear, protecting perhaps the real baby from the overly specific fantasized baby-to-be. Brazelton (1993) comments that mothers are undoing their more positive representations to prevent disappointments and to keep their babies unburdened. While often positive and luscious, there are representations and fantasies that are not always so. Mothers might also fantasize about deformity and handicap, monsters and invaders. In these fantasies they imagine themselves not as the paradigmatic caring maternal presence, but as the mother with split-off hostile fears. These more frightening reveries (Bion, 1962a) also get undone in these last months. Premature babies are born as early as 23 weeks' gestation, barely into the sixth month of pregnancy. Imagine, then, giving birth at the height of these richly formed highly specific fantasies – both the idealized ones *and* the horrifying ones. This sick tiny infant may not only be a devastating shattering of a hope but an actualization of a nightmare (Brazelton & Cramer, 1991).

For those most at risk during their pregnancy, the experience may be less one of settling in than of suspended animation, of the long wait between blood tests or ultrasound results, of the collapsed moments of time that follow an ambiguous finding or unexpected prenatal diagnosis. Or, like Ms. Y in the vignette above, breath held until the weeks move past the number at which the cervix had previously shortened, the membranes prematurely ruptured, or the pregnancy was lost. Bed rest, a common scenario for many mothers whose babies need NICU care, becomes another instance where the rhythms of pregnancy are disrupted. Friends and family may greet this with, "wow, you get to watch all those movies," but parents describe this time as an enforced, endless, and isolated engagement with one's ruminative mind. Googling endlessly and praying fiercely, these women are hoping their body does not betray them again. They submit to regimens of medications to forestall labor, and shuttle back and forth between levels of critical care within the hospital, or back and forth to their home with their hearts in their throats. This holding pattern is shattered abruptly when the baby's heart beat slows or the mother's blood pressure dangerously rises, and she is rushed to delivery. Infants born out of time, hurried off to the NICU, without a moment for the mother to glimpse her newborn. Once in the NICU, some proudly say, "I held them until 32 weeks," while others are meek and shamed, disoriented, at failing and falling out of synch with time.

The relationship of past, present, and future is endlessly entangled in the NICU. Beset by the extremes of unbearable anxiety carried by Ms. F (above), parents are counseled to take "one day at a time." They try to narrow their focus, struggle to quarantine the past, to limit questions about the future and make peace with the long hours and days and even weeks or months of waiting and the profound uncertainty of the present. Some do this with exquisite skill, especially those with babies that have an easier NICU course and those who haven't had prior losses. But for those whose past years are littered with losses, images creep into the imagination. Ms. F sits at the side of her baby's isolette with her arms wrapped around her middle, as if holding her fragile insides together, shuddering against the ghosts of both past and future. When her baby gets an infection, she heaves with guilt as she had a cold the week before. “She can’t die from this. I can’t have killed her. She has to live.” No amount of reassurance from nurses comforts her. The NICU is inevitably a palimpsest where the past bleeds through the best intentions to start over, to take each day as it comes.

> “I have premonitions that he will die,” says another mother, of a 24-weeker, now 1 month old. “When I arrived this morning and saw him swaddled, I had images of his dead twin. When she died, the nurse had swaddled her and put her in my arms and I held her. Now what if this baby dies too? I couldn’t see him this morning. I only saw him dead and swaddled. Will these thoughts make him die? I fear that God hears my thoughts. Are these premonitions? Is something wrong with me?

Others rail against the admonition to narrow their focus on the present moment, insisting that memory be invited in. Ms. Y and Ms. F both memorialized their prior dead babies, naming, celebrating, creating rituals and, even for Ms. Y and her husband, permanent bodily markers. That helped them, though Ms. Y’s mother found it hard to bear and the nurses wondered if this was odd, maybe a tad eerie.

Ms. F asks in the parents’ group if she has one baby or three. What should she answer when people ask how many children she has? “The two babies that died are real to me; I named them, had a wake and buried them.” Another mom says, “You sacrificed for them. You are their mother.”

And what of the future, the other side of this stifling present moment? Just as there can be, on the part of staff, what seems like a conspiracy of silence around prior losses, the future is sidestepped, entering in with jolts. “She doesn’t orient to my face, doesn’t track,” says an attuned neonatologist about a now 4-month-old baby, still in the NICU. But the fact that the parents have barely been around is not linked up. Or the parent who says,

> I know I have a long way to go before we are home, many surgeries and hurdles, but no one will answer this question, “Will she be neurologically normal?” I can deal with anything but a severely cognitively handicapped child.

Unanswerable questions. “We can’t know,” followed quickly perhaps by a story about a former very sick NICU baby who is now in college. The closed *claustrum* is now given some air. Yet, we fret. These babies are at high risk of impairments and most parents in this age of Google know that. Is this anecdote of normality a gift or a mirage? Can we do better while also protecting the parents’ fragile sense of a future they can now, in the present, bear? (See e.g., Groopman, 2003.)

Like a tsunami that reverberates through the ocean for days, bouncing back and forth between continents, the feelings of shame and abjection that began with infertility can echo throughout the *claustrum* that is the NICU. The shame of the betraying body that couldn't hold the baby to term becomes one with the shame of not being able to suckle the baby at one's breast. This shame coils itself around the unexpected ambivalence felt about this longed-for baby and spirals around the lack of confidence one feels as woman or man, or as mother or father. There is the cruel shame of the mother who recoils in fear from her baby who turned blue in her arms and the shame of the father who withdraws because he feels helpless in the face of her shock and depression or because he is one of the almost 40% of males that are infertile. The stigma that silences this statistic compounds the lonely shame and grief of these fathers. The envy these mothers feel toward women with healthy babies and full-term pregnancies also leads to unforgivable shame. "Every belly and baby is a painful reminder of what I lost and most especially of what I am not," says still another mom.

We have come to call this a complex form of gender shame, and it affects the narrative arc of oneself as creative and procreative or toxic and barren, and within the *claustrum*, which is the NICU, speaking these feelings is never easy.

> "OK, tell me," whispers one woman in the parent group, "are you getting enough milk to feed your baby? I mean, I pump and I pump and all I get is a few drops. This electric machine pulls at my boobs but still, hardly anything. Today I was so embarrassed that I covered the bottle as I took it to the refrigerator. I didn't want anyone to see how little milk I produce." The ice is broken. "Oh, you too!" says another mom. "What's with me? I couldn't get pregnant naturally and I couldn't hold my baby until she was full-term. I never felt her kick. I never had that full, can't-see-your-toes feeling. And now I don't get enough milk to feed her. I get so jealous when I see pregnant women on the street." Another confides: "It's so hard for me that my breast milk is not good enough for my baby, that they need to supplement with formula. I actually avoid visiting at feeding times, but I do call, and the nurse says I am interrupting and she sounds so annoyed with me. Like I am failing again, this time for not being there."

Coincidentally, this nurse had shared her frustration about parents calling all the time – the wrong times, like feeding times when she is so busy. We wondered aloud about the mom calling at feeding times, about her possible sense of increased failure, about feeling that she couldn't be a good-enough provider for her baby. Perhaps her staying away but calling right at feeding time was mom's "uncanny" attempt to "be there"? And could she (the nurse) find a way to tell mom that she and her baby looked forward to seeing her soon? Might she perhaps encourage her, saying:

> I can tell you are thinking about him and I can speak to you more in a half-hour when I am less busy. Perhaps you wish you were here. Can you come later today? Soon you will be able to fully feed your baby and he will really like that.

For so many possible reasons, this suggestion didn't seem to penetrate. The nurse didn't seem open to thinking more complexly, to considering the mother's potent sense of shame. Perhaps in time, with more conversation, greater reflection might be possible, so that this caring nurse could better consider the mother's state of mind and reflect to the mother what she understood so as to help her move closer to her baby.

Shame leads to secrets and secrets lead to shame. Both proliferate in the NICU. With all the fetal and then sometimes newborn losses these women are left feeling that their body has become a "house of death." Selective reductions, so often kept secret, haunt. "Is this baby, now so sick, a punishment for that?" Male infertility, still more shameful than that for women, may be a component of the unspoken strain in the relationship between moms and dads in the NICU. (See Chapter 6 for a discussion of the cultural and interpersonal disavowal of male vulnerability.)

> My husband was very ashamed and certainly couldn't talk about it. So we didn't tell either of our families that we were doing IVF. Now they see these sick babies, but they don't know all that we went through. No one does. And we are so very tense with each other too.

In the sketches above, each woman was feeling cut-off from her husband. Ms. F made clear that her husband had no patience for all her questions and loops of thinking; she felt alone, her mother also very unavailable to her. Ms. Y's husband is more or less absent. "When our baby comes home, then I will be there. Now I can't." Ms. F says she understands, though her loneliness is palpable. "He was thrown by the twins' deaths. He won't let that happen again."

The potentially procreative couple is now abject, shamed, deadened, and destructive.

"Mother blaming" finds new life in diagnoses of "incompetent cervix" and women seem to "cover" for their spouses, whispering anxiously and confidentially, "his sperm motility was poor." Women and men too can feel degraded and isolated, aspects of themselves cut off and held in secret, all the "incorrigible badness" (Willoughby, 2001) and terrible, brittle sadness trapped in the fear, speculation, and imaginings of that which is too often held in solitary silence.

"Hi, I'm so glad to meet you. I'm the psychologist and I meet *all* the new families." Saying this, "*all* the new families," we learn, is essential, so wary are parents of being exposed as not good enough, lacking, wanting, crazy even. Normalizing their experience, no, their selves, is vital. "Are these your babies?" "Congratulations!"

Invariably, we see a look that seems to meld surprise, confusion, and maybe pleasure that reads as "is this baby *worth* congratulations? this 'unfinished' infant?" And then "thank you," they shyly smile.

In this medicalized high-tech critical care unit, the "act of beholding" has been replaced by the "act of scrutiny" (Boyer and Sorenson, 2009). So too was sex during infertility treatments. Hormones were measured, temperatures taken, calendars checked. Sperm evaluated, eggs rated, and indignities endured. Now these new parents, separated from their hard-won issue by beeping monitors and plexiglas, not to mention their traumatized shock, are facing a new language of numbers, tests, diagnoses, and treatments. It is barren and cold, this medicalization of birth. Where does wonder enter? Or awe? The counting of toes and nuzzling of necks? How does a parent's normal ambivalence survive this? How do they fall in love? We have come to think of nurses as the "emotional umbilical cord" connecting mothers and babies. They are situated to allow juicy vitality into the sterile, *claustrum*-like unit. They decide whether to place a baby on a mother's chest – skin to skin – an experience that is not only beneficial for the infant, but brings tears of joy to moms' and dads' eyes. "It's the first time I felt she was really mine. That I am her mother," they say. Some nurses are perhaps overly cautious, not yet aware of the latest research emphasizing the value of skin-to-skin care, maybe deadened themselves from the high-pitched hours with fragile babies and equally fragile parents. Some might feel uncomfortable putting a 2-lb infant between a mother's breasts, needing to touch the mom's breasts as she does this. Still others trained at a time when parents were not particularly welcome in the NICU, and they haven't yet understood the emotional linking role they can surely play. In the NICU, all are at risk of dissociative states of mind, knowing and not knowing, feeling and numbing.

When the suffocating spaces can be stretched through the relational matrix (Mitchell, 1988), it becomes more possible for the deepest fears to be articulated and responded to. When Ms. Y's daughter had a hard day (a little less active, needed a bit more oxygen, and had to have her feeds reduced), Ms. Y implored her nurse, "Is she going backwards or forwards? Is she going to die?" This nurse, understanding all that had transpired previously and how important this mom's vigilance was for her, addressed each one of her concerns patiently, carefully, and warmly, not leaving her abandoned to ruminations, nor offering false reassurances.

Despite the fragmentation of knowledge, the knowing and shadowed knowing that has accompanied these couples from the infertility clinic through to the NICU, the grave uncertainties that haunt each psyche, and the strong feelings aroused or dissociated, the relationship with knowing minds helps locate resilience and buffer easily aroused dread about future unknowns. Into this liminal space can be the world of women sharing tidbits about children and life; skilled moms helping new moms; women talking about leaky breasts and spit-up.

When Ms. Y could finally put her baby to her breast, she panicked that her "big boobs would smother" her still tiny baby. The lactation consultant gently reassured her and helped her safely position her infant. Within days, Ms. Y had formed a "breast-feeding club" with another mom. With the curtain drawn around them, you could hear their laughter, bringing pleasure back and at least for now allowing fear and shame to recede into the shadows.

Coda

> The multiple layers pile up like shadows, visible through the translucent onion skin of imagination.
>
> (Johnson, 2013)

Disrupted reproduction, disrupted pregnancy, disrupted birth. While the original story of "not yet, perhaps never" (Carson, 2002, p.180 and see above) has been rewritten and the feelings of grief and despair, shame and loss associated with infertility have been overlaid by hope and joy, the present is still clearly layered over the past and the future carries tremendous unknowns for these families. When we pay attention to the hauntings of, say, miscarriages past and shames suffered, decisions made through waves of trauma and longing leading to dissociated feelings; when we, along with the families, can dare to look straight into these shadows, we help these moms and dads develop a narrative of their experience that carries them through infertility and ART to life in the NICU and, finally, home.

Notes

1 Fathers can feel overlooked in the NICU. Much of the communications from staff is to the mothers. That is partially because fathers return to work so quickly, paternity leave being very uncommon in the United States. But there is literature that documents the often-unacknowledged emotions that fathers feel (see, e.g., Arockiasamy et al., 2008; Fegran et al., 2008; Hollywood & Hollywood, 2011).

2 We have also found ourselves subjected to this mindlessness and have written elsewhere about our own struggles with the breakdown of thought and reflection and the permeability of psychic space that is endemic to this traumatic environment (see, e.g., Kraemer & Steinberg, 2006, 2012).

3 Similarly, we have previously written about our own feelings of vulnerability, helplessness, and shame (see, e.g., Steinberg, 2006, 2012; Kraemer, 2012; Kraemer & Steinberg, 2016).

4 Gravida refers to the number of times a woman has been pregnant while para denotes the number of times a woman has given birth.

5 Michael Kamrava is the now infamous infertility doctor who transferred a dozen embryos to N. Suleman, yielding eight live embryos (*The New York Times*, 2011).

6 The author reports on a study by Boulet et al. (2015) showing that intracytoplasmic sperm injection, a procedure used to bypass male infertility, is being used increasingly despite a lack of increase in male infertility and despite that its use brings about a "1.5 to 4 times increased incidence of autism, birth defects, chromosomal abnormalities and intellectual disabilities when compared to pregnancies that result from conventional IVF".

7 In 2009 the Infertility Family Research Registry, a voluntary database funded by the National Insitutes of Health to collect information about the "health and well-being of family built with the help of infertility treatment" was founded. Thus far, about 800 people have participated. (Note that 1.5% of infants born in the United States per year are conceived using ART. In 2010, 3,999,386 babies were born in the United States: Martin et al., 2013.)

8 In 2010 the cost of an ART cycle in the United States was $13,775. In Canada it was $8,740, in Japan, $4,012 and in Belgium, $3,109 (Connolly et al., 2010).

9 It is important to keep in mind the inherent bias in the idea that children are necessary to the definition of family (see Chapters 1–4).
10 A tracheostomy is a surgical procedure to create an opening through the neck into the trachea (windpipe). A tube is placed through this opening to provide an airway.
11 RESOLVE is a national infertility association that offers information and support to families facing infertility.

Part III

Looking closely

A case study of egg donation

Chapter 9

Spoken through desire

Maternal subjectivity and assisted reproduction

Tracy L. Simon

A moment of practice

Nora[1] walked to the couch stiffly; thin and taut, she attempted self-possession. Gray-green eyes staring through me, with a blank, exhausted face, she said, "I'm aborting it." Her words hung between us in the ensuing exploding silence. "It" came to be only 2 weeks before, conceived via a donor's egg and her partner's sperm. "It" was Nora's first and only pregnancy after many years of suffering through infertility, a loss doubled by the many failures of assisted reproductive technology (ART). For 6 of those years, Nora and I sat together, waiting, steeped in the fantasies and confusions accompanying the ART process, situated uncomfortably between the possibilities and impossibilities embedded in it.

Eight years earlier, Nora entered the ART arena, beginning with intrauterine insemination (IUI),[2] then in vitro fertilization (IVF).[3] Between numerous failed IVF attempts, she tried IUI again. Doctors warned her of unresponsive eggs and very little chance of conceiving. Her daily rituals were the usual for women undergoing ART – racing to the doctor's office before work for blood tests and ultrasounds. Nightly, she administered the hormone injections into her stomach, always accompanied by waves of sweat and nausea. Like many women taking hormones, Nora watched herself change, horrified, unfamiliar in her body: weight gain and breast tenderness, agitation and itchiness, tearfulness, and explosions of frustration. Mitigating the waiting by acupuncture, not thinking, thinking, Chinese herbs, Mayan massage, blogs, wanting to be alone, not wanting to be alone, organic diets, no coffee, no exercise, silence. She spent tens of thousands of dollars. Still, there was no child.

ART embodies culture

With growing biotechnological advances, reproductive cells are migrating among bodies (Browner & Sargent, 2011). In the United States alone, about 10% of women between 15 and 44 are diagnosed with infertility (Centers for Disease Control and Prevention (CDC), 2015b). About half of these women use ART, the high-tech procedures that involve "surgically removing eggs from a woman's ovaries, combining them with sperm in the laboratory, and returning them to the woman's body or donating them to another woman" (CDC, 2015b), resulting in the birth of about 1.5% of all babies born in the United States per year (CDC, 2015a). However, ART is not always successful. Recent studies show that ART results in a live birth only "32% in women aged 35–37 years; 22% in women aged 38–40 years; 12% in women aged 41–42 years; 5% in women aged 43–44 years; and 1% in women aged 44 years and older" (CDC, 2015b).

Although these widespread practices have been used for some time (the first "test tube" baby was born in 1978), as has been described throughout this book, discourse surrounding reproductive technologies remains largely unarticulated in psychoanalytic writing, a silence that may reflect a collective struggle to process its meanings. As Dimen (2011) writes, "The power of discourse lies in its exclusions, in what it overtly or implicitly tells us we may not think" (p. 5).

No one goes through fertility treatments unscathed. Well aware of the extraordinary freedoms and possibilities ART offers to those wanting babies, I am not advocating for or against reproductive advances. Rather, my emphasis is on the significant cultural change ART has created for the reproductive body, always marked by the interpenetration of the bio-psyche-social, and how this change has generated new meanings that have been met with relative silence. In examining the social discourse around maternal subjectivity as it incorporates these technologies, I hope to create a space for thinking about infertility's bind with abject pain and loss, and technology's capacity for both creative, nonnormative potentials as well as for reproducing constricting, social practices.

For the purposes of this chapter, I focus specifically on the procedure of egg donation, which beautifully captures ART's complex embodiment. I only touch on maternal subjectivity as it is impacted by women identified as biologically infertile, even though there is much more to say about the use of ART for men with biological infertility as well as ART for single parents, same-sex parents, and those who choose not to have a genetic child.

Although ART has shifted our notion of control and certainty surrounding reproduction, it has also generated a new ambiguity. What was once full of uncertainty, surprise, disappointment, loss, and excitement is now met with a new degree of choice and control over timing (Mieli, 1999). Of course, not all of reproductive technology works when and how one wishes. Still, the developing technology dialogic continues to promote the implicit promise that anything and everything is possible,[4] introducing some illusion of control as well as an illusory antidote to loss surrounding reproductive disappointments from infertility (Mieli, 1999).

With all the potentials reproductive technology can offer – reversing infertility, reconfiguring normative notions of family, transforming culture, and rearticulating parental subjectivity – it can *also* carry with it loss and mourning that do not yet have a speakable place in culture (see Ehrenshaft, 2005, 2007; Murphy, 2006). Simultaneously, mourning occurs at two levels, for any individual's inability to conceive and in reaction to the cultural notion that one should have a baby in one particular way.

Some come out of the reproductive arena with a child but also without much help processing their experiences. Often people enter the fertility world dazed by the new language, technologies, and procedures. In fact, however, enormous new complexities challenge our thinking and ethics[5] (Browner & Sargent, 2011). Reproductive technology codes its new medical procedures in euphemism, "harvesting," "GIFTing," and "donation"[6] (Browner & Sargent, 2011). These terms obfuscate the psychic meaning as well as the actual and symbolic price for both donor and recipient participants, even when a wished-for child is born. Without having to undo parents, or damage their capacity for enjoyment of their child, the complex fantasies ART engenders in the space between imagining a child and having one has great psychic significance. Although this is true of all parenting, the cultural silence surrounding ART lends itself to particularly painful fantasies, as silence can haunt like a secret.

Furthermore, the cultural excitement around the technology encourages people to use it. But, this encouragement is subtly coercive. It is a choice, but not quite a free choice – to the procedures, to the doctor's recommendations, to giving up bodily control, to taking medications that wreak havoc on the body, because if the desire is to have a child, and ART is the only option, how could one not choose it?

Of crucial importance to this subtle coercion is the concept of "failure." The technology dialogic surrounding reproduction can latch on to an old discourse on motherhood, by reintroducing and reproducing the idealization of femininity and reinterpreting failure to have a child as failure to be a (real) woman (see Chodorow, 1978; Kristeva, 1982; Benjamin, 1998; Baraitser, 2009). Being (the right kind of woman) gets conflated with and concretized as having (a child). The child, then, becomes the sign of status and power. Eng (2006) writes:

> Indeed, I would go so far as to suggest that the possession of a child, whether biological or adopted, has today become the sign of full and robust citizenship – of being a fully realized political, economic, and social actor in American life.
>
> (p. 56)

Eng's point demonstrates that, in the traditional mandate of femininity, obligation masquerades (Riviere, 1929) as choice (I chose it, so I must want it), intensifying the coercion. With illusion of choice, there is illusion of control, which can be especially painful when ART does not work, exacerbating the pain of infertility with technological failure, particularly when it is necessary to repeat the process over and over again.

Discourse writes the subject

As Nora *speaks* her fantasies, fears, and protests via the assisted reproductive process, she names something about the cultural, intergenerational, and psychic transmissions speaking through her. Although operating at different levels, these discourses inevitably intersect. I take the position that subjectivity is constituted through culture, and discourse renders subjectivity intelligible or unintelligible (Butler, 1999, 2005; Dimen, 2011). By elaborating on Nora's speech, I bring ART and its silences *into* a psychic register, literally listening for discourse spoken through the unconscious.

To explicate this dynamic, I draw on Lacan's three registers of psychic experience – the Imaginary, the Symbolic, and the Real – and explore how subjectivity, or what Lacan calls "the subject's sense of life" (1957, p. 558), is negotiated within each register (see Lacan, 1957, 1973; Evans, 1996; Bailly, 2009). Although distinct from one another, the three registers of mental functioning always transect, simultaneously acting upon the psyche, and "together they cover the whole field of psychoanalysis" (Evans, 1996, p. 132).

The Imaginary is the order of identifications. It is, at first, a body image, as Lacan (1973) illustrates through the infant, an utterly dependent being, seeing itself whole and unfragmented in the mirror. The false wholeness reflected back becomes the basis of lifelong identifications and projections with others, such as love, hate, sameness, and difference (Lacan, 1973; Bailly, 2009). Although the Imaginary allows for critical attachments, Lacan argued that psychoanalytic theorizing has been reduced to the Imaginary order alone, with analysts highlighting attachment and identification (dual relations), while missing the important function of the symbolic third and its role in mediating duality (Bailly, 2009).

The Symbolic register functions as the place of culture (prohibition and social rules) and as the place of radical otherness (Other), which, for Lacan, is the unconscious (Lacan, 1957, 1973; Bailly, 2009). The unconscious is represented through language, which always carries the mark of the Other. The project of psychoanalysis is to symbolize "at least something of the Real" (Bailly, 2009, p. 98). Characterized by its impossibility, the register of the Real is unsymbolizable and unimaginable, which is what makes it, essentially, traumatic (Evans, 1996; Bailly, 2009). Through speech, Lacan (1957) illustrates how subjectivity *changes*, as the subject moves from terror to loss to signification, shifting between the Real, Imaginary, and Symbolic psychic registers. "Before Lacan, no one thought of locating the subject *within the very act of talking*" (Safouan, 2004, p. 3).

Lacan (1978) posits that all subjects are marked by lack-in-being. Manifesting differently in the three registers, lack appears as Real privations, Imaginary frustrations, and Symbolic castrations (Lacan, 1978). Entry into the Symbolic order of language and culture requires an acceptance of lack; in facing lack, we come into being, entering the social order as desiring subjects. The relation between lack and desire is relevant to this article: "It is a lack that causes desire to arise" (Lacan, 1991, p. 139). Desire is in paradoxical relation with the law of the Symbolic order: regulating desire in the form of prohibitions and social rules (we accept lack: being is always incomplete) also fuels desire by creating prohibition (by telling us what we are not, it informs us that something is missing and, therefore, we must desire it; Evans, 1996). As I illustrate, it is in this anxiety-filled gap between lack and desire that Nora and I collude and collide.

The unconscious is the discourse of the other (Lacan, 1957, p. 10)

Before Nora's sibling was born, their young mother had given birth to a stillborn baby. As the family story is told, the couple wanted only two children. Had the first baby survived, Nora would not exist. As a result, the family considered Nora a miracle, a name that marked her throughout her life.

The stillborn loss created a haunting fiction in the family that only one child could survive, and Nora was placed in the idealized position (the one who would compensate for loss) vis-à-vis her sibling, who was placed in the position of mourning (the one who would carry loss). Nora, charming and sassy, appealingly quick and bright, carried the burden of being born into this idealized position, her lifelong debt, with a certain energy and determination.

Nora loved her birth story, glowing from her "symbolic, cultural inheritance" (Mieli, 1999, p. 265), her mother's unconscious desire that Nora compensate for the loss of the stillborn baby by surviving and thriving. Born out of loss, the psychic "errand" (Apprey, 2013, p. 7) passed on to Nora was to "succeed," to live out the intergenerational transmission of her mother's haunting loss. However, because Nora had to carry something that did not belong to her, the impossible task of compensation in this fiction introduced, from the beginning, a sense of falseness and failure that ran through Nora's life. Nora had to keep thriving, in spite of pain and loss, unable to face mourning, carrying out her mother's desire, spoken through Nora's unconscious, in what Lacan (1957) calls the "discourse of the Other" (p. 10).

As Nora reflected, she loved her life, describing a playful, energetic relationship and productive, enriching work. She felt that she neither needed a baby nor necessarily wanted one. At 35, though, the pressure of age, with its threat of fertility problems, led Nora to opt to have a child. As occurs for many women, the pressure registered for Nora through the fantasy of baby as completion – the completion of being and the completion of femininity.

Lack

Infertility smashed into Nora. She entered therapy abject, sunken, and ashamed. She faced the traumatic confrontation with her body's limits. Then there was the symbolic debt into which she was born. The thread of falseness and failure was already present in her mother's fiction. Operating on Nora without her knowing it, infertility prevented her from being the miracle she was supposed to be, failing at the miracle of life. It incarnated the inchoate sense of insufficiency (James Ogilvie, personal communication, January 16, 2013) that she has carried her whole life. Nora's infertility embodied the loss she was meant to deny.

Because both the family and cultural-political stories were powerfully operating on Nora at once, it becomes impossible to separate them out. Simultaneously, she faced three failures, the first of which consisted of the limitations of having a healthy, vital body. Second, she was confronted with her inability to compensate for her mother's loss. And, third, she entered, through "failure," the discourse that idealizes motherhood and claims the child as the completion of this idealization. Nora was forced to register her own lack – the "castratedness" (Bailly, 2009, p. 134) or the incompletion of being – with which Lacan sees all subjects marked.

Clinically speaking, "failure" was the signifier Nora used most often: "I am a failure"; "I hate failing"; "My body is broken, it has failed me"; "My partner will be devastated, I've failed him"; "The doctors have failed me"; "My partner fails to see what I'm going through"; "I'm a failure as a woman"; "I've failed to stop"; "I've failed to get pregnant." Locking her into a cycle, each verbalization of failure brought Nora into contact with vulnerability and disappointment, hence to failure, flipping her original signifier, "success," on its head. Pregnancy, then, became the only solution to infertility's mark; embedded in ART's promise of success, Nora tried, compulsively and painfully, over and over again, IUIs and IVFs, repeating the refrain, "just one more try."

Nora and I entered a vortex, unable to articulate the multiple discourses at play in this problematic, lost in the ambiguities and contradictions. All we could do was claim confusion. Nora was a walking ghost, stripped of her vitality and propelled into blind action. She existed on the surface, each loss marking her psychically, but registering as blankness, which characterized me, too: we could not think. We tried, but meaning making quickly collapsed into details about medical information and inconclusive news. Our time felt urgent, driven, manic, bumbling through information we could not understand under the psychic weight of what could not yet be said.

The lack is lacking (Lacan, 2014)

Like many women who face multiple failed IVFs, Nora confronted her two remaining ART options: a donor's egg or adoption. Her partner pushed for the former, so the child would carry at least half of their genes while enabling Nora's body to nourish and sustain it. She pushed for adoption, so that both she and her partner would come to the child from the same, equal, outside place. They agreed to pursue both.

An adoption broker urged Nora to create adoption books depicting what the broker called the "all-American family," illustrated by photos of an "attractive couple, financial stability, and a spacious home." Ironically, this is the last thing Nora felt about herself. Conflicted and consumed, she set to the task of photographing her life, while at the same time feeling she was failing at this ideal life. Nora was made to become complicit with this fiction by then having to perform the very life she felt she was not leading. Making use of her status to attract those searching for adoptive parents only accentuated the emptiness and confusion she felt.

Simultaneously, Nora perused egg donor profiles, searching for women who physically resembled her with her dark-red waves, light freckles, and gray-green eyes. Her doctor encouraged her to search for sameness, someone with her physique; her hair, eye, and skin color; her ethnic background; her smile. Nora fiercely resisted egg donation as an option yet became consumed with the impossible task of finding a woman who could and would stand in for her – in her eyes, a miracle substitute. With little to go on save some medical details and a few photos, Nora fantasized about the donors' lives and identities, eventually selecting one.

Nora was riddled with anxiety and apprehension, strongly resisting egg donation and continuing to actively pursue adoption, even as she took the nightly hormone medications in preparation for the donor's egg to be transferred into her body. Dissociated and blank, she submitted to the egg transfer, which was bought at high emotional capital for her. Her ambivalent compliance with egg donation was, in part, an attempt to dissolve the paradox she faced. If she accepted the donor's egg, she had to accept her lack, which nullified her idealized miracle position. Yet, by accepting the donor's egg, she also found a solution that denied lack, a lack of lack (Lacan, 2014). Rather than being a subject of desire who accepts lack, the denial of lack subjects her to the loss of desire (Jessica Benjamin, personal communication, October 18, 2012). Manically defending against loss, Nora literally and symbolically bought into the fantasy that egg donation would make up for her lack, which, for Lacan (2014), can never be made up for. Instead, it exaggerated her lack, throwing her back into her symbolic debt to the stillborn sibling for the gift of life and to her older sibling for taking the place of mourning. Even after many exhausting years of failed fertility interventions, she persevered, unsure whether accepting the donor's egg would leave her lacking or having.

Two weeks after the donor's egg, fertilized with her partner's sperm, was transferred into her body, Nora learned she was pregnant. This was the day she told me, "I'm aborting it." She was enraged. She felt abducted, coerced, excluded, and invaded. In a state of abjection (Kristeva, 1982), her abortion fantasy edged on action, enlivening Nora: a protest.

Alienation is constitutive of the imaginary order (Lacan, 1981, p. 146)

Nora lived her pregnancy at the intersection of the three registers – the Real, Imaginary, and Symbolic – the place where, in Lacan's view, everyone exists. First, the nonviability of her own eggs in the Real would reduce her self-image in the Imaginary to that of a nonproductive, nongenerative "woman," which she conflated with "mother." The egg donor, in contrast, became a "real woman" possessed of the generative capacity Nora lacked, rendering her powerless and afraid while linking her to her own mother, reenacting her mother's loss, which her miraculous birth was meant to deny. Second, as a way to not face her Symbolic lack, Nora had to accept the donor's gift, which, upon turning into a debt, became her new sacrifice (Derrida, 1995). She felt she had to carry something that did not belong to her, a false possession, literally a foreign body, reappropriated from elsewhere. Not only did she feel like a thief, but her early burden of carrying the debt for her mother's idealization was recapitulated too.

Third, the healthy egg from another woman represented the Symbolic loss of a miracle child produced between her and her partner. Nora felt estranged in her experience of mourning because she felt her partner could not mourn the loss of the miracle child sufficiently. She also felt alone in mourning the loss of her genetic contribution to the baby; in her view, her partner wanted the baby even though the baby would not be carrying her DNA. If infertility fueled Nora's abjection, then the nongenetic question doubled it; she feared not only that she would be excluded from the father–child genetic bond, but also that the child's existence would continuously delegitimize her, exposing her lifelong story of falseness. Marked with its birth story, inscribed in its difference from her, Nora felt terrified of the child's imagined foreignness.

Bound in the Imaginary, Nora's fantasied relationship with the child became an imminent threat to her own annihilation, rendering her terrified, deeply alienated, and aggressive. Benjamin's (2004) "doer and done to" conceptualization captures Nora's bind; in a "kill or be killed power struggle," without an "intersubjective third" to intervene in the pair to prevent collapse, Nora and the child were separated by irreducible difference (p. 12). Nora faced lack at the level of mortality: her desire for sameness in reproduction and self-reproduction, flipped into difference, while the otherness of reproduction prevailed (Jessica Benjamin, personal communication, May 12, 2013). Therefore, Nora could hold on to just one truth: as only one of them could live, either the baby, as persecutor, had to be killed or she, Nora, would have to die (Benjamin, 2004).

Desire inscribes itself

> That the subject should come to recognize and to name his desire; that is the efficacious action of analysis. But it isn't a question of recognizing something which would be entirely given. . . . In naming it, the subject creates, brings forth, a new presence in the world.
>
> (Lacan, 1978, pp. 228–229)

Nora's loss and fear resisted symbolization, while she and I, equally embedded, colluded to avoid the despair and terror lurking in our work. These sessions were full of anxiety, burdened with waiting and uncertainty, balanced on the precipice of life and death, of trying to think the unthinkable. Instead, we spoke superficially about the long to-do lists and medical details, embodying lifelessness. Yet, through the deadness of Nora's speech, a critical shift in our work occurred. After many years of waiting together, Nora finally arrived in my office one day to announce she was pregnant. In the same breath, Nora elaborated her desire, "I'm aborting it," and, in doing so, she symbolized the violence of loss drowning us in the Imaginary.

All I could hear was the loud "No!" exploding in my head. My protest was in the name of the unsymbolized "it" that Nora carried. My prohibition was a Symbolic one, addressed to her Real life-or-death threat and to the imminent collapse in her Imaginary bind: "it" would have to be killed or "it" would kill her. In that clinical moment, the "no" spoke through me, in contradistinction to her manic motion, as a Symbolic plea to slow down, as an intervening third for an aliveness that must also carry with it deadness, and for the simultaneity of loss with possibility. Refusing to align with her do-or-done-to dynamic, my "no" was a rally for desire, one I would carry until Nora would eventually claim it for herself. It was also a thrust toward articulation, not only mine but for Nora as well. For the first time, Nora confronted her pregnancy as Real, which firmly grounded her in the Symbolic. Speaking as a subject, rather than being subjected, Nora named her choice, her desire: "*I'm* aborting it." In doing so, she dissipated some of the dyadic terrors of the Imaginary and moved into the freedoms and possibilities of the Symbolic.

Nora began to articulate her murderous wishes, terrifying fears, and, eventually, her desires. Previously haunted by the "ineffable and unimaginable" (Bailly, 2009, p. 98) terror of the Real, the intergenerational "errand" (Apprey, 2013, p. 7) of disavowing loss, Nora began to signify the losses she literally carried. Her pregnancy embodied the dead baby who could not be mourned, the miracle baby who had to disavow loss, the sibling baby who had to carry loss, and the loss of the baby that Nora could not conceive. Nora faced lack on all three registers:

> She was deprived of complete control over her body, her infertility was Real, as in biological. She was frustrated in the Imaginary that the baby was not all she wished it to be. And, she was Symbolically castrated by the missing signification that would make being a "mother" immediately assessable, such that she had to become one.
>
> (Jamieson Webster, personal communication, June 15, 2013)

For Lacan, acceptance of lack is necessary for the coming into being and "being . . . as an exact function of lack" brings forth desire (Lacan, 1978, pp. 223–224).

With some despair, but mostly freedom, Nora began elaborating curiosity about the child-to-be as well as imagining herself as a mother. She then was able to hold in tension the contradictory experiences: the donor and her eggs as both a miracle and as a threat. As Nora continued to speak for herself, she began to symbolize the pregnancy not only as a persecutory attack on her legitimacy, a burden to carry, and a debt, *but* also as a child she longed for, whom she wanted to know and watch grow. Together, we created a space of vitality, and, as we conceived new truths, a desire was birthed that inscribed itself on her body.

Birth of desire

Nora carried the baby to full term. She left me a message, "I am completely, madly in love." When she returned to her sessions a few weeks later, she proudly walked into my office carrying the sleeping baby. Reverberating from the significance, we stood looking at the baby together. She said with a smile, "Look what we did." Her "we" was doubly significant: she and her partner, she and I.

Yet, Nora worries almost daily – sometimes she panics, "When will the baby 'know'? When will the baby ask for the 'real mother'? Will the baby hate me?"

Even though worrying is part of all parenting – it is not just a product of ART – nevertheless, the strangeness of ART and the ambiguity it creates deepen such fears. In Nora's case, her anxieties centered on whether the community would police her, catching and delegitimizing her, rendering her a "false" mother. Nora smiles awkwardly when others say, "Look, the baby has your eyes, your smile." As much as she takes pleasure in this sameness, she also wonders if she can fully claim the rights to motherhood. When plagued with doubts, Nora wonders, "Why am I consumed with other people's interpretations of me and my baby?" When the donor agency relayed a message from the donor, Nora spiraled into a panic. Suddenly, in Nora's fantasy, the donor became an embodied person with her own desires for the baby. As Nora despairingly said, "The existence of the donor out there in the world is a constant threat to my claim as the mother."

Signification

Birthing Nora's claim on subjectivity via our work, Nora, like all mothers, struggles in relation to her child – how she locates and loses herself in everyday maternal subjectivity, which is being defined and redefined by a culture that increasingly incorporates new technologies, continuously exposing contradiction and possibility (see Baraitser, 2009; Browner & Sargent, 2011; Sheehy, 2011). As Corbett (2009b) reminds us, "The family is less a fortress, more a clearinghouse, open to the currency of social forces (both majority and minority); the 'outside' society is indelibly 'inside' the family" (p. 361).

Advancement in reproductive technology has always called intelligibility into question, pushing up against and resignifying discourse and its imperatives (Butler, 2005). ART scrambles bodily and biological demarcations in previously unimaginable ways. On the one hand, its mixing of bodies and bloods through bodily fluidity, expansion, and hybridity creates a global citizen (Browner & Sargent, 2011). On the other, it generates diffusion, fusion, and confusion of bodies (Browner & Sargent, 2011). Corbett (2009b) proposes that resignification occurs "through collective intersubjective fantasies and terms: bonds are forged" (p. 366). Nora, like us, must hold and tolerate these tensions, contradictions, and ambiguities to live within the paradoxes inherent in mapping maternal subjectivity and the reproductive body (Baraitser, 2009; Sheehy, 2011). And, as we continue to consider these paradoxes in a psychic register, we can begin to symbolize that which eludes us.

Acknowledgments

I am deeply grateful to "Nora" for granting me permission to use material from our work together for my writing.

I also want to thank Julia Beltsiou, Jessica Benjamin, Muriel Dimen, Orna Guralnik, Kirsten Lentz, James Ogilvie, Olga Pugachevsky, Avgi Saketopoulou, Maura Sheehy, Jamieson Webster, and Jeanne Wolff-Bernstein for reading drafts of this paper.

Notes

1 A pseudonym.
2 Intrauterine insemination is a medical procedure in which washed sperm are injected directly into the uterus for the purpose of pregnancy (Centers for Disease Control and Prevention (CDC), 2015b).
3 In vitro fertilization is a surgical procedure in which eggs are removed from the ovaries, fertilized outside of the body, and then transferred back to the uterus as one or more embryos (CDC, 2015b). Injectable hormone medications are used to stimulate the ovaries for the purpose of retrieving eggs, and often cause uncomfortable, and at times painful, side effects.
4 An accruing discourse on capitalism and classism can be heard here as well, namely, that anything and everything is possible *at a certain price*, and ART carries an often prohibitively high price tag.
5 Ethics surrounding ART and commerce is much debated. Browner and Sargent's (2011) collection of essays examines commerce in reproductive materials, which is quite lucrative as body parts, commodified, enter the international trade. They explore, to name a few debates, class dynamics that place the poor in positions as bioavailable suppliers of reproductive materials; the ethics of gifting "spare embryos"; gender politics surrounding reproductive choice; and gametes crossing religious, ethnic, and racial borders to enter other bodies.
6 Harvesting refers to the egg retrieval process, in which ovaries are hyperstimulated with hormones to produce multiple mature (ripe) eggs that are then gathered for donation, insemination, or freezing. GIFTing (gamete intrafallopian transfer) is a surgical procedure in which eggs are removed from the ovaries and placed in the fallopian tubes with sperm for purposes of insemination (CDC, 2015b). Donation is a heated issue. Sperm and eggs can be donated; however, egg donation is a much more complicated process, involving lengthy medical/psychological screenings and medically invasive IVF procedures. Compensation laws vary by country. For example, in the United States donors are always paid and compensation for egg donation is unregulated, raising ethical debates about egg donors' motives (i.e., monetary gain, withholding medical information to ensure compensation, as well as limiting egg donation to those who can afford it). Gendered dynamics are clearly at play, in which women who choose to donate for "monetary gain" are criticized over those who donate for "altruistic" reasons. See Chapter 5 for further discussion of egg donors.

Chapter 10

On viability and indebtedness – or "Get away from her, you bitch!" (after Roberto Bolaño)

Stephen Hartman

It took me quite a while to write this discussion of Tracy Simon's chapter.[1] I confess, I carried it for months and worried it would be stillborn. Other times, I feared or hoped or swore that it would pop out of me like the alien from the *Aliens* movies. I fussed over it, wanting to repay debts to mentors and colleagues who have fostered my development, and, most importantly, to Simon for offering her courageous paper as our muse. Much as I wanted to be able to think about Nora and Simon, I couldn't, somehow, and I festered. Envy overtook me: you see, I approach middle age childless, and usually I'm able to muffle my doubts and regrets, but carrying Simon's paper around, it was different. I kept confronting an image of myself foreshortened and bungled. As the pages became increasingly dog-eared, I could no longer tell if I had joined Nora among the nonreproductive or if I resented her purchase of the elusive infant-objet "ah!" so profoundly that, in *syncope* with her abortive fantasy, I jumped to lance the psychic boil only to have toxic ooze burn a hole in my mental floor.

To cast aside my brooding, I indulged my reverie. Not in pursuit of an analytic third (Ogden, 1994) that would enlighten me about the transference; this I glean from Simon's precise prose and Nora's clobbered affect. No, my aversion to Nora wants blood: permission to kill, not to kill and be killed, but to kill . . . and to be absolved (for whose guilt, I suppose, mother, right?), and all from a 12-page Google doc crammed with factual information. I can't help but engage Nora's fury from the position of my lack. In my reverie, I *cross-equate*, cross-pollinate, try not to dominate, not to hybridize, but to somehow allow our shared text, no matter how rarified in the unconscious, to also exist "enmeshed in circumstance, time, place, and society" (Said, 1981, p. 52) – which is, as Edward Said wrote, a viable text: one that is: "responsible to a degree of separation for articulating those voices dominated, displaced, rendered un-viable or silenced by the textuality of texts" (Said, 1981, p. 53).

I can't focus on Nora, though, and I disappear into a picture of Nora's siblings, themselves not miracles and dead baby and *noir* mother, and Nora seeing them interrogate her as they watch her, in Nora's mind's eye wandering aimlessly up and down Natoma Street, a back alley in the Tenderloin of San Francisco (that damp, foggy city known in psychoanalytical circles as "Britain by the Bay") among alpha males who notoriously strut about carrying an alien virus, primed to give the gift that no technology can quite take away: "*Sie haben ihr Kind Getötet*!" And she scurries down the block past the venerable San Francisco Center for Psychoanalysis where the remodeled halls of alpha function have colonized the space above a derelict bareback porn studio. Male prostitutes stalk Natoma Street while our Nora drags herself past them with downcast eyes and our Bionian colleagues soak up part-object representations from their perch above. Waiting for their interpellation of *analyzability*, I, as Nora, not seeing me, one foot trapped in the branding machine, as Orna Guralnik (Guralnik & Simeon, 2010) calls this moment, the other foot stomping out the door, search for Simon.

All the while, Simon is in the thick of it with Nora and, along with her, being bombarded by the incongruities of real life as well as the signifiers of lack. And there I am, mad at my colleagues and arriving in New York from foggy San Francisco on Masud Khan's white horse,[2] saber in hand, to restore Simon (one of San Francisco's own) to Melanie Klein. I'd position Simon in the transferential line of Nora's psychic fire: *envious Nora wishes to get inside Simon's healthy body and ravage it, but, fearing she would do violence to the object, she eradicates it*, and so on. I could go there, take a few hits at Lacan while I'm at it too, but there is something I would omit, targeting for self-immolation; my reverie is mocking me for thinking so hard in the presence of someone who can't think, and then I see an enraged precocious part of me that I have failed to abort. I think I get it! Nora's infertility is sublime, precious; it is as ineffable as the virus impregnating the replicants of Natoma Street. Her infertility is not a fantasy introject. It is Real. And yet the air is ionized with psychic bits that can't-because-they-won't comprehend. Nora's pain has a stark beauty that Simon will suffer with Nora body to body and psyche to psyche so that Nora may be connected to the bodies of other women, other mothers, other daughters, her siblings, live ones, dead ones, even though, for this, as of yet, Nora has no words of gratitude because she is trapped in her own inside.

As am I. I can't reach Nora as I feel I ought; I worry that my manic reverie is going to backfire. I summon Warrant Officer Ellen Ripley and command the dripping sinewy monster to back away from Simon as she struggles to protect Nora, or is it Newt, Ripley's surrogate daughter? I declare the mother of interpellations in a patch of phosphorescent eggs: "Get away from her, you bitch!" And then, as time folds in on itself and then starts to fold back out, I wonder, why had I done that? Why did I rush to protect a viable life when inviability is the lacuna that can't be represented? I work loose threads and deep associations to the bone so that I might liberate Nora so that she might honor Simon and thus fulfill the lofty promise of *this very moment*. I suffer emotional distress. My heroic strategy is doomed by hubris, but I hold on to it because it is so esthetically pleasing.

The more I sat with the text, the less I could read it – which I take to be a good sign, since Simon beautifully describes not being able to think: "we tried, but meaning making quickly collapsed into details about medical information and inconclusive news" (Chapter 9). Nor could they move: "our time felt urgent, driven, manic, bumbling through information we could not understand under the psychic weight of what could not yet be said" (Chapter 9). This graphic swatch of hypertensive standstill is all we really have to go on. Nora is a walking ghost – but ghosts fly, they don't walk. Or they permeate. Or they roll in and out like the fog, which is, I suppose, why our colleagues in London and San Francisco are so preoccupied with projective events and psychic microclimates.

Wanting to find beauty in Nora's pregnancy, I find myself waging a war against Simon's emersion in Lacanian theory as a relational salvo might present a counterpoint where there had been a void, a lack, a gap, a theory. It's not that the Real can't be represented, but that it has been alienated from representation, screened out, washed, assembled – in the form of "the gift" or the specter of HIV-infected sperm in the mind of the barebacker, for whom it is at least his and not a donation for the homeless (Bersani, 2008). Imagine being with a person whose persecutory fantasies are so vivid that she says of her child, "I'm aborting it!" Imagine not feeling much as she says that to you. And then you drift to a Calvary in your own head. Nora's internal world – so bleak and shameful. Relational authors who don't live so close to London shy away from this landscape. It is too unbearably disconnected, so internal, inert, bereft of intention, and lawless. No wonder I teamed Nora up with Sigourney Weaver, both of them playing Warrant Officer *Ripley*, wandering alone in a playless landscape so grisly and selfsame that the film's director, *Ridley* Scott, purportedly used a pseudonym to disguise that he had art-directed the film.

Nora is rich, but the story is poor. I want to assail lack. I want to have a child. I want Nora to die instead of Lady Sybil on *Downton Abbey*. I blame Simon for referring her to this panel. I have depersonalized and donned the straitjacket of the *claustrum*, an airtight crevice of the deepest internal world where, writes the Kleinian psychoanalyst, Donald Meltzer (1990, p. 72): "generosity becomes quid pro quo, receptiveness becomes inveiglement, reciprocity becomes collusion, understanding becomes the penetration of secrets, knowledge becomes information, symbol formation becomes metonymy, art becomes fashion." This is the outside seen only from the inside so that the inside is seen only from the inside too. Sensory experience is estheticized and misused as the *Ding an sich* playing out in the theater of the mind, and the body becomes at once prison cell and refuge (Chassay, 2012). There is no movement and no time. In the *claustrum*, all time is now. Susanne Chassay explains it this way: without the viability of the Other, the subject is unable to sustain the trustworthiness of her own senses as food for thought. Again, Meltzer: "the present object is seen to contain the shadow of the absent-object-present-as-a-persecutor" (1973, p. 228). The miracle spies the dead baby lurking about, oozing. Let it be, I think; Simon has wisely contained Nora's urge to alert the police. It would be like calling in an FBI psychopath to monitor a nutty CIA agent. I channel Simon and hold the intention of Nora's wish to abort, to paralyze, to feel "abducted, coerced, excluded, and invaded" (Chapter 9) until it is linked to what she does indeed lack, a viable egg.

Lest you think I'm a rogue Kleinian or worry that I have anything but admiration for Simon, who sat with Nora year after year and month after month and hour after hour of sheer terror, let me say this. One thing I have learned in my travels is that if you are trying to attack something that you don't fully understand, and your attack becomes esthetically pleasing to you, but you start to feel like a suicide bomber, you might want to take a second look. Projective implosion reins in the *claustrum:* relation is at best an afterthought. What is there in Mother's pregnancy that Nora hates and adores? Might Nora be shielding her beautiful baby from a beautiful mother disguised as an alien baby? Is assistive reproductive technology (ART) savior or abortionist? Our collective practice of mulling over these questions and arguing about them is not the *claustrum*. To scoff at a cliché may be rude, but it is also meaning. Even when we go for broke in an enactment, we hope to turn something stuck, something that has perhaps been perverted by an economy built on possession, into meaning. Exiles from meaning are not stuck in binaries relative to the law; they are binaries in and of themselves, cross-sections through prisms eyed in planar view. Objects are not in use. Does Nora want to destroy donor-assist? Simon? partner? baby? It doesn't matter (in this moment) until some shift presents the possibility of gratitude to it, them, me, . . . us for holding the intention of her viability.

Fortunately, I found a mother figure to work with. A woman whose pregnancy was no highlight of a long and brilliant career, whose marriage fell apart soon after the birth of her child, and who was quickly dispatched to Vienna as a way to regain her senses. In a potent aside in Joan Rivière's (1929) masterpiece, "Womanliness as a Masquerade," Rivière attempts to understand "a puzzle," a woman "who can play the part of a devoted and disinterested mother substitute among a wide circle of relatives and friends" (1929, p. 304), all the while brash and masculine in her confident, professional display. This woman, who "puts on a mask of womanliness to avert anxiety and the retribution feared from men" (p. 303), cannot, absolutely cannot, let you know that she feels just like Nora. Despite her *psychose blanche*, as Adrienne Harris (2012) describes the trauma that being an acolyte vests in her, she has so much to be thankful for and yet she cannot summon sufficient gratitude to relinquish a lifelong habit of obsessive excoriation for a crime she did not commit.

Rivière, though famously a treatment failure on the couches of Ernest Jones and Sigmund Freud, went on to become Donald Winnicott's analyst, and it is by standing in the spaces between Winnicott and Lacan that I found a way to connect with Nora and with Simon's elegant text. But full credit goes to Winnicott's analyst who, like my own analyst, guided me to the question of viability and its relation to the stumbling block posed by indebtedness, of which Rivière conceded, simply, "*this* has been my own experience" (in Jacobus, 2005, p. 57).

After conjuring insurmountable and ever-more inundating debts of gratitude to obtain recognition for her intellectual capacity (and absolution for her self-flagellating quest for reassurance), Rivière wrote (speaking as if of her patient): "her efforts to placate and make reparation by restoring and using the penis in the mother's service were never enough; this device was worked to death, *and sometimes it almost worked her to death*" (Rivière, 1929, p. 311, emphasis added). "Stay away from her you bitch!" In the *claustrum*, the Real is the Unreal. Is that

Rivière the mother dressed up as the father to hold the phallic mother at bay? And if the paternal phallus needed holding, the mother didn't need to be protected, and her dick wasn't such a big dick after all?

Holding an intention

I reread Simon's text, scouring it for a good-enough mother, a fallible human greater than any alien perfection whose subjectivity, whose desire, and whose intention of my viability, I might perceive, would only I allow that *she* were always already there standing beside *us* in the mirror, and not in limbo awaiting the debt-restructuring operation that I had both fantasized and lost her to. Simon moves in step with *amae*, described by Doi (1989) as the ineffable beauty of the collective mother, and by Taniguchi (2012) as unrequited maternal erotic desire. She aspirates sound into language but does not require that Nora signify her, not yet: even in what I imagine to be her most *noir* moment (Green, 1995), Nora's viability is held in Simon's best intention.

We hoard our phantasized debts, as we do the debts that have been telescoped into us (Faimberg, 2005), until one day, out from the accumulated and inert heap of losses so long chalked up, out pops a fantasmatic, now viable, alien – "a peanuts," as Ken Corbett tells, or as Adam Phillip opined and Muriel Dimen witnesses clinically, a good smelly fart that launches the body into potential space. Simon's affect is so stolid when she suggests that "as we continue to consider ART in a psychic register, we can begin to symbolize that which eludes us" (Simon, 2013, p. 298). But she need not hold caution so; Nora has given viable birth.

Viable, as we use it nowadays, comes to us in English from France in the same year that Karl Marx was writing the *Communist Manifesto* (1848). Beginning in 1828, *viable* asserted that a particular newborn was capable of living. Then, in 1848, *viable* took on a slightly different, generalized meaning. Infants who were "viable" survived *as planned.* The intention of viability was held with reference to the fact of survival. In the theory of natural selection, Darwin used the term in this way to imply that an inherited trait (no matter how pesky) destined the viable newborn for survival. A life that is viable is a life that is capable of *going on being* (Winnicott, 1965), and this life had already been hoped to be capable by the species even if it was necessary to imagine that this life might not survive so that its survival would be *fitted.*

If the object's vitality is in doubt and can only be perceived in some internal *claustrum* where the inside perceives the outside as the inside from the inside, time stands still, just as Warrant Officer Ripley drifts in space for 57 years with the alien gestating in her bosom. But, as Winnicott wrote in *Human Nature* (1954), his last text before a fatal series of heart attacks that began in a New York City hotel room after a ghastly duel at the American Psychoanalytic, the healthy among us, though ever preoccupied with inherited traits and tendencies, "are (by definition) the nearest to being what they came into the world *equipped* to be" (Winnicott, 1954, p. 19). Struggle for health we must: it is our nature.

Like Lacan, Winnicott can be seen as preoccupied with that piece of equipment that had *always already* been supplied to the viable such that they might desire to survive. Again, because there can be no time before a viable life except, perhaps, in the Garden of Eden – and there can be no before-the-fall without a transitional state of being alone enough to appreciate loss – one must imagine life as the possession of the solitary or the godly, only to be proven eternally wrong. This is a fact of life that we can also date to circa 1848 thanks to Karl Marx, because the possession of fulsome living as well as a life worth living can only be experienced socially. Our gaze upon mother's beauty is always already averted to masquerade the violence of birth and ensuing abjection inherent in material life (Kristeva, 1982). Hence, already in *The Origins of Table Manners* (Levi-Strauss, 1979) and the birth of the signifier (Saussure, 1959), we find the struggle to repay debts that are structural to the psyche no matter how hard we try to deconstruct them or how perversely we fail to represent them (Hartman, 2013). This we read with great humor and sadness in Eyal Rozmarin's (2010) account of playing Holocaust alphabet with Israeli parents of soldiers bound for the front: history reiterates the limitations of viability but, as we move through time, we learn to state our best intentions as we strive to improve connectivity.[3]

So where this leaves us is something like this: there can be no baby without a mother and no alien without a slew of parasitic eggs cleaving to the iron work of a donated, if not broken-down, vessel and so there is more: an Other to grab on to when the audience screams – and then you laugh while you cry. As Canadian critic Mari Ruti writes, "we purchase our social subjectivity at the price of narcissistic injury in the sense that we become culturally intelligible beings only insofar as we learn to love ourselves a bit less" (2011, p. 135). We lack, substitute, compensate, rinse and repeat, she writes: "the subject's ability to dwell within lack without seeking to close it is indispensable for psychic vitality" (p. 137).

Me, I call this searching (Hartman, 2012), and I imagine that searching is the prerequisite for what we relational folk call "multiplicity." In an effort to describe a relationally inflected, collectively minded reading of the *claustrum*, Susanne Chassay and Karen Peoples argue that it is precisely the Kleinian baby's phantasmatic probing of the mother's estheticized body that gave Winnicott the first whiff of potential space. If "the analyst's breathing skin," as Peoples (2012) writes, is "a seamless wrapping of receptor cells that sense density and intensity, tightness and spaciousness, coolness and warmth in the analytic womb in which the analytic dyad's breathing occurs" (p. 21), then we can hold the viability in the despairing self who pretends to have no need of air with the intentionality of the aging body's grace. Time is restored and so is thought. Nora, in Peoples' elegant prose, is "an infant who has *failed to be sufficiently lit from within* by a reciprocated sense of the baby's own beauty" (2012, p. 22). Nora takes in Simon's breath through the pores in her skin and, when she does, she will assimilate Simon's intention for her care, and something larger.

Like Lacan, Winnicott emphasized what will need to be lost internally so that the viable object has the symbolic capacity to become a vital subject. And I think it is utterly important to add, as French psychoanalyst François Villa writes (2011, p. 159), that "little humans enter actively into dependence on an environment that, [while] not anticipating this encounter, will not prematurely stamp out their creativity." The social world was always already there. Yet, for Winnicott, the encounter with the world "must happen in such a way that individuals do not have to take this reality into consideration too prematurely. This is necessary so that they can experience this encounter as a moment of personal creation." Villa concludes, "before being a singular representative of the species, they are the species itself, a virtual vehicle of all of its potentialities." Here is where ancestral memory eggs us on. As we become virtual subjects, we must recognize a debt to subjects who precede us in creating the potentials and practices that we live by: "our existence being the proof of their ability to survive" such that I am viable too.[4]

Indeed, maternity, cultivated as agrobusiness, poaches from a long-held intention to be generative, contained in baby's "viability." Capitalism makes no such investment; indeed, it obfuscates our faith in the other and turns maternal work into a commodity that can be farmed out and alienated from the mother, who requires no reparation because she is no longer *us*. This perverse scenario nonetheless has, as Masud Khan (1989) wrote, some purchase on reality. Simon isn't approaching ART as some kind of technophobic Luddite, but rather holding a spot for her patient in the depressive position. For ART is the prisoner's dilemma for those of us who can't have a child any other way but through *assistance*. And, how assistance is contained by society, it seems to me, has a great deal to do with whether a mother will experience birth technology within the *claustrum* or use it in the way that Warrant Officer Ripley, perhaps inspired by Jessica Benjamin (1988), stops cold upon recognizing that the alien is herself a pregnant mother, who, like Ripley, holds the intention of viability for her fetus. "Get away from her, you bitch!" is now a call to end suffering and it becomes starkly clear that "mother," the computer, is in reality Hal, the sadistic phallus of *2001: A Space Odyssey*. Repairing the mothership was a claustrophobic fantasy of surrrender gone very wrong, so Ripley blows it to smithereens.

Ripped out of the Imaginary order into the Symbolic army of mothers masquerading as men, Ripley slays the weary alien, restoring her to motherhood, as perhaps does Nora her mother, and Benjamin (1988) describes this moment of mutual recognition where kill-or-be-killed dynamics yield to access to the Other as a "constant." For orthodox Kleinians and Bionians, the politics of this moment are a primarily internal affair, the projective machinations of which we presume to conjecture because somehow or other the analyst is able to contain them. I rather prefer to travel closer to the social edge of care. As Karen Peoples notes (personal communication, 27 June, 2013), there is a social dimension to embodied containment, yet: "in some particularly encapsulated and *anaesthetized* psychesoma states it may only be through the pt's acting sensorily upon the analyst's body that communication (of the social) is made representable." Our duty is to allow Nora to abort in the *claustrum* so that, in the Real, she may use whatever technology gives her time to plan parenthood: time to *bricolage* useless bits of horror into a life usable and sustainable and connected. It is only then that we can begin to reconcile our real indebtedness to our mother's long-held intention of our inevitably viable and spontaneous gestures. Might Simon's prose be so spare and Nora's alexithymia so savage at the intent of collective unconscious desire?

Now, I refer you to IMDB to get the whole twisted plot of the *Aliens* series, and I've already gone on way too long, but know this: the men who work for the company just keep going on back to the mothership because they want to own a piece of the rock. Unlike Ripley and unlike Simon, they have not found a way to generalize from the 1828 sense of viable as specific, to the 1848 definition of it as generalized and collective. These woeful company men are deluded to imagine that if you have a piece of the rock, you own it because, if you believe you've finally got it, you can only have it in a symbolic and therefore melancholic relation to the rock's viability. In other words, you can only be viable in debt at which point you have to choose, it seems to me, between a reality where you continually search for meaning alongside Others and one where you continually rack up debt on a 3-hour tour to the *Claustrum*.

Nora has a tremendous burden of indebtedness. She also has many fantasies about her indebtedness that Simon eloquently retells. I suggest we cast Sigourney Weaver in her role – tall, thin, angry, and self-possessed, just like Nora and rather like, I imagine, Joan Rivière having a chortle with the cigar-smoking luminaries whom she addressed in Vienna on the occasion of Freud's 80th birthday. To whom, I immediately ask, must Nora repair? Who must she fix so that she need not abort her child? Why, for the sake of the child's viability, must she cede her own? And so on. Too much for one script, and maybe Simon's treatment is the more accurate one, leaner, closer to the bone.

Final scene: Nora is in this alone. Simon tells us that approximately one in six American women who seek to become pregnant use ART. Where are they? Nora cannot use them. She is too busy dodging the police, like Nicole Kidman in Lars von Trier's *Dogville*.[5] She masquerades as the viable child that she was intended to be. This will restore mother to beauty, dispense with her siblings' envy, perhaps even kill the partner who is now merged with the likely male child obliging her to stay home from work. There she is, a tall, lanky, sassy mommy. Rich too. Out of breath. Inside, nothing but debt.

Simon's body comes into view. Breathing. Two bodies now. Simon hearing. Deadness drowning. All of these percepts register in the sensorium which is now alive and has the intention of the body's going on breathing. Susanne Chassay (2013) explains that the analyst's breath is the patient's as-yet-unspeakable sign that we are called to heed, a sign that must first make itself known through the analyst's senses.

I think Susanne is right. In order to do relational work, the analyst must often sit on the edge of her seat, skin crawling – quietly *knowing* that the alien always comes twice (which might be the only thing we know as analysts) – so that the patient can at last encounter an indebtedness to an internal that is held externally to its internal regurgitation. Nora escapes her lawless refuge (Guralnik, 2011), anticipates time, and rejoins the collective project. No doubt Simon's affect penetrated Nora as meaning. "No!" Simon yells, albeit in silence, "Keep your hands off my baby, you bitch!" and Nora hears it, knowing that Simon is not speaking about the fetus. Among Nora's internal cast of characters, there is now a viable baby gasping for air. Now Nora can live "the miracle" instead of having to be "it": "Look what we [mothers] did," she declares triumphantly, "we had a baby without a man" (Chapter 9).[6]

Notes

1 This discussion is the text of an oral presentation. The first section was intended to depict being inside a meltdown trying to elaborate an argument but stymied by the interiority of the meltdown. In keeping this written version close to the original, I hope to vocalize some of the flavor of an antiverbal madness.
2 M.M. Khan (1924–1989) was a British psychoanalyst legendary for erratic behavior at the British Psychoanalytical Society.
3 Versus the Lacanian simultaneous fascination with and defamation of the internet on the grounds that it presents the Imaginary as if Real, I emphasize how searching, like playing, for Winnicott constructs the subject.
4 Hence the title of a documentary depicting the devastation of the Castro district in San Francisco at the height of the AIDS epidemic takes the depressive position title: We Were Here.
5 I'm indebted to Cynthia Sailors for this reference.
6 This quotation appeared in an earlier draft of Simon's chapter.

Chapter 11

Teleplastic abduction

Subjectivity in the age of ART or delirium for psychoanalysis: Commentary on Simon's "spoken through desire"

André Lepecki

Whose body?

We owe to Gilles Deleuze the following insight: "Delirium is always geographical-political" (in Boutang, 2007). My response to Tracy L. Simon's article (Chapter 9) is framed by Deleuze's insight and by my work in the fields of dance studies and performance studies – because I am a total outsider to the field of psychoanalysis. However, and following Gilles Deleuze's insight that a concept is an "object of an encounter" (Deleuze, 1968, p. xx), I hope that by facilitating (or precipitating) an encounter between Tracy's article and some notions of corporeality and subjectivity coming from experimental dance and performance art, a few productive concepts may erupt – concepts that may help us reflect further on the question of "embodiment."

I do not want to sound as if I am forcing an encounter between such distinct fields and disciplines. Because concepts are also endowed "with their zones of presence" (Deleuze, 1968, p. xx), what I am proposing is that the encounter between dance and psychoanalysis is occasioned by a shared zone of conceptual co-presence between these disciplines: a zone defined by the question, or main problematic, traversing the entire case study Tracy analyzes – the question: "Whose body?"

Indeed, the interrogation "Whose body?" sutures the whole analytical exchange between Tracy and her patient, Nora. It is indeed an interrogation that titles the whole drama of the case, the whole drama of the analysis, but also Nora's anguish. A drama, a question, an anguish – all derived from one single event: the quasi-impossibility of delineating neat boundaries between all the main elements at play in Nora's anxieties and conflicts: between Nora's body and the body of assisted reproductive technology (ART), where, as Tracy tells us, "body parts, commodified, enter the international trade" (Chapter 9, footnote 5) as well as "legal, financial, governmental, global, medical, and technological worlds"[1]; between Nora's body and the egg donor's body; between Nora's body and her familial body (including the body, and ghost, and corpse, of her stillborn older sibling). But also, as I explore further down, it is an analysis whose drama in and as transference lies on the undecidability of both patient and analyst in defining the limits of their bodies in relation to each other – the limits of Nora's body with regard to Tracy and all of her bodies.

As a main premise to my arguments, I take the question "Whose body?" to be the main question traversing and structuring the whole field of contemporary sociability, of contemporary panicking as sociability, thus defining our daily "social choreographies," to use Andrew Hewitt's expression.[2] Indeed, "Whose body?" is one of the fundamental questions informing the notion of choreography as a general system of (corporeal) transmission. It is through this particular understanding of choreography (as a system of transmission of corporealities that instills social order into, on to, and across bodies) that I hope to contribute in thinking on the status of contemporary embodiment as it emerges in the analysis of Nora.

Dancing with psychoanalysis, with Tracy's article, and with Nora's and Tracy's bodies, as well as with all the bodies they invoke, let's see whose body is at stake when we talk about embodiment via ART.

Telepathy

Nevertheless, I start closer to psychoanalysis than perhaps I should. Or rather, I start with some observations on what, in psychoanalysis, I am most attracted to: the famous "private affair" Freud confesses to be having in a letter addressed to Ernst Jones dated March 7, 1926 (Gay, 1988, p. 445). Referring to a "Fall into Sin," Freud reveals to Jones the object of that potentially scandalous affair and orients Jones on how deal with it in the event of any public inquiry. To quote the perhaps too familiar passage,

> If someone should reproach you with my Fall into Sin, you are free to reply that my adherence to telepathy is my private affair like my Jewishness, my passion for smoking, and other things, and the theme of telepathy – inessential for psychoanalysis.
>
> (Freud as cited in Gay, 1988, p. 445)

It seems to me, however, that the famous and certainly intriguing association Freud makes in that letter between his affair with telepathy, his vices, and addictions (cigars and "other things"), and his Jewishness (all of which had to be foreclosed for the sake of the future of psychoanalysis as a "proper" science) has more to it than meets the eye. It seems to me that there is something else at stake here than just a legitimate concern about ensuring the respectability of psychoanalysis – something else that may be of relevance to our discussion. The challenge telepathy poses to psychoanalysis is not only about a possible crisis involving its "respectability" as scientific and clinical endeavor. Perhaps more profoundly, telepathy's challenge is to dare psychoanalysis to occasion, precipitate, and fully embrace a deep (epistemological) crisis in its definition of subjectivity – and consequently, in its understanding of embodiment.

For it seems obvious that, contrary to Freud's concession that (at least for the general public) telepathy is "inessential to psychoanalysis," the fact remains that telepathy is indeed absolutely essential to psychoanalysis – in fact, this may be the reason Freud reportedly remained faithful to his private affair throughout his life. And, I dare venture this hypothesis here, perhaps Freud's affair derived not out of an idiosyncratic passion for the occult but rather from an intuition that telepathy is an absolutely essential concept for understanding subjectivity (and the unconscious) as essentially porous, permanently traversed, opened, and captured by the calls (and, by extension, by the bodies) of others – subjectivity as a permanent being-on-call, to use Avital Ronell's expression (Ronell, 1991). This is exactly John Forrester's point when he writes, "The telepathic question par excellence, one which immediately *reveals its kinship to psychoanalysis* is: 'Whose thoughts are these, inhabiting my inner world?'" (Forrester, 1990, p. 252; italics added).

This is the fundamental question telepathy poses: "Whose thoughts?" A question addressing directly the ontological nature, or ontological correspondence, between self-identity and self-control over one's own inner world; between subjectivity and ownership over one's thoughts; between a subject perceived as an autonomous and private being and a subject perceived as porous multiplicity, as pack, as proliferation and conglomeration (Deleuze & Guattari, 1987, pp. 6, 26–38, 238–243); and therefore a subject already troubled by the impossibility of determining clearly an answer to the proprietary question posed by telepathy: "Whose thoughts are these, inhabiting my inner world?"

By pressing the question, "Whose thoughts, whose thoughts?", telepathy reveals subjectivity as generalized abduction. This insight allows us to start addressing some of the issues brought up by Tracy's article, namely, Nora's anguish regarding the source of her desire (Who desired her pregnancy? Herself? Her partner? ART? Heteronormativity? Something else?); the odd appearing of the egg donor (against all regulations) after the birth of Nora's child, which relaunched the property question, "Whose child? Whose child?"; the political-symbolic power of that abstract machine called "assisted reproductive technology" along with its "legal, financial, governmental, global, medical and technological worlds"; and the interesting confusion, or conflation, between Nora and Tracy at certain key points of the analysis. Hopefully, by attempting to answer the double question, "Whose body? Whose thoughts?" via an expanded notion of subjectivity (subjectivity as telepathic abduction) and an expanded notion of embodiment (embodiment as "teleplastic" abduction), we may start addressing the question of embodiment not only in the analytical situation but also in the broader field of subject formation.

Teleplasty

As mentioned earlier, what is being proposed here is to explore what happens when we promote an encounter between apparently radically different disciplines (dance studies, performance studies, psychoanalysis) and identify through their encounter how all share a zone of conceptual co-presence expressed by the double question, "Whose body? Whose thoughts?" What I am proposing is that perhaps the practice of choreographing and the experience of dancing could allow us to answer these central questions, so present in Tracy's analysis of Nora.

What does choreography do? As I said earlier, choreography is, first of all, a technology of transmission. But what choreography transmits is not only information, imperatives, or commands (commands such as "jump," "stay," "run," "count to ten and leap"). Choreography also transmits bodies: living and dead ones; actual and virtual ones; and not always whole, integral bodies but quite often only body parts (when Tracy refers to ART as creating a global market for "body parts," this logic of transmission and commodification is already choreographic, even if not in the esthetic sense of art). In this sense choreography is both productive – it produces specific bodies ready to perform specific acts – and reproductive – it assists bodies to reproduce themselves across time and space, by the means of a kind of body abduction. Choreography indeed is a "body snatcher", to use German dance theorist Franz Anton Cramer's expression. We can see its powerful effect in endless cohorts of young girls and boys gathered across the globe in dance studios where they collectively step into the legs of Merce Cunningham, or receive Martha Graham's pelvis, or turn their spines into Steve Paxton's spine, or make their solar plexus into Isadora Duncan's solar plexus. Historically, and perhaps even ontologically, choreography (understood as a project through which modernity as scene of mobilization first forces itself upon bodies to turn mobilization itself into modernity's privileged emblem[3]) erupts quite literally as a kind of telepathic machine where what is embodied by the dancer is not only the body of the dance master but even, and this is very important, the bodies of those dancers who are already dead. At the formation of choreography, in the first book that prints for the first time, a neologism fusing writing and movement into one single word, *Orchesography*, by Thoinot Arbeau (1589), we can find the plea of a dancer to his dance master. Before the disappearing body of dance, in a position of melancholia before dance's ephemerality, the student dancer begs his dance master to write a book so that, by setting "these things down in writing to enable me to learn this art," the dance master "will seem reunited to the companions of [his] youth" (Arbeau, 1589, p. 14). Choreography does not allow the lost object to depart. Its body must return over and over in order to be reembodied in/as my own, or in/as someone else's – even after I am dead. Again and again, choreography seals its social contract that a body will always be transmitted.[4]

In other words, choreography erupts as a practice of corporeality predicated both on the transmission of esthetic intentions (choreographic thoughts) and also on the transmission of gestures, acts, affective forces, and body parts (body forms) – including bodies of dancers already dead. As Japanese dancer and choreographer, and founder of Butoh, Tatsumi Hijikata once said, when dancing one must be aware of the corpse one always drags along. A dancer, then, lives and works with this particular understanding of subjectivity: her body is not only hers, her body is a composite of living and dead body parts, assembled under the provisional exercise of activating embodied transmitted intention or choreographic thought. Indeed, there is no other subjectivity for the dancer than to be a host – and to experience his or her body as already a condensation and an amalgamation of endless series of other bodies. This is why a dancer knows her legs are not quite only her legs; a dancer's intentions are not quite only his; just as their bodies, even if flailing like crazy, are not quite fully only alive because they continuously must remain open to receive and express what Avery Gordon called "ghostly matters" (Gordon, 1997).

Telepathy for sure, then – but also teleplasty: a word coined by Roger Caillois in his essay "Mimicry and Legendary Psychasthenia" (Caillois, 1935, p. 23), to describe a kind of morphological transmission at a distance, across space and time, of someone's or something's form – and the concomitant reception of that form by an organism or subject.[5] Teleplasty, telepathy, body snatching, fantasmagoria, being always already multiple – these must not be seen as metaphors but as precise and very concrete expressions of a dancer's experience of how subjectivity meets embodiment. We can now rephrase Forrester's (1990) diagnosis. If he wrote that "the telepathic question par excellence, one which immediately reveals its kinship to psychoanalysis is: 'Whose thoughts are these, inhabiting my inner world?'" choreography and dance supplement his question with another, correlative, which can be phrased thus: "Whose words, voices, gestures, and movements are these, inhabiting my body?"

It is in this sense that choreography offers ways to delineate what is "spoken through desire" (Simon, Chapter 9) in an open, rhizomatic, telepathic–teleplastic way. And what choreography reveals, through its fusion of telepathy and teleplasty, is how what is "spoken through desire" is not an existential question laced by mortality, that is, not Hamlet's "to be or not to be" but the more contemporary realization that subjectivity is essentially abduction and its existential question is one laced by an excess of living: how to negotiate being inhabited; moved; spoken by and through the thoughts, desires, and body parts of (so many) others. If telepathy operates theoretically and critically at any level, it is to reveal how subjectivity is predicated on the model of "the body-sieve" (Deleuze, 1969, p. 87).[6] In other words, telepathy exposes how a normative notion of subjectivity as the only desirable, prized subjectivity, as the only one where something like health and happiness may perhaps be achieved, is one of the subject-as-idiot – the word idiot being used here in its etymological sense.[7]

But the fact remains that reality constantly assaults us with the dancer's dilemma. Facing the impossible dream of always wanting to be an individual (i.e., unique, original, autonomous, private, personal, self-sovereign, indivisible), the idiotic subject cannot help but to fall into a state of panic (which is precisely that other name for our contemporary condition) once confronted with the clear, inevitable, and therefore absolutely alarming question that overcomes this subject in the middle of the night, robbing him or her of sleep: whose thoughts, words, voices, gestures, movements, and body parts are these, inhabiting my body? Teleplastic–telepathic as well as choreo-existential question. Thus, we are back to the (choreographic) refrain at the root of Nora's anxiety: "Whose body? Whose body?"

Abduction

Let's go back to Freud's wish to detach telepathy from psychoanalysis. The question is to know how the future of psychoanalysis was secured by paying the price of foreclosing that which it should directly address – namely, a radical clinical and critical project aimed at dismantling subjectivity as inextricably tied to the normative primacy of the private. By refusing telepathy and teleplasty psychoanalysis prizes only one position to subjectivity: the idiotic position.[8] Teresa Brennan (2000) defines her project of "exhausting modernity" by precisely unworking and extracting subjectivity from the notion of privacy. In a radical shift of our common understanding of the relations between embodiment, affect, and psychic life, Brennan proposes that our contemporary state of anxiety, exhaustion, depression, and particularly the panic syndrome pandemic must pass through a philosophical, political, clinical, and esthetic dismantling of understanding subjectivity as a "private affair" between me, myself, and I (or as a "private affair," eventually, with an analyst, as long as I can afford, obviously, an analyst who, moreover, will be paid to address my problem, my symptom, my anxiety, my neurosis . . . private properties everywhere).

Could psychoanalysis perhaps gain something by learning from the dancer's subjectivity? From the understanding of how the body as sieve may be not a symptom of (or a path toward) psychic dissolution and regression but could be seen as grounding a different understanding of subjectivity and embodiment – where both are always already traversed by the world, already conceived as world? Being always plural: a way out of the panic of having to be always a self-contained, self-authored, privately regulated self attached to a singular private body. As French choreographer Xavier LeRoy puts it, in a "self-interview" conducted in 2000:

> There must exist another alternative to the body image than the anatomical one. . . . For instance, the body could be perceived as space and time for trade, traffic, and exchange.
>
> (LeRoy, 2002, p. 46)

We can recognize in LeRoy echoes of Paul Schilder in his *The Image and Appearance of the Human Body* (1950). Indeed, LeRoy acknowledges Elizabeth Grosz and Deleuze and Guattari as inspiration to his insights, which are not too far from Schilder's views on the spatial–temporal distributions of the body image.[9] But what I particularly like about LeRoy's language is how the body dissolves its depth to become a transtemporal surface for trafficking, perhaps even smuggling. Any artist whose work is to embody another understands very well how embodiment is always transgression of economy, how embodiment is always a question touching the heart of private property. Any artist who embodies another body (living or dead) knows very well the discontinuous misalignments between property, subjectivity, and corporeal autonomy – the subject as sole author of his or her life; of his or her thought processes; of his or her desires, babies, marriages, and even analysis emerging as a fantastical fantasy – a taxing one, however. In fact, boundaries between self and others are, indeed, permanently being trespassed to the point in which "self" and "others" name pure ideals, illusions – albeit taxing ones.

In her analysis of Nora, Tracy describes this collapse of boundaries between herself and her patient (or between her self and Nora's self). Determining the entire narrative of this case study is Tracy's initial acknowledgment that, at the moment of crisis, that is to say, at the moment when something singular is indeed taking place, both she and Nora become one and the same. I see this confusion, this fusion, as the work of a kind of empty, or blank, or contentless, telepathy where what is transmitted is the fact of a co-abducted subjectivity being teleplastically co-formed: "Nora was a walking ghost, stripped of her vitality and propelled into blind action. She existed on the surface, each loss marking her psychically but registering as blankness, *which characterized me, too* [emphasis added]: we could not think" (Chapter 9).

What is being transmitted here, to form a particular embodiment whose name can only be "TracyNora," is a shared nonthought: pure transmission. Through this transmission, a lifeless desert spreads across and through both women and becomes the conjunctive tissue of the analysis, characterizing not only Nora's psychic life but also the analytical encounter. However, on this desert surface, TracyNora's shared nonthinking could be seen as a symptom that goes far beyond the particularities of their specific interaction in the context of their analysis. Tracy tells us that the desert operates as a surface for telepathic crisscrossing, where their role is to become frantic conduits to exchange endless logistical information:

> meaning making quickly collapsed into details about medical information and inconclusive news. Our time felt urgent, driven, manic, bumbling through information we could not understand under the psychic weight of what could not yet be said.
>
> (Simons, Chapter 9)

The desert becomes rather a surface where an event (telepathy) takes place, so it may reveal how it is that our times impale subjectivity through an unbearable choreographic demand of always being in a permanent state of frantic agitation, of producing and reproducing without creating. Despite all the commotion, this impetus's aim is to prevent the creation of a movement that truly matters.

The hyperactivity of TracyNora – choreographed and (re)produced via the hyperactivity of the informational superhighway of medical decisions, fertility tests, parental options, reproductive technologies, monetary decisions, adoption brokers, and cliché photo shoots staged to represent heterosexual white American financial-familial success – becomes in itself a reproductive machine for a generalized "nervous system" (to use Michael Taussig's (1993) expression) that now can be located as existing, operating, and twitching precisely in the nonspace of pervasive telepathic transmission of endless logistical details and of teleplastic imposition of "prized" body types (pregnant body, maternal body, healthy body, heterosexual body, blond body, "all-American" body), which are vehicles (i.e., dancers) for the reproduction of biopolitical norms and social-choreographic imperatives.

But once the fact of intersubjective telepathic–teleplastic transmission has been accepted, then the subsequent proposition must follow: embodiment is not only a phenomenon of incorporation but also a matter of excorporations. Embodiment would then be defined as the endless work of incor-excorporating, telepathically and teleplastically (in other words, choreographically), endless series of other excorporations and incorporations permanently crisscrossing, weaving the social.

Copyright anxiety

Whose body? Whose thoughts? Whose gestures? Whose pregnancy? In any context that prizes a proprietary notion of subjectivity, the answer to these questions can only end up in anxiety. This is because any question regarding creative property in our neoliberalist nervous system ends up being a question about determining who owns exclusive rights over one's productions – in other words, maternity and paternity under ART become a matter of exclusive copyrights and well-defined authorship. The progenitor is an author, and we know how every subject is condemned to be a creator, in neoliberal capitalism, as long as creativity, above all, conforms.[10] But because the model for creativity we have is still sadly theological, Nora's anguish is also the anguish of the author violating copyright laws: her baby may not be entirely hers genetically; her desire for it, just as her desire to abort it, may not be entirely hers – her anxiety comes from the suspicion that her partner's or her doctors' or the world's, perhaps even Tracy's, desires are already implicated in her desire. Which, of course, they are. But, for the private subject, the contemporary, educated, highly accomplished idiot, these intrusions (this inescapable parasitism, haunting, or telepathic teleplasty) are seen not as constitutive of living but as copyright infringement.

Whose body? Whose thoughts? Whose desire? You may hear echoes of Alice – the one in Wonderland – when she asks herself, "Which way? Which way?" only to discover that the only answer to her question is – all ways, every direction! That's where your body goes: everywhere; that's where your body is: all over; that's where your body has always already been: excorporating (across) time and space; incorporating (across) space and time.

Whose body, whose thoughts, whose subjectivity, whose illness, whose panic, whose frustration, whose depression? In this endless exchange, in this series of excorporations and incorporations, a poliplastic, transtemporal intercourse ensues. For aren't we even told that Nora and Tracy made a baby together? And is it not true that, indeed, they did make a baby together? Whose baby? Whose love? Whose desire? Whose assistance? Nora's sentence may be a joke, a sign of joy, but it is not at all a metaphor. It is a precise description of a joyful situation of confusion: love. As Deleuze and Guattari (2007) say, "We always make love with worlds" (pp. 428–432). How does an analyst make love to her patients' worlds? What other worlds does this love make?

Thus, rather than to say, "I do not know what my neurotic, my depressive, my anxious nucleus is," it should perhaps be better to say, "I do not know from where in the world a neurotic, a depressive, an anxious nucleus is coming." This is where analysis becomes cartography, not of the unconscious of a subject but of the world as telepathic–teleplastic machine whose main vital function is to excorporate as much as it is to incorporate. Abductor and abductee always existing in all directions at once and irrespective of property rights and propriety issues. The question of desire then becomes one of identifying how it is reduced from being multidirectional and multitemporal, and it is turned into a domesticated unidirectionality, into a logic conformity. Tracy's analysis suggests how we could name this logic. For instance, we could call it "prosperous-heteronormative-north-American-white-success-story-under-pressure-to-fill-in-the-space-of-its-pre-assigned-maternal-image-as-the-(re)producer-of-human-beings." This name expresses the main elements in the generalized social choreography of conformity already snatching up Nora's body, her partner's body, but also all of our bodies because we all assist, one way or another, more or less willingly, more or less unwillingly, in the making of a world that makes ART.

Against conformity's unidirectional force, one possible answer for subjectivity and embodiment is to actively multiply counterforces, to be a dancer, that is to say, to be a subjectivity willingly trafficking at the border between things and words, thoughts and bodies, to be a subjectivity open to be abducted, telepathically, teleplastically, and yet agentially, actively, critically, politically, lovingly, and willingly by the unexpected delirium of something else.

Notes

1 This quotation appeared in an earlier draft of Simon's article.
2 "I use the term social choreography to denote a tradition of thinking about social order that derives its ideal from the aesthetic realm and seeks to instill that order directly at the level of the body" (Hewitt, 2005, p. 3).
3 On the relation between modernity, choreography, and transmission, see Lepecki (2006), particularly Chapters 1, 2, and 6.
4 For a discussion on Arbeau and the melancholic transmissibility of dance, see Lepecki (2006, pp. 25–29).
5 "a reproduction in three-dimensional space with solids and voids: sculpture-photography or better teleplasty, if one strips the word of any metaphysical content" (Caillois, 1935, p. 23).
6 "Freud emphasized this aptitude of the schizophrenic to grasp the surface and skin as if they were punctured by an infinite number of little holes" (Deleuze, 1969, p. 87).
7 From the Greek, *idiotes*: the private individual; *idios*, private. On dance and idiocy, see Lepecki (2006, Chapter 2).
8 What strikes me as amazing is this: had Freud written back to Jones affirming rather than denying the essential role of his Jewishness, his addiction, and of telepathy for psychoanalysis, he would have embraced the three pillars of schizoanalysis, or rhizomatics, namely, the understanding that: (1) all subjectivity is already captured by, and must deal with, the judgment of God (Artaud and the body without organs); (2) desire is also an impersonal affair between things and organs, between matters and body parts (addiction as desire of the organ: Wilhelm Reich); and (3) every subject is simultaneously host and guest of other subjects (the body as a pack, as assemblage always in "unnatural nuptials" (Deleuze & Guattari, 1987, p. 273).
9 "I have specifically pointed out the fact that whatever originates in or emanates out of our body will still remain part of the body-image. . . . The body image incorporates objects or spreads itself into space" (Schilder, 1950, p. 213).
10 See, for instance, Virno (2004, pp. 47–72) and Berardi (2009).

Chapter 12

Zen and the ART of making babies

A discussion of Tracy Simon's paper

Orna Guralnik

"Today is a bad day," Drew announces as he sits down, "The heart beat is gone." The fetus had a short life. "I feel sad but it's hard to know where to localize it. We all seem to be confused about which one of us is the primary mourner: Gillie [the surrogate], David [Drew's partner], or me?" This would have been Drew and his husband's third child through egg donation and surrogacy. "Their baby" growing in another woman's belly confuses the location of loss. "Who needs to console who?" Drew asks. As if to convince me of the urgency of writing this chapter, my next patient, Avery, arrives, announcing that she and her fiancé have decided to abort their new pregnancy. She has been worried about interrupting what she calls the "blood line" of her first two kids, both conceived with the sperm of the same anonymous donor. She chose to have her second child with the same donor sperm and not her fiancé (who entered her life after she had her first child), hoping that it would enhance her first child's ability to understand who he is, by having a "like me" sibling. She was deeply ambivalent about introducing a third child, conceived with her fiancé, into the family and relieved to discover that he did not feel an urgent need for a biological link to his children. The day continues. Late that afternoon I see a gay couple; they are excited about starting a business together. Being of an older generation, they never felt having kids was an honestly thinkable option and are newly melancholic about it.

Later that week I saw Gene, who wants to have kids with his girlfriend; however, for a variety of posttraumatic reasons, they will not have sex. He wonders whether to consider their asexual life a prohibition on having children. The week ends with a trans patient sharing with me the dilemmas of an F-to-M friend who accidentally got pregnant while off hormones (to prepare for surgery). He ended up keeping the baby and completed his surgery only after birth, resulting in a family of two dads having their biological child. Their dilemma was about disclosing their biological link to their child. And on it goes. In the process of writing this paper, as my days with patients go by, I could not help but feel amused. From where I sit, the traditional family is somewhat of a fantasma; a powerful one, but Object-*a*-ish (Lacan, 1994) and increasingly harder to find. In real life, a revolution has taken place, much of it afforded by medical technology. This is true in my practice, as well as with my friends and family.

Yet our ideologies and theories (and the sets of affects and thoughts they permit; Guralnik & Simeon, 2010) remain stubbornly linked to a traditional portrait of the family. In this gap, Simon's paper was conceived.

Simon's analysis with Nora is deeply moving. She describes the difficult task of tuning into muted affects, and enduring the brunt of brutal ones, as she travels with Nora the range of melancholic disavowal to the rage of infanticide. I deeply respect her nimble read of these shifting experiences employing a multitude of theoretical frames. Courageously delving into relatively unexplored terrain, infertility and technology, Simon continues the project of linking psychoanalytic and political frames of reference. She contextualizes Nora's individual struggles in the matrix of global biopolitics and the patriarchal imperative to conflate womanhood with motherhood, bringing to life the cruel toll of exclusion this imperative inflicts on Nora ("Being (the right kind of woman) gets conflated with and concretized as having (a child)": Simon, Chapter 9). Fueled by my admiration of her work, I feel compelled to write about an aspect of the discourse on assisted reproductive technologies (ARTs) that has bothered me for a long time, and will hopefully complement Simon's insights.

Oedipal anxiety and the ART of making babies

Let's start with a declaration of my own subject position: I love ART. I love the wild fantasies, possibilities, and new realities it affords. But mostly I love the unabashed indifference ART demonstrates toward the sacred cow of Oedipal law. (See Chapters 1, 2, and 7 for further discussion of ARTs and Oedipal configurations.) I use the term Oedipal law here to refer to the theoretical assumption that the "threefold" structure of the family (Fenichel, 1931) – father, mother, and child – is predetermined (supporting the continuation of the human species) and protected by the incest prohibition, which in turn is enforced by castration anxiety.[1] Oedipal law is reinforced by state law. It is implicitly based on the bedrock association of sexual desire with reproduction, with roots in the patriarchal order. ART offers us the possibility of "unknowing what families are" (Corbett, 2009a, p. 55). In this chapter I will be referring to the options ART offers people who want to have children, and not to the choice to be childfree, which is a different break-away from the Oedipal spell.

Technology, medicine, ethics, and regulatory anxiety

Simon invites us to think of individual struggles within their biopolitical context. As with any technology, ART presents possibilities that are being continually examined for their ethical, psychological, and political implications. By virtue of still being an expensive technology, ART discriminates by class. Since there is so much money involved, many vulnerable populations – donors and surrogates in particular – can be pushed into a form of "consent" to offer their bodies, while being coerced or exploited by material need and power dynamics (Saketopoulou,

2011, writes about the complexity of consent in reference to sexual encounters). Simon sensitizes us to the ways want-to-be parents can be vulnerable to the seduction of ART's promise, caught in the despairing web of desire and social pressures. She also draws our attention to how ART feeds on the "old discourse on motherhood" and reproduces the idealization of femininity as motherhood. Other ethical concerns that often come up with the topic of ART include how it could be employed in the service of eugenics (the wish to "improve" the genetic load of a population and "purify" it of its various Others).

I relate to these concerns, yet am repeatedly surprised when the dread of misuse of technology takes on a certain tense urgency when it is put to the use of reproduction. I can think of many other types of new medical technologies that evoke anything from sheer apathy to admiration, and rarely this kind of panic, as for example when people turn to expensive medical practices aimed to prolong life (e.g., the heroic struggles of cancer or heart disease patients) or for cosmetic desires. The transferences towards such patients tend to be idealizing to neutral, rather than intensely paranoid.[2] In my practice I find that transferences tend to get particularly hostile when applied to the medical teams in the ART sector; they seem to come ready-made: the medicine men/researchers/embryologists take their place on stage as bad objects: money-hungry and heartless bastards, out to exploit their patients' weakness/pathology. For the longest time several of my patients who could not get pregnant avoided even going for a fertility consult, assuming they'd be pressured into an assembly line. I interpret this bias to ultimately reflect the distaste people feel when the traditional Oedipal family is threatened. This observation is not to absolve medical practitioners from unethically taking on this very exploitative role and feeding off patients' needs, dependency, and vulnerability.

ART isn't only in the service of certain biopolitical interests. It also poses a major threat to heteronormative, patriarchal biopolitics. ART ("noncoital reproduction," as used in some legal documents; Robertson, 1986) destabilizes the sanctity of the traditional family. We no longer need the (Oedipal) composition (fantasy) where to have a baby you need husband and wife to perform intercourse,[3] the wife needs to carry the baby, give birth, and nurse her child (and ideally they'd live together happily ever after, as a legally protected economic unit). Instead, ART carves a demarcation between previously collapsed categories: eggs, uterus, mother, sperm, father, parent. It opens up the field to many possible permutations on family. People previously ruled out from reproduction (the biologically and socially infertile, including factors such as age, disabilities, sexual orientation, and aversions to sex) are now in the game. There are new types of possible parents: single parents, several parents, of any sex, with varying degrees of genetic relationship to the baby. The child's genetic load, sperm and egg, can each come from anonymous donors, or substitutes (e.g., a lesbian patient used the sperm of her girlfriend's brother). Genetic contribution, gestation, and parenthood can effectively be separated and assumed by different individuals. Those assisting the parents, such as donors and carriers, can assume different positions and kinship relationships in the new family, from receding to the background to a very involved presence.[4]

ART complicates the relationship between how parents wish to construct their family, what is possible, and what state law confirms. Prior to recent advancements, the law was aligned with biological ideals, protecting the heterosexual family while delegitimizing/excluding alternatives (although access to ART is still regulated and can differ by state in the United States). However, the underlying facts that justify legal rules have changed, and the law has been slowly adjusting (depending on state, and varying widely between countries[5]). A "contractual" or "bargaining" theory of parenthood has been gradually replacing the "biological" legal doctrine (Baker, 2004). Legal "ownership" of a child can no longer be assumed to correlate with biology. Surrogates and donors often have to sign documents relinquishing their legal rights to the future children. Of course, legal regulation is bound with more subtle forms of regulation that operate implicitly, through ideology and the various ways it shapes intelligibility and affect (Guralnik & Simeon, 2010). We know that psychoanalytic notions of health and cure typically align with state law, each reifying the other (Foucault, 1965; Dimen, 2010) – a topic I will return to later in this discussion.

Thus, while remaining vigilant to how ART can be used to discriminate and coerce, I'd like to notice how it also undermines the very conservative ideologies and politics that fiercely protect traditional families. I suggest that some of the queries and regulatory practices around the ethics and politics of ART be reinterpreted as a righteous cover-up of reactionary anxieties. These anxieties fuel a particular brand of suspicion and hostility towards ART that parallels the cruel attacks the Kleinians have attributed to the superego, whose goal is to enforce Oedipal law upon the ego, aiming the powerful ammunition of guilt, shame, and disavowal at transgressive desires. I meet such hostility in my patients, friends, and colleagues. And perhaps in Nora's aversion to her own noncoital fetus.

The hostile dread of anything different from the traditional family is deep. Golombok of the Centre for Family Research in Cambridge, United Kingdom, published a longitudinal outcome study on the welfare of surrogacy children, basically concluding that they were "doing extremely well" (Golombok et al., in press). A comparison group of those conceived through reproductive donation (sperm/egg) showed particularly low levels of emotional or behavioral problems. A reporter covering the publication for a popular audience skewed the findings so badly that Professor Golombok was moved to distribute an open letter to the reporter, protesting the biased reporting.

People in Nora's position, who are using ART to have a baby, will inevitably meet comments such as: Have you thought about why you want a child so badly? Why do you need another child? Have you thought that maybe it's just not meant to be? Perhaps you don't want it for the right reasons? Perhaps you should be talking to your analyst about this? And I wonder: how will your analyst be listening to you, while you're imagining nontraditional ways of making babies? Should you be talking to him or her?

"With such friends, who needs enemies?" asks Drew, in response to an organized group of "enlightened" queer friends who put out a Facebook "calling" to all gay dads: "work on your intimacy issues with women" ("Gay Dads" Facebook forum). Apparently, the psychologically healthy gay man should not deprive his children of a real mother and should let go of the selfish wish for a one-household family, in favor of a two-men-and-a-woman family. In this version of the new good family, maternal functions are still equated with biology, and gay dads are lacking. This goes back to the basic psychoanalytic belief, as expressed by Boehm in 1931: "For, even in cases where patients have never known their father or mother, analysis always brings out again that in their unconscious the typical Oedipus complex can be uncovered" (pp. 450–451). Or to Fenichel (also 1931), describing children who did not grow up in a typical "Oedipal family." Sooner or later they learn that the institution of the family exists and wherein it consists: that other children have a father and mother, and that they themselves are the inferior exceptions. They too have their Oedipus complex, i.e., phantasies about father and mother phantasies which closely resemble the Oedipus complex of other children, only drawing a special form from their phantastic character (pp. 428–429).

Nora and Simon

Simon's paper is one of a very few in the psychoanalytic literature even touching upon the subject of ART (Chapter 9). ART is oblivious to the very Shibboleth of psychoanalytic theory: the fantasma of the Oedipal family. Can we even consider ourselves psychoanalysts if we are not loyal to Oedipal ideology? The few papers on ART and psychoanalysis interpret the omnipotent fantasies ART can unleash (Zalusky, 2000). Simon refers to ART's promotion of an "implicit promise that anything and everything is possible," an "illusion of control," and "an illusory antidote to loss surrounding reproductive disappointments" (Chapter 9). She sees the use of ART as masking loss and mourning that do "not yet have a speakable place in culture" (Chapter 9). In psychoanalytic discourse omnipotence means: defensively rejecting limits and loss; going beyond what is real, and thus healthy; not accepting the correct version of "reality"; hubris, for which there is always a price. Simon attends to the generous language coding ART's procedures (harvesting, GIFTing, donation) as obfuscating the psychic meaning and price for the participants. From the Oedipal perspective, the price is high.

Simon is deeply attuned to Nora, and thus able to immerse herself in their field, fall situationally ill with Nora's frozen silence, and work her way out of this muted space relying on her analytic and Lacanian sensibilities, as well as her political curiosity. I have no doubt that Simon's willingness to immerse herself and seek meanings where Nora's mind refused was incredibly helpful to Nora. In Nora's silence, blankness, numbness, concreteness, and It-ness around infertility, Simon finds the unspeakable lack.

I do wish to take some liberty here and use this case material to illustrate my view. If we keep an eye on a treatment's ties to dominant discourse, we can read

Simon and Nora's field as "bastioned" (Baranger et al., 1983) by the Oedipal ideological persuasion I have been describing (Guralnik, 2010). The fantasies and affects available to patient and analyst may be limited to what falls within this hermeneutic-ideological circle, whilst other desires and excitements are foreclosed from generating other meanings (see our work on interpellation and dissociation; Guralnik & Simeon, 2010). When "the cultural notion that one should have a baby in one particular way"[6] prevails, any other option can only register as loss and mourning. Hartman (2011) commented on how difficult it is for the psychoanalytic literature to accommodate the new realities of cyberspace. He refuses to simply assume that technology and its cyberspace are to be equated with the not-real, and thus loss and limit. Instead, he suggests: "what appears to be a psychic retreat to nonreality (using a traditional frame of reference) may also be appreciated as a mode of psychic advance in a new kind of reality" (p. 470).

Nora and Simon's horizon is drawn in the opening sentences: "It", an abject embryo, "conceived via a donor's egg and her partner's sperm." The plot is engined by the power of genetic origins and their implied lines of legitimacy and possession to declare Nora as lacking. Nongenetic is abject. It can only be understood in terms of what it is not: a genetic coital baby. If we follow this suggested plot line, Nora is cast as the resentful woman, "abducted, coerced, excluded, and invaded," pressured into submission by a "curious cast of characters"[7] – the faceless medical specialists, and their long lists of invasive procedures ("Dissociated and blank, she submitted to the egg transfer": Simon, Chapter 9). Within this discursive circle women can only "consent to ART"[8] and only have an "illusion of choice." They could not be desiring subjects.

From the perspective I'm exploring here, the blankness that Simon describes so chillingly may be nesting unspeakable passions. What may be hidden in the silent gaps, the unthinkable, what Simon interprets as a refusal to mourn, may be Nora's desire, a desire that exceeds what sex will produce (a noncoital baby). Simon describes Nora feeling as if "she had to carry something that did not belong to her, a false possession, literally a foreign body, reappropriated from elsewhere." Did Nora experience her desire as kleptomanic and criminal? An illegal immigrant crossing the border for a job in the United States? When Simon writes about "reproductive cells migrating among bodies," I hear the whisper of anxiety about transgressive migration across legal (Oedipal) boundaries. Experiencing certain desires as transgressive, and thus foreclosed, may be part of what leaves both Nora and Simon flat, numb, lost in concrete operations. I find it particularly interesting that when this noncoital baby makes her first live appearance (a positive pregnancy test), the veil is temporarily dropped and we get a peek at the fire below: Nora explodes with fury, and Simon's whole being shouts "No!" to the idea of abortion. So much passion hidden behind their shared blankness! Passion for life, for a baby, conceived through the egg of another woman, or who even cares how and by whom. A baby. Indeed, Nora falls "madly in love" with this baby when she is born.

Simon turned to Lacanian theory for some reflective space between the subject and her body. I would find Lacan to be a tricky partner to engage on the topic of reproduction. Lacan, who returned to Freud with the supposed aim of keeping psychoanalysis separate from biology, studied how the human subject is constructed in language. However, in his view of the penis as the transcendental phallus, the signifier of sexual difference (phallic versus castrated), it is revealed that Oedipal law is always already presumed. Lacan did not disconnect unconscious desire from the Oedipal narrative, constrained by the implicit link between desire and reproduction: reproduction as it was imagined pre-ART. To quote Simon on Lacan (through Evans):

> Desire is in paradoxical relation with the law of the Symbolic order: regulating desire in the form of prohibitions and social rules (we accept lack: being is always incomplete) also fuels desire by creating prohibition (by telling us what we are not, it informs us that something is missing and, therefore, we must desire it).
>
> (Simon, Chapter 9)

Per Lacan, Oedipal law first announces Nora as lacking, which then fuels in her a certain kind of desire. Accordingly, egg donation performs a "denial of lack," or/and "lack of lack." It is not a thing; it's a no-thing. A donor egg baby is not an honest possibility. In employing Lacanian theory, Simon gains many sensibilities. However, the Lacanian "lack," a lack that is expressly nonbiological but located in language, actually reproduces the very biologically based ideology it is to critique. The Lacanian read interpellates its user to continue the reproduction of the law of the father. To understand Nora's process as a journey through lack can also be read as Lacan's failure of imagination, rooted in "what was possible" technologically and ideologically during the years that preceded the era of ART. Within the bastions of Lacanian theory there is no way for Simon to queer her "understanding" of Nora's distress.

Putting Lacan's theory through the feminist shredder and ending up in queer land, Butler resignified the Oedipal narrative as regulatory psychobiographic fiction. From this perspective the Oedipal narrative serves to define how bodies are to be understood (e.g., gendered), and, by extension here, families, desire, and kinship. The Oedipal ideology of the good life and the good family becomes unconsciously embedded in our ways of seeing the world. It resides in us in the form of procedural knowledge, governing our affective, moral, and cognitive systems. I wonder if Nora's deep sense of failure and falseness would morph if, in addition to its mournful qualities, it were explicitly interpreted as an expression of her loyalty to centrist Oedipal ideologies, and the affects, wishes, and self-states they interpellate.[9]

Psychoanalytic treatments are glass-ceilinged by what the analyst can imagine. We work with implicit notions of the normative/healthy (Dimen, 2010), against which we interpret. On some level, we are frequently called to determine whether a wish is an expression of growth or a fixation, whether a fantasy is creative or omnipotent. Not long ago mourning the impossibility of having children was part and parcel of many treatments. However, as Simon states: "the technology around reproduction has created a cultural change."[10] ART offers the infrastructure to create new kinds of psychobiographical narratives. Babies born through ART are anything but fantasy. They are true, live, in-reality babies that psychic reality may have trouble coming to terms with. A melancholic preoccupation with the lost coital baby can be interpreted as servicing a defensive, reactionary foreclosure of other possible "real babies."

With the changing landscape of what is actually possible in the world, we must listen differently to our patients' wishes, plans, and actions. Even in 1931, while pontificating about how embedded Oedipal structure was in the human psyche, Fenichel had the foresight to add: "In any case, to assume that the Oedipus complex has this phylogenetic root is by no means to contradict the notion that the complex itself is bound to change when the institution of the family disappears or changes" (Fenichel, 1931, p. 430). For us to change with culture, we may have to come to our patients having "forgotten," in the Bionian sense, some of the ideologies that are rooted in us. Working from a place deeply informed by ART would mean having allowed for technological possibilities to become psychologically viable possibilities. We might be able to hear wishes and fantasies that, due to technology, have long switched category from omnipotent to possible and viable. A baby. Not necessarily a baby that is a substitute to the lack: a subject in its own right, a sovereign subject who does not have to be so automatically interpellated by Oedipal ideology. Wild wishes and new psychobiographic narratives: for Drew and his husband – two twin babies, one yours, one mine! For an infertile partner – a baby with the mixed DNA of your family and mine! For Dina and her husband – a baby free of our genetic lineage! A baby where we thought none could be! A baby to love!

I will conclude with one of Simon's quotes of Lacan:

> That the subject should come to recognize and to name his desire; that is the efficacious action of analysis. But it isn't a question of recognizing something which would be entirely given. . . . In naming it, the subject creates, brings forth, a new presence in the world.
>
> (Lacan, 1978, pp. 228–229)

Notes

1 Freud (1924) introduced the concept of the Oedipus complex to denote the biologically and phylogenetically based sexual attraction of the child to the parent of the opposite sex, with concomitant jealousy and hostility to the other parent. Supposedly, "as the result of many thousands of years of evolution, it appears to have become a hereditary possession of our world" (Boehm, 1931, pp. 450–451). In joining society, the child has to give up early attachments, and is commanded to accept a feminine or masculine identity according to the norm of sexual difference and the threat of castration.

2 I am thinking of a well-to-do (financially) friend who is a war-veteran amputee. He was recently invited to receive three new hyper-designed and hyper-expensive prosthetic legs that will allow him to walk, run, and cycle faster. Large teams of doctors and techs have been tailoring such extensions for a lucky few. People who know him or have

heard of his story have nothing but admiration. One would have to stretch hard to hear a parallel *class* protest about his being coerced to spend so much on new technology.

3 Only in the 1600s did scientists figure out that the woman's orgasm was not necessary for conception (Bergner, 2013).

4 Just *naming* the participants is an interesting process – e.g., MaMa, Mommy, and Birth-mom.

5 For instance, the United States is a unique country with a mixed legal landscape concerning surrogacy, resulting in an entirely unregulated surrogacy industry; most relevant activities take place in a few extremely permissive states. Internationally, laws vary widely. Israeli legislation has changed rapidly in the past two decades, starting from surrogacy being illegal, to being legal for straight couples, and more recently to gay couples, but only if done on an "altruistic" basis – no fees involved. See Svitnev (2011) for a review of international law.

6 This quotation appeared in an earlier draft of Simon's chapter.

7 This quotation appeared in an earlier draft of Simon's chapter.

8 This quotation appeared in an earlier draft of Simon's chapter.

9 Nora's ART baby may be recruited to replace and substitute her Oedipal baby, reenacting her impossible role as substitute to her mother's stillborn baby, thus returning her to her sense of falseness. I wonder whether interpreting out of this paradigm, deconstructing the Oedipal interpellation by imagining other kinds of wished-for babies, may have served to *Nachträglichkeit* undo Nora's debt to her mother.

10 This quotation appeared in an earlier draft of Simon's chapter.

Chapter 13

Reply to commentaries

Hartman, Lepecki, and Guralnik

Tracy L. Simon

I am grateful to Stephen Hartman, André Lepecki, and Orna Guralnik for their perceptive, profound discussions. Their articles consider assistive reproductive technology (ART) in its cultural surround, raising questions about subjectivity, normativity, embodiment, and transmissions of meaning. Thanks to their willingness to join Nora and me in being lost, desirous, infuriated, hopeful, and terrified, each of these three discussions beautifully captures the elusive and ineffable landscape of ART. ART is a relatively new practice, beginning in the late 1970s, and we are among the first generation to know its practices and procedures as well as to think through its implications. Reflecting on a cultural struggle to integrate ART's discourse as it plays catchup to the widespread technological developments, these discussions explore the gap in which ART has developed faster than our collective capacity to process it.

Hartman, Lepecki, Guralnik, and I approach cultural discourse from a similar theoretical stance, passionately taking the position that subjectivity is constituted through culture. We mine ART's discourse for its capacity to both reproduce and subvert normative imperatives. Within this shared framework, we each pull on different threads to explicate the paradoxes and silences embedded and embodied in ART. In the following reply, I address three of these threads: viability, telepathy–teleplasty, and normativity, as elaborated by Hartman, Lepecki, and Guralnik respectively.

Hartman addresses reproduction, ART included, from its position between debt and viability. He critiques our "economy built on possession," and he elaborates my argument that ART can reproduce gendered imperatives. Hartman writes, "maternity, cultivated as agrobusiness, poaches from a long-held intention to be generative, contained in baby's 'viability.'" We are born into debt, he argues: we owe our viable, livable lives to the vitality of those who imagined us coming into the world. We embody this debt; we must carry it; and, without it having to undo us, it will act upon us "no matter how hard we try to deconstruct" it. Furthermore, Hartman substantially captures ART's coercive push, arguing that it can represent "the prisoner's dilemma for those of us who can't have a child any other way but through *assistance*." Holding the dialectical tension, Hartman articulates the bind: ART is a choice and an opportunity, a possibility previously foreclosed. Yet, when it is the *only* option, it bears a melancholic loss. He writes, "Nora's infertility is sublime, precious . . . ineffable . . . It is Real."

Willing to wrestle with Nora and me, infuriated and distressed by his "manic reverie," Hartman enters the *claustrum* (Meltzer, 1992) and its terrors, unsure if he "had joined Nora among the nonreproductive or if [he] resented her purchase of the elusive infant-objet 'ah!'" Critically reflecting on his reverie, Hartman describes the lacuna, the "graphic swatch of hypertensive standstill" in which Nora and I could neither move nor think. Yet, thinking his way out of the paralysis, Hartman wonders if our silence does not represent something in and of itself, a "collective unconscious desire." He writes,

> Our duty is to allow Nora to abort in the *claustrum* so that, in the Real, she may use whatever technology gives her time to plan parenthood: time to *bricolage* useless bits of horror into a life usable and sustainable and connected. It is only then that we can begin to reconcile our real indebtedness to our mother's long-held intention of our inevitably viable and spontaneous gestures.

From his background in dance and performance, Lepecki anchors us in the language of choreography: "a system of transmission of corporealities." Lepecki explores how a body is transmitted across time and space, always inhabited by the bodies of others. He makes a significant contribution to our understanding of subjectivity in general, by describing, "subjectivity as telepathic abduction" and "embodiment as 'teleplastic' abduction." Here, Lepecki argues for the multiplicity, multidirectionality, unknowability, and porousness constitutive of all subjectivity. He bridges psychoanalysis with dance theory by pointing out that both disciplines address the question: "Whose thoughts are these, inhabiting my inner world?" Critical of the notions of private self and "private property," Lepecki explores the price psychoanalysis has paid for its supposed legitimacy – the exchange of Freud's original radical insight of subjectivity as otherness for a thesis of the private, knowable self. Psychoanalytic theories have evolved and subjectivity as multiplicity is now a commonly held theoretical assumption. However, as Lepecki argues in his moving illustration of the confusion-fusion of bodies, acts, desires, and thoughts in my encounter with Nora, a private self ideology prevails.

Poignantly, Lepecki likens Nora's anguished bind to that of "the author violating copyright laws." More generally, he argues, "maternity and paternity under ART become a matter of exclusive copyrights and well-defined authorship." Nora, abducted by her family fiction, normative imperatives, and the exchange of reproductive body parts, is lost in confusion, unsure whose baby she carries and in what body she carries it. Characterizing the psychic landscape between Nora and me as an "empty, or blank, or contentless telepathy," Lepecki interprets our manic motion and unthinking states as reflective of culture. He writes:

> our times impale subjectivity through an unbearable choreographic demand of always being in a permanent state of frantic agitation, of producing and reproducing without creating. Despite all the commotion, this impetus's aim is to prevent the creation of a movement that truly matters.

Lepecki gets to the heart of ART's potentials and confusions, its conformity and subversion, through his rich metaphor of the body as "a transtemporal surface for trafficking – perhaps even smuggling," where "[a]bductor and abductee always [exist] in all directions at once and irrespective of property rights and propriety issues."

Guralnik argues that, in separating sexual desire from reproduction, ART "poses a major threat to heteronormative, patriarchal, biopolitics" and "destabilizes the sanctity of the traditional family." Guralnik proposes that ART produces a cultural paranoia, a "regulatory anxiety" (Corbett, 2009b, p. 354) in reaction to ART's breach of normativity. Through ART, various family forms and "noncoital" babies proliferate, where "[g]enetic contribution, gestation, and parenthood can effectively be separated and assumed by different individuals." Linking the traditional "threefold" family to a biologically predetermined "Oedipal" theory, Guralnik suggests that ideology recognizes and legitimizes only one family form and one mode of reproduction. This ideology renders babies born of ART unintelligible. Guralnik highlights how both state laws and psychoanalytic discourse are equally embedded in this ideology. While state laws are changing in response to ART's widespread use, laws still largely validate norms. Likewise, she wonders whether, insofar as psychoanalysis maintains its loyalty to father Freud, psychoanalysis can even conceive of a noncoital, non-Oedipal baby, let alone help our patients to imagine one.

Guralnik's discussion is an important ideological critique in its own right. It situates us in, and reminds us of, the heteronormative and biopolitical imperatives operating always in culture, which shape "intelligibility and affect." However, the "liberty" Guralnik tells us she will take with the case material overlooks the actual salient dynamics at play in my encounter with Nora. Her argument polarizes our positions: mine is to mourn ART, "'bastioned' (Baranger et al., 1983) by the Oedipal ideological persuasion" of reproduction, whereas hers celebrates "the unabashed indifference ART demonstrates toward the sacred cow of Oedipal law," sidestepping ideology. Curiously, staging this divide undoes her claim that one cannot live outside of norms. This move in turn misses the point of my paper, which is to hold the polarities of loss *and* possibility, ideological embeddedness *and* subversiveness in dialectical tension. Collapsing the dialectic into a split reproduces some of the confusions and disavowals ART can engender, three instances of which I highlight here.

First, although paranoia of ART's doctors and ethics may be, in part, "regulatory anxiety" (Corbett, 2009b), we can also still appreciate why people are hesitant to pursue it. ART's procedures are unpleasant, painful, intrusive, costly, time consuming, and, most of all, anxiety provoking – the outcome always balanced on the precipice of hope and despair, life and death. Yet, people pursue ART in droves, filling up and overflowing the doctors' waiting rooms. By turning all loss into a "melancholic preoccupation with the lost coital [Oedipal] baby," Guralnik forgets that it was Nora who first considered remaining childless, and then pushed for adoption after her infertility was diagnosed, two options which do not presume a genetic link or produce a coital child. What predominantly required recognition and mourning for Nora was her impossible position as miracle substitute for a dead sibling. Infertility and egg donation signified for Nora her *failure to compensate,* not necessarily the loss of a baby produced through sex.

I wholeheartedly support and celebrate ART's potential for the transformation of families, subversion of social norms, and its capacity to fuel social and legal change. However, we cannot overlook the pain that comes from living with an infertile body, even as we recognize that pain to be produced by ideology's tight regulatory grip on family and reproduction. ART cannot shield us from grieving for a lost child, the anguish of feeling that we are "failing" at our "gender." And it cannot contain the psychic impact of the projections childlessness evokes and which are hurled in the direction of the childless subject, all of which Nora faced during her 8 years of ART. By conflating the diagnosis of infertility in women with ART's procedures (in vitro fertilization, egg and sperm donation, surrogacy), Guralnik omits the actual losses that infertility and ART's failures can embody, reproducing ART's manic disavowal of loss, which encourages women to repeatedly try, over and over again, no matter its toll.

Finally, thanks to cultural, feminist, psychoanalytic, and queer critiques, a biologically predetermined Oedipal theory is now largely accepted as a fiction. If the term "Oedipal" is to be retained at all, it may be redefined as a subject's symbolic entry into and position within culture, including its patriarchal mandates (Grosz, 1990). I use Lacan precisely for his emphasis on the Symbolic, in which he situates the subject in a "socio-linguistic genesis of subjectivity" where subjects are "seen as social and historical effects, rather than pre-ordained biological givens" (Grosz, 1990, p. 148). Lacan emphasizes subversion and the celebration of social censorship, a position I use to explore Nora's experience with ART (Grosz, 1990).

In biologizing Lacan, Guralnik concretizes his symbolic lack-in-being (the Otherness of subjectivity) (Lacan, 1978) with the lack of an anatomical penis, and she equates the "Real" with "reality." The effect of these conflations leads Guralnik to view Nora's lack as the lack of a penis-genetic baby and my view of egg donor babies as not "real" possibilities. Lacan's "Real" refers to psychic experience that is inherently traumatic *because* it is unsymbolizable. This view is different from some psychoanalytic theories that describe "reality" as a given, such that a patient who refuses to accept it (i.e., has fantasies of omnipotence) is deemed unhealthy because the goal of analysis is to accept reality and its limitations. I regard reality as construction and, thus, do not subscribe to the analytic goal of forcing a reality on a patient, an act that presumes knowledge and authority. My approach to analysis is from the position of questioning and naming desire and its relation to lack-in-being, which my paper described in detail.

As meaning is signified, we may begin to name and celebrate what cannot be said, speaking as desiring subjects (Butler, 2005). "Desire is marked by the search for particular meaning. What we love and desire is what is meaningful to us in our social context" (Grosz, 1990, p. 81). ART transgresses and subverts binaries. It is celebration, affording possibilities that liberate and free us. ART is also loss; it requires our appreciation of its melancholic, painful aspects, which too produce freedom and creativity. It is the recognition of both its losses and gains that will allow ART to have a transformative role. We witness this powerful unfolding as Nora navigates ART, submitting to it, protesting it, and subverting its norms, as she eventually comes to claim something for herself – desire.

Part IV

Epilogue

Chapter 14

Epilogue – embodying the gaps in the face of catastrophe and hyperobjects

Katie Gentile

I hope this book has succeeded in painting a realistically complicated picture of assistive reproductive technologies (ARTs), one that holds both their promise and their "shadow sides" (Steinberg & Kraemer, Chapter 8). These shadows include not just the neonatal intensive care units, as described in Chapter 8, but also those apparitions that usually remain hidden: the experiences of retraumatization; the ongoing unacknowledged losses; the liminal spaces of uncertainty that engulf patients; the "confusion of tongues" (Ferenczi, 1933/1980) that blame the patient while mandating the manufacturing of hope and optimism; and the bankrupting failures to conceive. ARTs open up the notion of family to include more diverse configurations while reinforcing a reproductive mandate for everyone. They have ushered in new frontiers of science as well as of kinship, but nearly 20 years after Franklin's (1997) ground-breaking book, ARTs are still described as a "wild west science," where patients are urged to do anything to conceive. These pushes and pulls of progress and regression remain stunningly fascinating and disturbing and untenable. Engaging with ARTs requires holding these contradictions and more, as the chapters in this book illustrate.

The world of ARTs is growing exponentially. The proliferation of ARTs also has global consequences in terms of harvesting and selling sperm and eggs, the outsourcing of surrogacy to women living in the southern hemisphere, and the continuing growth of the human population that is crowding out the rest of the planet's inhabitants. While feminist and cultural studies have critically analyzed these technologies in books and articles, psychoanalysis has remained relatively mute and unreflective. In this book I have tried to simultaneously explore this silence, and some of its causes, while breaking it via chapters that describe different facets of the technologies. Thus, this book has sought to hold the cultural and the psychological to create a form of inquiry capable of exploring our ambivalent attachments to, and experiences of, ARTs.

I hope this book will stimulate more interest and critical psychoanalytic engagement and writing in this area. But, given what we have learned in the chapters here, this will not be an easy task. The field and our patients experience a contradictory emotional whirlwind around ARTs and a corresponding ambivalence that is tough to name, address, hold, and analyze. The cultural values of reprofuturity (L. Edelman, 2004), which can render ARTs an unquestionable requirement (see Chapters 1–4 and 8), are reflected in our Oedipal-based theories (Chapters 6 and 7), which continue to shape our therapeutic interactions (Chapters 9–13). Given that context is key to approaching and formulating any inquiry around ARTs, I end this book with an Epilogue that brings the global to the clinical, and the clinical to the global, in order to formulate different ways to sit within liminal spaces of temporal uncertainty, the tenuous futures that are continually reshaping our presents and pasts.

Starting global – hyperobjects

As has been described, the proliferation of ARTs is in part related to cultural affective networks attempting to find certainty in the face of a tenuous future. Another way of looking at this is to use psychoanalytic theory to explore the desperate and dangerous narcissism of the cultural body that is using fetal bodies to disavow knowledge of what Morton (2013) calls a "hyperobject."[1] Hyperobjects, such as global climate change and human overpopulation, are "massively distributed in time and space relative to humans" (p. 1). They are viscous, meaning they stick to and alter all beings involved with them. They are nonlocal in that their effects are dispersed and what is experienced by us is a displacement. Their effects are detected by us only interobjectively as they impact relational or interobjective spaces. So, for instance, flooding is a manifestation of global warming but it is not global warming itself, and flooding is only experienced when one sees previously dry land covered in water. Hyperobjects occupy a different temporality such that they cannot be seen or grasped fully by us.

Not surprisingly, hyperobjects emphasize the limits of human existence. They do so by intensifying the gap between phenomenon and thing – the profound limits of our experience and representational systems – and by reminding us that existence and our very forms of meaning making rest upon fragility (Morton, 2013). Related to this, hyperobjects force us to reconsider what it means to exist. Thus, hyperobjects are humiliating, bringing us back "down" to earth (p. 17). Like the Copernican revolution and Freud's unconscious, hyperobjects are "being-quake[s]" (Morton, 2013, p. 19), decentering humans, rendering them merely one type of object in a world of objects. Hyperobjects also exert a force downward, a "causal pressure" on those objects that are shorter lived (Morton, 2013, p. 67), reminding us that we are merely a speck of time for the earth, and even less for the universe.

But narcissistic defenses against reality and accountability are thick and unyielding. Thus, as Morton (2013) observes in relation to hyperobjects, it is not reasoning but media like art, and, I would hope, psychoanalysis and psychotherapy, that can break through denial by "walk[ing]" people through a space that is difficult to "traverse" (p. 184). These spaces are made difficult to inhabit because they render omnipotence a fantasy, replacing it with "intimacy, grief, and overwhelmingness" (p. 184), and, I would add, shame. Walking through means holding the split-off parts of vulnerabilities and humiliations. It requires a new form of "ecological being-with" cultivating a gap of intimacy (Morton, 2013, pp. 193–194). So to Morton it is not oneness that we need to cultivate but the capacity to "stand in the spaces" (to reference Bromberg, 1998, in a different context), feeling and embodying the gaps between things and essences, words and affects, intentions and actions, actively decentering ourselves within the world. Thus, it is not a goal to close the gap but to mind–body it, while holding the inconsistencies and fragilities of being (Morton, 2013).

Traversing spaces of "intimacy, grief, and overwhelmingness" (Morton, 2013, p. 184), as well as of shame, is key to holding and exploring the experiences of infertility and ARTs.

Psychoanalysis and cultural theories of splitting off catastrophe

According to Cooper (2006), catastrophic risk is unlike other forms of risk. Catastrophe is based on speculation and disrupts traditional rational forms of decision making. There is no exact "when" (p. 125) in a catastrophic future. According to Cooper, the only way to face up to such a future is to become "immersed in its conditions of emergence, to the point of actualizing it ourselves" (p. 125). In other words, our collective psychic defense to attempt to continue any semblance of going on being in the face of catastrophe is to live in a state focusing primarily on conditions of the emergence of that catastrophe – i.e., a state of hypervigilance that functions to both soothe and rile the nervous system. The brilliance of using the fetus as a fetish object in the face of catastrophe is that it enables the cultural body to actualize these conditions not just *within the fetal body*, but *within the fetal body as it is gestated within maternal body,* the space rendered abject (Kristeva, 1982) within the culture. Like any truly useful and, thus, intractable defense, projecting future catastrophe into the fetal body provides important secondary gains. First, it maintains a fantasy of masculine impenetrability in the face of catastrophe by projecting all vulnerability not just *on to* the identified female body, but *into* it, where it can be embodied by the fetus *and* the potential fantasy fetus. Second, all threats to the fetus – domestic violence, which is the leading cause of birth defects, environmental toxins, and other dangerous conditions – can be projected on to the maternal, who then becomes the threat to her current or potential fetus. This maternal threat can then be managed through biomedicalized surveillance or/and criminal justice interventions. The fetal fetish also works successfully as a defense because it enables this disavowal, projection, and containment of vulnerability and threat, while functioning to secure a more certain future embodied by the fetus. The fetus then functions as the only available container that can possibly hold us individually and collectively, in time, reinforcing reprofuturity and the need to go to extremes for a baby. After all, time and space are central to the production of subjectivity (Chapter 2). If catastrophic not-knowing disrupts our capacities for expectation and anticipation, it threatens our very psychic organization, such that a future of catastrophe and the resultant annihilation anxieties can function as a seismic disruption to being.

As has been described in Chapter 2, memory and meaning making emerge from expectation. Expectation is not a cause-and-effect prediction, nor is it an internal capacity, as it is in a continual state of re-emergence within the social spaces between things, objects, and beings (see Gentile, 2015). Expectation enables the "future to come" to remain both with us and ungraspable (Braun, 2007, p. 17), always unfolding and multiple. This differentiation of expectation from prediction is imperative to understanding the difference between facing catastrophe as annihilation and attempting to use it to generate the space necessary to create multiple futures, thus, multiple presents and pasts. It is this understanding of psychoanalytic-based capacity (integrated with cultural theory) that can help illuminate how it is that networks of affective communication in the face of catastrophe can form both the potential spaces of resistance and those of social control.

One could also integrate psychoanalytic and cultural theories to interpret the obsession with fetuses and babies as a very dangerous displacement of the guilt of realizing the devastated planet these fetuses will inherit.[2] In this context, controlling the uterine environment through the manic proliferation of ARTs and personhood amendments and fetal rights laws could be seen as displacement, attempts to cleanse our guilt. Such a displacement in the face of the hyperobject of environmental destruction is easier than doing the work necessary to provide a healthier, less toxic, postnatal environment, and it evacuates and projects the blame for toxin-related health issues to the maternal. In the face of environmental destruction and ungraspable hyperobjects, who wouldn't run to the futurity of the fetus to gain some semblance of control and a fantasy of going on being?

Braun (2007) cites of Cooper: "when biology comes to be known in terms of 'emergence' the future can only be 'speculative' and political calculation must become 'future invocative', actively intervening *within* the disorder of biological life in order to produce a desired future" (p. 19). With this temporal layering, the catastrophic future is used to generate the present and past (Gentile, 2013), an experience of memory in the present (Cunningham, 2014).

Actively intervening to create and monitor fetal lives enables both acts of preemption and the management of time and space. And, of course, doing so by controlling not just the timing but the process of pregnancy enables the fantasy of dominating (mother) nature during a time when our relationship with nature is constructed like a war, with nature staging destruction everywhere and humans as the innocent, childlike victims. The Oedipal returns as we split off responsibility and accountability.

The ART fetus, as has been observed in this book, is not made of what we usually consider to be the flesh, but of chemically treated cells in a Petri dish. It may in fact embody the space between the human and nonhuman object, similar to "My Baby Frankenstein," on the cover of this book. The only sexual act involved is the male orgasm, and even that is not always necessary and is rarely described as being pleasurable, so much as being a carefully timed chore. This ART fetus is not made of original sin. It has a purity for our Puritan culture. This purity may provide a secondary gain for the cultural body, that of a fantasy of cleansing our sins, starting anew again and again, like any other obsessive psychological defense. In this context, the US cultural body is operating like a psyche in terror, displacing anxieties, hypervigilantly obsessing over identified risk factors, splitting off violent threat into segments of the population that can be imprisoned and contained in some way. Here, obsession over the fetus needs to be seen as yet another form of splitting off and containing anxieties, but this one comes with the added benefit of a fantasy of containing, protecting, and controlling the future, manufacturing a sense of duration, time's movement, in lieu of the collapsed spaces that render time repetitive, but not creative or generative.

Embodying some gaps in psychoanalysis

Creating space through linking and linking through space is the job of psychoanalysts. It's what we are trained to do. Yet the mainstreams of US psychoanalysis still privilege insularity in terms of the discipline and the clinical relationship. Many of these psychoanalysts have challenged certain aspects of traditional analytic sensibility, specifically the assumption of analytic neutrality. This capacity to challenge certain aspects (the idea that the analyst does not participate in the analytic relationship) while clinging to others (splitting the clinical from the cultural and political) demonstrates that some ideologies are easier to deconstruct than others, and destroying links to the external is a form of splitting that is difficult for psychoanalysis to shake.

As described in Chapter 2, subjectivities only exist as assembled moments of coherence that are always necessarily emerging in relation to not only other people, but to environments – objects, spaces, other animals, social practices and rituals, beliefs, and networks of affect. The separations we experience between ourselves, affective networks, and the collection of objects surrounding us is the space of ideology. Ideologies function to split and hierarchically structure objects and affects, the social networks and webs within which we emerge. These emergent webs, shaped by ideology, construct human needs as being isolated from and taking priority over everything else, including the environment, nonhuman[3] animals, and objects. If we deconstruct these ideologies of human exceptionalism (Haraway, 2008) that function to split – split culture from the analytic space and analytic work; split humans from our environments – we lose our dominion, our fantasies of dominance and centrality, but gain a new level of relationality, just as we did when we (analysts) loosened our grip on the fantasy of analytic neutrality that split and elevated the analyst above the analysand. Similarly, if we experience and conceptualize the energy and life in all of our surroundings producing us, as we reproduce these surroundings, we are faced with being immersed and emergent within what Morton (2013) calls "an intimacy" and what Haraway terms "being-with." If the table top I see as merely a desk is actually coaxing me to approach it, to sit in certain ways as it holds my wrists while I type, as it multitasks as a tempting cat bed, then I might take better care of it and be less likely to throw it out when I do not really need a new one. This intimacy of being co-emergent with all of the objects in our surroundings can function as an antidote to the alienation and splitting required in neoliberalism, and renders us better equipped to engage in reflective, responsible, and caring action. But such an antidote requires creating and maintaining active links between the inner and outer, personal and cultural, psychological and the political, understanding these links are often formed not just around ambivalence, but around conflicts of interest.[4] Acknowledging these conflicts means acknowledging as legitimate the interests of nonhuman others, de-centering humans. With this active linking we open our eyes to the wider relational spaces within which we emerge. Thus, these "links," then, are not connections between distinct entities but spaces of differentiations that are in continuous motion.

This approach to subjectivity casts selves as not only emergent within relations, but also as, to use Oliver's (2001) word, "response-able" agents with impact. In these response-able relationships, the "needs of others obligate us to do something" (Oliver, 2009, p. 305), to be accountable "for the lively relationalities of becoming of which we are a part" (Barad, 2007, p. 393). But here I would push this idea further. Morton's (2013) approach of a co-emergent intimacy and Barad's intra-activity are wonderful concepts, but they can be used to flatten and disperse agency. Certainly, I am shaped by my relationships with objects and it is differentiations like these within which I come into being. But as a human I have a level of agency and power desks may not have in a world that is shaped by and for humans. And this level of power and agency needs to be acknowledged and used to generate response-able interactions – interactions that cultivate the space for the other to be able to respond and be heard as a valuable subject in his or her own right (Oliver, 2001), to be intra-active (Barad, 2007). Thus, we need to see, acknowledge, and take response-ability for our effects on the world around us and we need to expand our horizons in order to engage with the vast world of objects that sustain us. Creating the capacities to recognize our effects on all the others that enable us to come into being is a step toward being better able to acknowledge and engage with the hyperobjects we face.

Within psychoanalysis, such an approach requires that we push ourselves further, not only to conceptualize a more complex level of relationality, but to formulate better practices to address human-centered narcissism. Just as we would empathetically challenge a patient struggling with narcissistic responses to consider the impact of her actions on others and to find ways to create compassionate links to others, we need to challenge ourselves and our patients to consider the impact of our/their actions on others and our/their environments, understanding these environments to be shared with nonhuman animals and objects. After all, if we take linking and differentiation to the outside world seriously, we have to do the work necessary to deconstruct the malignant narcissism of humankind and recognize and take responsibility for the destruction reaped by us not only as individuals but as a species, without collapsing into a puddle of debilitating shame. Shame is merely a convenient defense designed to reinforce the destruction of links and maintain the narcissism. It can be paralyzing and silencing, but it is also a primary affective and effective form of social control. We should be ashamed of what we have done and continue to do to each other, the planet, and its inhabitants. Our lives and our lifestyles depend upon the active and conscious "extinguishing" of animals (Oliver, 2009, p. 11) and of all objects in and of our ecological surroundings. This *is* shame-full. Avoiding shame because it can be collapsing reinforces the destruction of links and the denigration and destruction of the environment and all its inhabitants. We need instead to harness this shame, model ways of holding it, using it to fuel accountable and responsible action. We as a species need to learn to share (Oliver, 2009), not just with other people, but with all entities on the planet. This new form of response-able subjectivity can also be seen as emerging from a new form of caring, where one is "subject to the unsettling obligation of curiosity, which requires knowing more at the end of the day than at the beginning" (Haraway, 2008, p. 36), even when that knowing is inconvenient, destabilizing, painful, and demands action.

I am not stating anything radical to say the biggest threat to the planet is humans: FINRRAGE (www.finrrage.org/) already used this argument in the 1970s as part of their critique of ARTs (see Chapter 3). We have populated the planet beyond what it can sustain. In this context, and with the more expansive approach to engagement described above, we must find ways to hold ambivalence around each pregnancy we see. We need to recognize that a pregnancy may be a celebratory or/and frightening event; it might be a mistake; and it might need to be terminated for any number of reasons. And adoption, while being at times immensely difficult, needs to be held as just as important as biological parenting. Imagine adults having the equally accessible and valid options of adoption, ARTs, or/and other social and communal forms of parenting. Imagine giving equal value and celebration to those who commit themselves to caring for nonhuman animals and other forms of life. In weighing these options and making decisions, we need to also hold the perspective and care of the multiple "others" that make our existence possible, consciously recognizing the impact of our reproductive decisions on the animals who are being crowded into extinction with each human being that is created; the environment that is overwhelmed by the garbage of human life; the planet that just cannot sustain this many human bodies. As psychoanalysts we are trained to hold multiple divergent experiences simultaneously. Pregnancy, attempts at reproduction, and decisions to not reproduce are actions that need to be explored within these complicated, interrelated, and interdependent spaces. Even if we do not state these multiple divergent experiences verbally within sessions to our patients, holding them in mind and body are an important step toward linking and interrupting the splitting, to embody the gaps.

In relation to reproduction, we need to create spaces for alternatives to reproduction that are not cast as alternatives, but as legitimate paths to meaningful lives. We need to articulate the force of the reproductive mandate in the Oedipal and deconstruct it, as we do the traditional family structure. Why does a patient want a child? How do cultural ideals shape desire for children? How much is a patient avoiding other anxieties, choices, or decisions by having or seeking to have a child? We need to recognize that not everyone should reproduce and not everyone should be a parent, and these choices do not reflect some psychopathology or lack of maturity or growth. Successful case studies could end not with "and the patient is now happily married with children," but instead with "the patient chose not to reproduce and has a full and meaningful life." How are annihilation anxiety, fears, or realities of meaninglessness and existential dread defended against through reproduction? Can there ever be consent around these issues and what are the ramifications of this incapacity? How can other spaces of meaning be nurtured so that babies are not the main focus of generativity, especially for women?

How can our theories grow so the Oedipal mandate is not the center of psychic development? Even as Ehrensaft (Chapter 7) opens the Oedipal into a generative circle, it is still reproductive. ARTs can shake up the horizontal and vertical generational structure of the Oedipal, allowing grandmothers to birth their own grandchildren, uncles and aunts to donate sperm or eggs to create their own nieces or nephews. But, regardless of the complexities of configurations, the central Oedipal mandate – to desire and pursue reproduction, is reinforced at all financial, emotional, and physical costs. Thus, ARTs become yet another device to service the Oedipal, and vice versa. How can we better theorize childfree lives of creativity that are not seen as displaced parenting but generativity for its own pleasures? In order to truly displace the Oedipal, how can we conceptualize lives not referenced to children at all? How can we create a psychoanalytic relationship that heals the splits of ideology and holds and cultivates the multiple levels of response-ability required of us all?

Although I pose these questions, I too am filled with uncertainty, ambivalence, and conflict about how best to engage and hold these depths of subjectivities and complex relations within the clinical space. But beginning to link the complicated desires and motivations for ARTs with the contradictory experiences and psychological, physical, environmental, and global consequences of engaging with them is a necessary start. Perhaps the goals of therapy are to stand in the collective spaces of intolerable and overwhelming grief, contradiction, ambivalence, and annihilation and nothingness. In so doing, we become more aware of how the technologies of ARTs as objects "cast their spells" (Morton, 2013) on human bodies, rendering them more and more pliable and dependent upon their interventions in part as a way of avoiding these nearly intolerable affective experiences. Here, the analyst can function as a link not only to the unbearable void of nothingness from which we fled as infants, but also to the cultural body, our surroundings, and the inevitable and potential futures we have made possible through our narcissistic greed and destruction and our beauty and creativity. The analyst, then, functions to disassemble the dissociations that manufacture splits between affects, bodies, objects, worlds. In so doing, humans lose their fantasy of dominance and transcendence over all, but gain an intimacy (Morton, 2013), a caring and enlivening sense of being-with (Haraway, 2008), that can buffer the terrors of annihilation with faith in ongoing connections, thus, differentiations, through times.

Notes

1 I thank Ann Pellegrini for introducing me to this concept/object.
2 I thank Steve Botticelli for highlighting the complicated role global climate change and environmental destruction could play here.
3 Of course, this term demonstrates how difficult it is to get beyond human-centric thinking and language.
4 Joan Tronto (1994) describes the ramifications of sustaining caring links to our local and global communities and conflict.

References

Ahmed, S. (2004). *The Cultural Politics of Emotion.* New York: Routledge.

Ahmed, S. (2007/2008). The happiness turn. *New Formations*, 63: 7–14.

Ahmed, S. (2010). Killing joy: Feminism and the history of happiness. *Signs,* 35(3): 571–594.

Alexander, M. (2010). *The New Jim Crow: Mass Incarceration in the Age of Colorblindness.* New York: New Press.

Allen, E.C., Manuel, J.C., Legault, C., Naughton, M.J., Pivor, C. & O'Shea, T.M. (2004). Perception of child vulnerability among mothers of former premature infants. *Pediatrics*, 113(2): 267–273.

Almeling, R. (2011). *Sex Cells: The Medical Market for Eggs and Sperm.* Los Angeles: University of California Press.

Ammaniti, M. (1991). Maternal representations during pregnancy and early infant–mother interactions. *Infant Mental Health Journal*, 12(3): 246–255.

Apprey, M. (2013). *Representing, Theorizing and Reconfiguring the Concept of Transgenerational Haunting in Order to Facilitate Healing.* From the unpublished paper presented at The Wounds of History Conference: Repair and Resilience in the Trans-Generational Transmission of Trauma (March 2, 2013), Sponsored by NYU Postdoctoral Program in Psychotherapy and Psychoanalysis, The Psychoanalytic Society of the Postdoctoral Program, and the NYU-GSAS Trauma and Violence Transdisciplinary Studies Program.

Arbeau, T. (1589). *Orchesography: A Treatise in the Form of a Dialogue Whereby All Manner of Persons May Easily Acquire and Practise the Honourable Exercise of Dancing.* New York: Dance Horizons, 1966.

Arockiasamy, V., Holsti, L. & Albersheim, S. (2008). Fathers' experiences in the neonatal intensive care unit: a search for control. *Pediatrics*, 121(2): e215–e222.

ASRM (American Society for Reproductive Medicine) (2012). *Fact Sheet: Egg Donation.* Retrieved on August 14, 2015 from: http://www.asrm.org/uploadedFiles/ASRM_Content/Resources/Patient_Resources/Fact_Sheets_and_Info_Booklets/Egg%20donation%20FINAL%204-23-12.pdf.

Atwood, M. (1986). *The Handmaid's Tale*. Toronto: McClelland & Stewart.

Bailly, L. (2009). *Lacan*. Oxford, England: One World.

Baker, K.K. (2004). Bargaining or biology? The history and future of paternity law and parental status. *Cornell Journal of Law and Public Policy,* 14:1–69.

Baor, L. & Blickstein, I. (2005). Enroute to an "instant family": psychosocial considerations. *Obstetrics and Gynecology Clinics*, 32(1): 127–139.

Baor, L. & Soskolne, C. (2010). Mothers of IVF and spontaneously conceived twins: A comparison of prenatal maternal expectations, coping resources and maternal stress. *Human Reproduction*, 25: 1490–1496.

Baor, L., Bar-David, J. & Blickstein, I. (2004). Psychological resource depletion of parents of twins after assisted versus spontaneous reproduction. *International Journal of Fertility and Women's Medicine,* 49: 13–24.

Barad, K. (2007). *Meeting the Universe Halfway: Quantum Physics and the Entanglement of Matter and Meaning.* Durham, NC: Duke University Press.

Barad, K. (2010). Quantum entanglements and hauntological relations of inheritance: Dis/continuities, spacetime enfoldings, and justice-to-come. *Derrida Today,* 3(2): 240–268.

Baraitser, L. (2009). *Maternal Encounters: The Ethics of Interruption.* New York: Routledge.

Baranger, M., Baranger, W. & Mom, J. (1983). Process and non-process in analytic work. *International Journal of Psycho-Analysis, 64*: 1–16.

Barrington, K.J. & Janvier, A. (2013). The pediatric consequences of assisted reproductive technologies, with special emphasis on multiple pregnancies. *Acta Paediatrica,* 102(4): 340–348.

Bartlam, B. & Woolfe, R. (1998). Working with survivors of sexual abuse within the context of infertility. *The European Journal of Psychotherapy, Counselling and Health,* 1(2): 183–193.

Batcheller, A., Cardozo, E., Maguire, M., DeCherney, A.H. & Segars, J.H. (2011). Are there subtle genome wide epigenetic alternations in normal offspring conceived by assisted reproductive technologies? *Fertility and Sterility*, 96(6):1306–1311.

Beck, U. (2007). *World at Risk.* Trans. C. Cronin. Malden, MA: Polity Press.

Becker, G., Butler, A., & Nachtigall, R.D. (2005). Resemblance talk: A challenge for parents whose children were conceived with donor gametes in the US. *Social Science & Medicine*, 61(6): 1300–1309.

Beebe, B. & Stern, D. (1977). Engagement–disengagement and early object experiences. In Freedman, M. & Grand, S. (Eds.), *Communicative Structures and Psychic Structures* (pp. 35–55). New York: Plenum Press.

Beebe, B., Lachmann, F., Markese, S. & Bahrick, L. (2012). On the origins of disorganized attachment and internal working models: Paper I. A dyadic system approach. *Psychoanalytic Dialogues, 22:* 253–272.

Beeson, D. & Lippman, A. (2006). Egg harvesting for stem cell research: Medical risk and ethical problems. *Reproductive Biomedicine Online*, 13(4): 573–579.

Behrman, R.E. & Butler, A.S. (Eds.) (2007). *Preterm Birth: Causes, Consequences and Prevention.* Washington, DC: National Academies Press.

Benjamin, J. (1988). *The Bonds of Love: Psychoanalysis, Feminism, and the Problem of Domination.* New York: Pantheon.

Benjamin, J. (1998). *Shadow of the Other: Intersubjectivity and Gender in Psychoanalysis.* New York: Routledge.

Benjamin, J. (2004). Beyond doer and done to: An intersubjective view of thirdness. *The Psychoanalytic Quarterly*, 73:5–46.

Benjamin, O. & Ha'elyon, H. (2002). Rewriting fertilization: Trust, pain, and exit points. *Women's Studies International Forum,* 25(6): 667–678.

Bennet, J. (2010). *Vibrant Matter: A Political Ecology of Things.* Durham, NC: Duke University Press.

Benoit, D., Parker, K.C.H. & Zeanah, C. (1997). Mothers' representations of their infants assessed prenatally: Stability and association with infant attachment classification. *Journal of Child Psychology and Psychiatry and Allied Disciplines,* 38: 307–313.

Berardi, F. (2009). *The Soul at Work: From Alienation to Autonomy*. Los Angeles, CA: Semiotext(e).

Bergh, C. (2005). Single embryo transfer: A mini review. *Human Reproduction*, 20(2): 323–327.

Bergner, D. (2013). *What Do Women Want? Adventures in the Science of Female Desire.* New York: Ecco/HarperCollins.

Bergson, H. (1913/2001). *Time and Free Will. An Essay on the Immediate Data of Consciousness*. Mineola, NY: Dover Publications.

Berlant, L. (2008). *The Female Complaint: The Unfinished Business of Sentimentality in American Culture.* Durham, NC: Duke University Press.

Berlant, L. (2010). Cruel optimism. In Gregg, M. & Seigworth, G.J. (Eds.), *The Affect Theory Reader* (pp. 93–117). Durham, NC: Duke University Press.

Bernstein, A. (1994). *The Flight of the Stork.* Indianapolis: Perspectives Press.

Bersani, L. (2008). Shame on you. In Bersani, L. & Phillips, A. (Ed.), *Intimacies* (pp. 31–56). Chicago, IL: University of Chicago Press.

Bion, W.R. (1962a). *Learning From Experience*. London: Heinemann.

Bion, W.R. (1962b). The psycho-analytic study of thinking. *The Psychoanalytic Quarterly,* 43: 306–310.

Blackman, L. (2007). Psychiatric culture and bodies of resistance. *Body and Society*, *13*(2): 1–23.

Blackman, L. (2008). Affect, relationality and the 'problem of personality'. *Theory, Culture & Society,* 25(1): 23–47.

Boehm, F. (1931). The history of the Oedipus complex. *International Journal of Psycho-Analysis*, 12: 431–451.

Bollas, C. (1987/1989). *The Shadow of the Object*. New York: Columbia University Press.

Bordo, S. (1993). *Unbearable Weight: Feminism, Western Culture, and the Body.* Berkeley: University of California Press.

Borrero, C. (2001). Gamete and embryo donation. In Vayena, E., Rowe, P. & Griffin, D. (Eds.), *Medical, Ethical and Social Aspects of Assisted Reproduction* (pp. 166–176). Geneva: World Health Organization.

Boulet, S., Mehta, A., Kissin, D., Warner, L., Kawwass, J. & Jamieson, D. (2015). Trends in use of and reproductive outcomes associated with intracytoplasmic sperm injection. *Journal of the American Medical Association,* 313(3): 255–263.

Bourdieu, P. (1977). *Outline of a Theory of Practice*. Cambridge: Cambridge University Press.

Boutang, P.-A. (Director) (2007). *Gilles Deleuze from A to Z* (DVD). Los Angeles, CA: Semiotext(e).

Boyer, D. & Sorenson, P. (2009). Adapting the Tavistock model of infant observation to work in the neonatal intensive care unit. *Psychoanalytic Inquiry*, 19(2): 146–159.

Bradow, A. (2012). *Primary and Secondary Infertility And Post Traumatic Stress Disorder: Experiential Differences Between Type of Infertility and Symptom Characteristics.* Dissertation. Abstracts International: Section B. Louisville, KY: Spalding University.

Braun, B. (2007). Biopolitics and the molecularization of life. *Cultural Geographies,* 14: 6–28.

Brazelton, T.B. (1993). Personal communication. In Stern, D. (1995). *The Motherhood Constellation: A Unified View of Parent–Infant Psychotherapy*. New York: Basic Books.

Brazelton, T.B. & Cramer, B. (1991). *The Earliest Relationship: Parents, Infants and the Drama of Early Attachment.* London: Karnac Press.

Brennan, T. (2000). *Exhausting Modernity*. London: Routledge.

Bretherick, K., Fairbrother, N., Avila, L., Harbord, S. & Robinson, W. (2010). Fertility and aging: Do reproductive-aged Canadian women know what they need to know? *Fertility and Sterility*, 93(7): 2162–2168.

Britton, R., Feldman, M. & O'Shaughnessy, E. (2007). *The Oedipus Complex Today: Clinical Implications.* London: Karnac Books.

Bromberg, P. (1998). *Standing in the Spaces: Essays on Clinical Process, Trauma and Dissociation*. Hillsdale, NJ: The Analytic Press.

Brown, W. (2005). *Edgework: Critical Essays on Knowledge and Politics.* Princeton: Princeton University Press.

Browner, C.H. & Press, N.A. (1995). The normalization of prenatal diagnostic screening. In Ginsburg, F.D. & Rapp, R. (Eds.), *Conceiving the New World Order: The Global Politics of Reproduction* (pp. 307–322). Berkeley, CA: University of California Press.

Browner, C.H. & Sargent, C.F. (2011). *Reproduction, Globalization, and the State: New Theoretical and Ethnographic Perspectives.* London: Duke University Press.

Bryan, E. (2003). The impact of multiple preterm births on the family. *British Journal of Obstetrics and Gynaecology,* 110 (suppl.): 24–28.

Bryan, E. (2005). Psychological aspects of prenatal diagnosis and its implication in multiple pregnancies. *Prenatal Diagnosis*, 25(9): 827–834.

Budgeon, S. (2003). Identity as an embodied event. *Body & Society*, 9(1): 35–55.

Bukulmez, O. (2009). Does assisted reproductive technology cause birth defects? *Current Opinion in Obstetrics and Gynecology*, 21: 260–264.

Burtman, R. (2014). *Contrasts in Conducting Treatment While Childfree and Not.* Panel Childfree by Choice, for the American Psychological Association's Division 39 Annual Conference Presentation. New York.

Butler, J. (1990). *Gender Trouble*. New York: Routledge.

Butler, J. (1993). *Bodies that Matter: On the Discursive Limits of "Sex".* New York: Psychology Press.

Butler, J. (1999). *Gender Trouble: Feminism and the Subversion of Identity.* New York: Routledge.

Butler, J. (2004). *Undoing Gender*. New York: Routledge.

Butler, J. (2005). *Giving an Account of Oneself.* USA: Fordham University Press.

Caillois, R. (1935/1984). Mimicry and legendary psychasthenia. *October*, *31*: 16–32, 1984.

Cain, M. (2001). *The Childless Revolution: What it Means to be Childless Today*. New York: Perseus Books.

Campbell, J. (2006). *Psychoanalysis and the Time of Life: Duration of the Unconscious Self.* London: Routledge.

Carson, R.A. (2002). The hyphenated space: Liminality in the doctor–patient relationship. In Charon, R. & Montello, M. (Eds.), *Stories Matter: The Role of Narrative Medicine in Medical Ethics* (pp. 171–182). New York: Routledge.

Carsten, J. (2007). Constitutive knowledge: tracing trajectories of information in new contexts of relatedness. *Anthropological Quarterly*. 80, 403–426.

Casper, M.J. & Moore, L.J. (2009). *Missing Bodies: The Politics of Visibility.* New York: New York University Press.

Cath, S., Gurwitt, A. & Munder-Ross, J. (1982). *Father and Child: Developmental and Clinical Perspectives.* Boston: Little, Brown.

Centers for Disease Control and Prevention (CDC), American Society for Reproductive Medicine, Society for Assisted Reproductive Technology (2011). *2009 Assisted Reproductive Technology Success Rates*. National Summary and Fertility Clinic Reports Atlanta, GA: US Department of Health and Human Services, Centers for Disease Control and Prevention. Retrieved from: http://www.cdc.gov/art/reports/archive.html.

Centers for Disease Control and Prevention, Division of Reproductive Health, National Center for Chronic Disease Prevention and Health Promotion (2015a). *Assisted Reproductive Technology (ART)*. Retrieved from: http://www.cdc.gov/art/reports/index.html, last updated June 23, 2015.

Centers for Disease Control and Prevention, Division of Reproductive Health, National Center for Chronic Disease Prevention and Health Promotion (2015b). *Reproductive Health: Infertility FAQs*. Retrieved from: http://www.cdc.gov/reproductivehealth/Infertility/index.htm, last updated April 16, 2015.

Chanter, T. (2006). *Gender: Key Concepts in Philosophy*. London: Continuum International Publishing Group.

Charon, R. & Montello, M. (Eds.) (2002). *Stories Matter: The Role of Narrative Medicine in Medical Ethics*. New York: Routledge.

Chassay, S. (2012). 'Tis beauty kills the beast: Aesthetic and sensory transformations of encapsulated states. Paper presented to the Psychoanaytic Institute of Northern California, San Francisco, 19 May, 2012.

Chassay, S. (2013). 'Tis beauty kills the beast: Aesthetic and sensory transformations of encapsulated states. *Studies in Gender and Sexuality*, *16*: 5–17.

Chodorow, N. (1978). *The Reproduction of Mothering: Psychoanalysis and the Sociology of Gender*. Berkeley: University of California Press.

Chodorow, N. (2003). "Too late": Ambivalence about motherhood, choice, and time. *Journal of the American Psychoanalytical Association,* 51(4): 1181–1198.

Choi, Y., Bishai, D. & Minkovitz, C.S. (2009). Multiple births are a risk factor for postpartum maternal depressive symptoms. *Pediatrics*, 123(4): 1147–1154.

Clarke, A.E., Mamo, L., Fishman, J.R., Shim, J.K. & Fosket, J.R. (2003). Biomedicalization: Technoscientific transformations of health, illness, and U.S. biomedicine. *American Sociological Review* 68(April): 161–194.

Clarke, A.E., Shim, J.K., Mamo, L., Fosket, J.R. & Fishman, J.R. (2010a). Biomedicalization: A theoretical and substantive introduction. In Clarke, A.E., Shim, J.K., Mamo, L., Fosket, J.R. & Fishman, J.R. (Eds.), *Biomedicalization: Technoscience, Health, and Illness in the U.S.* (pp. 1–44). Durham, NC: Duke University Press.

Clarke, A.E., Shim, J.K., Mamo, L., Fosket, J.R. & Fishman, J.R. (2010b). Biomedicalization: Technoscientific transformations of health, illness and U.S. biomedicine. In Clarke, A.E., Shim, J.K., Mamo, L., Fosket, J.R. & Fishman, J.R. (Eds.), *Biomedicalization: Technoscience, Health, and Illness in the U.S.* (pp. 47–87). Durham, NC: Duke University Press.

Clough, P. (2004). Future matters: Technoscience, global politics, and cultural criticism. *Social Text* 22(3): 1–23.

Clough, P. (2008). The affective turn: Political economy, biomedia and bodies. *Theory, Culture & Society,* 25(1): 1–22.

Colebrook, C. (2000). From radical representations to corporeal becomings: The feminist philosophy of Lloyd, Grosz, and Gatens. *Hypatia*, 15(2): 76–93.

Collins, P.H. (1990). *Black Feminist Thought: Knowledge, Consciousness, and the Politics of Empowerment*. London: Routledge.

Connolly, M., Hooren, S. & Chambers, G. (2010). The costs and consequences of assisted reproductive technology: an economic perspective. *Human Reproduction Update,* 16(6): 603–613.

Conway, K. (2007). *Illness and the Limits of Expression.* Ann Arbor, MI: University of Michigan Press.

Cooper, M. (2006). Pre-empting emergence: The biological turn in the war on terror. *Theory, Culture & Society,* 23(July): 113–135.

Cooper, M. (2008). *Life as Surplus: Biotechnology and Capitalism in the Neoliberal Era.* Seattle, WA: University of Washington Press.

Connor, S. (2011). *Paraphernalia: The Curious Lives of Magical Things.* London: Profile Books.

Corbett, K. (2009a). *Boyhoods: Rethinking Masculinities.* New Haven, CT: Yale University Press.

Corbett, K. (2009b). Boyhood femininity, gender identity disorder, masculine presuppositions, and the anxiety of regulation. *Psychoanalytic Dialogues,* 19: 353–370.

Corea, G. (1985). *The Mother Machine: Reproductive Technologies from Artificial Insemination to Artificial Wombs.* New York: HarperCollins.

Crawford, A. (2008). *Born Still: Euphemisms and the Double-Taboo of Women's Bodies and Death.* Retrieved from: http://homes.chass.utoronto.ca/~cpercy/courses/6362-CrawfordAllison.htm.

Culley, L., Hudson, N. & Lohan, M. (2013). Where are all the men? The marginalization of men in social scientific research on infertility. *Reproductive Biomedicine Online.* Retrieved from: http://www.rbmojournal.com/article/S1472-6483(13)00354-4/pdf. Downloaded December 1, 2013.

Cunningham, K. (2014). *(Remember) The Future: The Preemptive Governance of Memory in the Age of Mass Catastrophe.* Dissertation for Doctorate, Graduate Center of the City University of New York.

Cunningham, M. (2013). Michael Cunningham. In McCann, C., Cabot T. & Consiglio, L. (Eds.), *The Book of Men: Eighty Writers on How to Be a Man* (pp. 69–73). New York: Picador.

Curtis, A. (2010). Giving' til it hurts: Egg donation and the costs of altruism. *Feminist Formations,* 22(2): 80–100.

Cvetkovich, A. (2012). *Depression: A Public Feeling.* Durham, NC: Duke University Press.

Daniels, C.R. (2006). *Exposing Men: The Science and Politics of Male Reproduction.* New York: Oxford University Press.

Daniluk, J.C. & Tench, E. (2007). Long-term adjustment of infertile couples following unsuccessful medical intervention. *Journal of Counseling & Development,* 85: 89–100.

Davies, M.J., Moore, V.M., Wilson, K.J., Van Essen, P., Priest, K., Schott, H., Haan, E.A. & Chan, A. (2012). Reproductive technology and the rise of birth defects. *New England Journal of Medicine,* 366(19): 1808–1813.

Davoine, F. (2012). The psychotherapy of psychosis and trauma: A relentless battle against objectification. *Psychoanalysis, Culture and Society,* 17(4): 339–347.

Declercq, E., Luke, B., & Belanoff, C. (2015). Perinatal outcomes associated with assisted reproductive technology: The Massachusetts outcomes study of assisted reproductive technologies. *Fertility and Sterility, 103*:888–895.

Deleuze, G. (1968). *Difference and Repetition.* New York: Columbia University Press, 1994.

Deleuze, G. (1969). *The Logic of Sense*. New York: Columbia University Press, 1990.
Deleuze, G. (1991). *Bergsonism.* New York: Zone Books.
Deleuze, G. (1995). Postscript on control societies. In *Negotiations, 1972–1990* (pp. 177–182). New York: Columbia University Press.
Deleuze, G. & Guattari, F. (1977/2009). *Anti-Oedipus: Capitalism and Schizophrenia.* New York: Penguin Classics.
Deleuze, G. & Guattari, F. (1987). *A Thousand Plateaus*. Minneapolis: University of Minnesota Press.
Deleuze, G. & Guattari, F. (2007). We always make love with worlds. In Lock, M. & Farquhar, J. (Eds.), *Beyond the Body Proper: Reading the Anthropology of Material Life* (pp. 428–432). Durham, NC: Duke University Press.
DeOcampo, A.C., Macias, M.M., Saylor, C.F. & Katikaneni, L.D. (2003). Caretaker perception of child vulnerability predicts behavior problems in NICU graduates. *Child Psychiatry and Human Development*, 34(2): 83–96.
Derrida, J. (1995). *The Gift of Death and Literature in Secret,* 2nd edn, translated by David Wills (2007). Chicago: The University of Chicago Press.
Diamond, N. (2013). *Between Skins: The Body in Psychoanalysis – Contemporary Developments.* Chichester, UK: Wiley-Blackwell.
Dimen, M. (1991). Deconstructing difference: Gender, splitting, and transitional space. *Psychoanalytic Dialogues,* 1: 335–352.
Dimen, M. (2010). Reflections on cure, or 'I/thou/it'. *Psychoanalytic Dialogues,* 20(3): 254–68.
Dimen, M. (Ed.) (2011). *With Culture in Mind: Psychoanalytic Stories*. New York: Routledge.
Dinshaw, C. (2012). *How Soon Is Now? Medieval Texts, Amateur Readers, and the Queerness of Time*. Durham, NC: Duke University Press.
Dinshaw, C., Edelman, L., Ferguson, R.A., Freccero, C., Freeman, E., Halberstam, J. & Hoang, N.T. (2007). Theorizing queer temporalities: A roundtable discussion. *GLQ: Journal of Lesbian Gay Studies,* 13(2–3): 177–195.
Doi, T. (1989). The concept of *amae* and its psychoanalytic implications. *International Review of Psycho-Analysis*, 16: 349–354.
Donovan, J. & Adams, C.J. (Eds.) (1996). *Beyond Animal Rights: A Feminist Caring Ethic for the Treatment of Animals.* New York: Continuum.
Downing, L. (2011). On the fantasy of childlessness as death in psychoanalysis and in Roeg's "Don't look now' and von Trier's "Antichrist." *Lambda Nordica,* 2–3: 49–68.
Dubow, S. (2011). *Ourselves Unborn: A History of the Fetus in Modern America.* New York: Oxford University Press.
Edelman, G.M. (2004). *Wider Than the Sky: The Phenomenal Gift of Consciousness*. New Haven: Yale University Press.
Edelman, L. (2004). *No Future: Queer Theory and the Death Drive.* Durham, NC: Duke University Press.
Ehrensaft, D. (1980). When men and women mother. *Socialist Review,* 10(1): 37–73.
Ehrensaft, D. (1987). *Parenting Together: Men and Women Sharing the Care of Their Children.* New York: Basic Books.
Ehrensaft, D. (2005). *Mommies, Daddies, Donors, Surrogates: Answering Tough Questions and Building Strong Families*. New York: Guilford.

Ehrensaft, D. (2007). The stork didn't bring me, I came from a dish: Psychological experiences of children conceived through assisted reproductive technology. *Journal of Infant, Child, and Adolescent Psychotherapy,* 6(2): 124–140.

Ehrensaft, D. (2008). It ain't over until the fat lady sings: Commentary on the Oedipus complex in adolescence by Marsha Levy-Warren. *Studies in Gender and Sexuality,* 9(4): 349–364.

Ehrensaft, D. (2011a). *Gender Born, Gender Made: Raising Healthy Gender-nonconforming Children.* New York: The Experiment.

Ehrensaft, D. (2011b). Boys will be girls, girls will be boys: Children affect parents as parents affect children in gender nonconformity. *Psychoanalytic Psychology,* 28(4): 528–548.

Ehrensaft, D. (2012). From gender identity disorder to gender identity creativity: True gender self therapy. *Journal of Homosexuality,* 59: 337–356.

Eigen, M. (1984). The area of faith in Winnicott, Lacan and Bion. *International Journal of Psychoanalysis,* 62(4): 413–433.

Eng, D.L. (2006). Political economics of passion: Transnational adoption and global woman: Roundtable on global woman. *Studies in Gender and Sexuality,* 7: 49–59.

Ettinger, B.L. (2006). *The Matrixial Borderspace.* Minneapolis: University of Minnesota Press.

European Society of Human Reproduction and Embryology (2014). *ART Fact Sheet.* Retrieved from http://www.eshre.eu/Guidelines-and-Legal/ART-fact-sheet.aspx.

Evans, D. (1996). *An Introductory Dictionary of Lacanian Psychoanalysis.* New York: Routledge.

Faimberg, H. (2005). *The Telescoping of Generations.* New York: Routledge.

Farquhar, D. (1998). Feminist politics of hagiography/demonology? Reproductive technologies as pornography/sexworks. In On, B.A.B. & Ferguson, A. (Eds.), *Daring to Be Good: Essays in Feminist Ethico-Politics.* New York: Routledge.

Fausto-Sterling, A. (2005). The bare bones of sex: Part 1 – Sex and gender. *Signs,* 30(2): 1491–1527.

Fegran, L., Helseth, S. & Fagermoen, M.S. (2008). A comparison of mothers' and fathers' experiences of the attachment process in a neonatal intensive care unit. *Journal of Clinical Nursing,* 17(6): 810–816.

Feldman, R. & Eidelman, A. (2009). Triplets across the first 5 years: The discordant infant at birth remains at developmental risk. *Pediatrics,* 124(1): 316–323.

Fenichel, O. (1931). Specific forms of the Oedipus complex. *International Journal of Psycho-Analytics,* 12: 412–430.

Ferenczi, S. (1933/1980). Confusion of tongues between adults and the child. In Balint, M. (Ed.), *Final Contributions to the Problems and Methods of Psycho-Analysis* (pp. 156–167), trans. E. Mosbacher. London: Karnac Books.

Firestone, S. (1970/1979). *The Dialectic of Sex: The Case for Feminist Revolution.* New York: Farrar, Straus, and Giroux.

Forrester, J. (1990). Psychoanalysis: Gossip, telepathy and/or science? In: *The Seductions of Psychoanalysis.* Cambridge: Cambridge University Press.

Foucault, M. (1965). *Madness and Civilization: A History of Insanity in the Age of Reason,* trans. by R. Howard. London: Tavistock

Foucault, M. (1970). *The Order of Things: An Archaeology of the Human Sciences.* New York: Vintage Books.

Foucault, M. (1978). *The History of Sexuality, Vol. 1: An Introduction.* New York: Random House.

Foucault, M. (1988). Technologies of the self. In Martin, L.H., Gutman, H. & Hutton, P.H. (Eds.), *Technologies of the Self: A Seminar with Michel Foucault* (pp. 145–162). Amherst, MA: University of Massachussetts Press.

Frank, A. (1995). *The Wounded Storyteller*. Chicago, IL: University of Chicago Press.

Franklin, S. (1991). Fetal fascinations: New dimensions to the medical-scientific construction of fetal personhood. In Franklin, S., Lury, C. & Stacey, J. (Eds.), *Off-Centre: Feminism and Cultural Studies* (pp. 190–206). London: HarperCollins.

Franklin, S. (1995). Postmodern procreation: A cultural account of assisted reproduction. In Ginsburg, F.D. & Rapp, R. (Eds.), *Conceiving the New World Order: The Global Politics of Reproduction* (pp. 323–345). Berkeley, CA: University of California Press.

Franklin, S. (1997). *Embodied Progress: A Cultural Account of Assisted Conception.* London: Routledge.

Franklin, S. (1998). Making miracles: Scientific progress and the facts of life. In Franklin, S. & Ragoné, H. (Eds.), *Reproducing Reproduction: Kinship, Power and Technological Innovation* (pp. 102–117). Philadelphia: University of Pennsylvania Press.

Franklin, S. & Ragoné, H. (Eds.) (1998). *Reproducing Reproduction: Kinship, Power and Technological Innovation*. Philadelphia: University of Pennsylvania Press,

Freeman, E. (2007). Introduction to queer temporalities. *GLQ: A Journal of Lesbian and Gay Studies,* 13 (2–3): 159–176.

Freeman, E. (2010). *Time Binds: Queer Temporalities, Queer Histories.* Durham, NC: Duke University Press.

Freud, A. (1965). *Normality and Pathology in Childhood.* New York: International Universities Press.

Freud, S. (1924). *The Dissolution of the Oedipus Complex.* The Standard Edition of the Complete Psychological Works of Sigmund Freud.

Freud, S. (1925). Some physical consequences of the anatomical distinction between the sexes. *Standard Edition V,* 19: 248–260.

Gallese, V. (2007). Before and below "theory of mind": Embodied simulation and the neural correlates of social cognition. *Philosophical Transactions of the Royal Society B,* 362: 659–669.

Galvin, R. (2002). Disturbing notions of chronic illness and individual responsibility: Towards a genealogy of morals. *Health: An Interdisciplinary Journal for the Social Study of Health Illness and Medicine* 6(2): 101–137.

Gannon, K., Glover, L. & Abel, P. (2004). Masculinity, infertility, stigma and media reports. *Social Science and Medicine,* 59(6): 1169–1175.

Gay, P. (1988). *Freud: A Life for Our Time*. London: Papermac.

Gentile, K. (2006). Timing development from cleavage to differentiation. *Contemporary Psychoanalysis*, 42(2): 297–325.

Gentile, K. (2007). *Creating Bodies: Eating Disorders as Self-Destructive Survival.* New York: Routledge.

Gentile, K. (2010). Is the old psychoanalytic story part of the problem? Invited response to Keylor and Apfel's "Male infertility: Integrating an old psychoanalytic story with the research literature." *Studies in Gender and Sexuality,* 11(2): 78–85.

Gentile, K. (2011). What about the baby? Baby-philia and the neo cult of domesticity. *Studies in Gender and Sexuality,* 12(1): 38–58.

Gentile, K. (2013). Biopolitics, trauma and the public fetus: An analysis of preconception care. *Subjectivity,* 6(2): 153–172.

Gentile, K. (2014). Exploring the troubling temporalities produced by fetal personhood. *Psychoanalysis, Culture, and Society,* 19(2): 1–18.

Gentile, K. (2015). Generating subjectivity through the creation of time. *Psychoanalytic Psychology*. Retrieved from: http://dx.doi.org/10.1037/a0038519.

Ginsburg, F.D. & Rapp, R. (1995). *Conceiving the New World Order: The Global Politics of Reproduction.* Berkeley, CA: University of California Press.

Goldner, V. (1991). Toward a critical relational theory of gender. *Psychoanalytic Dialogues,* 1: 249–272.

Goldner, V. (2011). Editor's note: Transgender subjectivities: Introduction to papers by Goldner, Suchet, Saketopoulou, Hansbury, Salamon & Corbett, and Harris. *Psychoanalytic Dialogues*, 21(2): 153–158.

Golombok, S. & MacCallum, F. (2003). Practitioner review: Outcomes for parents and children following nontraditional conception: What do clinicians need to know? *Journal of Child Psychology and Psychology,* 44:303–315.

Golombok, S., Blake, L., Casey, P., Roman, G. & Jadva, V. (in press). Children born through reproductive donation: A longitudinal study of child adjustment. *Journal of Child Psychology and Psychiatry.*

Golombok, S., MacCalllum, F. & Goodman, E. (2001). The "test-tube" generation: Parent–child relationships and the psychological well-being of in vitro fertilization children at adolescence. *Child Development*, 72: 599–608.

Golombok. S., Murray, C., Brinsden, P. & Abdalla, H. (1999). Social vs. biological parenting: Family functioning and the social-emotional development of children conceived by egg or sperm donation. *Journal of Child Psychology and Psychiatry*, 40: 519–527.

Gordon, A. (1997). *Ghostly Matters: Haunting and the Sociological Imagination.* Minneapolis: University of Minnesota Press.

Green, A. (1995). Has sexuality anything to do with psychoanalysis? *International Journal of Psycho-Analysis*, 76: 871–883.

Greil, A.L. (1997). Infertility and psychological distress: A critical review of the literature. *Social Science Medicine,* 45(11): 1679–1704.

Grewal, I. (2006). "Security moms" in the early twentieth-century United States: The gender of security in neoliberalism. *Women's Studies Quarterly,* 34(1&2): 25–39.

Groopman, J. (2003). *The Anatomy of Hope: How People Prevail in the Face of Illness.* New York: Random House.

Grosz, E. (1990). *Jacques Lacan: A Feminist Introduction*. London: Routledge.

Grosz, E. (1994). *Volatile Bodies: Toward a Corporeal Feminism.* Bloomington, IN: Indiana University Press.

Grosz, E. (1995). *Space, Time, and Perversion: Essays on the Politics of Bodies*. New York: Routledge.

Grosz, E. (2004). *The Nick of Time: Politics, Evolution, and the Untimely*. Durham, NC: Duke University Press.

Gupta, J.A. & Richters, A. (2008). Embodied subjects and fragmented objects: women's bodies, assisted reproduction technologies and the right to self-determination. *Bioethical Inquiry*, 5: 239–249.

Guralnik, O. (2010). Reading classical theory in the 21st century: a discussion of Leon Hoffman's "The impact of opposite-sex younger siblings: a hypothesis concerning gender differences." *Journal of Infant, Child, and Adolescent Psychotherapy*, 9: 86–93.

Guralnik, O. (2011). Raven: Travels in reality. In Dimen, M. (Ed.), *With Culture in Mind: Psychoanalytic Stories* (pp. 67–74). New York: Routledge.
Guralnik, O. & Simeon, D. (2010). Depersonalization: Standing in the spaces between recognition and interpellation. *Psychoanalytic Dialogues*, 20: 400–416.
Gurevich, M., Bishop, S., Bower, J., Malka, M. & Nyhof-Young, J. (2004). (Dis)embodying gender and sexuality in testicular cancer. *Social Science and Medicine*, 58(9): 1597–1607.
Halberstam, J. (2005). *In a Queer Time and Place: Transgender Bodies, Subcultural Lives.* New York: New York University Press.
Halberstam, J. (2011). *The Queer Art of Failure.* Durham, NC: Duke University Press.
Haraway, D. (1997). *Modest_Witness@Second_Millennium.FemaleMan©_meets_OncoMouse™: Feminism and Technoscience.* New York: Routledge.
Haraway, D. (2008). *When Species Meet.* Minneapolis: University of Minnesota Press.
Hardt, M. & Negri, A. (2000). *Empire.* Cambridge, MA: Harvard University Press.
Harris, A. (2005). *Gender as Soft Assembly.* Hillsdale, NJ: The Analytic Press.
Harris, A. (2012). A house of difference, or white silence. *Studies in Gender and Sexuality*, 13: 197–216.
Hartman, S. (2011). Reality 2.0: When loss is lost. *Psychoanalytic Dialogues*, 21: 468–482.
Hartman, S. (2012). Cybermourning: Grief in flux from object loss to collective immortality. *Psychoanalytic Inquiry*, 32: 454–467.
Hartman, S. (2013). On making reparation to the analyst's idolized countertransference: A relational riff on Dana Amir's Chameleon Language of Perversion. *Psychoanalytic Dialogues*, *23*(4): 408–417.
Hashiloni-Dolev, Y., Kaplan, A. & Shkedi-Rafid, S. (2011). The fertility myth: Israeli students' knowledge regarding age related fertility decline and late pregnancies in an era of assisted reproductive technology. *Human Reproduction*, 26(11): 3045–3053.
Hassinger, J. (2014). Dangertalk: Why do we avoid real conversation about widespread assaults against women's reproductive freedoms in the United States and why is this a problem for the psychoanalytic community? In *Conflict Avoidance Within Psychoanalysis: A Collaborative Discussion Panel.* American Psychological Association's Division 39 Annual Meeting, New York City, April 24.
Haughney, C. (2007). Mansions in the sky. *The New York Times,* Sept. 9.
Haylett, J. (2012). One woman helping another egg donation as a case of relational work. *Politics and Society*, 40(2): 223–247.
Hedwick, C. (2012). Assisted reproductive technologies linked to birth defects. *Medscape*, October 20, 2015.
Helmreich, S. (1998). Replicating reproduction in artificial life: Or, the essence of life in the age of virtual electronic reproduction. In Franklin, S. & Ragone, H. (Eds.), *Reproducing Reproduction: Kinship, Power, and Technological Innovation* (pp. 207–234). Philadelphia: University of Pennsylvania Press.
Henderson, D. (2013). Earliest of early term births at higher risk for mortality. *Medscape*, September 30.
Henderson, D. (2015). Injecting sperm more popular but does not improve outcomes. Retrieved on January 21, 2015 from www.medscape.com.
Hesford, V. (2008). Securing a future: Feminist futures in a time of war. In Hesford, V. & Diedrich, L. (Eds.), *Feminist Time Against Nation Time: Gender, Politics, and the Nation State in an Age of Permanent War* (pp. 169–184). New York: Lexington Books.

Hesford, V. & Diedrich, L. (2008). Introduction: Thinking feminism in a time of war. In Hesford, V. & Diedrich, L. (Eds.), *Feminist Time Against Nation Time: Gender, Politics, and the Nation-State in an Age of Permanent War* (pp. 1–22). New York: Lexington Books.

Hewitt, A. (2005). *Social Choreography: Ideology as Performance in Dance and Everyday Movement.* Durham, NC: Duke University Press.

Hollywood, M. & Hollywood, E. (2011). The lived experience of fathers of a premature baby on a neonatal intensive care unit. *Journal of Neonatal Nursing*, 17(1): 32–40.

Huyssen, A. (2000). Present pasts: Media, politics, amnesia. *Public Culture,* 12(1): 21–38.

Inhorn, M.C. & Birenbaum-Carmieli, D. (2008). Assisted reproductive technologies and culture change. *Annual Review of Anthropology,* 37: 177–196.

Inhorn, M.C. & Van Balen, F. (Eds.) (2002). *Infertility Around the Globe: New Thinking on Childlessness, Gender, and Reproductive Technologies.* Berkeley, CA: California University Press.

Jacobus, M. (2005). *The Poetics of Psychoanalysis in the Wake of Klein.* London: Oxford University Press on Demand.

James, P.D. (1992). *The Children of Men.* London: Faber & Faber.

Janvier, A., Lorenz, J.M. & Lantos, J.D. (2012). Antenatal counseling for parents facing an extremely preterm birth: Limitations of the medical evidence. *Acta Paediatrica*, 101(8): 800–804.

Janvier, A., Spelke, B. & Barrington, K.J. (2011). Epidemic of multiple gestations and neonatal intensive care unit use: The cost of irresponsibility. *Journal of Pediatrics*, 159(3): 409–413.

Jeanjot, I., Barlow, P. & Rozenberg, S. (2008). Domestic violence during pregnancy: Survey of patients and healthcare providers. *Journal of Women's Health,* 17(4): 557–567.

Johnson, J.C. (2013). Online review of *Chalk the Sun.* Posted September 9, 2013 at Chalkthesun.org/2013/09.

Johnson, S., Hollis, C., Kochhar, P., Hennessy, E., Wolke, D. & Marlowe, N. (2010). Autism spectrum disorders in extremely preterm children. *Journal of Pediatrics*, 156(4): 525–531.

Jones, C. (2005). Looking like a family: Negotiating bio-genetic continuity in British lesbian families using licensed donor insemination. *Sexualities*, 8(2): 221–237.

Jong, E. (2010). Mother madness. *Wall Street Journal.* http://www.wsj.com/articles/SB10001424052748704462704575590603553674296. Downloaded December, 2010.

Kalbian, A.H. (2005). Narrative *ART*ifice and women's agency. *Bioethics,* 19(2): 93–111.

Kalfoglou, A.L. & Gittelsohn, J. (2000). A qualitative follow-up study of women's experience with oocyte donation. *Human Reproduction, 15*(4), 798–805.

Kaplan, A. (2014). Recalibrating a psychoanalytic compass: Searching for flexibility in the midst of grief and loss. *Psychoanalytic Perspectives*, 11: 229–242.

Kargman, J. (2007). *Momzillas.* New York: Broadway Books.

Katz, S. (2008). Mindful care: An integrative tool to guide holistic treatment in enhancing fertility. *Perspectives in Psychiatric Care,* 44(3): 207–210.

Katz-Rothman, B. (2004). Motherhood under capitalism. In Taylor, J.S., Layne, L.L. & Wosniak, D.F. (Eds.), *Consuming Motherhood* (pp. 19–30). Pisctaway: Rutgers University Press.

Keylor, R. & Apter, R. (2010). Male infertility: Integrating an old psychoanalytic story with the research literature. *Studies in Gender and Sexuality,* 11(2): 60–77.

Khan, M.M. (1989). *Alienation in Perversions*. London: Karnac.

Klein, J.U. & Sauer, M.V. (2010). Ethics in egg donation: Past, present, and future. *Seminars in Reproductive Medicine*, 28(4): 322–328.

Klein, M. (1959). *The Psycho-analysis of Children.* London: Hogarth Press.

Klein, R.D. (Ed.) (1989). *Infertility: Women Speak out About Their Experiences of Reproductive Medicine*. London: Pandora Press.

Klock, S. (2004). Psychological adjustment to twins after infertility. *Best Practice and Research Clinical Obstetrics and Gynecology*, 18(4): 645–656.

Knoblauch, S. (2011). Contextualizing attunement within the polyrhythmic weave: The psychoanalytic samba. *Psychoanalytic Dialogues,* 21(4): 414–427.

Koehler, B. (2011). Psychoanalysis and neuroscience in dialogue: Commentary on paper by Arnold H. Modell. *Psychoanalytic Dialogues,* 21(3): 303–319.

Kovacs, P. (2012). In search of safer IVF. *Medscape,* April 4.

Kovacs, P. (2015). Does insurance coverage of IVF lead to better outcomes? *Medscape.* Retrieved from http://www.medscape.com/viewarticle/850158 on September 4, 2015.

Kraemer, S. (2006). So the cradle won't fall: Holding the staff who hold the parents in the NICU. *Psychoanalytic Dialogues*, 16(2): 149–164.

Kraemer, S. (2012). *Imaginations at the Threshold: Psychoanalytic Consultations in Newborn Intensive Care.* Presented at IARPP spring meeting, New York, New York.

Kraemer, S. & Steinberg, Z. (2006). It's rarely cold in the NICU: The permeability of psychic space. *Psychoanalytic Dialogues*, 16(2): 165–180.

Kraemer, S. & Steinberg, Z. (2012). Creating tolerance for reflective space: the challenges to thinking and feeling in a neonatal intensive care unit. In O'Reilly-Landry, M. (Ed.), *A Psychodynamic Understanding of Modern Medicine* (pp. 194–203). London: Radcliffe.

Kraemer, S. & Steinberg, Z. (2016). Empty arms and secret shames: Reverberations of relational trauma in the NICU. In Harris, A., Kalb, M., & Klebanoff, S. (Eds.) *Ghosts in the Consulting Room: Echoes of Trauma in Psychoanalysis (Vol. 1).* New York: Taylor & Francis.

Kristeva, J. (1982). *Powers of Horror: An Essay on Abjection.* New York: Columbia University Press.

Kulkami, A., Jamieson, D., Jones, H., Kissin, D., Gallo, M., Macaluso, M. & Adashi, E. (2013). Fertility treatments and multiple births in the US. *New England Journal of Medicine,* 369: 2218–2225.

Lacan, J. (1957). *Ecrits: The First Complete Edition in English,* transl. by B. Fink (2006). New York: Norton.

Lacan, J. (1973). *The Four Fundamental Concepts of Psychoanalysis, The Seminar Book IV, 1973,* edited by J.A. Miller, translated by A. Sheridan. New York: Norton, 1988.

Lacan, J. (1978). *The Ego in Freud's Theory and in the Technique of Psychoanalysis, The Seminar Book II, 1954–1955,* translator S. Tomaselli (1991). New York: Norton.

Lacan, J. (1981). *The Psychoses, The Seminar Book III, 1955–56,* translator Russell Grigg, with notes by Russell Grigg. London: Routledge, 1997.

Lacan, J. (1991). *Le Séminaire, Livre VIII, 1960–1961, Le Transfert.* Paris: Seuil.

Lacan, J. (1994). *The Four Fundamental Concepts of Psycho-analysis.* London: Norton.

Lacan, J. (2014) *Anxiety: The Seminar of Jacques Lacan, Book X,* edited by J.-A. Miller. Cambridge, UK: Polity Press.

Lampic, C., Svanberg, A.S., Karlstrom, P. & Tyden, T. (2006). Fertility awareness, intentions concerning childbearing and attitudes towards parenthood among female and male academics. *Human Reproduction*, 21(2): 558–564.

Lantos, J.D. & Meadows, W. (2006). *Neonatal Bioethics: The Moral Challenges of Medical Innovation.* Baltimore, MD: Johns Hopkins University Press.

LaScala, S. (2009). *Small Wonder: The Story of a Child Born Too Soon.* Gill, MA: Barton Cove Publishing.

Lau, C., Ambalavanan, N., Chakraborty, H., Wingate, M. & Carlo, W. (2013). Extremely low birthweight and infant mortality rates in the United States. *Pediatrics*, 131(5): 855–860.

Layton, L. (2010). Irrational exuberance: Neoliberal subjectivity and the perversion of the truth. *Subjectivity,* 3: 303–322.

Layton, L. (2014). Some psychic effects of neoliberalism: Narcissism, disavowal, perversion. *Psychoanalysis, Culture, and Society,* 19(2):161–178.

Leckman, J., Feldman, R., Swain, J. & Mayes, L. (2007). Primary maternal preoccupation: Revisited. In Mayes, L., Fonagy, P. & Target, M. (Eds.), *Developmental Science and Psychoanalysis: Integration and Innovation* (pp. 89–108). London: Karnac Books.

Lefkowitz, D.S., Baxt, C. & Evans, J.R. (2010). Prevalence and correlates of post traumatic stress and postpartum depression in parents of infants in the neonatal intensive care unit (NICU). *Journal of Clinical Psychological Medical Settings*, 17(3): 230–237.

Lehrer, J. (2009). Don't: The secret of self-control. *New Yorker,* May 18.

Lemke, T. (2011). *Biopolitics: An Advanced Introduction.* New York: New York University Press.

Lepecki, A. (2006). *Exhausting Dance: Performance and the Politics of Movement.* London: Routledge.

LeRoy, X. (2002). Self-interview 27.11.2000. In: *True Truth About the Nearly Real.* Frankfurt am Main, Germany: Künstlerhaus Mousonturm.

Letherby, G. (2002). Challenging dominant discourses: Identity and change and the experience of "infertility" and "involuntary childlessness". *Journal of Gender Studies,* 11(3): 277–288.

Leve, M., Rubin, L. & Pusic, A. (2012). Cosmetic surgery and neoliberalisms: Managing risk and responsibility. *Feminism and Psychology*, 22(1): 122–141.

Levi-Strauss, C. (1979). *The Origins of Table Manners: Mythologies, Vol. 3.* New York: Harper and Row.

Levy-Warren, M.H. (2008). Wherefore the Oedipus complex in adolescence? Its relevance, evolution, and appearance in treatment. *Studies in Gender and Sexuality,* 9(4): 328–348.

Liebert, R., Leve, M., & Hui, A. (2011). The politics and possibilities of activism in contemporary feminist psychologies. *Psychology of Women Quarterly*, *35*(4): 697–704.

Loewald, H.W. (1980). *Papers on Psychoanalysis*. New Haven, CT: Yale University Press.

Loftin, R., Habli, M., Snyder, C., Cormier, C., Lewis, D., & De Franco, E. (2010). Late preterm birth. *Reviews in Obstetrics and Gynecology*, *3*(1): 10–19.

Lombardi, R. (2003). Knowledge and experience of time in primitive mental states. *International Journal of Psychoanalysis,* 84(6): 1531–1549.

Lombardi, R. (2008). Time, music, and reverie. *Journal of the American Psychoanalytic Association,* 56(4): 1191–1211.

Lorber, J. (1989). Choice, gift, or patriarchal bargain? Women's consent to in vitro fertilization in male infertility. *Hypatia,* 4(3): 23–36.

Love, H. (2007). *Feeling Backward: Loss and the Politics of Queer History.* Cambridge, MA: Harvard University Press.

Lowry, F. (2015). *Fewer Multiple Births May Cut Autism Risk in ART Kids*. Retrieved from: www.medscape.com, March 25, 2015.

Ma, J. (2014). 25 famous women on childlessness. *New York Magazine,* September 15. Retrieved on September 20, 2014, from http://nymag.com/thecut/2014/08/25-famous-women-on-childlessness.html.

MacDorman, M.F. (2011). Race and ethnic disparities in fetal mortality, preterm birth and infant mortality in the United States: An overview. *Seminars in Perinatology*, 35(4): 200–208.

Mahjouri, N. (2004). Techno-maternity: Rethinking the possibilities of reproductive technologies. *Thirdspace: A Journal of Feminist Theory and Culture*. Retrieved from: http://journals.sfu.ca/thirdspace/index.php/journal/article/view/mahjouri/157.

Mahoney, A.D., Minter, B., Burch, K. & Stapel-Wax, J. (2013). Autism spectrum disorders and prematurity: A review across gestational subgroups. *Advances in Neonatal Care*, 13(4): 247–251.

Mamo, L. (2007). *Queering Reproduction: Achieving Pregnancy in the Age of Technoscience.* Durham, NC: Duke University Press.

Mamo, L.. (2010). Fertility, Inc.: Consumption and subjectification in U.S. lesbian reproductive practices. In Clarke, A.E., Shim, J.K., Mamo, L., Fosket, J. & Fishman, J.R. (Eds.), *Biomedicalization: Technoscience, Health, and Illness in the U.S.* (pp. 173–196). Durham, NC: Duke University Press.

Manterfield, L. (2011). *I'm Taking my Eggs and Going Home: How One Woman Dared to Say No to Motherhood.* Redundo Beach, CA: Steel Rose Press.

Marino, J., Moore, V., Wilson, K., Rumbold, A., Whitrow, M., Giles, L. & Davies, M. (2014). Perinatal outcomes by mode of assisted conception and sub-fertility in an Australian data linkage cohort. *PLOS oNE*, 9(1): e80398.

Martin, E. (1991). The egg and the sperm: How science has constructed a romance based on stereotypical male–female roles. *Signs,* 16(3): 485–501.

Martin, L.J. (2010). Anticipating infertility egg freezing, genetic preservation, and risk. *Gender and Society*, 24(4): 526–545.

Martin, J., Hamilton, B., Osterman, M., Curtin, S., & Mathews, T.J. (2013). *Births: Final Data for 2012. National Vital Statistics Reports.* Atlanta, GA: US Department of Health and Human Services. Centers for Disease Control and Prevention.

Massumi, B. (2002). *Parables for the Virtual: Movement, Affect, Sensation*. Durham, NC: Duke University Press.

Massumi, B. (2014). *What Animals Teach Us About Politics.* Durham, NC: Duke University Press.

Matte Blanco, I. (1988). *Thinking, Feeling and Being*. London: Routledge.

Matthews, T.J. & MacDorman, M.F. (2013). Infant mortality statistics from the 2009 period linked birth/infant death data set. *CDC: National Vital Statistics Reports,* 61(8): 1–27.

McGregor, S. (2001). Neoliberalism and health care. *International Journal of Consumer Studies,* 25(2): 82–89.

McKenzie-Mohr, S. & Lafrance, M. N. (2011). Telling stories without the words: 'Tightrope talk' in women's accounts of coming to live well after rape or depression. *Feminism and Psychology*, 21(1): 49–73.

McLeod, C. (2002). *Self-Trust and Reproductive Autonomy.* Cambridge, MA: MIT Press.

Meltzer, D. (1973). On the apprehension of beauty. *Contemporary Psychoanalysis*, 9: 224–229.

Meltzer, D. (1990). *The Claustrum: An Investigation of Claustrophobic Phenomenon.* London: Karnac Books.

Meltzer, D. (1992). London, UK: Karnac Books, 2008.

Merritt, T.A., Goldstein, M., Philips, R., Peverini, R., Iwakoshi, J., Rodriguez, A. & Oshiro, B. (2014). Impact of ART on pregnancies in California: An analysis of maternity outcomes and insights into the added burden on neonatal intensive care. *Journal of Perinatogy,* 34(5): 345–350.

Mieli, P. (1999). Some reflections on medically assisted reproduction. In Houis, J., Mieli, P. & Stafford, M. (Eds.), *Being Human: The Technological Extensions of the Body* (pp. 257–276). New York: Agincourt/Marsilio.

Miller, T. (2013). Grandmother, 53, gives birth to her own twin granddaughters. *New York Daily News,* August 15.

Mishler, E. (1984). *The Discourse of Medicine: The Dialectics of Medical Interviews.* Norwood, NJ: Ablex.

Mitchell, S.A. (1988). *Relational Concepts in Psychoanalysis.* Cambridge, MA: Harvard University Press.

Modell, A.H. (2011). The unconsciously constructed virtual other. *Psychoanalytic Dialogues,* 21(3): 292–302.

Morton, T. (2013). *Hyperobjects: Philosophy and Ecology After the End of the World.* Minneapolis, MN: University of Minnesota Press.

Mundy, L. (2007). *Everything Conceivable: How Assisted Reproduction is Changing Our World.* New York: Random House.

Muñoz, J.E. (2009). *Cruising Utopia: The Then and There or Queer Futurity.* New York: New York University Press.

Murphy, M. (2006). Frozen dreams: Psychodynamic dimensions of infertility and assisted reproduction. In Rosen, A. & Rosen, J. (Eds)., *Fort Da,* Vol. 12A (pp. 82–83). Hillsdale, NJ: The Analytic Press.

Murphy, M. (2012). *Seizing the Means of Reproduction: Entanglements of Feminism, Health, and Technoscience.* Durham, NC: Duke University Press.

Murray, L., Fiori-Cowley, A., Hooper, R. & Cooper, P. (1996). The impact of post-natal depression and associated adversity on early mother–infant interactions and later infant outcome. *Child Development,* 67(5): 2512–2526.

Nahman, M. (2008). Nodes of desire: Romanian egg sellers, "dignity" and feminist alliances in transnational ova exchanges. *European Journal of Women's Studies,* 15(65): 65–82.

Newman, C.E., Bonar, M., Greville, H.S., Thompson, S.C., Bessarab, D. & Kippax, S.C. (2007). "Everything is okay": The influence of neoliberal discourse on the reported experiences of Aboriginal people in Western australia who are HIV-positive. *Culture, Health and Sexuality,* 9(6): 571–584.

Nosarti, C., Reichenberg, A., Murray, R.M., Cnattingius, S., Lambe, M.P., Yin, L., MacCabe, J., Rifkin, L. & Hultman, C.M. (2012). Preterm birth and psychiatric disorders in young adult life. *JAMA Psychiatry,* 69(6): 610–617.

Ogden, T.H. (1994). The analytic third: Working with intersubjective clinical facts. *International Journal of Psycho-Analysis,* 75: 3–19.

Ogden, T.H. (2012). *Creating Readings: Essays on Seminal Analytic Works.* London: Routledge.

Oliver, K. (2001). *Witnessing: Beyond Recognition.* Minneapolis: University of Minnesota Press.

Oliver, K. (2004). *The Colonization of Psychic Space.* Minneapolis: University of Minnesota Press.

Oliver, K.. (2007). *Women as Weapons of War.* New York: Columbia University Press.

Oliver, K. (2009). *Animal Lessons: How They Teach Us to Be Human.* New York: Columbia University Press.

Oliver, K.. (2012). *Knock Me Up, Knock Me Down: Images of Pregnancy in Hollywood Films*. New York: Columbia University Press.

Ostfeld, B.M., Smith, R.H., Hiatt, M. & Hegyi, T. (2001). Maternal behavior toward premature twins: Implications for development. *Twin Research*, 3(4): 234–241.

Paltrow, L. (2013). Roe v Wade and the new Jane Crow: Reproductive rights in the age of mass incarceration. *American Journal of Public Health,* 103(1): 17–21.

Papadimos, T.J. & Papadimos, A.T. (2004). The student and the ovum: The lack of autonomy and informed consent in trading genes for tuition. *Reproductive Biology and Endrocrinology*, 2(56). Retrieved on August 14, 2015 from: http://www.rbej.com/content/2/1/56.

Parikh, R.K. (2012). In preemies better care for babies also means hard choices. *The New York Times*, August 13.

Parisi, L. (2004). Information trading and symbiotic micropolitics. *Social Text,* 22(3): 25–49.

Peoples, K. (2012). Body to body: discussion of "'Tis Beauty Kills the Beast" by Susanne Chassay. *Studies in Gender and Sexuality*, *16*: 18–32.

Petchesky, R.P. (1995). The body as property: A feminist re-vision. In Ginsburg, F.D. & Rapp, R. (Ed.), *Conceiving the New World Order: The Global Politics of Reproduction* (pp. 387–406). Berkeley, CA: University of California Press.

Peterson, B., Pirritano, M., Tucker, L. & Lampic, C. (2012). Fertility awareness and parenting attitudes among American male and female undergraduate university students. *Human Reproduction*, 27(5): 1375–1382.

Phillips, R.M. (2013). Multidisciplinary guidelines for the care of late preterm infants. *Journal of Perinatology,* 3: S3–S4.

Pierrehumbert, B., Nicole, A., Muller-Nix, C., Forcada-Guex, M. & Ansermet, F. (2003). Parental post-traumatic reactions after premature birth: implications for sleeping and eating problems in the infant. *Archives of Disease in Childhood, Fetal & Neonatal Edition*, 88(5): 400–404.

Pilgrim, D. & Rogers, A. (1997). Mental health, critical realism and lay knowledge. *Body Talk. The Material and Discursive Regulation of Sexuality, Madness and Reproduction*, 33–49.

Pinto-Martin, J.A., Levy, S.E., Feldman, J.F., Lorenz, J.M., Paneth, N. & Whitaker, A.H. (2011). Prevalence of autism spectrum disorder in adolescents born weighing 2000 grams. *Pediatrics*, 128(5): 883–891.

Pitts-Taylor, V. (2010). *Beyond Social Constructionism: The Body as Awkward Surplus.* Keynote address, Sociology Graduate Student Conference, University of Maryland.

Pollock, A. (2003). Complicating power in high-tech reproduction: Narratives of anonymous paid egg donors. *Journal of Medical Humanities*, 24(3): 241–263.

Probyn, E. (1993). *Sexing the Self: Gendered Positions in Cultural Studies.* New York: Routledge.

Probyn, E. (1996). *Outside Belonging.* London: Routledge.

Puar, J. (2009). Prognosis time: Towards a geopolitics of affect, debility and capacity. *Women & Performance: A Journal of Feminist Theory, 19*(2): 161–172.

Rapp, R. (2011). Reproductive entanglements: Body, state and culture in dys/regulation of child-bearing. *Social Research: An International Quarterly, 78*(3): 693–718.

Ratcliff, K.S. (2002). *Women and Health*. Boston: Pearson.

Reefhuis, J., Honein, M.A., Schieve, L.A., Correa, A., Hobbs, C.A. & Rasmussen, S.A. (2009). Assisted reproductive technology and major structural birth defects in the U.S. *Human Reproduction*, 24(2): 360–366.

Reeves, C. (2011). Redeeming time: Winnicott, Eliot, and the *Four Quartets. American Imago,* 67(3): 375–397.

Regalado, A. (2004). Could a sperm cell someday replace sperm or egg? *Wall Street Journal,* October 17, 2002, B1.

Reis, B., & Grossmark, R. (Eds.) (2009). *Heterosexual Masculinities: Contemporary Perspectives from Psychoanalytic Gender Theory.* New York: Routledge.

Reith, G. (2004). Uncertain times: The notion of "risk" and the development of modernity. *Time and Society,* 13: 383–402.

Richards, S.E. (2013). Alimony for your eggs. *The New York Times, OP-ED Contributor.* Downloaded, September 6 from: http://www.nytimes.com/2013/09/07/opinion/alimony-for-your-eggs.html?_r=0.

Riska, E. (2010). Gender and medicalization and biomedicalization theories. In Clarke, A.E., Shim, J.K., Mamo, L., Fosket, J.R. & Fishman, J.R. (Eds.), *Biomedicalization: Technoscience, Health, and Illness in the U.S.* (pp. 147–172). Durham, NC: Duke University Press.

Riviere, J. (1929). Womanliness as a masquerade. *International Journal of Psycho Analysis*, 10: 303–313.

Roberts, D.E. (2009). Race, gender, and genetic technologies: A new reproductive dystopia? *Signs,* 34(4): 783–804.

Robertson, J.A. (1986). Noncoital reproduction and procreative liberty. *Embryos, Families and Procreative Liberty: The Legal Structure of the New Reproduction, Southern California Law Review, 59*: 939–1041.

Rojas-Marcos, P.M., David, R. & Kohn, B. (2005). Hormonal effects in infants conceived by assisted reproductive technology. *Pediatrics*, 116(1): 190–194.

Ronell, A. (1991). *The Telephone Book. Technology, Schizophrenia, Electric Speech.* Lincoln: University of Nebraska Press.

Rosa, E. & Lahl, J. (2012). *Eggsploitation*. Retrieved from: http://www.amazon.com/Eggsploitation-Evan-Rosa-ebook/dp/B008RE1VV8.

Rose, N. (2001). The politics of life itself. *Theory, Culture and Society,* 18(6): 1–30.

Rosen, A. (2002). Binewski's family: A primer for the psychoanalytic treatment of infertility patients. *Contemporary Psychoanalysis,* 38(2): 345–370.

Rozmarin, E. (2010). Living in the plural. In Harris, A. & Botticelli, S. (Eds.), *First Do No Harm: The Paradoxical Encounters of Psychoanalysis, Warmaking, and Resistance* (pp. 305–326). New York: Routledge.

Rubin, L.R. & Phillips, A. (2012). Infertility and assisted reproductive technologies: Matters of reproductive justice. In Chrisler, J.C. (Ed.), *Reproductive Justice: A Global Concern* (pp. 173–199). Santa Barbara, CA: Praeger.

Russo, N.F. (1976). The motherhood mandate. *Journal of Social Issues*, 32(3): 143–153.

Ruti, M. (2011). Winnicott with Lacan. Living creatively in a postmodern world. In Kirschner, L.A. (Ed.), *Between Winnicott and Lacan* (pp. 133–150). New York: Routledge.

Ryan, M.A. (2009). The introduction of the assisted reproductive technologies in the "developing world": A test case for evolving methodologies in feminist bioethics. *Signs,* 24: 805–825.

Ryan, G., Zhang, S., Kokras, A., Syrop, C. & van Voorhis, B. (2004). The desire of infertile patients for multiple births. *Fertility and Sterility*, 81(3): 500–504.

Safouan, M. (2004). *Four Lessons of Psychoanalysis.* New York: Other Press.

Saketopoulou, A. (2011). Consent, sexuality and self-respect: Commentary on Skerrett's essay. *Studies in Gender and Sexuality,* 12: 245–250

Said, E.W. (1981). *The World, the Text, and the Critic*. Cambridge, MA: Harvard University Press.

Salamon, G. (2010). *Assuming a Body: Transgender and Rhetorics of Materiality*. New York: Columbia University Press.

Sampson, E.E. (1998). Establishing embodiment in psychology. In Stam, H.J. (Ed.), *The Body and Psychology* (pp. 30–53). London: Sage.

Sandelowski, M. & de Lacy, S. (2002). The uses of a "disease": Interferility as rhetorical vehicle. In Inhorn, M.C. & Van Balen, F. (Eds.), *Infertility Around the Globe: New Thinking on Childlessness, Gender, and Reproductive Technologies* (pp. 33–51). Berkeley, CA: California University Press.

Sassure, F. (1959). *Course in General Linguistics*. W. Bastkin, trans. New York: Philosophical Library.

Sawicki, J. (1991). *Disciplining Foucault: Feminism, Power, and the Body*. New York: Routledge.

Schilder, P. (1950). *The Image and Appearance of the Human Body*. New York: International Universities Press, 1978.

Seligson, H. (2014). Data murky on fertility rates. *The New York Times,* April 29, p. D6.

Sengupta, S., Carrion, V., Shelton, J., Wynn, R., Ryan, R., Singhal, K. & Lakshminrusimha, S. (2013). Adverse neonatal outcomes associated with early term birth. *JAMA Pediatrics*, 167(11): 1053–1059.

Shanley, M.L. (1998). Collaboration and commodification in assisted procreation: Reflections on an open market and anonymous donation in human sperm and eggs. *Law and Society Review*, 36(2): 257–283.

Shanley, M.L. (2002). Collaboration and commodification in assisted procreation: Reflections on an open market and anonymous donation in human sperm and eggs. *Law and Society Review*, *36*(2): 257–284.

Sharot, T., Korn, C. & Dolan, R. (2011). How unrealistic optimism is maintained in the face of reality. *Natural Neuroscience*, 14(11): 1475–1479.

Shaviro, S. The universe of things. http://www.shaviro.com/Othertexts/Things.pdf. Downloaded November, 2011.

Shaw, R., Bernard, R.S., DeBois, T., Ikuta, L.M., Ginzburg, K. & Koopman, C. (2009). The relationship between acute stress disorder and post-traumatic stress disorder in the neonatal intensive care unit. *Psychosomatics*, 50(2): 131–137.

Shaw, R., Bernard, R.S., Storfer-Isser, A., Rhine, W. & Horwitz, S.M. (2013). Parental coping in the neonatal intensive care unit. *Journal of Clinical Psychology in Medical Settings,* 20(2): 135–142.

Sheard, C., Cox, S., Oates, M., Ndukwe, G. & Glazebrook, C. (2007). Impact of a multiple, IVF birth on postpartum mental health: A composite analysis. *Human Reproduction*, 22(7): 2058–2065.

Sheehy, M. (2011). Melissa: Lost in a fog, or "How difficult is this mommy stuff, anyway?" In: Dimen, M. (Ed.), *With Culture in Mind: Psychoanalytic Stories* (pp. 11–17). New York: Taylor and Francis.

Sheldrake, R. (1990). *The Rebirth of Nature: The Greening of Science and God*. New York: Bantam.

Silverman, W. (2004). Commentary: Compassion or opportunism. *Pediatrics*, 113(2): 403–404.

Simon, T.L. (2013). Spoken through desire: Maternal subjectivity and assisted reproduction. *Studies in Gender and Sexuality*, *14*: 289–299.

Sims-Schouten, W., Riley, S.C., & Willig, C. (2007). Critical realism in discourse analysis: A presentation of a systematic method of analysis using women's talk of motherhood, childcare and female employment as an example. *Theory & Psychology*, *17*(1): 101–124.

Skora, D. & Frankfurter, D. (2012). Adverse perinatal events associated with ART. *Seminar in Reproductive Medicine*, 30(2): 84–91.

Spar, D. (2006). *The Baby Business: How Money, Science, and Politics Drive the Commerce of Conception.* Boston, MA: Harvard Business School Press.

Spar, D. (2007). The egg trade – making sense of the market for human oocytes. *New England Journal of Medicine,* 356: 1289–1291.

Spivak, G. (2010). "Can the subaltern speak?" In Morris, R.C. (Ed.), *Reflections on the History of an Idea: Can the Subaltern Speak?* (pp. 21–80). New York: Columbia University Press.

Steinberg, Z. (2006). Pandora meets the NICU parent or whither hope? *Psychoanalytic Dialogues*, 16(2): 133–148.

Steinberg, Z. (2012). *Empty Arms, Secret Shames: Relational Trauma and the Fate of the Imagination.* Presented at IARPP spring meeting, New York.

Steinberg, Z. & Kraemer, S. (2010). Cultivating a culture of awareness: nurturing reflective practices in the NICU. *Zero to Three*, 31(2): 15–21.

Stenner, P. (2008). A.N. Whitehead and subjectivity. *Subjectivity,* 22:90–109.

Stern, D. (1977). *The First Relationship*. Cambridge, MA: Harvard University Press.

Stern, M., Karraker, K., McIntosh, B., Moritzen, S. & Olexa, M. (2006). Prematurity stereotyping and mothers' interactions their premature and full-term infants during the first year. *Journal of Pediatric Psychology*, 31(6): 597–607.

Strathern, M. (1992). *Reproducing the Future: Essays on Anthropology, Kinship and the New Reproductive Technologies.* New York: Routledge.

Strathern, M. (1995). Displacing knowledge: Technology and the consequences for kinship. In Ginsburg, F.D. & Rapp, R. (Eds.), *Conceiving the New World Order: The Global Politics of Reproduction.* Berkeley, CA: University of California Press.

Strathern, M. (2005). *Partial Connections*. Landham, MD: AltaMira.

Sucksdorff, M., Lehtonen, L., Chudal, R., Suominen, A., Joelsson, P., Gissler, M., & Sourander, A. (2015). Preterm birth and poor fetal growth as risk factors of attention-deficit/hyperactivity disorder. *Pediatrics,* Aug. 24.

Svitnev K. (2011). Legal control of surrogacy international perspectives. In Schenker, J. (Ed.), *Ethical Dilemmas in Assisted Reproductive Technologies* (pp. 149–163). Berlin: Walter de Gruyter.

Taniguchi, K. (2012). The eroticism of the maternal: So what if everything is about the mother? *Studies in Gender and Sexuality*, 13: 123–138.

Taussig, M. (1993). *The Nervous System.* New York: Routledge.

Teitelbaum, M. & Winter, J. (2013). *The Global Spread of Fertility Decline: Population Fear and Uncertainty.* New Haven, CT: Yale University Press.

Tepper, N., Farr, S., Cohen, B., Nannini, A., Zhang, Z., Anderson, J.E., Jamieson, D. & Macaluso, M. (2012). Singleton preterm birth: Risk factors and association with assisted reproductive technology. *Maternal Child Health Journal*, 16(4): 807–813.

The New York Times (2011). California: Fertility doctor loses his license. Retrieved from http://www.nytimes.com/2011/06/02/us/02brfs-California.html?_r=0.

Thompson, C. (2005). *Making Parents: The Ontological Choreography of Reproductive.* Cambridge, MA: MIT Press.

Throsby, K. (2004). *When IVF Fails: Feminism, Infertility and the Negotiation of Normality.* New York: Palgrave MacMillan.

Tracey, N. (1991). The psychic space in trauma. *Journal of Child Psychotherapy*, 17B: 29–43.

Tracey, N., Blake, P., Warren, B., Hardy, H., Enfield, S., & Schein, P. (1995). A mother's narrative of a premature birth. *Journal of Child Psychotherapy, 21*: 43–64.

Trevarthen, C. (2009). The intersubjective psychobiology of human meaning: Learning of culture depends on interest for co-operative practical work and affection for the joyful art of good company. *Psychoanalytic Dialogues,* 19(5): 507–518.

Treyvaud, K., Ure, A., Doyle, L.W., Lee, K.J., Rogers, C.E., Kidokoro, H., Inder, T.E. & Anderson, P.J. (2013). Psychiatric outcomes at age 7 for very preterm children: Rates and predictors. *Journal of Child Psychology and Psychiatry*, 54(7): 772–779.

Tronto, J.C. (1994). *Moral Boundaries: A Political Argument for an Ethic of Care.* New York: Routledge.

Tsigdinos, P.M. (2010). *Silent Sorority: A (Barren) Woman Gets Busy, Angry, Lost and Found.* Self-published.

Twenge, J. (2013). How long can you wait to have a baby? *The Atlantic*, July/August, June 19.

Tyler, I. (2009). Introduction: Birth. In Tyler, I. & Gatrell, C. (Eds.), *Feminist Review*, 93: 1–7.

Tyler, I. (2011). Pregnant beauty: Maternal femininities under neoliberalism. In Gill, R. & Scharff, C. (Eds.), *New Femininities: Postfeminism, Neoliberalism and Subjectivity* (pp. 21–36). London: Palgrave McMillan.

Ussher, J.M. (1997). Introduction: Towards a material-discursive analysis of madness, sexuality and reproduction. In Ussher, J. (Ed.), *Body Talk: The Material and Discursive Regulation of Sexuality, Madness and Reproduction* (pp. 1–9). New York: Routledge.

Vanderbilt, D. & Gleeson, M. (2010). Mental health concerns of the premature infant through the lifespan. *Child and Adolescent Psychiatric Clinics of North America*, 19(2): 211–228.

van der Kolk, B.A. (1994). The body keeps the score: Memory and the evolving psychobiology of posttraumatic stress. *Harvard Review of Psychiatry,* 1: 253–265.

Van Leeuwen, F.E., Klip, H., Mooji, T.M., van de Swaluw, A.M.G., Lambalk, C.B., Korfman, B., Laven, J.S.E., Jansen, C.A.M., Simons, A.H.M., van der Veen, F., Evers, J.L.H., van Dop, P.A., Macklon, N.S. & Burger, C.W. (2011). Risk of borderline and invasive ovarian tumours after ovarian stimulation for in vitro fertilization in a large Dutch cohort. *Human Reproduction*, 26(12): 3456–3465.

Vaughan, S.C. (2007). Scrambled eggs: Psychological meanings of new reproductive choices for lesbians. *Journal of Infant, Child, and Adolescent Psychotherapy,* 6(2): 141–155.

Villa, F. (2011). Human nature: A paradoxical object. In Kirschner, L.A. (Ed.), *Between Winnicott and Lacan* (pp. 151–164). New York: Routledge.

Virno, P. (2004). *The Grammar of the Multitude.* Los Angeles, CA: Semiotext(e).

Waknine, Y. (2012). Sperm injection procedures may increase birth defects. *Medscape*, May 7.

Waldby, C. (2002). Biomedicine, tissue transfer and intercorporeality. *Feminist Theory*, 3(3): 239–254.

Waldby, C. & Cooper. M. (2008). The biopolitics of reproduction: Post-fordist biotechnology and women's clinical labor. *Australian Feminist Studies*, 23(55): 1465–3303.

Webb, R.E. & Daniluk, J.C. (1999). The end of the line: Infertile men's experiences of being unable to produce a child. *Men and Masculinities,* 2(1): 6–25.

Weibe, S. (2009). Producing bodies and borders: A review of immigrant medical examinations in Canada. *Surveillance and Society*, 6(2): 128–141.

Weinbaum, A. (1994). Marx, Irigaray and the politics of reproduction. *Differences: A Journal of Feminist Cultural Studies*, 6(1): 98–128.

Whiteford, L.M. & Gonzalez, L. (1995). Stigma: The hidden burden of infertility. *Social Science Medicine,* 40(1): 27–36.

Willig, C. (2008). *Introducing Qualitative Research in Psychology*. Maidenhead, Berkshire, UK: Open University Press.

Willoughby, R. (2001). The dungeon of thyself: The claustrum as pathological container. *International Journal of Psychoanalysis*, 82(5): 917–931.

Wilson, E. (2004). *Psychosomatic: Feminism and the Neurological Body*. Durham, NC: Duke University Press.

Wilson, E. (2011). Neurological entanglements: The case of paediatric depressions, SSRIs and suicidal ideation. *Subjectivity*, I4(3): 277–297.

Winnicott, D.W. (1954). *Human Nature*. London: Free Association Books.

Winnicott, D.W. (1956). Primary maternal preoccupation. In *Collected Papers* (pp. 300–305). New York: Basic Books.

Winnicott, D.W. (1960). The theory of the parent–infant relationship. In *The Maturational Processes and the Facilitating Environment* (pp. 37–55). Madison, CT: International Universities Press, 1965.

Winnicott, D.W. (1965). *The Maturation Process and the Facilitating Environment*. London: Karnac Books.

Winnicott, D.W. (1971). *Playing and Reality*. London: Tavistock/Routledge.

Wittmann, M. (2013). Opinion: The inner sense of time: How the brain creates a representation of duration. *Nature Reviews Neuroscience,* 14: 217–223.

WPATH (2011). *The World Professional Association for Transgender Health: Standard of Care for Transgender and Gender-Nonconforming People*, Vol. 7. Retrieved from http://www.wpath.org/site_page.cfm?pk_association_webpage_menu=1351.

Yardley, L. (1997a). Introducing material-discursive approaches to health and illness. In Yardely, L. (Ed.), *Material Discourses of Health and Illness* (pp. 1–24). London: Routledge.

Yardley, L. (1997b). Introducing discursive methods. In Yardely, L. (Ed.), *Material Discourses of Health and Illness* (pp. 25–49). London: Routledge.

Zachor, D.A. & Ben Itzchak, E. (2011). Assisted reproductive technology and risk for autism spectrum disorder. *Research in Developmental Disabilities*, 32(6): 2950–2956.

Zalusky, S. (2000). Infertility in the age of technology. *Journal of the American Psychoanalytic Association*, 48: 1541–1562.

Zoll, M. (2013). *Cracked Open: Liberty, Fertility, and the Pursuit of High-Tech Babies – A Memoir*. Northhampton, MA: Interlink Books.

Zoloth, L. & Charon, R. (2002). Like an open book: Reliability, intersubjectivity and textuality in bioethics. In Charon, R. & Montello, M. (Eds.), *Stories Matter: The Role of Narrative in Medical Ethics* (pp. 21–38). New York: Routledge.

Index